THE PRESIDENTIAL ELECTION SHOW

July 19, 1984—Republican Vice Presidential nominee George Bush, Ronald Reagan and Barbara Bush as they were greeted by Bush's neighbors at Houston. Reagan had lunch with Bush at his home before they attended their first rally of the campaign. (AP/WIDE WORLD PHOTOS)

THE PRESIDENTIAL ELECTION SHOW

CAMPAIGN 84 AND BEYOND ON THE NIGHTLY NEWS

Keith Blume

Foreword by Elliott Roosevelt

BERGIN & GARVEY PUBLISHERS, INC.
MASSACHUSETTS

To Jack and Maralyn, for everything
To Claire, for sharing so much
To Marya, for loving her country
And to Beau, for constant support

First published in 1985 by
Bergin & Garvey Publishers, Inc.
670 Amherst Road
South Hadley, Massachusetts 01075

6789   98765432

Printed in the United States of America

LIBRARY OF CONGRESS CATALOGING-IN-PUBLICATION DATA

Blume, Keith.
    The presidential election show.

    Bibliography: p.
    Includes index.
    1. Presidents—United States—Election—1984.   2. Television broadcasting of news—United States—Influence. 3. Television in politics—United States.
    I. Title.
    E879.B58   1985   324.7'3 '0973   85-13472
    ISBN 0-89789-080-9
    ISBN 0-89789-081-7 (pbk.)

This instrument [television] can entertain, it can inform. Yes, it can even inspire. But it can only do that to the extent that men and women are determined to use it for that purpose. Otherwise, it's just lights and wires in a box.

—EDWARD R. MURROW

Acknowledgments

My special appreciation to Elliott Roosevelt for honoring me by writing the foreword. I owe an enormous debt to Planet Earth Foundation, President Roy Prosterman, and Vice-President Jeff Reidinger, for the support necessary to complete the research for this book. Dan Levant of Madronna Publishers was forthcoming with perceptive and timely advice. Brad Fisher of the Institute for the Study of Human Issues was encouraging and instrumental in publishing contacts. Michael Dressler of Bogle and Gates generously donated legal advice. The Congressional Clearinghouse on the Future delivered important transcripts overnight, without compensation. Debbie Liceaga and Vickie Wall at Business Word Processing were always understanding in the face of last minute demands. And finally, the support of family and friends, with which I was blessed, is what makes the difference in the end, for all of us.

Contents

Foreword by Elliott Roosevelt   ix

Introduction   1

CHAPTER ONE   Presidential Politics, Television, and Democracy   5

CHAPTER TWO   Prelude: Reviewing the Campaign Before Labor Day   16

CHAPTER THREE   Campaign on the Nightly News: The First Half   26

Labor Day, Monday, September 3: A Prophetic Beginning   26

Tuesday, September 4: The Presidency or the Papacy, Part One   33

Wednesday, September 5: Issue-Blind Video   38

Thursday, September 6: The Presidency or the Papacy, Part Two   45

Thursday, September 13: The Hollywood Campaign   60

Friday, September 14: The No-Chance Candidacy   65

Tuesday, September 18: Talking TV   72

Friday, September 21: Dirty Tricks and No Questions   76

Tuesday, September 25: A Little Balance 83
Friday, September 28: Video Détente 88
Monday, October 1: The One-Minute Report 95
Thursday, October 4: Blackout on Blacks 99
Friday, October 5: Polls and Images 114
CHAPTER FOUR   Campaign on the Nightly News:
The Debates **121**
Monday, October 8: Media Shock 121
Wednesday, October 10: TV Giveth and TV
Taketh Away 129
Thursday, October 11: Making History 135
Monday, October 15: The Story Behind the
Picture 148
Friday, October 19: Self-Fulfilling Prophecy 158
Monday, October 22: The Last Hurrah 161
CHAPTER FIVE   After the Election: Looking Back,
Looking Forward **178**
CHAPTER SIX   TV's Invisible Issues, An Example:
World Hunger and U.S. Foreign Policy **204**
CHAPTER SEVEN   Reagan and the Media **217**
CHAPTER EIGHT   An Appeal to Conscience **232**
Appendix: The Televised Presidential and Vice-
Presidential Debates *243*
Selected Bibliography *333*
About the Author *336*
Index *337*

Foreword

Elliott Roosevelt

This book offers an in-depth examination of the role that television plays in the United States in shaping the course into the future that our country will follow.

Television has an extraordinary impact in shaping our opinions. Other media, newspapers and radio, at earlier periods in our history, also exerted great influence in shaping the opinions of our citizens. But the older media forced the voters of our democracy to understand and choose between the opposing issues put forward by our political leaders to a much greater extent than in the television era. After my father's presidency, television began to be a force in American politics, and by the end of the Eisenhower years it was fast becoming the preeminent force. The new medium of television has now completely wiped out the necessity for "we, the people" to evaluate the mental capacity of our leadership and to understand the candidates' different stands on issues and how they propose to lead us.

Television concentrates on providing images. Who is the most photogenic? Who projects the best and appears to be more natural? Who can deliver his or her lines in the most convincing manner? Who can come up with and deliver ad-lib replies most easily and convincingly? In other words, the harsh reality is, to be a successful political leader today means little more than being a great television actor.

What the book, *The Presidential Election Show*, brings forcefully to our attention is that the Democratic candidate for president in 1984, Walter Mondale, proved inadequate in using the medium of television effectively, compared with his opponent. The Republican candidate, Ronald Reagan, proved that he had mastered the medium, albeit exhibiting woeful ignorance of his facts on several occasions. Unlike any previous work, this book dramatically demonstrates the responsibility of television journalism itself in terms of creating and contributing to these images and perceptions. The only conclusion one can reach at the end of this book is that, thanks to the network nightly news programs, issues mean virtually nothing and personality projection means everything in presidential politics.

In terms of the 1984 campaign, the fact that the American public was in a fairly euphoric state of mind, with inflation significantly lower, the impact of the deficit not yet widely felt, and a general economic upsurge peaking during the campaign, led to the decision not to rock the boat. But a good performance by Mondale, coupled with TV news coverage that concentrated on the issues could have overcome these disadvantages, despite the almost universal theme found in postelection analysis stating that Reagan could not have lost. Mondale could have exploited Reagan's foot-in-mouth remarks and he could have capitalized on the administration's obviously weak foreign policy record. In modern-day politics, conservatives have generally championed the wealthy and upper middle classes and the benefits of trickle-down economics, and liberals have championed the worker, the underprivileged, and the need for government intervention. The dynamics of the 1984 campaign should have made for a historic debate before the American people on these different approaches. But Reagan, and to a lesser but still significant degree Mondale, both backed off from such a confrontation. The effect of TV politics was to blur where the candidates stood on issues. Reagan ran on images, and away from his right-wing history. Mondale was concerned about appearing too liberal, and at first made the traditionally conservative issue of deficit reduction the primary domestic concern of his campaign. When Mondale attempted to run a campaign based on issues, he failed in attacking the Reagan preference for right-wing philosophies, and in creating a real debate on policies. The television-news approach guaranteed this outcome, but it could have been different.

It would be disingenuous for any political observer to claim that he or she could discuss the media coverage of issues in politics without taking positions on these issues. Keith Blume does so in a manner in which no one escapes his critique, and which illuminates and contributes to his main focus, the approach television news takes in covering a presidential campaign. His conclusions are applicable regardless of partisan political perspective.

This book should be must reading for all in the business of television, particularly news departments. It is very revealing regarding the choices of news producers, reporters, and the performances of our famous and extremely high-paid network news anchors and commentators. Their contribution to the public's understanding of the issues during the campaign was practically nonexistent. The record does show that public television did a much more credible job.

The effect of the TV commercial in conjunction with the nightly news programs must also be mentioned. Madison Avenue produced, through the ad agencies involved, some of the most effective TV spots that have ever been used to sell a product. In terms of both "paid" and "free" TV time, the Republicans had two things going for them that were unbeatable. One was their star performer. With his years as a professional in the media, he made his opponent look like a wooden marionette. The decisive advantage, which greatly enhanced the effectiveness of the advertising campaign, was the fact that the network news programs reinforced the same images night after night, declared Reagan unbeatable from the start, and discussed issues only secondarily and in a shallow manner. On election day, the average householder bought the product that had been sold so frequently on his or her TV screen.

After reading this book I am deeply disturbed and troubled. Where are we headed as a democratic country? Does this newest medium of communication force us to consider reforms in campaign conduct? I, for one, think reforms are overdue.

When newspapers and radio provided us with our political coverage, campaigns were vastly less expensive. Television escalated these costs to where a congressional candidate today spends more than a presidential candidate did before 1948. Major-party candidates, and their so-called "independent" surrogates, should be limited in the media to equal expenditures of time and space. Then, if the clearly needed changes in news programming's approach called for in this book are not implemented voluntarily by the networks, other remedies must be analyzed and attempted. This would be a very complex subject in itself. But the need for change and the direction broadcast journalism ought to take in terms of preserving our democracy is persuasively outlined in this book. The people of this country must be given a chance to make up their own minds without being brain and "eye washed." The present combination of advertising dollar power and the lack of responsible TV journalism does not allow the voters a chance to really understand what each candidate is offering.

Again, I recommend this book to all in the television industry. I also recommend it to all political analysts, historians, journalists, students of government and public affairs, as well as every concerned citizen. We must truly understand this powerful medium and its effect on the future of our democratic process.

July 13, 1984—Presidential candidate Walter Mondale and running mate Rep. Geraldine Ferraro greet well-wishers on their arrival at Fairmont, Minnesota Airport.(AP/ WIDE WORLD PHOTOS)

Introduction

The election was over. The results had been totally predictable. Ronald Reagan was the most popular president since Dwight Eisenhower or even Franklin Roosevelt. He had been invincible. Walter Mondale represented the death throes of the Democratic party of the past. He never had a chance. President Reagan launched his second term with great expectations, a call for a "second American Revolution." It appeared possible that a historic realignment was occurring in American politics. The Democrats surveyed the wreckage and began scurrying in the direction of whatever politics seemed to be in vogue, whatever was perceived to be at the root of Reagan's phenomenal success.

Hold it. Not so fast. Play back the videotapes. How secure would these assumptions be in the long view of history? How wise would these certainties appear within even a few short years? To the degree these observations remained accurate, what were the factors responsible? Did the American people vote for a second American Revolution? What was reality and what was illusion? With the images of the campaign fading as crucial issues demanded attention, by mid-1985 the Reagan magic began to wear thin. Except for an event such as U.S. troops in Central America, Reagan's place in history depended on a budget process no longer in his control, and a choice between a nuclear arms treaty with the Soviets or his radical "Star Wars" program. In his speech before the nation on May 28, 1985, he finally affixed the symbol of a "second American Revolution" to the issue of tax reform, an issue on which at this point he pinned hopes for a successful second term. But whatever the ultimate outcome of these and other issues, Reagan would certainly have been in a stronger position to obtain what he wanted and the American people would have been in a better position to determine what they wanted, if symbol and substance had been linked during the campaign. Had the election been a referendum on fundamental national direction or a popularity contest? Time would be the ultimate judge. But many of the answers were already available. All you had to do was play back the videotapes of the television nightly news programs during the campaign, and the questions and answers would be visible on the video screens, where the contest, in essence, was waged.

Television is increasingly *the* crucial factor in politics in America. The images on the nightly news count for everything in a presidential election campaign, and beyond. The Presidential Election Show on the nightly news, for all practical purposes, *is* the electoral process. In this culture, if something is not on the TV nightly news, it didn't happen, it doesn't exist, it's invisible. Consider these words from Lance Marrow's Essay in *Time* (13 May, 1985): "Remember Walter Mondale? All spring and summer and fall of 1984, Mondale was a presence in American life, his words, his candances, his voice and visage and body English all injected electronically into the nation's consciousness. Then November. Poof. Mondale vanished, like the minute explosion of light on the screen when one turns off an old television set after the national anthem—the little death of a star. . . . Television is the principal theater in which the drama of vanishing is enacted."

In the past few years a virtual proliferation of television news programs has occurred. As an alternative to the commercial network nightly news programs, PBS offered "The MacNeil/Lehrer Report," then the expanded "MacNeil/Lehrer NewsHour." ABC's "Nightline," created in the wake of ABC's nightly coverage of the Iranian hostage crisis, pioneered the concept of late-night "in-depth" news programming. NBC created the superb one-hour news program "Overnight," and CBS aired its marathon early-morning show, "Nightwatch." Another major player was the revolutionary CNN, the Cable News Network, giving those on cable twenty-four hours of news programming. INN, the Independent News Network, was created to provide syndicated national and international news to independent local stations. At the peak of this trend, in 1983, ABC had expanded "Nightline" from thirty to sixty minutes, and it appeared the networks were heading in the direction of a CNN-type format in the late-night, early-morning hours. To those news and video junkies among us who also happen to have a nocturnal life-style, this all seemed too good to be true. It was. The audience just wasn't there to sustain this programming. "Nightline" was cut back to thirty minutes. "Nightwatch" saw a staff of several reporters reduced to two. And NBC's "Overnight," which many would call the best news program ever to grace the airwaves, was dropped altogether.

CNN continues its twenty-four-hour format, thanks to an expanding base of cable TV households and the tenacity of its owner, Ted Turner. CNN provides some interesting news-oriented programs in addition to the ongoing news updates. And a new cable network, C-SPAN, the Cable-Satellite Public Affairs Network, broadcasts twenty-four hours of public-affairs programming, such as the debates in the House of Representatives. C-SPAN was the only place you could see uninterrupted, gavel-to-gavel coverage of the Democratic and Republican national conventions in 1984. Unfortunately, only a small minority of viewers have the time to take advantage of this kind of programming, even if they have the cable access.

Additional news-oriented programming would include the old standby Sunday network interview shows, "Meet the Press" (NBC) and "Face the Nation" (CBS). Also included would be the commercial network early-morning news programs and, to a degree, the programs they precede: "Today" (NBC), "Good Morning America" (ABC), and the "CBS Morning News." Sometimes news oriented is the year-in and year-out huge ratings success "60 Minutes" (CBS) and its also successful clone "20/20" (ABC). "This Week with David Brinkley" (ABC) is an interesting combination of interviews with the "talking reporter" format of "Washington Week in Review" (PBS), the excellent long-running program hosted by Paul Duke. There are others, some of which have come and gone, or will.

Whatever may be on the horizon for news-oriented TV programming, it is likely that in the foreseeable future the evening news programs will continue to be the main source of information on national and international affairs for most of the public. In a great many cases it is the only source. The trend away from the written word toward the seen and heard images of video seems to be continuing, both for information and entertainment. And the so-called postindustrial era we are entering, although adding increasing flexibility of hours and place of work for many, continues to require most of society to operate within a nine-to-five context. It's a safe bet that at the millennium, and long after, most people will get their news from the nightly news on their video monitors.

This book will concentrate on the nightly national news programs, Monday through Friday, seen by and most accessible to the largest number of Americans. These are the national news programs available on what might be called "free" TV as opposed to cable, and include "The CBS Evening News," "NBC Nightly News," "ABC World News Tonight," and "The MacNeil/Lehrer NewsHour" of PBS. Periodic reference will be made to other programs.

The 1984 presidential election campaign will be followed here on the nightly news from the traditional Labor Day campaign kickoff to election day. It would be an entirely different, and equally interesting, endeavor to follow a presidential campaign through the primary season and before. Certainly such a task would be Herculean, to say the least. But this book will be limited to the formidable, though less tiring, journey through the nightly news of the two finalists as they campaign for eight weeks before the American people, to determine who shall be the next president of the United States. Given the stakes, for voters and nonvoters alike, an updated and thorough examination of the process through which the public receives campaign coverage in the video age seems a worthwhile undertaking. It is reasonable to assume that the impact of this coverage is substantial in influencing individuals to vote and, if they vote, as to the choice they make. It would be hoped that video journalism would be a positive influence, creating interest, in the former case, and in the latter, a source of both objective information and varied opinion, rather than a medium to be used to the benefit of the most telegenic, or for the purpose of creating the most sellable story. Keeping in mind that these potential influences are by no means totally under the control of the video journalists themselves, but are affected by the candidates and their campaigns as well, this book will focus primarily on the performance and options under the control of television journalism.

Having devoted much of my time for the past decade researching and producing public-affairs-related documentaries that have been broadcast on television, as well as having interviewed a number of presidential candidates and public figures on camera, I have some expertise and an acute interest in the TV medium, particularly in terms of how it informs and influences the public on the issues of our times. Few, if any, of us, unless videotaping and reviewing each day, as I have, will have an opportunity to see the nightly news programs of CBS, NBC, ABC, and PBS, and other news programming as well, on any given day, much less over an extended period of time. To do so in connection with what every four years is arguably the most important news story on the planet has been an epic informational adventure, a sometimes enlightening, sometimes disturbing, unfailingly interesting experience. My intent has been to document this experience objectively, as well as to comment subjectively; to give the reader a thought-provoking tour of how television news covers a presidential election campaign in particular, public-policy issues in general, and the impact on American democracy.

(Opposite page) NBC's Meet the Press broadcasts from the Kentucky Center for the Arts the morning of the League of Women Voters sponsored Reagan-Mondale debate on October 7, 1984 (LEAGUE OF WOMEN VOTERS EDUCATION FUND)

CHAPTER ONE

Presidential Politics, Television, and Democracy

It was October 5, 1978. I stood in the Roosevelt Room of the White House. A few feet away sat President Jimmy Carter. Behind me was the White House press corps, multiple cameras clicking, film and video recording, correspondents taking notes, and the bright camera lights shining on Carter and the assembled members around the table of the newly created Presidential Commission on World Hunger. Several memories from that day are indelibly imprinted on my mind. To see the president of the United States, the most powerful man on earth, on the flesh-and-blood side of the camera, instead of through the TV set, changed my perception of both politicians and press forever. It was not a new intellectual realization, but a visceral experience. This man who was president looked tired. The awesome responsibilities of the office appeared to be taking the expected toll. He talked so softly you could barely hear him. He also seemed intelligent, capable, and committed to the perceptive words he was speaking: "The United States has a stake in helping to solve this problem, not only because of our humanitarian concerns but for other reasons as well. We cannot have a peaceful and prosperous world if a large part of the world's people are at or near the edge of hunger." As I watched Carter, I realized that the technological gadgets behind and around me that were recording his words and image, when played back through the millions of TV sets through which the public experienced this man, and others of his stature, could not transmit his actual humanity. The video experience magnified or detracted from image and personality, but it just could not quite deliver the real human. Perhaps it is as simple as

5

the difference between actually being in someone's presence and not, but the realization struck me profoundly at the moment, because video is the medium through which we interact with our political leaders, our "media" stars, the famous and infamous.

There were two additional important lessons learned from that day in the White House.

I was there as the producer of a documentary film on world hunger and so, in a sense, had joined the White House press corps for a day. After the president's remarks we were all led out of the Roosevelt Room and back into the press briefing room so familiar to television viewers, where Press Secretary Jody Powell would introduce Sol Linowitz (Panama Canal and later Middle East special negotiator), the new commission's chairman, to answer questions. As we left the Roosevelt Room, ABC White House correspondent Sam Donaldson exclaimed loudly, "World hunger? Fuck world hunger! What about the veto!" The veto he was referring to was President Carter's surprise veto of a public-works bill earlier that day, which the press had not yet had an opportunity to ask questions about. The public-works veto was unquestionably the top story of the day. Nonetheless, I was appalled at Donaldson's apparent lack of understanding as to the importance of the issue at hand, world hunger. As many as 18 million people, mostly infants and children, die every year, directly or indirectly, because of it. Overpopulation, ironically, is fueled by it. El Salvador and Vietnam, among many others, would have been conflicts largely defused without a massive hungry peasantry to exploit. Foreign aid and foreign bank loans too often neglect the needs of the impoverished majorities in debt-ridden Third World nations, adding to international monetary jitters without improving economic productivity. The list could go on. One would not be too hard pressed to make the case that, other than the issue of war and peace in the nuclear age, world hunger is the most important problem facing humanity. Every few years, the number of deaths from world hunger alone surpasses the total fatalities of every war and calamity in recorded history.

But I was far more shocked that evening when none of the networks ran the story on their nightly news. The announcement of this commission was the culmination of a year and a half of preparation involving the president and many of his top advisers. As Martin Schram would report the following June 3 in a front-page article in the *Washington Post*, Carter had said at that White House meeting that if there was one thing he wanted to work on when he left the presidency, it was the issue of world hunger. But Carter's words were never heard on the nightly network TV news. The American people never found out about the commission and why it had been formed. Every few years, a severe drought or famine would bring the shocking images of starvation to our TV screens. But the ongoing every-day holocaust of world hunger was ignored by the media. And when a bipartisan presidential commission compiled all the pertinent research and fashioned workable solutions to eliminate the root causes of this greatest of human tragedies, television news coverage was nonexistent. The power of television to inform or not to inform had never been so clear to me.

There was one other significant lesson learned that day. The fact that the networks did not choose to run this story could not be laid entirely at their doorstep. Sam Donaldson's seemingly insensitive remark was in many ways a logical response from his point of view. Did the Carter administration expect the world hunger story to be paid attention to when they had chosen to address it on the same day the bombshell of the public-works veto had been dropped, and the press had not yet had an opportunity to address this issue? Furthermore, the only way to guarantee coverage on the world-hunger issue would have been for Carter himself to come to the press room and introduce Sol Linowitz. In addition, the press was not briefed beforehand as to why we were suddenly being rushed into the Roosevelt Room, in the middle of comments President Carter had already begun. There was plenty of incompetence and insensitivity to go around that day, and it was an informative baptism into the interrelated, high-stakes relationship between politics and press, and the process through which the public receives information.

My first glimpse of this process had come a decade earlier, during the 1968 presidential primary campaign. I was a student at the University of San Francisco at the time, and was working for Senator Robert Kennedy's campaign as chairman of USF Students for Kennedy. In that capacity, I had helped organize an appearance at USF by Kennedy on April 19, where he gave a major address on his ideas for dealing with the problems of the impoverished inner-city ghettos of America. A handful of hecklers from the Peace and Freedom Party interrupted his speech, apparently because Kennedy's opposition to the war in Vietnam was not sufficiently radical for them. They had managed to get onto the balcony behind the podium from which the senator spoke, and he turned and told them that he did not agree with them (their position was immediate unconditional withdrawal, his was more complex, in essence a ceasefire and a negotiated settlement with a coalition government, preceding U.S. withdrawal). His handling of the situation disarmed the hecklers and brought cheers from the crowded gymnasium in which he spoke. By the time he had finished speaking, the entire event seemed minor and forgotten. But the next day the *San Francisco Chronicle* headlined its story to the effect, "Hecklers Disrupt Kennedy Speech," and the television reports did the same, in their fleeting coverage. There was no mention of the substance of his remarks. The impression created by the "story" the media chose to emphasize bore little resemblance to the experience of actually being at the event. With the exception of those present at the event itself, the voting public did not hear the ideas of the candidate. To this lesson concerning the media's seeming predisposition toward sensationalism over substance, there was added another observation during Kennedy's speech. I sat only a few feet from him on the podium and was able to see him tensely hold a pencil in his hands, looking like he would break it at any moment. It seemed to me a symptom of the unique pressure of being under the media spotlight as a candidate for the presidency.

Over the past few years, I have met with or interviewed on camera several of those who have held or sought the nation's highest offices—Gerald Ford, Walter Mondale, Hubert Humphrey, Robert Dole, John Glenn, George McGovern, and Gary Hart. When the lights go on, the camera begins to record, and the questions are asked, one can easily imagine that any of us would be affected if we were sitting in the chair of the interviewed, the object of attention. But for those under the spotlight as public figures, and particularly for those aiming for the presidency, that seat becomes very hot indeed. No matter how many times they have been in the media spotlight, it has an indescribable impact that each individual responds to differently. The camera decides what the public sees, it creates an image, for better or worse, no matter how fair or unfair. The successful politician has no greater task than to learn to properly utilize this magical medium, to be aware of what his or her capacities, limitations, and potentialities are in this regard. Even then, the politician is to a large degree at the mercy of the video technicians and journalists.

Since the dawn of television, politicians, historians, journalists, and concerned citizens have been analyzing the impact of the medium on our electoral process. This area of analysis and commentary became particularly established, in fact almost enshrined, after the Kennedy-Nixon television debates during the 1960 presidential campaign, which were widely credited with tilting the election in favor of Kennedy. The impact of those debates was such that there were no subsequent television duels between presidential candidates for the next sixteen years, until Jimmy Carter and Gerald Ford debated in 1976. The experience of Nixon, who came off less than spectacularly on television in 1960, had chastened other presidential aspirants, as well as incumbents running for reelection. Media image had become a new and important political consideration, and debating one's opponent on national television could be a tricky equation. The candidate with charisma or good camera presence might want a televised debate, unless this candidate had a significant lead in the polls that a slipup on the tube in front of millions could endanger. Conversely, a candidate perceived to be lacking in charisma or camera presence might want to avoid a nationally televised debate, unless, of course, that candidate was trailing in the polls and had nothing to lose and perhaps everything to gain by a surprisingly stellar performance. Having had nationally televised debates between presidential candidates for three elections running now, not to mention record numbers of televised debates between presidential primary contenders, we may be on the verge of establishing a precedent difficult to reverse. However, the abovementioned considerations would indicate that nationally televised debates between presidential candidates are not likely to be automatically guaranteed every four years.

Two areas where presidential politics and television can be guaranteed to continue interacting are political commercials and news coverage, barring the outlawing of the former, which some might not think such a bad idea. Such an occurrence would be highly unlikely, however, and would probably at least indirectly, in terms of infringement of freedom of speech, threaten the latter, the reporting of the news by a free press. It is this most durable means of dispensing information to the public since the founding of our democratic republic, the press, in its most recent incarnation through the magic of video, and its coverage of a presidential election campaign, which this book will examine.

Clearly, the campaign managers and media specialists of any presidential candidate would prefer to limit their dealings with the world of TV to paid political commercials, at least to the degree that money is not an issue. Debates and news coverage are events and arenas beyond their control, which makes them nervous, naturally enough. Campaign commercials allow the candidate to be packaged in a totally controlled environment, exploiting the candidate's assets and avoiding any weaknesses, with the assistance of the best (so the candidate hopes) media specialists and advertising people that money can buy. In 1984, President Reagan's media advisers abandoned nearly all aspects of the issue-oriented political commercial, which had been accepted form in previous elections, and ran the most effective "mood and image" commercials ever seen in a presidential campaign. Standing alone, this may have had limited impact. But in combination with successfully communicating the same "message" through television news, a powerful new campaign approach may have been created. The American people may be much more sensible than they are sometimes given credit for when it comes to being influenced by commercial media techniques in political advertising. This was the conclusion of the well-documented book, *The Spot: The Rise of Political Advertising on Television*, by Edwin Diamond and Stephen Bates. Political commercials can be a powerful tool, but probably at best as a complement and at worst as a detriment to the overall perception of the campaign as reported by the press, because of its substantially larger scope and greater credibility. For this reason, as Kathleen Hall Jamieson has pointed out in her book *Packaging the Presidency: A History and Criticism of Presidential*

Campaign Advertising, the video-age presidential campaign apparatus is highly geared to utilizing television news itself as an advertising medium. In 1984, this was to prove true as never before.

The major source of information on national and international affairs for the largest segment of the American public is the nightly television network news. During a presidential election, this is where most Americans follow the candidates and the campaign. The same campaign managers and media specialists who in many ways yearn to be free of the press shape entire campaign schedules around coverage on the nightly news. It is both an opportunity for free advertising and an experience that cannot be avoided in any event, except to the peril of the candidate's image. Because of the size of the audience and the importance of the process, television network news coverage of a presidential election campaign is an awesome journalistic responsibility.

How well television journalism lives up to this responsibility is a question to be explored here. There are many factors to be considered. In terms of the nightly news on CBS, NBC, and ABC, a paramount question is whether form will inevitably overwhelm substance in a program only thirty minutes long. Is there time for more than fleeting images and brief impressions? If such is the case, then editing decisions take on a mammoth dimension in terms of impressions created and information received by the viewing audience. A related question is as old as the competition to sell newspapers, which in TV jargon is translated into ratings and advertising dollars: Does this pressure contribute to decisions about nightly news formats being made on the basis of commercial considerations, what might be called "image selling," instead of journalistic integrity? PBS has now given us a comparative alternative through "The MacNeil/Lehrer News-Hour." As a public television production, this program is free of commercial sponsor concerns, although perhaps not entirely. PBS does advertise in the sense that its corporate sponsors are acknowledged, and with increasing prominence and media flair as the years pass. Only time will tell whether ratings will play a major role in corporate support for Mac-Neil/Lehrer and what effect this might have on program content or format. For present comparison, the fact of sixty versus thirty minutes of programming alone is obviously a significant factor. And additionally, MacNeil/Lehrer's format is radically different from that of the commercial network programs. Guests representing different viewpoints on the daily news stories and larger issues appear nightly to give their perspective, spurred on by incisive questioning. By definition this adds a measure of objectivity and depth not available on the commercial networks. However, there are no absolutes, and a good narrative report can sometimes be more informative than a lengthy squabble between persons representing different positions. And bias is a factor in any newscast, no matter how honest the attempt to subdue it, because subjectivity is one definition of being human. This factor, along with other journalistic, intellectual, and communicative capabilities, will of course vary from one reporter or anchor to the next. However, outright partisanship is hardly a factor in TV news, which is a fairly recent development in terms of the press and American politics. For much of our history, the press was partisan with a vengeance, indeed almost an integral part of each camp, as Paul F. Boller, Jr., observes in his excellent book *Presidential Campaigns*. In more recent times, an honest, if imperfect, effort has been made to separate reporting from editorializing. The numerous critics of press bias on both the political Right and Left may be the best testament to a measure of success in this regard.

The founders of the republic envisioned a participatory democracy based on the active involvement of an informed citizenry. The Continental Congress, in 1776, instructed the various colonies to form new governments "under the authority of the people." As with any ideal, this one has never been perfectly achieved. A premise of this book is that it is a goal to be continually sought if democracy is to remain viable and vibrant. At the very least, the degree to which an informed citizenry participates will determine the degree to which a democracy functions optimally, regardless of whether we have in the past or will in the future "muddle through" despite shortcomings in this regard. To those who might suggest that too much participatory democracy may not be such a good thing, it can only be said that after all the potential philosophical, political, and sociological hypotheses have been advanced, ultimately one must either cast one's vote for democracy as a system or not, with all the attendant risks and promises. The better informed the citizenry, the less the risk and the greater the promise. A disturbing fact is that slippage from the ideal of participatory democracy has been occurring in recent years, evidenced most blatantly by decreasing voter turnout. The United States has the lowest voter turnout record of all the Western democracies. As *New York Times* political pollster Adam Clymer has pointed out (*New York Times Book Review*, 21 October 1984) this has occurred despite easier voter registration laws and has been concurrent with television's increasing dominance of the perceptions of presidential politics. In 1984, which had the most television-oriented campaign thus far, after the greatest voter registration effort in American history by both parties, their surrogates, and nonpartisan organizations, the voter turnout was essentially unchanged from 1980.

The only true test of the inferred correlation would be a concerted effort by television journalism to reverse the image-over-substance bias of its coverage of presidential campaigns. This would require the commercial network news programs to either cover fewer stories, at least during the campaign, or expand program length. A conscious decision would have to be made to refrain from the "sportscasting" approach to reporting, deemphasizing constant reporting about polls and their significance, campaign strategy, and candidate personality (as opposed to character), all of which tends to become self-fulfilling prophecy, images reinforced as fact by repetition. Instead, television journalism could decide to make the discussion of issues the linchpin of its campaign coverage, regardless of whether the candidates were doing likewise. If such were the case, the candidates would be forced to follow suit. The underlying assumption here is that the American people are not inherently disinterested or lacking in intelligence, but lacking in information. Even the already politically active voting citizen would likely be affected in unpredictable ways by a presidential campaign dynamic emphasizing a thorough examination of the issues, spurred by a new definition of television journalism. Speculation as to whether a campaign waged in this context would have altered the ultimate result, in 1984 or before, is pointless. The concern ought to be in terms of substantially increasing the participation of the citizenry as voters making an informed choice.

The argument is sometimes made that, contrary to the above-described premises, if anything, television coverage over the lengthy presidential campaign period not only makes the viewer thoroughly aware of the candidate's positions, but in fact contributes to an overexposure that is the true culprit in turning off public interest. A defense for the "horse-race" approach to media coverage might be that this is the only antidote to the above, indeed, the only kind of coverage the masses will respond to. In addition to the inherent elitism of this view, voter turnout, again, simply flies in the face of such an argument. The concerns surrounding the time frame of presidential politics are important, interesting, and complex in themselves. However, in regard to the subject of this book, television does cover policy issues and the candidate's positions on these issues, but how often and how well? And since time is experienced qualitatively as well as quantitatively, how does, and how might, television coverage interact with campaign length in terms of creating apathy or generating interest? At the conclusion of this book, the answer to that question should be apparent.

In the *Wall Street Journal*'s "Politics 84" series (24 September 1984), Jane Mayer pointed out, "By day, Walter Mondale and Ronald Reagan worked the crowds . . . but at night they got down to the real business of working the masses: the 43 million Americans who view the evening television news. . . . For all the time and effort the presidential candidates spend crisscrossing the country, they know that the only political performance that counts in these final weeks is what plays well on the network news." The cover of *Time* (22 October 1984) said it all: Reagan, Mondale,

Bush, and Ferraro were depicted as jockeys riding horses with television cameras for heads. Howell Raines observed in a *New York Times* article (23 September 1984), "In 1984, advances in the staging of campaign events, President Reagan's skill as a performer and the communicative impact of television seem to have combined to turn incumbency into a political weapon of awesome potency. . . . Moreover, a ride on the White House reelection express suggests that, for better or worse, Mr. Reagan is pointing the way toward the campaign techniques of the future. . . ." Raines described Walter Mondale's waging of a campaign on the issues as "reenacting the rituals of elections past." However, as Raines himself points out, there are other examples throughout American history of presidential elections being won on the basis of theme-over-substance campaigns, which did not lead to the permanent demise of successful campaigns based on issues. Only the medium of communication has changed, but in impact the video medium seems historically unmatched, and that, perhaps, could make past precedents irrelevant.

More than once during the 1984 campaign, the question was raised, Could Washington, Lincoln, or even FDR have been elected in the video age? Would the video monitors show, and TV journalists tell us, that Washington was too ineffective a communicator, Lincoln too ugly, and Roosevelt too feeble, in a wheelchair, to be accepted by the modern image-conscious American electorate? Of course, it would depend to a large degree on who was running against them. In the television era, Eisenhower regularly stumbled over his words, Johnson was no beauty, Nixon was self-conscious to the extreme, Ford seemed the definition of plodding, and Carter seemed overly earnest and lackluster. These were television images. But no one who ran against them had TV charisma either. The exception was Kennedy, against whom all politicians have since been compared. That is, until 1980, and particularly after 1984. What has engendered talk of new techniques and campaigns of the future has not been the sudden discovery of a new technique, but the refining and expansion of the television "image" campaign strategy by the first White House incumbent in the video age who had, for most of his career, been a professional actor in film and television. As a result, the impact of television was being looked at anew, as indeed it should be.

On the eve of the election, ABC News political director Hal Bruno said on ABC's "Nightline," "Television has increasingly dominated every campaign since 1960. And it was Kennedy who said originally, 'You know life itself is unfair,' and that's very true with political candidates when they have to compete using television as the medium in talking to people. Some of us just don't look as good as others do on television. And it has nothing to do with what the person's qualities may be. You know, the first debate in 1960, Nixon lost it, not because of anything he said, but because of the way he looked. Walter Mondale simply, usually, does not look as good on television, or come across as well, as Ronald Reagan does on television, and nobody can beat Ronald Reagan looking into that camera, just one on one, all by himself. You'd almost think he'd been an actor once." There was one moment during the campaign when Walter Mondale, surprising everyone, looked better than Ronald Reagan on TV: during the first presidential debate. With nothing to lose, Mondale succeeded at being himself on television, which caught Reagan off guard and contributed to a bad night for the president. In the second debate, Mondale's discomfort and Reagan's professionalism in front of a camera were clearly factors, although neither of them soared or bombed. But the more significant aspect of these debates, as well as the Bush-Ferraro encounter, was that, with all their limitations, they provided a far better look at the candidates and their positions than what was generally provided during the campaign on the nightly news programs. It was during these brief nightly snatches of video reporting that the impressions described by Hal Bruno were largely created.

Because the greatest impact on the candidates' images was the result of the manner in which television news covered the 1984 campaign. Howell Raines stated that the press was not guilty of the horse-race approach to the campaign that it was historically criticized for, that indeed it was covering the issues in detail in 1984. This was certainly not true in the case of television, and as the premise of Raines's article made clear, television was where the campaign was being fought and where the "techniques of the future" were being refined. The premise of this book is that the kind of future we have in regard to presidential politics and democracy itself will largely be determined by television journalism. The TV journalists have options, some of which have been mentioned above and will become more clear and be discussed further after reviewing the 1984 campaign.

A false argument is sometimes advanced as to whether we need presidents who are "leaders" able to mobilize the national will, or presidents with a firm grasp of the complex issues of their time. History has shown that our great presidents have always possessed both qualities. Fortunately, we have been blessed with great presidents at crucial times. But not at every crucial time. And a careful study of the continuum that is history makes clear that crisis situations do not occur in a time vacuum, but are often the result of events that occur, and can be affected, over a long period of time. In other words, we always need the most intelligent and capable leadership we can find, the corollary of which in a democracy is that we always need a well-informed public. Whether the American people perceive leadership as an image, or something more substantial, is largely in the hands of the television networks. It is not a matter of critiquing the candidates' campaign strategies, which TV news does in abundance. One-line criticisms of "using the media," while simultaneously allowing the media to be used, may, if anything, increase public distaste for the press, and perhaps increase cynicism regarding politicians. But given the format, the politician who is a successful media performer will likely come out smelling like a rose. This is not a partisan statement about the 1984 campaign, but an observation that would apply equally if a popular Democratic incumbent with a good national economy and TV charisma on his or her side played the same game President Reagan had in this campaign: creating "Hollywood" rallies for the evening news and avoiding press questioning and the issues to a greater degree than any presidential candidate in modern American history. It would take a candidate of more saintly dimensions than we have yet seen who would not take advantage of the means available, but rather, at his or her expense, defer to some higher motive as to what was best for the Republic. Walter Mondale deserved no special credit for running a campaign of issues. In a sense, he too was doing what he was best at, indeed the only thing that seemed to offer him a chance of winning. However, as the campaign would demonstrate, the only time the *media* gave him a chance was after he "outperformed" Reagan on television in the first presidential debate. And after the second debate, although acknowledging that Mondale prevailed on issues, the media universally declared Reagan the real winner, since he had improved his TV "performance" over the first debate. But the optimal functioning of participatory democracy requires presidential election campaigns that focus on *issues*. And the media, especially television, play the most significant role in determining whether or not that will happen. It is a role that by definition, as we shall see, goes beyond the campaign itself.

(Next page) March 22, 1984—Presidential candidate Walter Mondale speaks with members of the press upon his arrival at Los Angeles International Airport. (AP/WIDE WORLD PHOTOS)

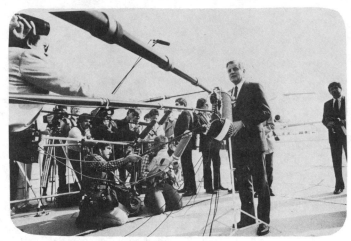

CHAPTER TWO

Prelude: Reviewing the Campaign Before Labor Day

As the 1984 campaign for the presidency began its final post-Labor Day sprint, Ronald Reagan seemed to hold the kind of commanding lead that had been seen in previous elections for Dwight Eisenhower in 1956, Lyndon Johnson in 1964, and Richard Nixon in 1972, all of which ended up being lopsided victories for the popular incumbents. On the other hand, the spread in most polls also resembled the leads of Nixon over Hubert Humphrey in 1968 and Jimmy Carter over Gerald Ford in 1976, both of which turned out to be very close elections, when early in the campaigns the outcome hardly seemed in doubt. Walter Mondale could only hope that the scenario more closely resembled the latter than the former. He could also hope that a year that had delivered its share of sobering political surprises to him would somehow do likewise for the seemingly invincible man he was challenging.

The bad news for Mondale was that Reagan's position more closely resembled Eisenhower's than Johnson's or Nixon's in their respective landslides. The country was simply in a good mood for the first time perhaps since the assassination of President Kennedy. America seemed, in the summer of 1984, ascendant again, economically, militarily, and politically. Reagan was the charming, reassuring grandfather figure, telling us that we were strong, safe, and proud, and the world looked up to us again, thanks to his policies. His communicative abilities—presence, delivery, the strong, warm, optimistic voice—were unmatched by anyone since Franklin Roosevelt. Inflation looked beaten and the stock market had reached all-time highs during his tenure. Unemployment had dropped dramatically since the depths of the great recession of 1982, even if only to the same level as when Reagan took office. If the most gargantuan federal deficits in history were an omen of disaster to come, it could not be felt in real terms by most people in the fall of 1984. And Reagan had changed his rhetoric to a softer tone as the election drew nearer, as far as relations with the Soviets were concerned. Public anxiety over the nuclear-war issue was being addressed somewhat more adroitly by the president.

The good news for Walter Mondale was that he was not perceived as the kind of ideologue of the Right or Left that Goldwater was in 1964 and McGovern in 1972, in their respective election burials. Ironically, the 1964 "Goldwater" convention was outdone by the 1984 Republicans in terms of a "right-wing ideologue" platform, which was clearly outside of the main- stream. But this was overshadowed by the personality of Ronald Reagan. In reverse contrast, the Democratic platform was the most centrist since at least 1968, and the greatest turn away from the New Deal since the Roosevelt presidency. Yet Ronald Reagan tried to personify Walter Mondale shortly after the Democratic Convention as "so far left, he's practically left America." This tactic had been successfully, if unfairly, used against George McGovern in 1972 by the Nixon campaign. McGov- ern's best chance at countering that image was lost when his first-rate acceptance speech at the Democratic Convention was broadcast early in the morning to a sleeping America. What America had seen on the TV screen in earlier hours was a Democratic party seemingly disorganized and in the turmoil of radical politics, which did for McGovern's image what right-wing booing of Nelson Rockefeller at the 1964 Republican Conven- tion had done for the image of Barry Goldwater. But Walter Mondale had always been perceived as a mainstream traditional liberal politician tied to the constituency groups of the New Deal, which were now labeled "spe- cial interests," and Reagan, who ironically had been the darling of the radical Right for two decades, quickly abandoned the unneccessary "far left" tactic. Mondale's position was not unlike that of Adlai Stevenson in 1952 and 1956, when he was overwhelmed by the popularity of Dwight Eisenhower. Mondale, however, was a better politician than Stevenson, more capable of waging a professional and, as he finally proved in the primaries, fighting campaign. In addition, Reagan was not Eisenhower, and the 1980s were not the 1950s, even though they were beginning to resemble each other. Perhaps, after all the traumas of the sixties and seventies—assassinations, Vietnam, Watergate, the erosion of America's dominant post-World War II economic, military, and political position in the world—Ronald Reagan was the perfect magic potion, taking the American people back to perceived better times. Perhaps, unless he was caught doing something shocking or illegal, or began to display severe senility, Reagan would simply benefit from the deep psychological need of the American people for calm and continuity, to complete a two-term presidency for the first time in over two decades.

On the other hand, the ensuing decades had left their mark on an entire new generation who were only children in the fifties. Their concerns were complex and changing, as well as somewhat difficult to predict politically, as the 1984 primary season had demonstrated. Gary Hart had largely reaped the benefit of this voting block, if it could be referred to as such. Ironically, it seemed many of these voters might swing to Reagan, which pointed out a major Mondale weakness exploited so successfully by Hart: He was widely perceived as the last of the New Deal liberals, an idea whose time was passing. It also seemed possible evidence of the impact of the "Great Communicator" on the first generation raised on TV. But this group of "yuppies" (young urban professionals) or "yumpies" (young upwardly mobile professionals) as they were dubbed by a label-prone media, were a potentially volatile and unpredictable group. Many were conservative on economic issues, and a segment were on foreign policy as well. But they were liberal on social issues, and many were deeply affected by the Vietnam experience. Peter Collier and David Horowitz, former editors of the sixties magazine, *Ramparts*, described in the *Washington Post* National Weekly Edition (8 April 1985) their journey from the quasi-Marxist left to voting for Reagan in 1984. But few contemporaries had shared their former, simplistic, leftist views any more than they now shared their new, equally simplistic, adherence to the right-wing foreign policy line. For as polls indicated, there was widespread apprehension in this generation about the arbitrary or unrealistic use of American military power, and the larger issue of the nuclear arms race. And Reagan's social agenda, on school prayer and abortion, for instance, was not popular with these voters. There was an opening here for Mondale, if he could expoit it. The high-flying economy, however, was a major plus for Reagan. The decision-making process between potentially conflicting inclinations on economic, social, and foreign policy issues would possibly decide the election. This baby-boom generation now comprised perhaps half of the electorate.

More solidly in the Reagan camp were the newest voters, the eighteen-to-twenty-four-year-old group. Polls showed the president getting 60 percent plus of this group. Such conservatism on the part of youth seemed historically odd to many, yet this group was probably responding less to ideology than to image and perceived economic self-interest. The argument was made that the political memory of the new youth didn't predate Jimmy Carter, and that the comparison with the Reagan presidency was working very much to Reagan's advantage, and naturally, Mondale's disadvantage. It also seemed that in the cyclical nature of things, much of this newest voting generation was focusing its youthful energy on the "new patriotism," with the "we're number one" consciousness being transplanted from the football field to the nation at large. On the other hand, the ideas and concerns of this generation were still being formed and, in a sense, up for grabs. There was a sizable number of this group concerned about the issue of nuclear war, for instance. And it was not known how many of them would actually vote.

Politics is timing, if it is anything, and timing was working in Reagan's favor. If the election had been held in 1982, with the economy a shambles and concern over nuclear war at a fever pitch, Ronald Reagan would have been in deep trouble, as all the polls indicated at the time. In 1984, although things had improved dramatically, there remained large constituencies who had been or were still hurting as a result of Reagan economic and budget policies. And the war-and-peace issue was still significant. Reagan had overseen the largest military buildup in peacetime in U.S. history. He was fighting a not-so-secret war in Nicaragua, and a larger Central American conflict involving American forces did not seem out of the question. Ironically, Reagan's largely popular invasion of Grenada may have latently enhanced the fear that he would get us involved in something bigger than an easy win on a dot on the map, if he was reelected. Two hundred and forty-one American marines had died in Lebanon, and no one knew why. He was the first president since Hoover not to meet with the leader of the Soviet Union. And he was the first president since Eisenhower not to have reached an arms-limitation agreement of any kind with the Soviets.

Reagan also had problems with women, the so-called gender gap, because of his record on women's rights, and almost total opposition from the black community because of his civil rights record, in addition to the concern of these groups over economic and war-and-peace issues. Also, concern about the environment was certainly working against Reagan, after the inglorious reigns of James Watt at the Interior Department and Anne Burford at the Environmental Protection Agency.

President Reagan looked strong in the polls despite these problems, however, as the personal charm of his oft-described "Teflon presidency," combined with economic recovery, seemed to be winning the day. Walter Mondale's greatest hope probably could be found in the fact that the Democratic primary season had proven just how totally wrong the polls and pundits could be. His greatest fear could have been in reflecting on the power of media image, particularly TV, and what it did for, then against, the remarkable phenomenon of Gary Hart's candidacy. Media image had never been Mondale's strong suit. On the other hand, there was solace to be found in the same example. Although not of Reagan's stature, Hart was far more telegenic than Mondale, and video was a great Hart asset until the media began to pick him apart. In the face of this,

Mondale became a more effective, if more negative, campaigner, ultimately coming out on top.

Coming out on top, of course, was what the pompous experts assured us all along was inevitable for Walter Mondale. Then the people of New Hampshire did something on primary day that all the media commentators had forgotten the whole process is about: It's called voting. The Hart trouncing of Mondale was a "shocking" media event, not in the least because for months the media had declared such an outcome virtually impossible. With the exceptions of John Glenn, who was at first pumped by the media, then abandoned for not having the right stuff for TV politicking, and Jesse Jackson, the historic candidate who had TV charisma, the media had always treated the remaining candidates—Hart, McGovern, Cranston, Hollings, and Askew—as mere inconveniences for Mondale on his way to the nomination. But New Hampshire changed all that. The power of video never being more obvious, along with the media at large, TV reporting went gaga over Gary, his image filling the screen constantly on the nightly news. This gave a huge boost to his campaign, and just as he was about to knock Mondale out of the race, the press seemed to come down with a case of panicky guilt. The media began to look more closely at Hart, dwelling on substantial issues such as whether he was a year older than he thought he was, and his name change. This gave Mondale enough time to think up his one slick media slogan of the campaign—"Where's the beef?"—which stuck to Hart enough for Mondale to eke out a nomination victory after a grueling primary campaign. It should be noted that the same experts who originally proclaimed his nomination preordained nearly declared Mondale dead after New Hampshire and subsequent losses to Hart in New England and Florida. Then, after Mondale's comeback victories in Illinois, Pennsylvania, New York, and finally Texas, Hart was all but declared a corpse. But then Hart won in Ohio, followed by California; if he had won in New Jersey, the Democratic Convention would have been an unpredictable affair.

So much for the experts. But though they should have been dead and buried forever after this series of failures in prophesying, they were at it again, hoping they were now on safer terrain, declaring Reagan invincible. This would seem harmless enough, given the record of voters paying attention to the media experts during the primary campaign. But it could also be argued that TV images were a major factor in voter volatility. And in the contest between the two finalists, many more people pay attention and vote. Those who vote in a primary are fairly well-motivated voters comparatively, and may be less influenced by the polls and images presented by the media than are voters during a general election. In any event, the media would certainly better serve the public by examining issues and contributing to a real contest, than by trying to predict the outcome, and thereby in a sense preempting the process.

The candidates, of course, share the responsibility for whether or not the media concentrates on issues. Jesse Jackson learned that the hard way. His candidacy was a milestone, and in addition his charisma made him the kind of story TV loves to follow. His rhetoric may have seemed simplistic to some, but it was strong, issue-oriented stuff, perfectly suited to the video medium. He came across as taking principled stands, and shortly before New Hampshire, he was beginning to successfully reach beyond the base of his black constituency. Polls showed that he was possibly shaping up as the surprise of New Hampshire. But then his remarks referring to New York City as "Hymie town" were made public, followed by supporter Louis Farrakhan's threats against the *Washington Post* reporter who made the disclosure, as well as Farrakhan's statement calling Judaism a "gutter" religion. Jackson was tentative and indecisive in dealing with the problems created, first by his own remarks, and second by his association with Farrakhan. The focus of the press shifted from the issues he represented to these problems, and his appeal outside the black community was never the same, although he went a long way toward reestablishing this appeal by his moving speech at the Democratic National Convention.

Shortly before the convention began, Walter Mondale exhibited within the same week the extraordinary dual capacity of utilizing the power of media to his greatest advantage and most inexplicable disadvantage. His announcement, on the eve of the convention, of his choice of Geraldine Ferraro as his running mate truly electrified the nation. He had made history. He had transformed his colorless, never-take-chances image overnight. He created a tremendous media opportunity to show himself as a "leader," without doubt the most important impression needed in a race against Ronald Reagan. Creating this kind of image can be indispensable in terms of getting the media to then focus its coverage on what the candidate has to say. Mondale had accomplished this. Even though the media coverage, which was awesome quantitatively, focused primarily on Geraldine Ferraro herself, it reflected by inference, and often in commentary, back on Mondale. Then, after a few short days of this media adulation, Mondale apparently decided that enough good news was enough, and proceeded to derail his leadership image by resurrecting Bert Lance from the politically dead. First he engendered a revolt of Democratic leaders by trying to install Lance as the national chairman of the party, in place of Charles Mannatt. Having been embarrassingly forced to back off from this attempt, Mondale proclaimed Lance a sort of superchairman of his campaign. A few weeks later, Lance would be unceremoniously dropped from this position as well, after someone not sleeping in the

Mondale campaign apparently successfully reminded the candidate that he already had more Jimmy Carter baggage than he needed, and the press was going to keep rubbing it in until Lance was dropped. Carter-bashing—one of the favorite media sports of the past decade—had begun with the banking irregularity allegations against Bert Lance, Carter's budget director. Carter suffered in general from what seemed to be the early post-Watergate journalistic ethos that the president was target number one. In addition, events beyond his control, such as the Iranian hostage crisis and skyrocketing oil costs, were laid at his doorstep. Being a Washington outsider didn't help much either. The populism and integrity in tackling hard issues that might have carried him through with the American people were never emphasized by the media. What *was* emphasized was that being an outsider meant not being able to get things done. As a result, in 1980 Ronald Reagan had a corner on the positive aspect of being an outsider—the American electorate's distrust of Washington politics. After the 1980 election, Carter's only media legacy was that he was a loser. His accomplishments were hardly mentioned. For Walter Mondale, association with him was the kiss of death. Never mind whether it was fair or not. It was reality.

Fortunately for Mondale, the Lance affair was overshadowed, and the Ferraro positive effect reestablished, by the enormously successful Democratic Convention. Here again was another lesson in the power of video. Mario Cuomo knocked everybody's socks off, coast to coast, establishing not only himself, but reestablishing the Democrats as a party of family and patriotism, along with compassion for the less fortunate and passion for nuclear sanity, in proclaimed stark contrast to Reagan Republicanism. Then Jesse Jackson disarmed everyone with his humility, and was inspirational with his powerful call for economic justice and political participation for all, and a united Democratic party. Gary Hart made crystal clear, if somewhat grudgingly at first, that he was totally behind Mondale-Ferraro in the crusade to unseat Reagan. Then, some as of yet unexperienced, indescribable new energy seemed to emanate from the video monitors as Geraldine Ferraro stood at the podium as the first woman in history to accept the nomination of a major party for the office of vice-president of the United States. And Walter Mondale, under tremendous pressure, did what he had to do, which was give the best speech of his life, a stirring call to eliminate those "God awful" nuclear weapons, and a thoroughly surprising challenge to Ronald Reagan on what to do about the deficit. The video images of the delegates were a collage of America, the diversity of a patchwork quilt, with huge American flags waving everywhere. It was such a stunning video success, that the media for the first time started talking as if the Democrats actually had a chance, however slim. And the infamous, fickle polls soon bore this out, as the first post-convention results showed Mondale-Ferraro pulling up to even with Reagan-Bush.

Now it was the turn of the new media star, Geraldine Ferraro, to stumble. She had only herself to blame for the onslaught of questioning about her family finances, after reneging on her previous pledge to release her husband's tax returns along with her own. On the other hand, the press had only itself to blame for the sickening post-Watergate orgy of overkill it indulged in. Fortunately, most members of the media realized this for themselves, after Ferraro released her own and her husband's returns after all, and delivered an extraordinary performance at a marathon press conference. Whatever mistakes she might have made, the purpose of public disclosure is to determine potential conflict of interest, and in this regard she came out with flying colors. It looked as if the campaign financing questions might ultimately work to her advantage, as the basic unfairness of her predicament seemed a clear result of the law, in effect, being sexist. The question of her claiming an exemption from reporting on her husband's financial affairs while in Congress seemed largely offset by her release of the information in question, and the total lack of any conflict of interest. Most important, in terms of public perception, she subjected herself to an unprecedented grilling by reporters for an hour and a half on television. At the end, many of her questioners applauded her. She had looked honest and tough. Clearly, Geraldine Ferraro had the stuff to be a top-rate national politician, and a telegenic one at that. Polls showed that the great majority of Americans considered the politics of her finances to be a successfully closed case.

Other polls, however, were not looking too good for the Mondale-Ferraro campaign. Mondale had disappeared from the TV screens since the convention, crowded out in effect by the negative coverage his running mate was getting. By the time Ferraro's ordeal was resolved, even if successfully, valuable time and momentum had been lost. The afterglow of the convention was not only gone, it was an opportunity squandered. What had been gained in the polls had now been given back. For a moment after the Democratic Convention, Mondale had caught the Reagan campaign off guard and put it on the defensive on the deficit issue. Reagan said he wouldn't raise taxes, Vice-President George Bush said Reagan might, Mondale said everybody knew taxes would be raised, it was just a matter of who would be taxed and how. He would do it fairly, and soon offer a specific plan. What was Reagan's plan? But the Ferraro-Zaccaro affair changed the media spotlight and gave the Reagan campaign time to get their lines straight for the Republican Convention.

The spotlight was now back on the Great Communicator. He told the nation that everything was rosy, so why be depressed by listening to those gloom-and-doom Democrats? Raising taxes, he said, was a last resort, and it would never be income taxes. (His right-wing Republican platform was even more restrictive, but we all know how the pages of platforms are used by presidents: to make paper airplanes with.) The Reagan campaign said that continued economic growth and additional spending cuts would reduce the deficit. They pointed out that, for a liberal Democrat like Walter Mondale, saying that you were going to raise taxes was stating the inevitable. How else could the big-spending liberals pay for the ever-expanding government Reagan was trying to cut? And Mondale converting to a belief in more austere government spending policies was a welcome, if difficult-to-believe, development.

The Mondale camp responded that the conversion of Fritz was necessitated by, and no more difficult to believe than, the great budget balancer, Ronald Reagan, having almost doubled the national debt through his program of radical tax cuts and increased defense spending. Ironically, the polls showed that on specific issues, such as fairness or war and peace, Mondale was more trusted than Reagan. But the voters seemed to prefer the president's upbeat vision, even if they were concerned with some of his specific policies. It seemed to be a matter of personality. Reagan was very much liked by most of his fellow Americans. His optimistic style of leadership was what many people had been longing for, and it seemed to be delivering results. Even though there were areas where those results were seriously questioned by a majority of Americans, Walter Mondale didn't seem appealing enough to drop a popular president for in the middle of a booming economy.

Martin Schram of the *Washington Post* reported (National Weekly Edition, 17 September 1984) that if image was Walter Mondale's weakness and issues his strength, then Mondale adviser Richard Leone had a novel idea: Go with the flow. Mondale could not make over his image or make himself telegenic without making himself look ridiculous and losing one of his main strengths, his integrity and sincerity. So the strategy was to let Mondale be Mondale and stick to the issues or, more appropriately, stick the issues to Reagan, until through repetition his message got through to the public. Ronald Reagan, on the other hand, would do what any popular incumbent does: Talk about how things were good and getting better, and avoid the potential pitfalls of specifics as much as possible. He would also continue to wrap himself in the themes of God and country more than any president in modern history, as well as run the most TV-image-oriented campaign since the beginning of the television era.

So there they were, poised at the arbitrary Labor Day starting gate, the most effective video communicator since JFK, and his loyal, seasoned running mate, versus the TV-flat but issues-strong challenger and the historic rookie choice, ready for the Presidential Election Show to begin.

How good a show would it be? The game seemed heavily weighted in Ronald Reagan's favor. Not only was he far ahead in the polls, but his entire professional career, mainly as an actor, then a politician, had been spent learning and applying the skills of communicating on screen and through video. Walter Mondale, although ironically possessing one of the more affable and engaging personalities in American politics, had never been comfortable in front of a camera, and the video journalists had added to his "colorless" image through months of commentary about it. TV journalism had not, in general, distinguished itself in past campaigns in terms of communicating about the issues. Television was by nature the medium of "image," yet this aspect of the medium was not all it had to offer. Issues could be covered in depth, imagery deemphasized. This was ultimately a conscious choice for which television journalism had to take responsibility. The 1984 campaign would test TV journalistic integrity as never before.

CHAPTER **THREE**

Campaign on the Nightly News: The First Half

Labor Day, Monday September 3: A Prophetic Beginning

If you had been watching ABC for your nightly news report on Labor Day, unless you made it through the first five stories and two commercials, you wouldn't have known that a campaign for election to the most important job in the world had officially begun this day. The top story on "ABC World News Tonight" was the $40 million winner of the Illinois Lottery, followed, in order, by stories on the Montreal train station bombing, the space shuttle *Discovery*'s "plumbing" problems (insignificant except for the toilet humor possibilities), the issue of the frozen embryo whose "parents" had died, and a gas truck collision fire in Virginia. The opening story on the lottery winner was given so much time that there was a commercial break after it, whereas the second commercial break came after the next four stories. This was followed, finally, by reports on the Labor Day election campaign kickoff. Ted Koppel, who was anchoring the news in place of Peter Jennings on this Labor Day, also covered the lottery story as the major story later that night on "Nightline." It was as if ABC was going for the *New York Post* Sensationalism Award instead of pursuing real journalism. The *New York Post* sells newspapers, however, and this appeared to be a classic case of the ratings-race-over-substance approach to TV news. ABC has sometimes been criticized for ratings-

26

over-substance fever in recent years, since Roone Arledge of "Wide World of Sports" took command of the news department, because ABC executives were concerned with their perennial third-place finish in nightly news ratings after CBS and NBC. Arledge turned this around, even hitting number one during the immediate aftermath of Walter Cronkite's retirement from CBS. Fortunately, it wasn't always the result of relying on flashy video technique or sensationalist journalism. This day was certainly not ABC's finest hour (or, more accurately, half hour). Some of what ABC did report on the election campaign will come later.

CBS, NBC, and MacNeil/Lehrer on PBS all covered the presidential election campaign as their top stories.

The "CBS Evening News" began with a very upbeat report from Bill Plante on the Reagan campaign rally in Orange County, California (Fountain Valley). Balloons filled the air and thousands chanted "four more years," to which the president answered, "Okay, you talked me into it." He went on to say, "Today we set out to achieve a victory for the future over the past, for opportunity over retreat, for hope over despair, and to move up to all that is possible and not down to that which we fear."

Since this was the excerpt of Reagan's remarks that was chosen, it would have been useful if Plante had commented on the themes and their meaning and purpose. For instance, the future-past theme is right out of the Gary Hart-versus-Walter Mondale play book. And the despair-fear theme was well established at the Republican Convention in Dallas as an attempt to label the Democrats and Mondale as the party and candidate of "gloom," since Mondale was talking about the future impact of the deficits, having to raise taxes, and the dangers of nuclear war.

Plante made an important and informative comment, however, by stating that "the Reagan campaign begins on such a high note, so high in the polls, that his campaign aides say he doesn't have to respond to Mondale on the issues," and that at this point the main concern was Republican apathy. He told us that the Reagan campaign strategy called for Vice-President George Bush to make any necessary trips along the "low road," and that Bush had accused Mondale of running a low-road campaign. These short statements were loaded with information and irony, but they were followed by a totally incongruous edit to Bush stating that "Walter Mondale's economic dream will be a return to the nightmare of Jimmy Carter." This did not sound like George Bush accusing Mondale of running a low-road campaign, nor was it much of an example of low-roading on his part. It sounded like Ronald Reagan's theme song, in 1980 as well as 1984. Nonetheless, Plante reported we wouldn't hear much of that from Reagan, but that we would hear about "prosperity, success, and better times for everyone" and that the Reagan campaign hoped for a "massive victory in November."

CBS then took us to Susan Spencer in New York City, reporting on the Mondale-Ferraro campaign. On our TV screen we saw the band playing and people marching, and Spencer told us that "the band tried to do its best, but for a campaign with nowhere to go but up, New York's Labor Day Parade was a puny way to start." She went on to say that the candidates "waved bravely," but the crowds were small and even New York Mayor Ed Koch didn't show up. However, she told us, "Mondale and Ferraro are determined to prove they are a clear alternative" and at their next stop on a cross-country Labor Day blitz, in the tiny town of Merrill, Wisconsin, the "crowds were better and parade peppier." A clip of Geraldine Ferraro was shown as she said to the cheering crowd, "I agree that the values we get from our different religions underpin our thinking about the great public issues. But you don't have to impose your religion or your morality on others in order to be religious or moral." Preceding this clip, Spencer had said, "Ferraro accused the president of flirting with nuclear war, unfair economic policies, and trying to interfere with religious freedom."

One can only speculate on why the clip chosen of Ferraro was of her speaking on the religious issue. It certainly was about to become the issue of the week, to say the least. But the question arises, To what degree are issues created by the media as opposed to the politicians, particularly in terms of priority? The nuclear war and economic fairness issues were already the major issues for the Democrats, but the tendency of the media is to emphasize the "new," particularly on the thirty-minute TV news program. It would seem that issues in the campaign are prioritized at least as much by the press as they are by the politicians. Theoretically, to the degree that such prioritizing was based on the public-policy significance of various issues, this would be a useful media function. But too often, the search for controversy overrides other considerations. Politicians, of course, often prefer this route as well, as long as the controversy is to their benefit or to the detriment of their opponents. In the end, both the politicians and the media, for somewhat different reasons, but each trying to sell to their markets, often tend to avoid detailed and prolonged attention to significant issues. And even when politicians attempt to run substance as opposed to sloganeering campaigns, the media is not often cooperative. Although the presidential campaign was just beginning in terms of the finalists, and the nuclear war and economic fairness issues had never been covered in depth, they were not new issues, and therefore didn't get the spotlight that the religion issue did. As the week progressed, the fact that this issue would be at the top of the agenda was only partly attributable to the candidates, who talked equally of other, and at times substantially more important issues. Not that the religion and politics issue wasn't important, or didn't deserve in-depth coverage. But the media prefers sparks flying to continuing sober consideration of difficult and complex public-policy questions, and so the media and the candidates engaged in a snowballing cycle of reinforcement in creating the church-and-state question as issue number one of the campaign. The unfolding of this story is to come.

Susan Spencer then turned in her report to Walter Mondale, as he took off his jacket and rolled up his sleeves, ignoring the chill, "to demonstrate his fighting spirit." She described him as "not always a dynamic speaker, [but] clearly trying today, at times sounding much like his mentor, Hubert Humphrey." Mondale was shown saying in a strong, lively, and fighting manner, "Let us end this uncaring, icy indifference to human need in American society and get a president who will stand up and lead us in a decent course in America again." Spencer pointed out that Mondale remembered with fondness Truman in 1948, when all the pundits were wrong, "but considering where they are in the polls, the Democratic fortunes will have to start changing soon if history is to repeat itself."

CBS followed with an interesting report on security around President Reagan, by correspondent Barry Peterson. It described how all 40,000 people who attended the rally for the president in the conservative bastion of Orange County, California, had to pass through metal detectors, an unprecedented occurrence. Peterson said the press corps was even being kept at a distance, allegedly for security reasons, "but that sources close to the Secret Service say its a nervous White House wanting to keep a talkative president away from the press in an election year." A scene was shown from the rally with Maureen Reagan, the president's daughter, standing next to him on the podium in the scorching sun, saying to her father, "It's hot, why don't you take off your jacket?" The president answered almost inaudibly that he couldn't because he had his long under-wear on. "Long underwear" is the euphemism for bullet-proof clothing. Peterson noted that challengers like Mondale took more chances than incumbents, wading into the crowd in traditional campaign style. But for Reagan, particularly after being shot, the name of the game was protection. It was a sad commentary on the campaign environment, which has become increasingly nervous over the years since President Kennedy's death and subsequent assassinations and attempted assassinations. It was also the first indication of the extraordinary measures the Reagan campaign would take to keep the press away from the president.

NBC and ABC aired reports similar to that on CBS. The upbeat nature of the Reagan kickoff versus the downbeat nature of Mondale's was emphasized in both broadcasts. NBC's Lisa Myers did give us one useful additional bit of information about the small turnout for New York's Labor Day Parade. She reported that Mondale's aides attributed it to the 9:00 A.M. start, which is when Mondale and Ferraro showed up. She and

Britt Hume of ABC both emphasized Mondale's remarks on the religion issue. NBC quoted him saying in his Merrill, Wisconsin, speech, "We didn't need government to tell us that we believed in our God." And ABC quoted from the same speech, "I want a government that watches out for you and not over you." Clearly, all the networks were jumping on the religion issue. The reports of Chris Wallace (NBC) and Sam Donaldson (ABC) on Reagan's rally in Orange County were very similar to Bill Plante's on CBS. Sam Donaldson, however, in his inimitable style, added some spice to his report by confronting White House chief of staff James Baker and asking him whether atypically conservative Orange County was the place to launch a campaign, in terms of "reaching out" to the rest of America. Baker responded, "We will be."

DONALDSON: *But not today.*
BAKER: *We are today. This is the heartland of America.*

That would certainly be news to most political demographers. On the other hand, there were signs that the accepted political demographics of the past were possibly being rewritten this year.

One curious difference between all three networks was the reporting on the size of the crowd at Reagan's rally. ABC reported 30,000; CBS reported 40,000; NBC reported 50,000. Interestingly, Associated Press reported 20,000 and said reports of up to 50,000 were the estimates from the Reagan campaign. The inference in terms of where "objective" journalism was in some cases getting its figures is not particularly comforting.

By far the best coverage of the day was to be found on "The Mac-Neil/Lehrer NewsHour" on PBS. There was extensive coverage of Reagan's and Mondale's remarks. Both were shown at their best, with Reagan talking about the values of faith, work, family, and peace in vintage form, and Mondale making a strong statement about the fact that if one false move is made in the nuclear era human history is over. Bush was reported as stating that Mondale's attacks on religion were a sign of desperation, and Ferraro was reported as accusing Reagan of Madison Avenue patriotism and stating that real patriotism required creating jobs and ending the nuclear arms race. The candidates' remarks were followed by random interviews with people on the streets of Manhattan at New York City's Labor Day Parade, giving their views about the candidates and the campaign. A wide spectrum of views was represented and the entire segment was a refreshing and interesting counterpoint to the political speeches. A couple of interesting images were a young white man, probably in his twenties, saying, "The labor union is people, hardworking people, and Mondale is definitely for the working people and we need a man like that," and a young black man, perhaps in his early thirties, a computer operator, saying, "My wife and I both were Democrats, but we're definitely going to vote for Reagan. . . . I don't even believe in unions. They breed complacency." A middle-aged woman said that a lot of people didn't realize that if it weren't for the unions they wouldn't be getting what they are, followed by a woman in her thirties stating that Mondale meant unions in her mind, and that was a negative. One woman talked about how excited she was about the union support for Mondale-Ferraro, gesturing to the people turning out at the parade. Unlike the other networks, MacNeil/Lehrer reported that the crowds had been sizable at the beginning of the parade, but had tapered off later.

Jim Lehrer then interviewed Paul Locigno of the Teamsters Union, who had endorsed President Reagan, and Edward Carlough of the Sheet Metal Workers Union, who along with virtually all other unions had endorsed Walter Mondale. Locigno claimed that the country in general and Teamster workers in particular were much better off under Reagan than under the "malaise" of Jimmy Carter. Carlough responded that Reagan was a radical president who had created 70,000 new millionaires through tax cuts that had created huge deficits, to the detriment of the rest of the country. In summation, Locigno said that people would vote for Reagan because they were better off than they were four years ago, whereas Carlough stated that if people thought about the future and their children, they would vote for Mondale.

Robert MacNeil followed with a moving report about unemployed middle-class manufacturing workers who had lost their jobs during the 1982 recession and remained unemployed or underemployed even though the national employment statistics had been improving. Several people in the Pittsburgh area were interviewed, people who were working at minimum-wage jobs, making one-quarter their former salary. They couldn't afford retraining programs, much less pay the mortgage and feed the kids. They felt that they had been betrayed, that the American Dream had been a lie. One man observed that the TV news reports on unemployment were misleading because so many people had taken a drastic step down to minimum-wage jobs. "The anchorperson smiles and says everything's wonderful in America now. And I just—I don't understand it." A woman interviewed declared that soon there would be no middle class, just "the guys at the top and the guys at the bottom."

Barry Bluestone of the Social Welfare Research Institute and Robert Ortner, the chief economist for the Commerce Department, were then brought on to debate this point of a shrinking middle class. Mr. Bluestone claimed it was indeed shrinking and Mr. Ortner claimed the opposite.

BLUESTONE: *If you go back to 1969, you'll find that less than half of all jobs were in industries that had had an average wage of $13,500 or less in 1980* *dollars. Between 1969 and 1982, however, two-thirds of all the new jobs that were created paid that little. The reason for that is that many of these jobs are part-time jobs, and of course many of them are in the service industries, which are the industries fastest growing in the country, which generally pay much lower wages. . . .*

ORTNER: *If we were really shifting from $12-an-hour jobs to $3-an-hour jobs, you would see it in the income statistics in this country. Real wages are growing now. They shrank in the last two years of the Carter administration. Real, disposable, personal income in the last two years is up 11 percent.*

Both Bluestone and Ortner seemed well prepared with figures to support their positions, but there simply was not enough time to explore the meaning of their claims, which for the viewer meant not only an unresolved debate, which is often the case in any event, but no real opportunity to absorb enough information from either of them to come away from the experience with much other than confusion. An additional truly nonpartisan expert was needed to explain the terms and sort out the facts, to whatever degree possible, in language understandable to most people. This approach is sometimes used on MacNeil/Lehrer, and it would have greatly enhanced this segment.

All in all, however, MacNeil/Lehrer did an excellent job of presenting both the campaign kickoff story and the related Labor Day issues. They spent the entire first half hour on these stories. The other networks would had to have spent fifteen minutes (minus commercial time, of course) on the same issues to match this, which they certainly came nowhere near doing.

MacNeil/Lehrer's last story, which was carried by the other networks also, was a perfect ending to this Labor Day. It reported that former President Jimmy Carter and Rosalyn Carter had gone to New York City to "labor" in the slums as part of a housing rehabilitation program. Carter was shown putting his carpentry skills to good use. This scene of the "ex-president" was more inspiring than anything seen this day from either the present White House occupant or his challenger.

Overall, it was not an impressive television debut for the 1984 campaign. If you had the opportunity to watch the broadcasts of every network, then you would have been fairly well informed, particularly from the MacNeil/Lehrer broadcast. But CBS, NBC, and ABC all seemed more like fast-paced sports wrapups than serious journalistic reports on the beginning of a presidential election campaign. To a certain degree this was a built-in format malady. Even within the given format, however, there was much room for improvement. For instance, it would seem reasonable for the commercial networks to delegate half of their news broadcast time to election-related reporting, *at least* on the opening day of a presidential campaign. In fact, given the import of the ongoing story, the "news" rationale was certainly there for such an approach, indeed, for spending the majority of the nightly news programs on election-issue-related reporting throughout the campaign. And short clips of a candidate's one-liners, commentary concerning campaign strategy, or what the polls say, may be someone's idea of good reporting, but journalistic integrity would seem to demand examination of the issues first and foremost. From what the viewers saw on the commercial network nightly news on this opening day of the 1984 presidential campaign, they would probably conclude that the most important and decisive issue was which candidates drew the largest crowds and had the most balloons at their respective rallies and parades.

Unfortunately, Labor Day was not the exception, but the model, for much of the coverage to come.

Tuesday, September 4: The Presidency or the Papacy, Part One

On this day the question of the week came into full focus: Was this election campaign, only two days old, for the presidency or the papacy?

Observe the opening statements by the anchors of the three major networks.

TED KOPPEL (ABC): *Religion and politics, already one of this campaign's dominant themes, was center stage again today.*

TOM BROKAW (NBC): *Tonight President Reagan has a softer line on religion and politics. When he tied religion directly to politics at a prayer meeting in Dallas, the president touched off a wave of criticism . . . today the president had a different tone.*

DAN RATHER (CBS): *It was campaign-trail combustion by long distance today for Ronald Reagan and Walter Mondale both had high-octane rhetoric ready about who was mixing politics and religion improperly, and who has the tax policy that will sock it to those least able to pay.*

Rather's was a more balanced opening than Koppel's or Brokaw's, as it also made reference to the issue addressed by Mondale on this day. As the first week of the campaign continued, however, religion and politics would certainly become the initial major issue to be focused on by both candidates, fueled by media coverage. And this was the day it began in earnest.

Bill Plante (CBS), Sam Donaldson (ABC), and Chris Wallace (NBC) all reported on President Reagan's speech to the American Legion in Salt

Lake City, leading their stories with his remarks about the religion issue in an unusual forum for such a subject, indicating that the heat was on. Reagan was shown saying, "We must protect the rights of all our citizens to their beliefs, including the rights of those who choose no religion. That is why our administration opposes any required prayers in schools; at the same time we call for the right of children once again to pray voluntarily in our public schools." Chris Wallace immediately pointed out that, in fact, Reagan supported a constitutional amendment for organized prayer in the public schools and that his tone was very different than in Dallas, where he said that opponents of school prayer were intolerant of religion. These were very important statements, as they were at the heart of the religion-and-politics controversy, which otherwise must have seemed very confusing to much of the public. Mr. Reagan had, in his Dallas statement, accused by inference mainstream religious groups—Christian, Jewish, and others—that opposed the school prayer amendment of intolerance toward religion. This amounted to accusing religious groups and individuals of being intolerant toward religion, the logic of which escaped many, unless religion was being narrowly defined by the president to mean only the right-wing Christian fundamentalists, in itself an incredible inference for anyone to make, much less a president of the United States. Chris Wallace reported that those remarks "sparked a heavy Jewish protest" in particular and handed Walter Mondale an issue. None of these nuances were reported by Sam Donaldson or Bill Plante, which were serious ommissions. It should also be noted that in the CBS report, after Dan Rather's opening remark about "high-octane rhetoric" in regard to religion and politics, it was somewhat contradictory to hear nothing fitting that description.

All three reporters moved on to the rest of Reagan's speech before the American Legion, introduced most eloquently by Sam Donaldson: "But if the president tried harder today to hold religion at arm's length, he went to great lengths with both hands to scoop in patriotism." ABC then showed Reagan saying, "What a change from a few years ago when patriotism seemed so out of style. How about those young men and women on our Olympic team this summer. Who has ever said more about this country than those young Americans?" Donaldson reported that the president gave other examples of the new patriotism, including the U.S. hockey team at the 1980 Lake Placid Olympics, the Grenada student's homecoming, the TV show "Call to Glory," and then delivered a roll call of dead military heroes: "Nimitz, Halsey, MacArthur, Bradley, Patton, Ike. They're all gone now. Well, I know you join me in a prayer today that for America, such days and places are gone forever." Donaldson then pointedly commented that "after only two days in the West, the president, leaving for Chicago, is convinced he's nailed down his base and is ready to do battle in the critical industrial states of the East, carrying with him a message of patriotic fervor, suggesting that voting for the Democrats is not only unwise, it's un-American." Presumably, such a strong statement by Donaldson was based on something said in Reagan's speech that we did not see. We should have. Otherwise, Reagan's speech was best covered by Donaldson. Wallace and Plante had similar, but shorter segments on it.

NBC and CBS then pursued a story that ABC ignored, the remarks that day of Treasury Secretary Donald Regan. Bill Plante of CBS stated that "elsewhere on the political battlefield . . . people were down in the trenches. Treasury Secretary Donald Regan delivered a blistering attack on Mondale's plan to raise taxes." CBS then cut to Regan saying, "He has not asked for any increase in taxes and we don't intend to ask for any increase in taxes. Mondale does. That's our whole point. He's asking for massive increases, the largest increases in the history of mankind." For the second day in a row in a Plante story, a nonsensical edit was made. At the beginning of the Regan quote, the first word, *He*, would grammatically have to refer to whatever subject had immediately preceded it, which in Plante's narrative was Mondale. Clearly, Regan was referring to the president and later refers to Mondale. It is particularly confusing because Plante says that Mondale is being attacked for his plan to raise taxes, then we hear Secretary Regan say "he" has not asked for any increase in taxes. In addition, Plante should have commented on the "largest increases in the history of mankind" comment. Is it true? And if so, should it not be put in the context of the "largest" tax cuts, then deficits, then tax increases under President Reagan? On NBC, Regan was shown saying that Mondale's tax plan would cost the average American household between $360 and $660 per year. But Tom Brokaw put the story in context, noting that Mondale's plan was a response to the huge deficits of the Reagan administration years and that Regan gave no administration plan for cutting the deficit.

Brokaw then effectively moved on to Mondale's day by saying that he had an answer for both "Regan and Reagan," cutting to Mondale talking to a group of meat cutters in a Long Beach, California, grocery store: "Under Mr. Reagan the rich will get richer and average Americans will get poorer. I think that's dead wrong. Yesterday Mr. Reagan said that when I talk this way I'm appealing to envy. In other words I should shut up is what I think he's saying, and if I were him I'd want me to shut up, because people don't agree with this. I wouldn't blame you for being envious when you see that your taxes went up and those wealthy went clear down, but I don't think *envy* is the real word, I think it's *anger*. I'm mad, I'm angry, I'm damn mad, because I don't think it's right." It would have been useful here to get some background, however briefly, on the actual effect of the Reagan tax programs of the past three years. We should not have to rely solely on the short clips of the candidates and their surrogates for "factual" information. Unfortunately, this is a common failing of the networks in these kind of reports.

Britt Hume of ABC covered this story using only the end of the above quote, but added some interesting footage of Mondale joking with the meat cutters about how many fingers they had, showing that Mondale was campaigning with the kind of people with whom he was most comfortable. Mondale was also shown referring to charts and saying to the group, "If you were here, you got enough tax relief to get a free Lincoln every year, with all the stuff. But if you were here, they didn't even give you a hubcap." It was interesting to see Mondale talking like this with these workers, as it seemed his best shot at creating a media event and, at the same time, showing that he can be comfortable campaigning. But Hume should have given us some analysis as to the context and accuracy of these remarks, the typically rhetorical type of one-line comments that TV news reporting such as this encourages. Hume finished his report with the comment that Mondale would like to "cast this race as a class struggle between him and the working people and President Reagan and his rich friends. With the economy in a booming recovery that has generated millions of jobs, it won't be easy to get Americans to see it that way. But it could be Mondale's only chance."

Susan Spencer of CBS had almost none of Mondale's remarks in her report, but it was an interesting narrative approach: "While the President had the flag-waving throngs cheering, Walter Mondale stayed in his suite on the *Queen Mary* [apparently docked near Long Beach], working on speeches, not even appearing until midday, his staff still down after yesterday's faltering Labor Day kickoff. A rally last night in Long Beach had done little to cheer anyone up. The sound system failed, the crowd was nowhere near President Reagan's 50,000 [there's that figure again] earlier in the day. But Mondale's aides insist such comparisons are meaningless, that this is to be a campaign of ideas, not media events. But today Mondale did do what advisers think works best for him on TV; he talked informally with a small group of workers, and in blasting President Reagan's tax policies as unfair, he seemed to be trying to follow advice to loosen up."

MONDALE: *I'm mad, I'm angry, I'm damn mad, because I don't think it's right.*
SPENCER: *Before a made-for-cameras chart, which he said made it clear that the president's tax program socked it to the middle class [again, no background, but at least she put in the qualifier "he said"], Mondale repeated his demand for debates.*
MONDALE: *Why shouldn't the two of us have to stand there toe to toe? If he*

says that chart is wrong, let's debate about it. [This is not only an important quote, which NBC and ABC left out, but it took the journalist off the hook somewhat for having to give background, at least until it was determined whether Mondale and Reagan would engage in a detailed debate of the issues themselves. The format and number of debates was still being negoti-ated at this point. But some objective background was still called for.] If he thinks the average American ought to pay more taxes while his rich friends are running free, let him argue it. I'll be glad to take him on. [Audience applauds.]

SPENCER: *In the meantime, Mondale will take on the tough issues, like religion and politics, the next day. The idea: Make people think beyond the president's great communicating.*

NBC's Don Oliver gave a report on the Mondale campaign's attempt to contest California even though it's Reagan's home state. He mentioned the not-very-good start of the Mondale campaign, including a comment about this day's "curious visit to a grocery company," where Mondale spoke to the workers, which seemed a very curious comment on Oliver's part. He also mentioned the 50,000 figure as the number for Reagan's Labor Day rally. It seemed that this curious figure was becoming the cross-network acceptable count (although ABC had used 30,000, which was closest to the Associated Press estimate of 20,000). Oliver reported a mock vote at the California State Fair that had Reagan-Bush leading Mondale-Ferraro by 7 percent as part of the evidence for why Mondale might be wasting his money in California. But considering the spread of most polls, 7 percent didn't sound too bad; and it isn't much of a spread in a political race with almost two months to go. Oliver said that to write off California may be to write off the election, that things didn't look much better in other states, so the Mondale people were moving in for a fight, hoping for Reagan overconfidence and help from the wide support in California for the nuclear freeze, concern about environmental issues such as offshore drilling, "the Ferraro factor," and help from Gary Hart (who defeated Mondale in the California primary), who was campaigning for Mondale eight days in California in September alone. Hart was shown saying, "There are miracles in politics and I believe one could happen here."

The real disappointment of the day, ironically after the previous day, was "The MacNeil/Lehrer NewsHour." It just goes to show, a good for-mat doesn't guarantee quality. The beginning of the report was fine, covering the same ground as the other networks on Reagan's and Mondale's day, but with more footage of their remarks, which is generally the case on this program. But then Judy Woodruff interviewed Mondale campaign manager Jim Johnson, and she just couldn't seem to get off the theme established in her first question: "First of all, the *Los Angeles Times*, as you know, has put out a poll today saying that your candidate is twenty-seven points behind President Reagan. How in the world do you make up a gap like that? No candidate ever has." One felt like saying, "Well, Judy, what's the point of having this interview, other than torture, since there's apparently no reason to even have an election?"

Jim Johnson did an admirable job in the face of this incessant "how can you possibly win?" questioning, pointing out that the polls had been constantly changing during the primary campaign and since the conventions, that different polls said different things, and that the issues, such as arms control and the deficit, were what mattered. He said the American people would pay attention to the issues, and this was how they would win. Whether it would have helped Mondale or reaffirmed support for Reagan would never be known (and for the author is not the point), but one wondered, after the TV "journalism" Johnson had just experienced, how he imagined the American people would be given a chance to pay attention to the issues. He must still have been dreaming that the Reagan campaign would agree to six debates with only a moderator, and the candidates going at it toe to toe.

A story that turned out to be very important was reported only by NBC. Top Reagan campaign advisers said that before the president held another press conference, they wanted to make sure Mondale wouldn't be given equal time by the networks. The last Reagan press conference had been in July. Tom Brokaw said sternly that NBC policy had always been that a news conference is *news*, and does not require equal time, in other words, the explanation about no more news conferences did not have a "valid premise." That, of course, wouldn't stop the Reagan White House from following through. The president's next press conference wouldn't be until January 1985. How did the other networks manage to miss this one!

Wednesday, September 5: *Issue-Blind Video*

The third day of an eight-week presidential election campaign was too soon to abandon all hope of the possibility that television news would make a positive contribution to the democratic process. The facts, however, were quickly snowballing in the direction of that inevitable conclusion. This day of TV news seemed almost as if it had been consciously constructed to supply evidence for such an opinion.

The only program to headline a campaign story was ABC. Unfortunately, this was not the result of ABC exhibiting a more responsible civic-mindedness than its fellow broadcasters, but an illustrative example of scoop-over-substance disease, in deadly combination with controversy-over-substance fever, for which no cure has yet been found. Ted Koppel began the report: "ABC has obtained a copy of a speech Walter Mondale plans to give tomorrow to the Jewish service organization B'nai B'rith in Washington, D.C. It is a ripsnorter of a speech. Mondale accuses Reagan of creating a 'holier than thou climate by gift-wrapping political issues in the name of God. . . . There are some in our midst today who insult religion by seeking to invoke God for political ends . . . and yes, Mr. President, I'm speaking of you.' " CNN reported later that evening that Mondale's press secretary, Maxine Isaacs, stated that ABC's report was not accurate, but that ABC stuck by the story, saying that the draft had been obtained from a reliable source. The following day, Mondale did give a strong speech on the religion and politics issue, an issue that will be examined at length in subsequent pages. But it was not the same speech that ABC quoted from. In a retraction the following day, Ted Koppel stated, "We should have and could have checked with the Mondale campaign. We did not. We formally apologize to Mr. Mondale and his supporters." To ABC's credit, there was no hedging there. But the incident pointed to something even more significant than a basic journalistic lapse in checking sources. While trying to report the future in an essentially sensationalist fashion, the present, which was filled with important events this day, was not given the attention it deserved, by ABC or anyone else. The tendency of TV news to try to report the future instead of concentrating on the present was exemplified in its broadest and most damaging form by the constant dwelling on controversy, strategy, and the probable outcome of the election, as opposed to examining in depth the issues at hand during the campaign.

On this day, the media got some help from a politician in avoiding the important issues at hand. For reasons known perhaps not even to himself, Speaker of the House and Democratic party leader Thomas P. "Tip" O'Neill decided to publicly discuss his feelings about Walter Mondale's strategy in the campaign thus far, with emphasis on his perception of its shortcomings. He would seem this day to have forfeited any right to leadership of his party, since it would be equally damning whether he did or did not understand the impact of what he was doing. The leads on NBC and CBS, along with all the stories on Mondale's day on all the networks, were ultimately dominated by this story. ABC and NBC had essentially the same clips of O'Neill saying, "He's [Mondale] being too much of a gentleman, let me put it that way. He's trying to talk issues, and while they're out cutting you up you just can't talk issues. You've got to tell the truth about them in a tough, a severe manner."

Consider the following by Lisa Myers of NBC: "Meanwhile in Washington, Mondale took a *beating* [my emphasis] from the leader of his own party. . . . Mondale was already having trouble persuading voters that he was a viable candidate and a strong leader. It certainly doesn't help to have O'Neill question his *toughness* [my emphasis], nor is it likely to enhance confidence in his ability to deal with the Soviets to have it said he's being pushed around by George Bush."

This was one of the more irresponsible narratives by a reporter to be encountered among much competition during the campaign. Myers's reference to George Bush is totally unintelligible to the viewer, as there is no previous mention of Bush. Upon examination of the report, it becomes apparent by inference that O'Neill had probably referred to Bush, but these remarks were not included in the clip shown of O'Neill. That some-one—the reporter, an editor, or the producer—didn't catch this, demonstrates gross amateurism, which happens remarkably often on these network reports. It's the perfect example of the intellectual vacuum in which so much of the "whiz-bang" reporting of network news seems to occur. The use of the words *beating* and *toughness* is highly questionable and is certainly not justified based on the clip of O'Neill that is shown. The "viable candidate and strong leader" comment was typical of the references to Mondale, which served only to create and reinforce these very images and preempt a process that the *campaign*, not reporter opinion or even current public opinion, was supposed to determine. But most outrageous was the "ability to deal with the Soviets" comment. This illogical leap was not likely to occur to any viewer, until Myers put it into the minds of millions.

This kind of damage also illustrates how politicians can utilize the media to commit political suicide or to politically assassinate their allies. Undoubtedly the truth of the old adage "With friends like these, who needs enemies" was evident to Walter Mondale this day. The ultimate irony of O'Neill's advice to Mondale to stop "talking issues" was that his comment helped take the media spotlight away from one of the most important proposals made by a candidate for the presidency, or a sitting president, in two decades. The fact that this story was missed entirely, for all practical purposes, by television news, was inexcusable. It was, among other things, a prime example of the predilection of TV news for controversy over substance, as Hedrick Smith pointed out in the *New York Times Magazine* ("The Politics Of Blame," 7 October 1984), where he noted that the O'Neill story got the attention this day instead of Mondale's important policy proposal.

The proposal that should have made the headlines was announced by Mondale during his speech to the American Legion convention. All the networks covered the speech and several of Mondale's points. Mac-Neil/Lehrer had an extensive segment on defense and arms-control issues based on Mondale's and Reagan's remarks the previous day before the

American Legion. But with the exception of a one-liner from CBS's Susan Spencer, all the networks, including MacNeil/Lehrer, completely missed the most significant and newsworthy item in Mondale's speech. He stated that, if elected, he would initiate a moratorium on all testing of nuclear weapons and antisatellite weapons, challenging the Soviets to do the same. This unilateral initiative (not to be confused with unilateral disarmament) would be implemented for six months. If there was no response from the Soviets, it could be abandoned. But that would not be the likely outcome. This aggressive approach to an arms-control breakthrough would have followed a landmark historical precedent.

The last time an American president had taken such an initiative had been in June 1963, when John Kennedy delivered his famous speech at the American University, perhaps the best and most important speech he ever gave. Kennedy announced that the United States would immediately cease testing nuclear weapons in the atmosphere and appealed to the Soviet Union to do likewise. His speech, which in a brilliant play on Woodrow Wilson's words called for making the world "safe for diversity," appealed to the common humanity and interests of Americans and Soviets in the nuclear age, pointing out that the potential for nuclear holocaust overshadowed our significant differences. Soviet Premier Khrushchev responded positively to Kennedy's initiative, which led to the nuclear Test Ban Treaty, signed in Moscow on August 5, 1963, by the United States, the Soviet Union, Great Britain, and later 113 cosigning nations. In addition, the United States and the Soviet Union entered into other economic and cultural agreements. But most important, Kennedy's initiative was the beginning of the entire arms-control process as we know it. The Test Ban Treaty, which outlawed nuclear tests in the atmosphere, underwater, and in space, has never been violated. But the remaining legal testing area, underground, has been utilized hundreds of times by both the United States and the Soviets. Walter Mondale's proposal would have made this, too, off limits, leading to a comprehensive test ban treaty. A Gallop poll in October would show that sixty-one percent of the American people supported a six-month unilateral freeze on not only testing, but production and deployment of nuclear weapons as a strategy for reaching a long-term agreement with the Soviets. In addition, the antisatellite moratorium would have been a potentially major step in halting an arms race in space.

The chances of Mondale's proposed initiative actually leading to an agreement with the Soviets outlawing all nuclear testing would be excellent. Because of the nature of the Soviet politburo, the conservative influence of collective decision making even under a strong leader in the USSR, it is likely that such a bold initiative would always have to come from the American side. There are advantages to such an approach for an American leader as well, which was demonstrated by Kennedy, and by subsequent arms-treaty negotiations. When an agreement is being sought through painstaking negotiation, the politics of the Congress, and particularly the Senate, which must ratify any treaty, invariably complicate the negotiating process itself. In the case of the Test Ban Treaty of 1963, Kennedy, by moving boldly and quickly, was able to bring a signed treaty to the Senate within two months. There was not much to argue about, although conservatives (including Ronald Reagan) made plenty of noise, some suggesting that the treaty verged on treason, for reasons unclear to most then and discredited since. (The argument was that the treaty would interfere with our defense capability and the Russians would cheat.) But public opinion and a majority of senators were behind Kennedy, who by the test ban agreement had ended fears of a strontium 90 environmental catastrophe (we will probably never know how much cancer was and is being caused by the atmospheric testing) and had brought new hope for an end to the nuclear reign of terror. A new initiative to make the test ban comprehensive would almost certainly receive a positive Soviet response, not only because indicated by historical precedent, but because the major points of such an agreement had already been worked out during the Carter administration.

The failure of television news, and to a large extent the print media as well, to even report, much less underscore, this as a major campaign issue was an incredible journalistic blunder. The Reagan administration had turned its back on negotiations for an end to testing, because it wanted to be able to test a new generation of weapons it intended to build. This was necessary, the administration argued, in order to "catch up" with the Soviets. Mondale and other military and arms-control experts said we weren't behind and some argued we were ahead, because of the Soviet reliance on land-based missiles and U.S. superiority in technology, submarines, and bombers. Still others wondered what meaning such arguments had when each side could incinerate the planet; they were concerned about the destabilizing effect of new weapons. On the issue of antisatellite weapons, the administration was concerned about Soviet advances and not interested in a precedent to stop space weapons testing, given the "Star Wars" initiative to devise a defense against nuclear attack. Mondale considered "Star Wars" to be a dangerous beginning of a new arms race in space. The stage was set for a classic political debate before the voters. But the media, particularly TV, was not to allow it to unfold this way. In many ways this was, unfortunately, to be expected. For over twenty years the following question had increased in relevance with the passing of time: Why had no other president taken Kennedy's approach, the most uncategorically successful initiative on arms control in the nuclear age? This was not a question that had been extensively examined over the years, particularly on television news programs. It was one of the great failings of broadcast journalism that it had such a poor record in either identifying or staying with and examining over long periods the crucial specific issues related to the broader major concerns of our times. Given this fact, it was not likely for a sudden metamorphosis to occur during a presidential election campaign. But one would expect that the journalistic minimum would require a more focused intellectual and civic-minded effort on the part of television news during a campaign, *at least* to the extent of reporting major policy proposals by the candidates.

This minimum expectation, however, did not seem to be in the cards. The "nail in the coffin" on this day of broadcast nonjournalism was the coverage, or rather lack of, on President Reagan's campaign activities. The only network with coverage of Reagan, including MacNeil/Lehrer, was NBC. Here is Chris Wallace's report.

WALLACE: *Addressing midwestern business leaders [in Chicago], the president launched one of his sharpest attacks yet on Walter Mondale's idea of raising taxes to cut the deficit. Mr. Reagan said the economic recovery will erase some of the red ink and that the rest of the answer is to cut government spending, although he offered no specifics. The president said tax increases don't work.*

REAGAN: *Today, to suggest a tax increase simply for the cure of the deficit, well, we've had any number of tax increases over the past fifty years and we have had regularly deficits every year for fifty years. Every year since World War II. In the five years before we came here, to office, the taxes doubled in those five years. And the deficits increased.*

WALLACE: *In fact, there have been federal budget surpluses in eight years since World War II. And while deficits generally increased under Jimmy Carter, they were higher under Gerald Ford and have more than tripled in the Reagan years following the huge tax cut. Despite those deficits, the president again blasted Congress for blocking a constitutional amendment requiring a balanced budget, and he urged the executives to lobby Congress to give him the power to strike individual items from the budget.*

REAGAN: *Please write letters, send wires, twist arms—we need the line-item veto—we're going to try for it all out.*

WALLACE: *After a rocky start, the Reagan camp now feels well positioned to handle Mondale on taxes. And aides say it's also smart politics for the president not to get any more specific about how he would cut that big budget.*

Apparently the "rocky start" comment was a reference to the period between the Democratic and Republican conventions when Reagan and Bush and other members of the administration were having trouble synchronizing their lines in response to Mondale's surprising challenge on raising taxes in his nomination acceptance speech. But it wasn't a very clear or useful comment. There was an edit, or "jump cut," in this report that was highly questionable, when Reagan referred to "deficits every year for fifty years" and then "every year since World War II." Even if you started counting from the German invasion of Poland in 1939 (and "since" implied after the war's end in 1945), it hadn't been fifty years since World War II. Was this edit an attempt at showing Reagan contradict himself or correct himself? If both comments were going to be used, then the latter should have been shown in its full context. Otherwise, Wallace did a fairly good job of packing the relevant information into the allotted time. He should particularly be credited for his dispassionate and factual rebuttal of Reagan's statements about the deficits. This was the kind of reporting that there should have been more of on both Reagan and Mondale equally. The first job of a journalist is to keep the facts straight, which contributes to keeping the candidates straight. Another noteworthy aspect of this report was the positive use of graphics, which is to say, of television's visual capacity. When Wallace spoke of the Carter, Ford, and Reagan deficits, there were excellent graphs onscreen illustrating the point. Graphics are a very useful tool, as they significantly increase the likelihood of the viewer absorbing the information being imparted in the reporter's narrative.

The drawback in even a well-done report such as this, however, is its brevity, and therefore its forced selectivity. There were several important factors related to Reagan's comments that were not discussed. First, there are other relevant concerns when discussing and measuring deficits besides amount of dollars, such as percentage of gross national product being consumed by federal spending. Reagan's expressed concern about raising taxes not helping to cut the deficit certainly had some historical justification, but it wasn't commented upon. The circumstances surrounding the budget-surplus years begged examination. And the issue of the line-item veto needed a full exploration in itself. Even with their half-hour time constraint, during a presidential campaign the majority of network nightly news time could be given over to followup on these kinds of questions, raised by the candidate's statements and records, which would greatly enhance the quality of election coverage.

But the truly dismaying fact was that on ABC, CBS, and MacNeil/Lehrer, there was no report at all on Reagan's remarks. MacNeil/Lehrer could fall back on the somewhat justifiable excuse that it covered issues in depth, and on this day they covered the defense issue extensively. The issues raised in Reagan's speech would also certainly be covered extensively on MacNeil/Lehrer, if not on this day, during the course of the campaign. But they still should have had a short report on the president's day. For the others, there was no excuse. The president of the United States gave one of his most specific issue-oriented speeches of the campaign (and one of his only) on one of the most important and controversial topics being debated before the electorate. But much of the electorate undoubtedly never heard about it, because it was nowhere to be found on the TV evening news program they were watching.

Thursday, September 6: The Presidency or the Papacy, Part Two

The religion-and-politics controversy that dominated the first week of the campaign reached its peak on this day. NBC, ABC, CBS, and Mac-Neil/Lehrer all headlined their news programs with remarks from Mondale and Reagan at the B'nai B'rith convention in Washington, D.C.

NBC's Lisa Myers reported on the Mondale speech before B'nai B'rith.

MYERS: *He chose a politically powerful Jewish organization to defend separation of church and state.*

MONDALE: *A determined band is raising doubts about people's faith. They are reaching for government power to impose their own beliefs on other people—and the Reagan administration has opened its arms to them.*

MYERS: *He spoke of an extreme fringe, with fire in the eyes, poised to capture the Republican party.*

MONDALE: *It is disquieting that a presidential aide dissatisfied with the religious purity of the White House staff has urged his colleagues to, quote, "Get saved, or get out." It is ominous when Reverend Falwell brags that if Mr. Reagan is reelected, quote, "We, we will get at least two more appointments to the Supreme Court."*

MYERS: *On Reagan's claim that religion needs to be defended from the state:*

MONDALE: *The queen of England, where state religion is established, is called defender of the faith. But the president of the United States is the defender of the constitution, which defends all faiths.*

MYERS: *On the suggestion that opposition to school prayer is un-Christian:*

MONDALE: *Instead of construeing dissent from him in good faith, Mr. Reagan has insulted the motives of those of us who disagree with him, including me.*

MYERS: *Mondale said he shared the concerns of those yearning for traditional values.*

MONDALE: *The truth is that the answer to a weaker family is not a stronger state, it is stronger values.*

MYERS: *Mondale's advisers insist that this speech was made more out of personal conviction than for political gain. But they believe Reagan has hurt himself among young, independent, and Jewish voters, and that Mondale has a much-needed opportunity to score points.*

Chris Wallace then covered Reagan's appearance before B'nai B'rith, which followed Mondale's.

WALLACE: *The president ignored Mondale's speech, but not the issue, trying to ease what aides admit is a deep Jewish concern about his recent statements. Mr. Reagan did not mention his support for school prayer or other religious measures B'nai B'rith opposes, emphasizing instead he rejects any state religion.*

REAGAN: *The unique thing in America is a wall in our Constitution separating church and state.*

WALLACE: *The president said his support for a religious revival is not limited to Christian fundamentalists, that all religions are included, and Jews have nothing to fear.*

REAGAN: *The ideals of our country leave no room whatsoever for intolerance, anti-Semitism, or bigotry of any kind—none.*

WALLACE: *But Mr. Reagan shifted quickly from religion to areas where he's on firmer ground with this audience. He said he will back a UN treaty against genocide that's been stalled in the Senate for thirty years. And he restated U.S. support for Israel.*

REAGAN: *Permanent security for the people of that brave state—in this great enterprise the United States and Israel stand forever united.*

WALLACE: *But the head of B'nai B'rith was concerned about church and state and disappointed the president did not back away from government support of religion.*

GERALD KRAFT: *Nothing he said today addressed that concern.*

WALLACE: *The Reagan camp says the religious debate has helped so far, firing up the president's conservative base. Now, aides say Mr. Reagan will disarm his critics, moving away from religion, and as in past campaigns, toward the center.*

One thing that should have been explained, since the UN treaty against genocide was mentioned, is the fact that the reason it hadn't been ratified for thirty years was opposition by conservative senators, which had made the United States look ridiculous at best in the world community for years. Given the right-wing opposition on obscure grounds of interfering with national sovereignty (the right to commit genocide apparently), it had also ironically handed the Soviets a propaganda weapon. (Of course, in terms of logic, rabid anti-Communists often seemed to be pro-Communist provocateurs in disguise.) In addition, it should have been pointed out that this was the first time Reagan had indicated support for the treaty. This issue, like so many others briefly alluded to or missed altogether in the nightly news reports, needed more attention.

On ABC's report, Sam Donaldson made a very important observation regarding the image-making, camera-conscious strategy of the Reagan campaign: "Two and a half hours after Walter Mondale left the hall, President Reagan took the same B'nai B'rith podium, behind which White House aides had carefully moved in the American and Israeli flags, so that unlike Mondale, Mr. Reagan would be seen on television flanked by those patriotic symbols. . . ."

If one reviews the videotapes of the news programs covering Mondale's and Reagan's appearances this day before B'nai B'rith, the importance of Donaldson's report becomes immediately apparent. The visual difference is like comparing black and white to color. Mondale appears drab in comparison to Reagan, even though he is clearly more comfortable and makes a better delivery in terms of his remarks. This, of course, makes sense, as he is speaking to an audience more receptive to his message than to Reagan's. But this advantage is completely offset in *visual* terms by the warmth and majesty of the flags surrounding Reagan as he speaks. Unconsciously, the image of Reagan as leader is reinforced, the image of Mondale as colorless and not on the same level as Reagan in terms of leadership is reinforced. These images are often more available to an incumbent president. After all, the White House is always available as a backdrop for visuals. But the kind of visual manipulation on "neutral" territory as described by Donaldson in this situation was raised to a new strategic level by the Reagan campaign in 1984.

Although, like the other networks, failing to make Donaldson's point, "The MacNeil/Lehrer NewsHour" did cover the religion-and-politics issue extensively, showing as it often does what television news can aspire to. The following lengthy excerpts illustrate the chasm between the commercial network nightly news programs and anything approaching in-depth reporting.

ROBERT MACNEIL: *The theme of religion in politics became an even sharper presidential campaign issue today. Walter Mondale used an appearance at the convention of B'nai B'rith to attack the president for encouraging religious groups he said wanted to use government power to impose their religious beliefs on the nation. Mondale said, "No president should attempt to transform policy debates into theological disputes." Mr. Reagan, speaking later to the same Jewish organization, referred only briefly to the religious issue, which he has raised twice in a major way. The president said, "The ideals of the country leave no room whatsoever for intolerance, anti-Semitism, or bigotry of any kind." As our first major segment tonight, we examine this rapidly emerging issue in depth.*

JIM LEHRER: *The first American politicians to debate religion in politics were Jefferson, Madison, and their fellow founding fathers. There is a debate now over who started it again in 1984. Republicans say it was Geraldine Ferraro, who said President Reagan's budget cutting doesn't jibe with his professed Christian beliefs. Democrats counter that, among other things, it was Reagan's friend and campaign chairman Paul Laxalt's "Dear Christian Minister" letter on voter registration. But there is no disagreement over when the issue was finally joined on the Reagan-Mondale level. That was in Dallas two weeks ago today when President Reagan talked of the connection between religion and politics at a prayer breakfast. Here is a reminder excerpt of what he said.*

REAGAN: *The truth is, politics and morality are inseparable. And as morality's foundation is religion, religion and politics are necessarily related. We need religion as a guide. We need it because we are imperfect. And our government needs the church because only those humble enough to admit they're sinners can bring to democracy the tolerance it requires in order to survive. We established no religion in this country, nor will we ever. All are free to believe or not to believe. All are free to practice a faith or not. But those who believe must be free to speak of and act on their belief to apply moral teaching to public questions. Without God there is a coarsening of society. And without God, democracy will not and cannot long endure. If we ever forget that we're one nation under God, then we will be a nation gone under.*

LEHRER: *Those words caused a furor in some religious and political circles—Jewish leaders and Democrats among those criticizing Mr. Reagan on grounds he was injecting religion into the 1984 campaign. [Strangely, the Reagan remarks categorizing as "intolerant" those who opposed the school prayer amendment, which caused the greatest controversy, were not used here.] The reaction caused Mr. Reagan to issue clarifying remarks, the major of those in a Tuesday speech to the American Legion. . . .*

REAGAN: *I can't think of anyone who favors the government establishing a religion in this country. I know I don't. But what some would do is to twist the concept of religion, freedom of religion, to mean freedom against religion. So let me repeat what I've always believed: Religion is one of the traditional values which deserves to be preserved and strengthened. We are and must remain a pluralistic society. When we speak of church and religion, we speak of them with a small "c" and a small "r" so as to include within the constitutional protection all churches and all religions. The unique thing about America is that every single American is free to choose and practice his or her own religion, or to choose no religion at all, and that right must not and shall not be questioned or violated by the state. We must protect the rights of all our citizens to their beliefs, including the rights of those who choose no religion.*

LEHRER: *Walter Mondale had been among those criticizing Mr. Reagan's remarks from the beginning. His toughest words came in a nationwide radio address from Minneapolis on Labor Day. He said then, "The Reagan approach will corrupt our faith and divide our nation." That was a prelude to his major address on the subject to the B'nai B'rith here in Washington today.*

MONDALE: *A few weeks ago on the eve of the Republican Convention, 45,000 ministers received a letter from the chairman of the Reagan campaign, Senator Laxalt, which was—which reads as follows: "Dear Christian Leader," it began, and before it ended, it had defined Mr. Reagan's supporters as "leaders under God's authority." Most Americans would be surprised that God is a Republican. And if Senator Laxalt's letter were an isolated example, one might dismiss it as partisan zealotry. Unfortunately, it is not an exception. Listen to Jerry Falwell, whose benediction at the Republican Convention called Mr. Reagan and Mr. Bush "God's instruments for rebuilding America." Or scan something called the "Presidential Biblical Scorecard," which as much as brands me as antifamily and un-Christian. I am alarmed by the rise of what a former Republican congressman called moral McCarthyism. A determined band is raising doubts about people's faith. They are reaching for government power to impose their own beliefs on other people, and the Reagan administration has opened its arms to them. And what I am doing here today is something that in twenty-five years of public life I never thought I would do. I have never before had to defend my political—my religious faith in a political campaign. I have never thought it proper for political leaders to use religion to partisan advantage by advertising their own faith and questioning their opponent's. I believe in an America where all people have the right to pursue their faith, not just freely, but also without insult or embarrassment. I believe in an America where government is not permitted to dictate the religious life of our people, where religion is a private matter between individuals and their God, between families and their churches and their synagogues, with no room for politicians in between.*

LEHRER: *Three hours later, President Reagan spoke before that same group. He ignored the Mondale charges directly and said only this about the issue.*

REAGAN: *The unique thing about America is a wall in our Constitution separating church and state. It guarantees there will never be a state religion in this land, but at the same time it makes sure that every single American is free to choose and practice his or her religious beliefs or to choose no religion at all. Their rights shall not be questioned or violated by the state.*

LEHRER: *We continue the discussion and the debate now with two United*

States senators with strong religious beliefs who strongly disagree on most things political, including religion in politics. They are Senator John East, Republican from North Carolina, and Senator Patrick Leahy, Democrat of Vermont. Senator Leahy, is there a rise of moral McCarthyism, to use the term that Vice-President Mondale used today?

LEAHY: *I think the term he used, of course, which is from a Republican, coincidentally, is an accurate one, and I really, in almost twenty years in political life, I have never seen anything quite like it. . . . It worries me when you see people in political life who go and start talking about what our religious beliefs should be, how we should do it, and so on, and give great speeches about it. I think if they really feel that strongly, they should worry about setting the example, a religious example, through their own lives and through their own way of doing things. I don't think that people in political office should be out trying to tell people how they should practice their religion. They should instead be talking about what their political stands are, and let their religion be a private matter and let it be by their own example. It sets far more example, for example, for somebody in public office that they truly believe in going to church and in practicing their religion, to do that—not to talk about somebody else doing it.*

LEHRER: *Is moral McCarthyism going on, Senator East?*

EAST: *Well, of course not, and it's absurd to say so. I think that we first need to put this in the context of politics. Mr. Mondale is way behind in the polls; he's grasping for political straws, and this is one of his straws. And politically, I think that it's a pretty slender reed that he's found to lean upon. First I would remind Mr. Mondale that Geraldine Ferraro, as you noted in the introductory comment, first raised the issue in San Francisco, where she said the president is un-Christian in terms of his social policies. So I think first he ought to lecture his own vice-presidential candidate before he turns to President Reagan. President Reagan, I think, has very clearly spelled out a responsible position here, namely, no one's calling for an established national religion. No one is trying to impose that upon the country—that was the intention of the First Amendment. What he is saying is, which I think is the commonsense thing, that the moral and ethical and religious values of people, whatever party they're in, whether they think of themselves as liberal or conservative, are bound to work themselves into their policy position on certain issues. We have examples of those on the liberal side. We think of the World Council of Churches, the National Council of Churches. We think of Martin Luther King's activities on behalf of civil rights. We think of William Sloane Coffin and the Vietnam War. We think of the Berrigan brothers and the Vietnam War. And then it only seems to be when there is a conservative activist—Mr. Falwell, for example—that all of a sudden we're told, "My, this is a very terrible thing that is occurring." I think it's interesting to note, the National Conference of Catholic Bishops, when they introduced their views on abortion, they are told, "Oh, now, you're mixing politics and religion." Yet if they issue a statement on the nuclear freeze, then those of the liberal side of the spectrum say, "Now, that is a very good socially conscious thing to do," where religion and politics clearly mix.*

LEAHY: *. . . The fact is—and I think just about everybody, left or right or middle, Republican or Democrat, agrees—that religion has been injected into politics more in the last couple of years than at any time, certainly since I've been old enough to vote. . . . We have a group, the ACTV, [American Coalition for Traditional Values] go down and meet at the White House. And they say that we don't have—the problem with America—we do not have enough of God's ministers running our country. . . . One of their members says that, for example, that Catholics, that's a false religion; that Jews are consigned to hell. Well, now, are we going back to the things we fought a revolution to get away from? Are we going to turn our back on the First Amendment of the Constitution? . . . I think it is wrong for religious leaders to tell people how they should vote, whether they're on the right or the left, whether it's a question of school prayer or Vietnam, whether it's a question of nuclear arms control or abortion. Every religious leader has a right—in fact I would say duty—to preach to their congregation what they feel are their moral values, to preach God's word however they see it and however they interpret it. But when they cross over and say that "Now we'll tell you how to run your country. Now we'll tell you how to have your political life," that's wrong. . . . I would not want the government to tell various religious groups how they must practice their religion, any more than those religious groups should tell the government how to run.*

EAST: *Well, I don't see that the president would disagree with Senator Leahy. What he is saying is, We believe in pluralism, we believe in diversity. And we simply are all agreed we will not have an established national church. He [Reagan] is expressing what I think is a legitimate concern that to some extent today, in contemporary American life—for example, in the public schools—anything that would reflect a religious symbolism of the Judeo-Christian heritage is denied access. The Ten Commandments cannot be posted, for example. . . .*

LEAHY: *When you look at the debate we recently had on school prayer in the Senate, it was very clear that the constitutional amendment that the president was espousing, certainly in the beginning of that debate, would have had the government dictate what kind of a prayer we we're supposed to say. . . .*

EAST: *That's not true. It was voluntary prayer, voluntary prayer.*

LEAHY: *No, that's not so. The first constitutional amendment that came up had a prayer dictated what it was going to be, and totally lost sight of the fact that children are now allowed to pray in school. You know, ask any*

child who's just gone through final exams if they've ever prayed in school.
They'll tell you they've prayed in school.

The discussion ended here and it was unfortunate there was no follow-through on this last point by Leahy. Polls showing a majority of Americans favoring "voluntary" school prayer were used to show support for a school prayer amendment. But it was not illegal for a child to voluntarily pray on his or her own impulse. The amendment was for "organized" prayer, which would always lead to the question, Who would organize and determine this group prayer? What kind of pressure would such a situation create for the children who may wish to "voluntarily" decline participation in this ritual?

Robert MacNeil then continued the debate with another twosome.

MacNEIL: *This heightened debate is not confined to the politicians, but is being waged at the grass-roots level by various groups which have sprung up to promote or protest the role of religion in government. People for the American Way started in 1980 to counter the rise of the religious Right. Its chairman is John Buchanan, a former Republican congressman from Alabama who blames the loss of his seat on efforts by Christian conservatives. On the other hand, Christian conservatives have banded together to form their own organizations, one of which is the American Coalition for Traditional Values. It claims it will deliver two and a half million fundamentalist votes to Reagan this year. Its chairman is evangelist Tim Lahaye. . . . Mr. Lahaye, as you heard, Mr. Mondale charged today that Mr. Reagan is reaching out to religious groups—and I presume he meant ones like yours—that want to use the power of government to impose their beliefs on the country. How do you respond to that?*

LAHAYE: *Well, I think it's a lot of smokescreen in the political campaign. Actually, I think this is all very healthy, where we have watched a pendulum swing in our country from being a nation under God and a nation that requires our public officials to swear their allegiance to America on the Bible, to where we have expelled God from public education, we've expelled prayer—we've become a secularized nation. And I think that the liberal secular humanists and secularists of our political mainstream have brought all of this on themselves. We believe that religion has a vital part of a person's life and makeup.*

MacNEIL: *What have they brought on themselves? You say all of this.*

LAHAYE: *This reaction. You see, we've had a pendulum swing to secularism, and the American people are not a hedonistic, secularist society overwhelmingly. I believe this is a country made up overwhelmingly of people that have a belief, a basic belief in God, and the civic, moral principles of God. But we've had public leaders that have led us contrary. And a good example is, the day that the U.S. Senate voted against the president's prayer amendment, the* New York Times *came out with a poll and said that 81 percent of the American people favored a prayer amendment in our schools, and yet 44 percent of our U.S. senators voted against it.*

MACNEIL: *Mr. Buchanan, . . . how do you see Mr. Mondale's charge that religious groups want to use the power of government to impose their beliefs on the country?*

BUCHANAN: *Well, I must confess, I was the Republican who talked about the dangers of moral McCarthyism, and I did so because I am concerned about that reality which Reverend Lahaye has just this moment demonstrated. He referred to those who disagree with his own narrow, far-right agenda as liberal secular humanists. Now . . . his field director, Gary Jarmin, began doing report cards on members of the Congress in 1980 and has continued ever since. And they are called "Moral Christian Report Cards." And they [members of Congress] were judged as to their morality and their Christianity, as to whether they were for or against the Equal Rights Amendment or the Department of Education. Equal Rights Amendment was an antifamily, anti-Christian position. The Department of Education was an anti-Christian position. . . .If you examine those reports, they are tests not of the members' piety but of their politics. All the clergy fail consistently Mr. Jarmin's tests. All the members of the Black Caucus consistently fail the test for morality of being profamily or for Christianity. Most of the Jews in Congress and many of the finest Christians in the Congress who happen to be more liberal than conservative in their politics fail this morality test.*

MACNEIL: *Let's get Mr. Lahaye's comment on that.*

LAHAYE: *No, I think that's a distortion of what we're trying to do. What we're trying to do is inform—*

MACNEIL: *Do you disown the pamphlet that the former congressman just quoted from?*

LAHAYE: *No, let me explain what that kind of thing is doing. It's educating the voters on how the politicians represented them. You see, too long in our country, we have let our congressmen and senators go back to Washington and vote any way they please just to suit themselves, and then come back and do a little political rhetoric and razzle-dazzle in the district and get reelected. We think that election day should be judgment day. It should be the day that the voter is well informed on how his representative represented him, and if he didn't represent him adequately according to the voter's beliefs, then he ought to replace him with someone who will. . . .*

BUCHANAN: *The real distortion is in taking the voting records of devout Christians like Pat Leahy and proclaiming them anti-God or anti-Christian or immoral because—*

LAHAYE: *That's not what we're doing.*

BUCHANAN: *That's precisely what you're doing.*

LAHAYE: *No one is called anti-God.*

BUCHANAN: *Oh, listen, your report is called "A Moral Christian Report Card." May I hold up the* Moral Majority Report, *Reverend Falwell's recent one right after the Democratic Convention, in which the whole Democratic party is characterized as against God? Now, you know, I was a member of the House prayer breakfast group for nearly all the sixteen years I was a member of the Congress—indeed, all of them. And one of the first things I noticed was that some of the finest Christians and religious persons who regularly attended those prayer breakfasts were conservative Republicans, and some of the finest Christians who attended them were liberal Democrats. They disagreed on all sorts of political issues, just like Senator East and Senator Leahy do, and yet they're both devout Christians. Now, what you folks are doing is you are mixing politics and religion in a new way. You are guilty of moral McCarthyism because you're branding all of us, millions of Christians in this country, most of the Jews in this country, most of the black community in this country, you're branding as liberal secular humanists because they disagree with your politics, Reverend Lahaye. And you do it consistently and I can bring forth a library in this television studio to illustrate that you do it, and you did it in this program. . . .*

LAHAYE: *Well, a person that votes for liberal things votes for liberal things because he has a liberal philosophy. And that's acceptable—*

BUCHANAN: *Is that secular humanism?*

LAHAYE: *That's where it comes from, secular humanism. Many liberals are not necessarily secular humanists. What they don't understand is their liberalism is based in secular humanism. But that's a whole other subject. The main point is—*

BUCHANAN: *You mean the Equal Rights Amendment is secular humanist?*

LAHAYE: *When a person votes on issues representing a clientele, he's going to reflect his philosophy. Let me give you an example of how we're not branding people as anti-Christian. Former President Jimmy Carter was a well-known born-again Christian, and yet he was rejected at the polls primarily because his voting record was too liberal, or his policies were too liberal. Not because he wasn't a good Christian. And so it's a bum rap to accuse us of labeling people as being anti-Christian because we believe their moral standards or voting records should be called into judgment on election day.*

MACNEIL: *Mr. Buchanan, can I ask you a question? You're a Republican, a former Republican congressman. Do you think that President Reagan is encouraging or abetting the McCarthyism you've just described by his joining the issue the way he did in Dallas?*

BUCHANAN: *I think the president has been very much under the influence of*

Jerry Falwell and of the religious Right, and for some good reasons if you want to talk about them. Certainly good political reasons, because this is a very powerful political force in the United States. Reverend Lahaye and his colleagues do represent a powerful political bloc, an organized, militant minority, well heeled and very highly motivated, which has political clout. I think the president also has become a pretty good fundamentalist Christian. But I liked what the president had to say today about the wall of separation and about the right of American citizens to worship according to their consciences or not to worship at all. And I really liked his language today, because he was reiterating what the First Amendment provides us, and we at People for the American Way are celebrants of our plurality, our diversity, and we seek to protect the constitutional rights of all Americans to do their thing in religion and politics, and not to brand them as anti-Christian or immoral or antifamily because they happen to disagree with a narrow, extremist, far-right agenda.

MACNEIL: *Mr. Lahaye, has President Reagan made it easier for you to fulfill your promise of delivering two and a half million fundamentalist votes to him by the stand he took at Dallas? Has he helped you in that?*

LAHAYE: *Actually, I think both candidates have made it easier, because Walter Mondale has thrown his weight into the liberal camp, which is the idea that there are no fixed moral absolutes, and the president refers to traditional values that have always been helpful to the American family. . . .*

BUCHANAN: *He just did it again.*

MACNEIL: *What did he do again?*

BUCHANAN: *He just branded those who are liberal as having no fixed standards. All of us support the traditional values of family. We are patriots. Many of us are Christians, devout believers. We disagree with your politics, Reverend Lahaye. We think you're wrong. . . .*

LAHAYE: *We're not blaming them as individuals. What we're saying is, liberal philosophy is antifamily and liberal determinations. For example, pornographic literature . . . is antifamily.*

The debate ended at this point. It would have been interesting to pursue Lahaye's "liberal determinations" remark to discover its meaning. More important, it was unfortunate to have the discussion end on Lahaye's assertion that liberals supported pornographic literature. It would also have been useful to coax a response from Lahaye in regard to Buchanan's questions about the Equal Rights Amendment, the Department of Education, and Buchanan's remarks about Lahaye's extremist, far-right agenda. And it would have been particularly informative to get some kind of definition of the apparent bugaboo of the religious Right, "secular humanism."

Both the strength and the weakness of MacNeil/Lehrer's interview format is the fact that so many questions are raised and then go unanswered or unresolved. There is no question that exploring issues in the format just examined stimulates the viewer to *think*, whereas the commercial network nightly news programs generally stimulate the viewer to *watch* the images, but not to think about the words, because the reports are much too short and choppy to concentrate on in terms of idea content.

Periodically, the commercial networks had lengthier special reports on a given issue, although still quite short compared to MacNeil/Lehrer. Bob Schieffer of CBS delivered such a report on the religion-and-politics subject this day, which had some interesting points.

SCHIEFFER: *When candidate John Kennedy went to Texas in 1960, his mission was to tell Protestant ministers he would never have Catholic church leaders tell him how to run the presidency. But Reagan's campaign chairman, Senator Paul Laxalt, took a different tack last month when he sent a "Dear Christian leader" letter to evangelical preachers, asking them to get on the Reagan team to, quote, "help assure that those in your ministry will have a voice in the upcoming elections . . . a voice that will surely help the reelection of President Reagan and Vice-President Bush." That raised some eyebrows, but it was a comment from the president himself at a Dallas prayer breakfast that really brought the issue to a boil.*
REAGAN: *And as morality's foundation is religion, religion and politics are necessarily related.*
SCHIEFFER: *Even some in the Reagan White House worry that some of the president's comments lately are edging too close to the line separating church and state as spelled out in the Constitution. But not the pastor of Dallas's huge First Baptist Church.*
REVEREND W. A. CRISWELL: *Well I think this thing of separation of church and state is a figment of some infidel's imagination. Now those Democrats, they can organize every ghetto and every Hispanic and every black and every down-and-outer and every welfare recipient—they can organize them all to get them all to vote and nothing's said about it at all, but here comes a man trying to get Christian people to vote, and man alive, that must be terrible. There's not anything wrong with trying to get God's people to vote. [Being introduced to Reverend Criswell made this entire report worthwhile. A recurring theme with the commercial network reports, however, was that they never allowed time for the obvious followup questions, such as, in this case, having Criswell identify who "God's people" are, since Democrats, blacks, Hispanics, every down-and-outer, and welfare recipients evidently have all been ruled out. Criswell's heaven seems to have a "White Republicans Only" sign on the Pearly Gates.]*
SCHIEFFER: *Democrat Jimmy Carter made no secret of his fundamentalist*

faith, but some political scientists say the Reagan approach to the funda-mentalists is different.

WILLIAM SCHNEIDER *(American Enterprise Institute): Reagan endorses their social positions. Reagan says that he agrees with them on prayer and cen-sorship and women's rights and gay rights and abortion. He's very different from Carter. Reagan appeals to them on political grounds, not on religious grounds.*

SCHIEFFER: *Although the president seldom attends church, his political strat-egists believe his appeal to fundamentalists could cut into a blue-collar vote that might otherwise go Democratic, especially in some southern states. But the approach can also be a two-edged sword. Some presidential supporters warn that Mr. Reagan's rhetoric could leave the impression that he wants a Christian Republican party. And various religious groups took issue with the president this week, including speakers at the B'nai B'rith convention, who were lambasting the Reagan view long before he and Mondale spoke today.*

RABBI DAVID SAPERSTEIN: *The fact is the president of the United States has explicitly chosen forums of people who are not committed to the separation of church and state, that have been spending much of their lives in battering down the walls separating church and state, some of whom explicitly want to create a Christian country.*

SCHIEFFER: *A campaign that contrasted two candidates with clearly different philosophies was expected. What's surprising is that the sharpest differences to emerge so far are not over issues such as war and peace and the need to control government spending, but on their views on the relationship between church and state.*

In fact, it was not at all surprising that the religion-and-politics issue had emerged as the most charged of the early stages of the campaign, because television and the media at large had made it so. It was an important issue that the candidates themselves, for various reasons, had brought up and become embroiled in. But it was not the only issue being discussed by Reagan and Mondale. There were others they were addressing and on which they were equally divided. At least as much time had been devoted by the candidates in previous days to exactly the issues that Schieffer referred to, war and peace and government spending, and the related issue of taxes. As we have seen, on September 4, 1984, Mondale didn't address the religion issue at all, but talked about the differences between Reagan's tax policies and his own proposals. Reagan, although drawing attention to the religion issue by discussing it in his speech at the Ameri-can Legion, spent most of his speech talking about defense policy and the "new patriotism" in America. But all the networks headlined their reports in a manner that guaranteed that the religion issue would overwhelm everything else. On the following day, Reagan's remarks on Mondale's tax plan weren't reported by any network, with the exception of NBC. And even more distressing in terms of "news," Mondale's noteworthy proposal for a comprehensive nuclear-testing moratorium was completely missed, with the exception of a one-liner on CBS. The issues were there, but TV news wasn't covering them. The zeroing in on the religion issue began on Labor Day, and was totally arbitrary, as has already been pointed out. It seemed as if the media were looking for something "new" to add fireworks, to make the "show" more interesting. There is no question that the religion-and-politics issue deserved the kind of coverage it received this day on MacNeil/Lehrer, for instance. But on the previous day, MacNeil/Lehrer devoted the same amount of time to defense and arms-control issues (although even they managed to miss the nuclear-testing-moratorium story), while the commercial networks were all "bottom lining" their leads with Tip O'Neill's bizarre meanderings about Mondale not attacking Reagan and Bush sharply enough. During the entire first week of the campaign, there were five election-related special reports from the combined evening news programs of NBC, ABC, and CBS. Three of these reports were concerned with campaign logistics and strategy. The remaining two covered the issue of religion and politics.

A few days later, on September 12, CBS commentator Bill Moyers addressed the religion-and-politics issue in what seemed to be the last reference to the subject in the context that dominated the first week of the campaign. The commentator on network TV news is akin to the editorial page writer of a newspaper. This association seemed to be lessening over the years, as the commentaries on network news became less editorial and somewhat more sterile in nature, playing more a role of giving an overview of some aspect of the news, somewhat opinionated, but not taking a strong stand. There were exceptions, and this was one of them. Opinions should be part of the newscast business, albeit as varied as possible. The human mind could in many ways be described as a collection of opinions, and to hear those of others is a catalyst for the examination of one's own. Bill Moyers commentary follows.

"The free exercise of religion has long presupposed the right of believers to press their view in the public square. And politicians almost always go hunting for votes in the precincts of the faithful. Lyndon Johnson did not invite Billy Graham to skinny dip in the White House pool because he wanted to test the Baptist doctrine of total immersion, he wanted to carry the Bible Belt. Jimmy Carter was elected with the born-again vote and then defeated when Ronald Reagan trumped him at his own game. Jesse Jackson orchestrates a black congregation as if it were the choir of heaven. So what's new in this campaign? This is new. Conservative Catholics and Protestants have openly allied themselves with the Republican party in a way that threatens to turn the public debate on morality into a partisan crusade, and make of Mr. Reagan's party the party of religion. That would be a profound change in American politics, in and of itself. But consider their ultimate goal. You'll find it expressed in a column by the conservative journalist Patrick Buchanan, himself a former speechwriter for Republican politicians. Writing of the school prayer crusade, Mr. Buchanan says, and I quote, 'It is the first great counteroffensive of a badly routed Christian community to recapture *their* occupied public schools, and reestablish *their* beliefs as the *legitimate* moral foundation of American society.' He goes on to say that Christians have every right to do this, and are under some obligation to try, as many are trying already. In Minnesota, for example, conservative Christians have gained control of several local Republican organizations and are demanding that school board candidates meet a religious test. But the Christian community of America is not of one mind, and the Republican party has been a tent of many stripes. In time, nothing but trouble is likely to come of a major political party's commitment to the doctrinal triumph of one sectarian notion of God's will for America. We have in this country an admirable alternative to civil war, and holy civil war at that. It's called the Constitution. Religion and politics mix in this delicate balance, but only if they serve to check one another's pretensions."

The religion-and-politics issue was to maintain a certain hold during the campaign, but it soon began to take a more specific twist, with Geraldine Ferraro's position on abortion becoming the focus. When Ferarro made the remark about Reagan's budget cuts in terms of impact on the poor not being the kind of policy implemented by a "good Christian," she was responding with apparent frustration to antiabortion hecklers in the crowd who were questioning her faith. The heckling was to continue and dominate the television cameras following her appearances for the first weeks of the campaign. Her faith, and that of other Catholic politicians, would soon be questioned also by two Catholic bishops, O'Connor of New York and Law of Boston. Ferraro's position was that she had no right as a public official to impose her private beliefs on others, even though she "accepted" the church's teaching on abortion. Much as John Kennedy had done in another context, she was affirming that her religion would not interfere with her constitutional duties. She had also been associated with a group called Catholics for a Free Choice who stated that there was not a historic or present theological or popular consensus among Catholics to support the absolute stand taken by the Vatican on abortion. After the election, the religious women members of this group were given an ultimatum from the Vatican to retract their statements or be expelled from their religious orders. In retrospect, it seems that Ferraro found herself at the cutting edge of a religious and political struggle that included elements of authoritarian male dominance versus women's equality, and church plurality, involving both the Vatican and American society.

The relationship of television news and the media at large to the unfolding of this story is a strange one indeed. Both the media and American Catholic bishops as a group share the responsibility for the dominance during the campaign of a few bishops speaking only about the abortion issue, when the bishops as a group had been emphasizing equally the nuclear arms race, poverty, and other issues related to the "sanctity of life" for some time. But the story behind this story, the most ominous "church and state" story, which was first brought to light by television news and then quickly abandoned without explanation by both TV and the media in general, should be recorded as one of the strangest happenings in the history of campaign journalism, as we shall see.

Thursday, September 13: The Hollywood Campaign

This day was noteworthy as a prime example of the Reagan campaign using television news as a forum for free, produced-in-Hollywood advertising. Other presidents and other politicians had utilized similar techniques, but President Reagan's acting ability, his stage presence, in combination with the event planning and staging of his campaign apparatus, raised this strategy almost to the level of an art form. And no one previously in the television age had relied so overwhelmingly on such an approach, such a total submersion of substance in favor of style. It is also worth examining in another respect, which is the dominance of visual impression over the spoken word in the nightly news report format, allowing the Reagan-style campaign strategy to be successful in spite of reporter commentary intended to objectively expose it.

On ABC, the campaign reports began with coverage of Mondale making a passionate plea for the votes of those over sixty-five, stating that if Reagan was reelected, he'd try to cut Social Security and Medicare. But whatever impression he made on the TV screen was lost on the following report on Reagan. Sam Donaldson was straightforward and pointed in his remarks, but the pictures overwhelmed his words. The scene was in Nashville, Tennessee, at the Grand Ole Opry, country music's national showcase.

DONALDSON: *President Reagan, campaigning in Nashville today, ignored Mondale's charges about his future economic plans and instead patted himself on the back for the good times at hand.*

REAGAN: . . . *We've had twenty-one straight months of economic growth—that is the best expansion since World War II. Some people have labored so long at making government bigger, they've developed a knee-jerk addiction to tax increases. And every time their knee jerks, we get kicked. [Reagan is standing on the stage and the place is packed. His comment elicits roaring laughter and applause.]*

DONALDSON: *The president failed again today, however, to say exactly how he intends to reduce the deficit, if not through higher taxes. None of this talk about deficits and taxes is the essence õf the Reagan campaign.* The essence of the Reagan campaign is a never-ending string of spectacular picture stories, created for television and designed to place the president in the midst of a huge throng of wildy cheering patriotic Americans *[my emphasis]. And today's occurred here in Nashville at the Grand Ole Opry.*

The meaning of Donaldson's words is quickly lost under the visual tidal wave that follows. Reagan is shown surrounded by country musicians (the event is also a birthday party for country star Roy Acuff), all of whom are singing together, along with the audience, Lee Greenwood's patriotic hit song "God Bless the USA," backed by a big band belting out the music. As the song's climax is reached, confetti is dropped from the ceiling on cue and the audience cheers with emotion. Words cannot do justice to the audiovisual impact. Donaldson's concluding words are, "God, patriotism, and Reagan. That's the essence this campaign is trying hard to project." It is not likely that the viewer even hears the "trying hard to project" part of the statement, for at this point, the audiovisual emotional impact has already put "God, patriotism, and Reagan" on more or less equal footing and made them somewhat synonymous. It seems easy to see through when the transcript is *read*. But *seeing* the report on television is a totally different experience.

The same scene was also shown on the other networks. NBC's report by Chris Wallace opened with what would become increasingly unsuccessful attempts by reporters to ask Reagan specific questions. Reagan's response was to emphasize the one thing he and the press had in common: their favorite subject, the polls.

WALLACE: *The president kept refusing today to get specific about how he would cut the deficit, but there were numbers that he did want to talk about. New polls that show him leading Mondale by as much as 16 percent.*
REAGAN: *How come none of you want to talk about the polls?*
REPORTER (unidentified): *What do you think of them?*
REAGAN: *Goodie.*

Again, when reading the transcript, Reagan's "Goodie" comment seems to warrant either howls or concerns about senility. But when delivered on TV in his "Aw shucks" style, it had a very different impact. It effectively made the election seem a question of this nice grandfatherly man being able to keep his job, as opposed to a debate about policy choices of extraordinary impact on millions of Americans and the future of the planet.

Wallace's report also showed Reagan at the Grand Ole Opry giving one of the perfectly crafted-for-TV one-liners that was to be the hallmark of his campaign: "I think we all better remember that the other side's promises are a little like Minnie Pearl's hat. They both have big price tags hanging from them." CBS had this Reagan quote from the same setting: "There's an old country-and-western song called 'Home on the Range' where seldom is heard a discouraging word. I guess they [Mondale-Ferraro] haven't campaigned there yet. [The audience cheers.] But they probably couldn't perform here anyway, because all they do is sing the blues." Then another on NBC: ". . . I want to offer a little friendly advice to our critics. Rather than saying things that always seem to run America down, how about giving the American people a pat on the back?" Reagan was, of course, transparently associating criticism of him or his policies with criticism of the American people. He might as well have said, Who needs democracy? After this comment, NBC ran the same scene at the Grand Ole Opry as ABC had. After the last Reagan statement, it was a perfect one-two punch. Wallace ended his report saying, "What the president has done very skillfully is to wrap his campaign in what appears to be a new wave of good feeling about this country. So the Democratic attacks against him are made to seem almost unpatriotic." When read, it is evident that Wallace is stating the obvious. But when seen and heard in the context of what had preceded, it is easy to miss the "made to seem" part, or even know how to interpret it. Although clearly not intending to, Wallace, like Donaldson, may simply have added an exclamation point to a powerful Reagan "commercial" on the nightly "news."

As usual, the reports on CBS, ABC, and NBC this evening were both shallow and extremely short. In addition, none of the commercial networks had their campaign stories at the top of the news. ABC, for instance, started with Hurricane Diana (as they all did), which went on until the first commercial. TV news had decided that the hurricane was the most nationally and internationally significant story of the week, making it the top story every day! It made good video. On this day, ABC continued with the surrender of American Indian Movement cofounder and fugitive Dennis Banks, the Agriculture Department's embargo on citrus from Florida, the potential United Auto Workers strike of General Motors, the sale of "airbus" airplanes, and the stock market. As with CBS and NBC, which ran some of the same reports, the campaign stories were aired after the second commercial. Some of these other reports were significant, but there is no excuse for not headlining election-related reports for eight weeks every four years.

Also as usual, MacNeil/Lehrer was the exception, running as the lead story a lengthy issue-and-debate segment on the elderly, Social Security, Medicare, and the Reagan and Mondale records and positions. As it was Senior Health Action Day around the country, the segment concentrated primarily on Medicare, the fast-approaching financial crisis for the hospital-benefits trust fund, and the difficult choices at hand. It was a refreshing counterpoint to the Mondale attacks and Reagan silence on the issue this day, both for political reasons. For nearly forty minutes, two-thirds of the program, the issues were discussed and argued. The politicking of Mondale and the Hollywood antics of Reagan were not the focus of this coverage. There were no image-over-substance commercials from the Grand Ole Opry here. And the segment made clear that Mondale's easy pledge of no Medicare cuts would not be so easy to keep.

"The MacNeil/Lehrer NewsHour" was offering a sharp contrast to the Presidential Election Show on the commercial network nightly news. One hoped the embarrassing comparison would eventually lead to emulation. Even within the half-hour time frame if the networks ran in-depth issue reports for at least half of their programs during a presidential campaign, leaving the visual trash, strategy, and the polls behind, it would be an evolutionary jump in the right direction.

On the following Monday, September 17, however, two potentially important stories were missed by all the news programs, proving as had been and would be shown again, that even good formats cannot guarantee good journalism.

On this day Walter Mondale gave a wide-ranging foreign policy speech to a group of Jewish supporters in Washington, D.C. MacNeil/Lehrer zeroed in on the Middle East element of his speech and the September 6 B'nai B'rith speech of President Reagan as the jumping-off point for another issue-and-debate segment on Middle East policy. It was a somewhat revealing look at the lack of leadership provided by either candidate in this difficult arena. The best summation came from Philip Stoddard, nineteen-year veteran of the State Department and executive director of the Middle East Institute, a nonpartisan research organization in Washington, D.C., when asked by Judy Woodruff, "Which candidate do you think has the better notion of what U.S. policy toward the Middle East should be?" Stoddard replied, "I think I'd have to say neither. I think what we're seeing is understandable, but it seems to me a lamentable exercise in ethnic politics basically, where both sides are trying to outdo the other in support of Israel. . . . It's too tough because we're dealing with the heart of the issue—the Israeli desire to retain the West Bank and the Arab desire to put some kind of an autonomous state for the Palestinians in that area. That's the nub of the whole issue. . . . It involves painful compromise on both sides, and no one so far has demonstrated the slightest idea of how to get there."

The commercial network reports were absurdly brief, but ABC had the most "extensive" coverage. In Britt Hume's report on Mondale's speech, a one-line clip on another aspect of the Middle East cauldron was an eyebrow raiser.

HUME: *[Mondale] blamed Mr. Reagan for the continuing spread of nuclear weapons.*
MONDALE: *How would you like to live in a world in which Kaddafi had his own bomb?"*

That's it, no more explanation. This was either an outrageous statement by Mondale or an outrageous editing job by ABC, or both. Clearly, Ronald Reagan would sooner be eternally damned than see Kaddafi with nuclear weapons. That's one issue that the United States, the Soviets, and nearly everyone on the planet would have little difficulty agreeing on. It may be that some aspect of Reagan administration policy or, more likely, lack of nonproliferation policy, could inadvertently contribute to such an outcome, in which case the entire context of Mondale's remarks should have been left unedited. In addition, such a statement by Mondale raises such important questions that he shouldn't have been let off the hook on it, nor should Reagan, if there was anything substantial to Mondale's remark. This was one time when the TV news addiction to controversy could have served the public well, had this controversial statement been followed up on. But it wasn't, on any of the news programs, including MacNeil/Lehrer.

However, in some ways there was an even more disturbing comment this day, if only because the implications were more readily tangible, a comment that seemed to be missed by everyone.

It was in conjunction with another example of the "campaign by commercial on the nightly news" strategy of the Reagan-Bush team. The scene was the largest naturalization ceremony ever held, with 9,706 residents, mostly Cubans, in the Orange Bowl in Miami. ABC's Carol Simpson reported, "After the Pledge of Allegiance, what was supposed to be a nonpartisan event took on the appearance of a campaign rally for President Reagan with the introduction of Vice-President Bush. And the crowd became partisan, chanting, 'Reagan, Reagan.' " The video showed the large crowd, chanting Reagan's name, and "spontaneously" producing hundreds of small flags to wave. George Bush was then shown saying hello in Spanish, followed by a few words on the importance of *voting.*

Covering the same event, CBS's David Dowe, to his credit, had an interview clip that should have sent journalists scurrying in several directions demanding answers to important questions. Dowe's report showed Dade County Democratic chairman Richard Pettigrew saying that a "major effort" had been made to convince the Cuban community that somehow or another "Castro was going to go away in the next four years."

If Pettigrew's remark was accurate, which there was no way of knowing since neither CBS nor anyone else ever followed up on it, then there were serious questions to be answered: Who was making this "major effort"? To the degree that the Reagan campaign was involved, how did this reflect Reagan policy intentions? Making Castro go away would not happen with any magic wand. The policy choices would be essentially either a return to the CIA's infamous attempts on his life, or, given the record of success in that effort, more likely a "Bay of Pigs II," with full American support this time, but facing a vastly improved Cuban military capacity. That would involve, at the least, a lot of American boys coming home in boxes. At worst, it could mean World War III. There were also other questions, such as the impact throughout Latin America of such an action. It would potentially be the most significant U.S. foreign policy decision in the post-World War II era. Granted, for all the above reasons, such a policy decision seemed unlikely, but the journalist's task is to get the answers. Even if the "major effort" in the Cuban community had nothing to do with reality, but was cynically creating expectations to get votes, which seemed more likely, this was a story worth following up. It would be a cruel play on the hopes of these Cubans, and potentially a dangerous one, given the history of anti-Castro Cuban violence and terrorism. Why didn't CBS explore this assertion by Pettigrew further? It was also never covered in any way on NBC, ABC or MacNeil/Lehrer.

One wondered if there was anyone awake at any of the networks. Didn't they even bother to watch each other's newscasts? It was difficult to believe that no one picked up on the obvious implications of Pettigrew's stunning statement. Again, even on the level of controversy, it would have seemed an obvious story to explore. It would apparently be too much to hope that such stories would be examined for the proper reasons.

Friday, September 14:
The No-Chance Candidacy

This day, the end of the second week of the campaign, offered an illuminating illustration of two facts of TV news reporting during the 1984 campaign. First, television consistently reinforced the image of Walter Mondale's campaign as "in trouble." Second, even when the commercial nightly news programs focused on an issue at some length (by their standards), they often shed no light on the issue they were supposed to be examining.

On ABC's report, Britt Hume, covering Mondale's day, began with, "Walter Mondale got an enthusiastic reception today at a college in St. Louis. But he also got a blunt question, one that is in the minds of many worried Democrats." The video then showed a young man saying to Mondale, "[Many people are having] a difficult time getting excited about the Mondale campaign. What changes do you have in mind to fire up the Mondale campaign, now that we're in the home stretch, to defeat Reagan?" Mondale's reply: "I've got only one approach. And that is to tell the truth and be who I really am."

In the face of such a vapid question, Mondale's response came across as strong and sincere, making one wonder, Where was this preoccupation with his "problems" coming from? What were these constantly referred to problems? The crowd responded with spontaneous enthusiasm to Mondale's statement. If his media advisers had been on their toes, this scene would have been a commercial in days, as the most effective way to deal with the "issue."

But the question germane to this observer was, Why did ABC open their report with this clip? This kind of thing happened time and again and was certainly the main reason for the perception of Mondale as being boring, or ineffective on TV, or having campaign problems, or in a hopeless struggle against Reagan. TV determines the images by what it decides to report about, therefore ending up reporting about what it has created. The media in general play the same game, but none with the impact of television.

MacNeil/Lehrer was certainly not immune from this tendency, as has already been pointed out. A September 14 report titled "Mondale's *Troubled* Campaign" was a case in point. It concentrated entirely on various "problems" the Mondale campaign had encountered. This report was followed by Jim Lehrer asking guests for their analysis of Mondale's "problem." The following week, there was a report on the Reagan campaign's "smooth-running machine," which will be examined later in this book. It wasn't a matter of one report being anti-Mondale and the other being pro-Reagan by any means. In fact, both reports tended to emphasize the negative, in one way or another. But the contextualizing of the campaigns in terms of one being basically hopeless and the other essentially invincible obviously created a tremendous impression and sets the tone for the whole campaign. The only thing that ever changed this tone was the shock of the first debate, in which Mondale and Reagan each displayed characteristics that, according the media, they should never have displayed. But that story is farther down the line.

There were, in any event, some interesting observations in the Mac-Neil/Lehrer report by Judy Woodruff. Mondale's release of his deficit-reduction plan and his offensive designed to get Reagan to respond in kind had dominated his campaign strategy the preceding week. Mondale was shown saying, "All the presidents since George Washington had added about $17,000 to your 'charge account.' And Mr. Reagan, in four years, has added an additional $13,092 to your share, the share of the average family . . . to the national debt."

WOODRUFF: *It was the theme of the week that the Reagan deficit is costing average Americans. Mondale press secretary Maxine Isaacs says making the point only once is not enough.*
ISAACS: *He feels some obligation, when he's raised a complicated issue, to bring it home to the American people. And you do that by talking about different aspects of it, and he's going to do that. Our experience has been—and maybe someday somebody will prove us wrong on this—that it takes a while for—it really is sort of a new idea—and it takes a while for something like that to sink in. . . . [Isaacs was absolutely correct here. Although the Mondale campaign took this approach for political reasons, the maxim is true in general, and needs desperately to be applied by broadcast journalism on issues of national importance. This subject will be explored further in the campaign postmortem, but it should also be mentioned here that one of the primary reasons Mondale's strategy backfired was that the public was not conditioned by TV news in general to pay attention to and examine complex issues.]*
WOODRUFF: *Many of the stories that appeared later in the press stressed the higher taxes the Mondale plan would mean for the middle class, exactly the opposite of the message the Mondale people wanted to get across. A chief political reporter for the* New York Times, *Howell Raines, says they simply didn't package their presentation very well.*
RAINES: *The problem I think they had was similar to the problem they had on Labor Day, where they did not make that event the centerpiece and the focal point of the day in a way that would make sure that a concentrated message that carried their idea directly to the voter via television got through.*
WOODRUFF: *Tom Oliphant of the* Boston Globe *agrees.*
OLIPHANT: *Now, Mondale is doing three, four, or five things a day. He is out in the open all the time, where we can get at him, where the public can get at him. You can shape a story about a day in Walter Mondale's campaigning life on your own, using your own frameworks. Often what happens is that his message gets lost in that effort.*

WOODRUFF: . . . *An appearance at a paper plant in Green Bay, Wisconsin, was downright embarrassing. What was supposed to be a chance for the candidate to shake hands with hundreds of blue-collar workers at their shift change—nice TV pictures for the evening news—turned into a half-hour wait for just a couple dozen laborers, most of whom were in a hurry to get home. . . . Linda Wertheimer, who has covered Mr. Mondale much of this year for National Public Radio, says the campaign invites these sort of incidents.*

WERTHEIMER: *These are these little serendipitous things that happen in a campaign. When you take your case out like that and you get out among the people, you run those risks: It's not a controlled situation. And you know, things go right and things go wrong.*

RAINES: *One of the striking things about this week to me is the Mondale people have been in politics a long time, they know how to run campaigns, and their advance people are really not producing much action for them on the ground out here. And I don't know the details of why that is, but it's very late in the campaign season to be having those kind of problems when you're up against people on the Reagan team who never, or very seldom, make a mistake when it comes to advancing an event, turning out a crowd. As you know, at the airport last night in Davenport, Iowa, there were more antiabortion demonstrators there than there were Mondale supporters. And that's just simply a failure of the organization to support the candidate. If I were Walter Mondale, I would have been a very angry man when I got off that airplane last night. . . . [Raines had a point about the advance work, but Oliphant and Wertheimer were more to the point. If he had been on the road, doing several events a day, open spontaneous engagements with people and the press, Reagan would certainly have encountered his difficulties as well. And Raines's example of the antiabortion demonstrators would prove to likely have as much to do with Reagan campaign subterfuge as with Mondale advance work mistakes, as will be seen.]*

WOODRUFF: *What Mondale is faulted for as much as anything in this campaign is a low-key speaking style that only rarely seems to turn on crowds, and even more rarely comes across as dynamic television. . . . [Ironically, in response to this very perception, Mondale had both "turned on" the crowd and been very dynamic on TV this day, in the ABC report referred to. Mondale was no video star, but comments like this one by Woodruff had less to do with reality than with the media's reporting its own reports, continually reinforcing the perception, just as the same was done with the image of Reagan as the Great Communicator.] Despite a series of events obviously designed for the TV cameras, Linda Wertheimer says Mr. Mondale deliberately avoids packaging himself for television, in contrast to his opponent.*

WERTHEIMER: *I think that the president campaigns almost entirely on television for television, for the effect of television. Mr. Mondale spends a lot more time talking and thinking about issues in ways that he regards as more serious. And he would think—does think, I believe—that campaigning just for television is somehow something that grownups shouldn't do. . . . [One week later, on PBS's "Washington Week in Review,"* Newsweek *correspondent Howard Fineman said of Mondale, "He said in that interview with the* Washington Post, *(National Weekly Edition, October 8, 1984), which is one of the most interesting and revealing interviews that I think any presidential candidate has given in the middle of the campaign, he said, 'I'm not comfortable in front of television, and I'm afraid I never will be. I can't stand studying to be a good salesman for myself. So what I'm going to do is just stand there and say what I believe in and take the results, whatever they happen to be.' Now there's kind of an endearing, almost noble quality to that. But the irony is in order to make even that point, you have to be able to sell yourself, including on television.]*

WOODRUFF: *But even when the Mondale campaign is running like clockwork and the candidate is belting out his message, there are still occurrences that prevent it from reaching the public, as this week, when the White House announced plans for President Reagan to hold his first meeting with Soviet Foreign Minister Gromyko.*

The Reagan announcement of the Gromyko meeting was the trump card of the campaign in many ways, which will be examined in pages to come. But one of the things it effectively accomplished, as Woodruff noted, was to take the focus off the deficit issue, which Reagan didn't want to talk about. One of the great shortcomings of network news is the inability, given the format, to stay focused on more than one issue at the same time, and the tendency to play up the new, making "old" what was "new" only days or hours before. There is no depth or staying power, and therefore nothing but facile information passed on to the viewers.

Periodically, the commercial news programs would have special reports that dealt with issues. ABC's were called "Issues 84," and on this day Richard Threlkeld offered a report on the issue of the deficit, which was a step in the right direction, since it had been the most discussed issue of the week, by Mondale at least. Threlkeld described the impact of the deficit on the credit markets, driving interest rates up, as economists almost unanimously agree it does, and the impact on the economy, in terms of lack of financing for the housing market, for instance. He also described the resulting inflated value of the dollar, which led to decreased exports, a whopping trade deficit, and the United States being on the way to becoming a debtor nation. "All that's why most economists wring their hands over the threat of the structural deficit," reported Threlkeld. Because of these problems, and the ultimate choices between inflation or recession (or hyperinflation or depression), Threlkeld stated that the business community considered the situation "so threatening that this week a Who's Who of businessmen implored the politicians to do something about the total national debt of about a trillion and a half dollars, now equal to all the deposits in all U.S. banks."

C. ROBERT BRENTON *(American Bankers Association): Now I would have to say that's one hell of a lot of debt for the public to be lugging around on their backs.*
THRELKELD: *The Democrats agree.*
MONDALE: *While you're working to build your future, the Reagan administration, through their deficit policies, is working very hard to mortgage your future. [These one-liners without examination are useless. The report started out all right in terms of describing the problem, but it never describes where the red ink is coming from and what the choices are. A report like this should go through the history of the issue, including both the impact of years of expanding government entitlement programs, led by the Democrats but with substantial Republican support, and the hyperdeficits created by Reagan's tax cuts and defense increases, also passed by Republicans and a good number of Democrats in Congress.]*
THRELKELD: *That mortgage will reach $263 billion by 1989, so the Congressional Budget Office estimates. Walter Mondale plans to cut it by two-thirds through a combination of spending cuts and tax increases, mostly for the wealthier half of Americans who earn more than $25,000 per year. . . . [This is a somewhat confusing representation of Mondale's plan, which called for no tax increase at $25,000 or below and only a $95 increase at the $35,000 level. The details should have been given. In addition, no information is given on spending cuts. But most important, there is no mention of the heart of Mondale's proposal, which was that any new taxes be put in a trust fund for deficit reduction only, to allay any fear of the money simply being spent on new programs.]*
THRELKELD: *President Reagan and the Republicans are pledged to at least making some sort of down payment on the deficit, which they don't think will be nearly as high as Congress predicts. [First, the "down payment" occurred long before the campaign began, in 1984 tax bill changes, which were forced on the White House by Republicans and Democrats. What is Threlkeld referring to? Second, why isn't the comparative record of the Congressional Budget Office and the Reagan administration brought out? The administration had counted on a supply-side economic-theory miracle that gave us megadeficits instead, and as the upwardly "revised" deficit*

figures the administration released days after the 1984 election showed, the miracle was nowhere in sight.]

THRELKELD: *One thing for sure, Mr. Reagan doesn't think much of the Mondale plan.*

REAGAN: *His plan would hurt working Americans by raising their taxes and by stifling economic growth. With your support, we'll make sure that no one puts that ball and chain around America's neck. [Mondale's plan wouldn't have hurt working Americans of moderate income. The "stifling economic growth" question should be examined on all sides; Reagan may have something there, but the deficit stifles economic growth and is a ball and chain around America's neck as well. What are the measurable tradeoffs?]*

THRELKELD: *But is the president going to reveal his own plan, if any?*

TREASURY SECRETARY DONALD REGAN: *No, he's not going to do it. Walter Mondale hasn't done it. This is not a real budget that Walter Mondale has put out. There's an awful lot of things in there that are just adjectives. [This statement was ludicrous, particularly coming from the people who still hadn't sent a budget to Congress when Reagan was innaugurated for his second term. There wasn't anyone in the Reagan campaign who wouldn't admit that Reagan wasn't matching Mondale's specifics because it wasn't deemed politically wise. As we later discovered, it was also because the administration couldn't decide what it was going to do.]*

THRELKELD: *It is a weird campaign. The incumbent, a fiscal conservative, has become the biggest deficit spender in American history. His challenger may be the first man ever to run for president on a tax increase. In any event, here's what the parties promise to do on the economy. On the deficit, the Democrats offer the Mondale plan. The Republicans promise to erase the deficit [nobody promised to "erase" the deficit], but won't say exactly how until after November. They'd raise taxes only as a last resort. They also want a constitutional amendment to balance the budget. [While helping to run up a trillion-dollar debt in a few short years. Where's the journalistic truth check?] The Democrats oppose that as too inflexible. [As do many Republicans, some even voting for it for political reasons, because it was not in danger of passing.] The Democrats want a more progressive income tax so the wealthier pay more of the tax load. The Republicans want to substitute one single tax rate, so the wealthy presumably pay less. . . . [This was a ridiculous oversimplification. Depending on the plan, the rate, the remaining deductions, everyone might pay less, more or the same individually. In fact, the trial-balloon plan released by the Treasury after the election was bitterly opposed by much of corporate America because corporate tax rates would go up substantially, in effect raising the taxes of many of the "wealthy." This could, in fact, be a move toward undoing some of the more regressive aspects of Reagan's original tax changes.]*

THRELKELD: . . . *On the deficit issue, you have to pity the poor American voter. It's hard to get worked up about something so complicated that seems to pose no clear and present danger. [Yes, to all of the above, thanks in part to this report.] What to make of it all? After a while you feel as if you're trapped between the pages of* Gone with the Wind *with Scarlet O'Hara, right after Rhett Butler walks out for good.*

The report then ends with a clip from the movie *Gone with the Wind*, showing Vivien Leigh as Scarlet O'Hara saying, "I'll think about it tomorrow."

Cute video, terrible report. "Let us entertain you, but never inform you" could be an applicable motto. The report should have been a catalyst for the American public to think about this enormously important issue during the campaign, not "tomorrow." Instead, it simply contributed to the sense of the issue being too complicated and not enough of a present danger to be concerned about.

This is a representative example of what was served up by the networks when they decided to air "in-depth" reports concerned with campaign issues on the nightly news. The commentary and editing are presumably designed to showcase someone's concept of wit, but are certainly not designed to impart useful information. To be useful, these reports would either have to be stretched over days, covering different aspects of the issue raised, or would have to take up a large section of the program. In either event, the reports would have to be intellectually geared to exploring and answering basic questions, not raising them, much less being a vehicle for the simplistic sloganeering of both presidential candidates.

Tuesday, September 18: Talking TV

Once in a while, commercial network news would offer a pleasant surprise. This was one of those days. The following special report from Dan Rather of CBS, consisting primarily of an interview with Walter Mondale, gave an inkling of what could be done on television news. The subject of the interview, campaign coverage by the media, particularly television, is obviously of interest here. But it is intriguing to imagine the possibilities if this format was offered on a nightly or seminightly basis, covering the major issues of the campaign. For one thing, under those circumstances it is difficult to imagine one candidate continuing to decline participation, as President Reagan unfortunately did in this case. In addition, the format, if lengthened, would allow television to be utilized to listen to the candidates calmly discuss their ideas, give us an insight into them as people, in a way that visual events or campaign oratory obviously never can. It would seem to offer an eminently civilized vehicle for the candidates to communicate at some length to the people of the nation as a whole, with the journalist acting not as an antagonist, but as a balancing force, to insure that the communication does not simply lapse into a rehearsed spiel.

Here is the complete report. Dan Rather began, "President Reagan last week again fired on the favorite target of many politicians, the press.

REAGAN: *There's never a good-news economic story on the evening news that is not accompanied by or buried by finding some individuals who have not yet benefited from the economic recovery.*

RATHER: *Such complaints are not new, but in this election year, in this television age, we thought we should address such criticism directly and specifically. We invited both President Reagan and former Vice-President Mondale to speak their minds about the news media. President Reagan declined. Walter Mondale agreed to talk about political coverage and his image.*

MONDALE: *The image I want is of an honest man, telling the truth, willing to take the questions, wanting to be with people, feeling their needs, speaking for them, and able to lead.*

RATHER: *Isn't your campaign of issues, as you call it, getting the hell beaten out of it by what's being called President Reagan's campaign of images?*

MONDALE: *What we have now is very frustrating and I'll be honest about it. I'm out every day answering questions at news conferences, maybe two or three times a day, sometimes more. The president, I believe, and I think the records will show this, is the most isolated president in modern history.*

RATHER: *Mondale criticized what he called President Reagan's "cameo" appearances, that is, choosing a backdrop to project a desired image. He specifically cited President Reagan's trip last week to a senior citizens center in Buffalo, New York. [Video was shown of Reagan at this site, which had been run on the all the nightly news programs.]*

MONDALE: *There was one good question to be asked, but no one could ask it of him, and that is, "Mr. President, if your budget had passed, there wouldn't have been that high rise there at all, you'd have cut the money out for senior citizens."*

RATHER: *Mondale said that reporters could not get to the president to ask such questions because [Reagan] was kept at a distance.*

RATHER (*talking with Mondale*): *Any number of philosophers and political realists say, Those who control the images, those who control the symbols, control the society, certainly to the extent that they can win in the election.*

MONDALE: *I think this is not just my problem. I think it's yours as well, it's all the media. Isn't that a threat to open journalism? Isn't that a threat to the right of people to know? I think Americans understand that if politicians are protected from the questions, all we'll ever hear out them is good news. And all the politician will hear is what he wants to hear. Leadership requires listening as well as talking, answering as well as speaking. And I think there's a vital fault line in American politics, and we should never let any politician get to where I think the president is now, where we can hear him, but he can't hear us.*

RATHER: *Mr. Vice-President, the other day on the evening news, you had the contrast between Walter Mondale in Tennessee standing in a barn, coat off, perspiring—*

MONDALE *(laughing)*: *It was 110 degrees in there!*

RATHER: *—and President Reagan was at the Grand Ole Opry singing "Happy Birthday" to Roy Acuff. This is a specific example of what the so-called experts and reporters who follow you say is happening day after day with your campaign—that you once had the Mondale juggernaut that has become a Mondale Edsel, because time after time you suffer by comparison on these kind of occasions.*

MONDALE: *Did I really suffer, Dan? Would they rather have a leader stand out in the heat and take questions from farmers who are in their worst year since the Great Depression, or stand next to Minnie Pearl and sing "Happy Birthday"?*

RATHER: *Mr. Vice-President, for people who watch the evening news night after night, who are interested in the campaign, want to know what the campaign is really about, as opposed to what it may appear to be about, what's your advice or counsel?*

MONDALE: *Try to listen to substance, trust your own judgment. When you think you're hearing baloney, discount it. If they do those things, which I think most Americans do, I think they'll come out all right.*

RATHER: *The marriage of politics and television is an uneasy arrangement, campaign coverage is a sensitive subject. We emphasize that we invited both President Reagan and Vice-President Mondale to share their views on this with us. So far, only Vice-President Mondale has said yes.*

Although the pace of the report was leisurely, it was still much too brief. One wished that there had been less editing and that the interview had gone on much longer.

Mondale appeared on all the network nightly news programs during the campaign. Reagan, of course, appeared on none. Even so, during the campaign, Ralph Nader was critical of Mondale for not appearing on other TV programs as well. Mondale certainly could have used the visibility, and continuous appearances might have finally forced Reagan to reconsider his strategy of always avoiding uncontrolled media events. But

Mondale was understandably tentative about TV, considering how it generally treated him and his campaign. It was the responsibilty of TV news to create a climate in which the airwaves could not be so easily used for or against candidates in terms of image, emphasizing instead, for example, the live interview format in terms of air time for the candidates, and interviews that emphasized issues, not image and strategy.

Mondale's expressed faith during the Rather interview in the American people's capacity to sift through the TV news images and find the substance would be largely lost by the end of the campaign. In his news conference the day after the election, he stated that he thought he would probably be the last candidate to run for the presidency who was not expert in the art of TV image making.

If that turned out to be true, then 1984 may have been a turning point that would ultimately prove George Orwell more on the mark than it seemed he was, during the year itself. For, as Dan Rather pointed out, those who control the symbols control the society, and in a society increasingly being taught by the incandescent tube that symbols, not substance, are what matters, the maxim becomes increasingly true. This is, in effect, the reverse of the evolutionary view of humanity on which the Republic's founders based their belief in democracy. To be sure, they were acutely aware of human imperfection, which accounts for our constitutional system of checks and balances. But they also believed thoroughly in the revolutionary concept of popular sovereignty, the individual and social ability to be governed democratically, to make informed and wise decisions. A central factor in this equation was not only freedom of the flow of information, but the assumption that the quality of information would be intellectually stimulating to the majority of people. In their time, the printed word was the only means of mass communication, and remained so until the advent of radio, which was quickly overtaken by television. But the problem, stated most simply, is this: Where on television does one find the equivalent of the Federalist Papers? Where are the great issues discussed and debated in intellectual depth?

Dan Rather made what seemed an extraordinary admission of the failure of the institution he presides over when he asked Mondale what advice he had for people "who watch the evening news night after night" and who "want to know what the campaign is really about, as opposed to what it may *appear* to be about." When watching the program, it was even more crystal clear by his expression and intonation that Rather was saying that television news was failing to do its most fundamental job during a campaign. He deserves credit for making the statement. But it put him even more on the spot, along with his colleagues throughout broadcast journalism, to demonstrate the integrity and courage to do something about it.

Friday, September 21:
Dirty Tricks and No Questions

The top story this day was continuing followup on the Beirut bombing of the American embassy annex, and the potential political fallout. NBC, ABC, CBS, and MacNeil/Lehrer all had nearly exactly the same concise report on Mondale stating that the facts pointed to Reagan being responsible for the security lapse that led to the bombing, and White House press secretary Speakes saying that, based on the information he had, the president was satisfied with the security arrangement that was in place.

ABC's Britt Hume stated, "Mondale has been criticized in the past for being too hesitant to criticize the Reagan administration when things went wrong in the Middle East. This time his hesitation lasted only twenty-four hours."

MONDALE: *The president is not responsible for the way in which bolts are put on a gate somewhere in Beirut. I'm not asking that of a president. But in light of what we've been through [the previous bombings of the American embassy and marine barracks], it surely is a matter of presidential concern and responsibility to order and support those changes that would enhance the security and to place top priority on the implementation of those orders. . . .*

SAM DONALDSON: *Here at the White House, no one would respond to Mondale's charges at all. But deputy press secretary Larry Speakes said the president was still satisfied with the security arrangements in effect at the time. Speakes said there is no such thing as perfect security, summing it up in these words: "It is a very difficult world in which we live." The degree to which the most basic security precautions, as opposed to "perfect security," had not been taken was an issue that we would hear more about in the coming days, but that would ultimately be overshadowed by the "Reagan-Gromyko meeting" story.*

CBS ran a report by Bill Plante on President Reagan sending "conciliatory signals" to the Soviets in advance of his upcoming meeting with Foreign Minister Andrei Gromyko. Plante reported he was told by a senior official that "Reagan wants to first clear the air with Gromyko, then propose a renewal of regular cabinet-level meetings with the Soviets, and finally, urge that the two superpowers resume arms-control talks. The notion that this is all now possible has become the official administration position. . . . Asked why the Soviets should believe the friendly Ronald Reagan of this election year, instead of the hostile Ronald Reagan who has denounced the Soviet system as evil for the last thirty years, a senior official today replied that the Soviets don't make decisions based on the level of rhetoric, but rather on the relative strength of forces."

This was the extent, with one exception, of election-related coverage on the commercial networks. It was very meager indeed.

The exception, however, was noteworthy. "NBC Nightly News" reported this day that the Reagan-Bush campaign, under the direct control of campaign manager Ed Rollins and long-time Reagan adviser Lyn Nofziger, was engaged in an "undercover" operation to discredit Geraldine Ferraro.

With a background logo that read "Target: Ferraro," Tom Brokaw began the NBC report.

BROKAW: *The campaign trail has to be a very rough road for Geraldine Ferraro. Nearly every day, she is confronted by antiabortion demonstrators. She has had a well-publicized exchange with the New York archbishop. Stories still appear about her family's finances. She is a special target in this campaign, a target of the president's campaign organization at the highest level. Jamie Gangel has learned who's involved and what they're up to.*

GANGEL: *According to high Republican sources involved in the campaign, the Reagan-Bush campaign has been running an undercover operation designed to undermine the Mondale-Ferraro campaign. It is being led by campaign director Ed Rollins and long time Reagan advisor Lyn Nofziger. And these sources have told NBC News there are almost daily planning meetings to organize political attacks, while keeping them at a distance so they cannot be traced to the president's reelection effort. The strategy is to have groups or individuals not officially connected to the campaign demand investigations of Geraldine Ferraro's finances, orchestrate a campaign of damaging leaks to the press, organize antiabortion demonstrations against the Mondale-Ferraro ticket, and encourage criticism by the Catholic hierarchy. Ed Rollins denies all this.*

ROLLINS: *There is not a master strategy laid out by this campaign to do the various things going on.*

GANGEL: *Lyn Nofziger initially agreed to an interview, then canceled it. The core of the strategy has been to attack Ferraro indirectly on two issues: her finances and her stand on abortion. On her finances, the Washington Legal Foundation, a conservative law firm, asked the House Ethics Committee and the Justice Department to investigate Ferraro. Our sources claim the reelection campaign was behind it. The Washington Legal Foundation denies that. Our sources also say that after her historic nomination, press leaks were carefully orchestrated so that a damaging story appeared almost daily. Rollins denies being behind the leaks, but is clearly pleased with the net effect.*

ROLLINS: *Today she is not the factor that she was a week after San Francisco.*

GANGEL: *On abortion, almost wherever Ferraro goes, she is confronted by antiabortion protestors. Again our sources, all top Republican staffers, say the protests are not an accident, and there is an organized strategy, coordinated by antiabortion groups who keep in touch with and are monitored by the Reagan-Bush team. In this campaign, the president has appeared with prominent members of the Catholic clergy, and the Catholic hierarchy has been openly critical of Ferraro's prochoice position. Our sources say Reagan-Bush intermediaries contacted high church officials, whom they would not name, to encourage their public criticism of Ferraro. The point was to get Ferraro without creating a backlash.*

TONY COEHLO *(Democratic congressional committee chairman)*: *Well, why don't they just come out and say that they're out discrediting Geraldine Ferraro? Why don't they just say that that is the aim of this campaign? Why don't they want to do that? They want those other people to do it so they can say, "We wouldn't do something . . . not, not us!"*

GANGEL: *The Reagan team believes that any advantage Ferraro brought to the ticket has been destroyed. There is nothing illegal about any of these activities. What it is, is hardball politics. But what the Reagan campaign did not want was for it to become public.*

If this story is accurate, which seems likely, unless one's imagination could encompass "highly placed Republican sources" attempting to sabotage their own campaign by lying, then the most damning aspect was probably the denials by Ed Rollins and Lyn Nofziger.

This story ended week three of the campaign with a bang, which looked as if it could potentially continue to reverberate throughout the remainder of the campaign. It appeared it might be the first "break," other than the upcoming debates agreement, for the Mondale-Ferraro campaign, one it so desperately needed. Although no apparent illegality was involved, the ethical aspects of the "dirty tricks" engaged in by Nixon's CREEP (Committee to Reelect the President) appeared to be having an unseemly resurrection from the Watergate-era graveyard.

On the following Monday, the *Wall Street Journal* reported on the "Newest Issue: Alleged Dirty Tricks" in response to the NBC report, adding a bizarre story about an attempt by a Mr. Trammel Crow, "a prominent Republican supporter who spent much time during the GOP convention in Dallas with high level Reagan Administration aides" to discredit Geraldine Ferraro with an anonymous analysis of Ferraro's financial statements. When the *Journal* refused to grant anonymity, Mr. Crow said the analysis "probably doesn't have any merit at all" and asked that the matter be dropped, saying he would be embarrassed if it became known, according to the *Journal* report.

On the following Wednesday, ABC carried a somewhat related report by Dean Reynolds, who began, "They were there again today at a big rally in Boston in the rain, abortion demonstrators dogging Geraldine Ferraro. But this time, the demonstrators were quiet for the most part, perhaps in response to warnings like this, just added to the local antiabortion telephone hotline."

RECORDING: *Remember, we come not to heckle but to witness. Respect the speaker's right to speak.*
REYNOLDS: *Their careful preparations for her visit have been under way for days, leading to Democratic party charges that the Republicans are behind them. The demonstrators deny it.*
ANNE FOX *(Chairperson, Massachusetts Citizens for Life)*: *No group, political or otherwise, within the state or outside the state, has urged us to be at this rally.*
REYNOLDS: *Nonetheless, charges of White House orchestration persist. This is an audio tape provided by a participant at a seminar for conservatives last month. The seminar was conducted by the Washington-based Leadership Institute, headed by former White House aide Morton Blackwell. The tape appears to suggest a link between demonstrators and the Reagan campaign.*
TAPE: *When the press starts asking around about who's holding up the signs about what group you are with, just say, "I'm just a concerned citizen." Don't say, "I'm with Students for Reagan."*
REYNOLDS: *Blackwell, who has no connection to the Reagan-Bush campaign, insists he's had no hand in the heckling incidents.*
BLACKWELL: *The American people do not like rudeness and unpleasantness, and I make that very clear in all my schools.*
REYNOLDS: *But Reagan-Bush officials, apparently trying to distance themselves from the flap, now acknowledge Blackwell's independent efforts may have provoked disruptions. If the protest and heckling continue, the charges of a Republican conspiracy will probably be kept alive by the struggling Democrats. But what's less clear is whether the Democrats can make something out of it, and turn the issue to their advantage.*

Reynold's narrative seemed to imply acceptance as fact that Blackwell's efforts were definitively independent of the Reagan campaign, which was by no means clear based on the rest of his report, not to mention the more significant report by NBC the preceding Friday. It was basically a solid report, but whether the Democrats can make something out of the issue was not as significant as the larger story of the ethics involved. And that larger story, of alleged involvement of the Reagan campaign at the highest levels in a multifaceted "undercover operation," as NBC had put it, and the ultimate veracity of the Reagan campaign, were the issues that all the networks and media at large should have been covering more seriously.

Also on Wednesday, Tom Brokaw told us that "Dr. John Wolkee, president of the National Right-to-Life Committee, told NBC News tonight that his group has been in close touch with the Reagan-Bush campaign, saying, 'They know more about our picketing than we do.' Dr. Wolkee also *confirmed* last week's NBC News story that groups such as his were in touch with and monitored by the Reagan-Bush campaign." This was the entire extent of the report.

Although NBC deserved credit for reporting this story to begin with, it was very difficult to understand why this report was not headlined and expanded. At worst, this confirmation, in effect, made liars out of the people running the Reagan-Bush campaign; at best, it meant that the campaign apparatus was totally out of control of the president and his managers. Why was there no reported attempt to reach Reagan campaign manager Ed Rollins for comment, after he had so angrily denied these very allegations? Why no further comment on the ramifications of this story by NBC News? After this report there was no followup by NBC or anyone else for the remainder of the campaign. The Reagan campaign was not talking, and no one was asking questions. It seemed inexplicable and uncharacteristic of the media at large to let such a story slide.

A related issue was the successful manner in which President Reagan was using the media, through television, to run his "show" but not "tell" reelection campaign, and the almost total embargo the White House and campaign staff had placed on Reagan's accessibility to the press. Conservative columnist William Safire had complained of the Nixon-like attitude of the Reagan White House, his natural ideological allies, long before the campaign began. This example helped illustrate a larger point: The press was not ill disposed toward Reagan, in fact most members of the media seemed to like him. There could be no accusations of a repeat of the "Nixon-hating" bias, which, though overstated by Nixon's defenders, had some basis in truth. But in Reagan's case, the increasing complaints of the press were clearly being aired strictly on their merits. A report by Judy Woodruff on MacNeil/Lehrer examined these issues in a report titled "Reagan Campaign: Smooth-Running Machine."

WOODRUFF: *With just a little more than six weeks to go before election day, you would expect the incumbent president to be out beating the bushes for votes, taking no chances that the electorate might somehow turn against him. But Mr. Reagan is spending most of his time these days not on the campaign trail, but at the White House, doing the things that presidents usually do and getting lots of TV coverage anyway. . . .*

REAGAN: *This we believe is a balanced approach that treats farmers as individuals and that recognizes our basic objective must be to help people through temporary difficulties. [Sound like a liberal Democrat? This scene in the White House was Reagan announcing a very modest farmer-subsidy program of the kind that he had resisted supporting throughout his first term. But the farm vote was now at stake, and he was dispensing the goods, in the fashion of his predecessors, during the reelection campaign.]*

REPORTER: *Mr. President, Walter Mondale says U.S. policy toward Nicaragua is not clear. How do you respond to that?*

REAGAN: *That doesn't have much to do with farming, but, no, I'm—I just am making it a point, I'm not going to respond to my opponent in these matters that he brings up. I'll be discussing them on my own and not in answer to his questions.*

WOODRUFF: *And when there's good news to reveal, as a long-sought meeting with a top Soviet official [long sought?] the president can drop by the White House press room to make the announcement himself.*

REAGAN: *I have invited Soviet Deputy Premier and Foreign Minister Andrei Gromyko to meet with me at the White House on September 28.*

WOODRUFF: *It's live on national TV, every newspaper's lead story the next day, but it ends before reporters can ask questions on many other subjects. Reporters, who point out Mr. Reagan has not had a full-blown news conference since July, acknowledge the White House is very much in control. Lou Cannon of the* Washington Post *has covered Ronald Reagan longer than any other reporter. . . .*

CANNON: *You have a person who is completely wrapped in the institution of the White House. His managers have cocooned him on the road more effectively and more completely than any other president, including Richard Nixon. You can go out with Ronald Reagan, spend a day with Ronald Reagan, and as you know, never get within a question of him. And if you do get within a question of him, you're going to have his aides and you're going to have the Secret Service—who are not supposed to be doing that, they're supposed to be out there protecting the president from danger, not from questions from the press—intervening. . . .*

WOODRUFF: *Reporters who have covered the Reagan White House for some time, like NBC's Andrea Mitchell, say the advance people [for Reagan's campaign stops] don't make mistakes.*

ANDREA MITCHELL: *They're using a lot of the Nixon people back from '72, from earlier Nixon campaigns, and they really have managed to turn out tremendous crowds. They don't have the kind of hecklers that Mondale has experienced. . . .*

SAM DONALDSON *(ABC News): Under the guise of security, they screen people coming in the rallies. Usually these rallies are only open to people with tickets, and they say they'll give out tickets to anyone who approaches them, but that's sort of a screening device. Second, you have to come through magnetometers. That is a little inhibition against people who want to come in and demonstrate. [True, although this may be appropriate in some situations for security. We're not given enough information to know.] Third, they don't allow any signs with poles on them, and in fact in one place they actually took away every sign of a person trying to enter the rally. So the result is that you have nothing but the faithful shouting "Reagan, Reagan, four more years."*

REAGAN *(at a rally): I'm willing if you are. . . .*

JAMES LAKE *(Reagan campaign spokesman): Today 45 percent of all the people get all their news through television. It's over 60 percent get the majority of their news through television. In order to be a leader, in order to be the president, you have to be able to convey your character, your leadership traits, and your programs, your ideas and your thoughts about the issues in that medium. [Of course, when it came to "thoughts about the issues" raised by Mondale or the press, Reagan felt no need to respond.]*

WOODRUFF: *Lake confirms that the campaign can get away with such an attitude because of the president's big lead in the polls.*

LAKE: *The people are already giving us their opinions of what they think of President Reagan and his record by virtue of the polling information that we all have available to us. They believe Ronald Reagan's record speaks for itself and deserves, at this point in their judgment, four more years of trial. And when they begin to feel differently, believe that he is not communicating with them in a way that is satisfactory, then those polling numbers will change.*

Reagan's White House and campaign staff had clearly analyzed the situation correctly. As long as they could get their message across through the appropriate images on TV, this would outweigh criticism for lack of substance or openness with the press. Even when the voiceovers on the nightly news might criticize the image over substance approach, the images themselves proved the stronger message. The nature of the medium, and the briefness and lack of substance covered in the reports themselves, combined to make this so.

Judy Woodruff ended the report this way:

WOODRUFF: *. . . Long-time Reagan watcher Lou Cannon says there is another aspect of the president's abilities as a performer that allow him to be packaged by the people who work for him.*

CANNON: *Because Reagan is kind of a paradox. He is in one sense a decisive leader, in that he has an agenda and he sticks to his agenda—and you know how hard it is to get him to change his mind on taxes or anything like that. But his personality is packaged. He's still the performer from his*

Hollywood days waiting for the "lights, camera, action" sort of direction, and he's not the kind of person who asserts himself with staff. He also doesn't say, "Hey, Larry [Speakes], hey, Mike [Deaver], I can answer that question perfectly well. I'll take that question." And he just doesn't do that. He never has done that, and he certainly is not going to start at the age of seventy-three.

Tuesday, September 25: A Little Balance

The top story on all the networks this day was the response of Soviet leader Konstantin Chernenko in a public speech, as well as the negative Soviet press reaction, to President Reagan's UN speech, and the related White House and Mondale campaign stories.

ABC, NBC, CBS, and MacNeil/Lehrer all made two points very clear in their reports: First, the Reagan White House was at least somewhat concerned with the negative public Soviet reaction to the president's speech and was therefore trying to decrease expectations of the Reagan-Gromyko meeting. Second, Walter Mondale's campaign had an excellent day, in part because the candidate himself gave perhaps his best performance of the campaign to this point in a speech at George Washington University in Washington, D.C.

There was also the fascinating report, which the White House had hoped to keep secret, of Reagan conferring with Richard Nixon in regard to the upcoming Gromyko meeting. This was in tandem with a White House meeting with Henry Kissinger, who afterward all but told the press corps that Reagan was returning to his [Kissinger's] and Nixon's old policy of détente, the very policy and architect that Reagan had run so fiercely against in his challenge to Gerald Ford for the Republican nomination in 1976. In a sense, this seemed a testament to *Foreign Affairs Quarterly* editor William Mayne's statement the previous day on MacNeil/Lehrer, that the doves were more important than the hawks as a voting block for the first time in a presidential election in the postwar period.

In his second appearance in several days, Soviet leader Chernenko gave a speech responding to Reagan's UN speech of a day earlier, saying, "People cannot hide from the nuclear threat, or turn it into a joke." The Soviet news agency, TASS, was even harsher, claiming that Reagan's UN remarks were merely aimed at the American voter. The networks showed Reagan responding in vintage style, saying jokingly, "I never get good reviews from TASS." NBC's Chris Wallace reported that "in fact, the

White House took the Soviet comments very seriously and, worried that Friday's Reagan-Gromyko meeting may go badly, immediately tried to lower public expectations. Spokesman Larry Speakes said the president's expectations are for no immediate results. . . .But former Secretary of State Kissinger, who briefed the president today, disagreed with this pessimism, saying he thinks Gromyko will move back toward negotiations. . . . Meanwhile, the White House had little to say about another Soviet briefing the president received yesterday in New York, from Richard Nixon. Even after Mr. Reagan confirmed it, aides refused to say officially the two men had met. Most aides here still see the Gromyko meeting as a political plus, but there is a minority view: That if after all this attention relations still don't improve, then playing the Gromyko card could backfire on the president."

All the networks carried virtually the same story. CBS played the most interesting give-and-take between reporters and Henry Kissinger, after his meeting with Reagan. CBS's Leslie Stahl asked, "Has the president changed his views?"

KISSINGER: *I think he is moving toward a negotiated coexistence with the Soviet Union.*
HELEN THOMAS (UPI): *Isn't that détente, easing of tensions?*
KISSINGER: *What I used to call détente.*

Now this was big news! Ronald Reagan lining up with Henry Kissinger, one of the archdevils of the right wing, and the hated words Reagan had attacked for so many years, *coexistence* and *détente*, used to describe the president's new policy with the Soviet Union? This would be a 180-degree shift from a lifetime of political rhetoric for Reagan, a far more significant shift than just the generally softer line he had adopted toward the Soviets in recent months. Why did none of the networks point this out or spend any time on the story?

NBC's Tom Brokaw followed the White House report of Chris Wallace with brief remarks about a group of experts on the Soviet Union, including former members of Democratic administrations, headed by former Secretary of State Cyrus Vance, which had concluded that relations between the United States and the Soviet Union had deteriorated to a dangerous point, and questioned whether the leadership of either country was equal to the job of improving them. Again, a potentially important and informative story, but no follow up. The other networks didn't even mention it.

On MacNeil/Lehrer, Judy Woodruff reported an important story unaccountably passed up by the other networks, dealing with the central dòmestic issue of the campaign, and featuring some of President Reagan's more substantive remarks.

WOODRUFF: *Two conflicting economic views were offered today. A group of economists headed by Wall Street guru Henry Kaufman of Saloman Brothers said the U.S. economy will not improve enough to wipe out the federal deficit. Kaufman, Felix Rohatyn, head of the New York City's Municipal Assistance Corporation, and Congressional Budget Office chief Ralph Penner told a congressional committee it was unlikely the U.S. economy would grow out of it's red-ink problems without raising taxes. President Reagan viewed the situation more optimistically. He told the International Monetary Fund improvements in the U.S. economy will benefit other nations.*

REAGAN: *We are heartened that the strength of the U.S. economy is helping lead the world from recession toward a new period of lasting economic expansion, with lower rates of inflation in many countries. And we're convinced we can continue to offer this leadership in the future. This broadening economic growth has had a significant impact on stimulating world trade. We sometimes hear complaints about U.S. interest rates, particularly by debtor nations, which are legitimately concerned about the additional debt-service costs that they must bear. But not enough mention is made of trade, and the far greater benefits developing countries receive from renewed economic growth and open market policies of the United States.*

WOODRUFF: *Mr. Reagan told the IMF that U.S. interest rates, which increase the payments owed by borrowing nations, would fall.*

The president had made an accurate observation about trade in this context. It would have been useful here to explore the flip side of the issue, the U.S. trade deficit, and the relationship, from the candidates' different points of view, between the federal deficit, interest rates, economic growth, and the need to raise taxes.

Turning to Walter Mondale's day, NBC's Tom Brokaw said that today he had stepped up his campaign against the Reagan foreign policy, "emphasizing the differences between what he called the old Reagan and the new Reagan. Mondale delivered his speech at George Washington University and to many traveling with him, it was his most impressive performance of this campaign." Certainly the reporters of the other networks agreed. ABC's Britt Hume described the speech as "strongly worded and strongly applauded." CBS's Susan Spencer told us that "Mondale found an overflow crowd, a teleprompter, and Gary Hart to introduce him, signs that with only six weeks left, things may be coming together for the Mondale campaign."

Coverage of the speech itself varied greatly. MacNeil/Lehrer ran a very lengthy segment. But for the commercial networks, NBC did an unusually good job of letting the candidate speak for himself beyond one or two lines: "The new Reagan supports economic aid to the developing world. The old Reagan slashed it. The new Reagan wants to settle regional differences. The old Reagan ignored them or made them worse. The new Reagan now praises international law. The old Reagan jumped bail on the international court. The new Reagan criticizes South Africa. The old Reagan cozied up to apartheid. Through four years, they failed for the first time in any modern presidency to reach a single arms-control agreement with the Soviets. In fact, they've proposed to extend the arms race into the heavens. But now, just six weeks before the election, they talk about arms control. They dust off the conference table and they brag about blunting an issue. This election is not about jelly beans and pen pals. This election is about toxic dumps that are poisoning our children. This election is not about the Olympic torch, it's about the civil rights laws that opened athletics to women and minorities and permitted us to win, in essence. This election is not about Republicans sending hecklers to my rallies. It is about Jerry Falwell picking justices for the Supreme Court."

All the networks emphasized the "Jerry Falwell" line, which illicited a thunderous response from the listeners, as did much of the speech. There was more passion in this crowd than there had been in any for either candidate so far, at least as shown on TV. ABC ran these quotes from Mondale's speech: "Six weeks before the election, he [Reagan] sprinkles his speeches with Roosevelt quotes, gives a medal to Humphrey, invokes Truman's name in Missouri, Kennedy's in Connecticut, asks Democrats to become Republicans as if it didn't matter. We know the difference. . . . The new Reagan now proposes regular consultations with the Soviets. The old Reagan is the first president since Herbert Hoover not to meet with his Soviet counterpart. My dad was a Methodist minister. He once told me to be skeptical of deathbed conversions." CBS offered these quotes: "Gone is the talk about winning nuclear war. Gone is the evil empire. How can the American people tell which Reagan would be president if he were reelected? . . . I would rather fight for the heart and soul of America, than to fight for the bonuses of the Fortune 500. . . . They may ask for our vote, but I'll be damned if they'll steal our consciences."

Even with narrative between the meager quotes offered on ABC and CBS, the reports were absurdly short, although they did run concurrently with the top stories on Chernenko and Reagan, unlike NBC, which ran the Mondale story after a commercial. NBC, on the other hand, had more substantive coverage. None of the coverage was truly substantive, of course, as the usual candidate one-liners were not used as a jumping-off point for examination of claims made and issues raised. But they were all, for a change, very upbeat about Mondale, which in a campaign defined by TV images, began to add some important balance. Given the quick-hit, image-making nature of TV news, this day was an oasis in the desert for Walter Mondale. ABC's Britt Hume ended his report saying, "There is growing hope in the Mondale camp tonight, partly because his events, like today's, have been going better, and partly because their own polls show that after three days on the West Coast last week he had cut the Reagan lead there dramatically."

Of course, it would have been too much to expect for a whole day to go by without some reference to Mondale's "hopeless" situation, which was supplied by Lisa Myers in an NBC report on the Mondale campaign's effort at a comeback. She started out positively enough, with, "The crowds are bigger and more enthusiastic. Mondale is more animated." But soon it was back to the same old theme: "By all accounts, Mondale is in very very deep trouble," preceded by "He is so far down that nothing but the biggest comeback in political history will beat Ronald Reagan." One would have been interested in Ms. Myers's research, backing up such a statement, going back not only to the 1796 election between Adams and Jefferson, the first "contested" presidential election, and examining every campaign since, but the even more formidable job of world history as a whole, implied in her statement. Presumably Ms. Myers meant to say, "modern American political history." Even this statement would depend on the reference point and which polls one was examining. And even so, would it be beyond imagining for the press to point out that elections that have looked like landslides have turned around dramatically and that precedents, like world records (since "news" journalists seem addicted to sportscasting rhetoric) and history itself, are constantly changing? Mac-Neil/Lehrer, which to its credit ran a very lengthy segment of Mondale's speech, unfortunately decided to follow with an even lengthier discussion of the "strategy" implications rather than the substance. Later that evening, on ABC's "Nightline," viewers were subjected to another horse-race analysis of the Mondale campaign. Again, the question, What contribution does this journalistic approach make to participatory democracy?

The last report on CBS this day, by Bernard Goldberg, was a welcome self-critique of television, titled "Television: A Nation Hooked." But it made one ponder, If the medium was capable of recognizing its failings, why wasn't it trying to correct them?

GOLDBERG: *In the beginning there was television and it was a window . . . a window we could look out and see the world. . . . A lot of what we see through the window is a carnival, a national amusement park.*
BRANDON TARTIKOFF *(NBC Entertainment): George Bernard Shaw once said the reason the Chinese like rice is that they've never tasted steak, and I*

think the more people see good television, the more they'll want good television.

TOM SHALES *(TV critic)*: *It's true, the working guy or gal who comes home after eight hours does not want to be bombarded with the problems of the world. But doesn't it seem a terrible waste of a miraculous invention to have it simply be this machine of silly dreams, foolish people, plastic characters, that have no real relevance to anyone's life? There's got to be a better use for it.*

NEWTON MINNOW *(CBS Board of Directors)*: *It is not enough to cater to the nation's whims. You must also serve the nation's needs [1961]. . . . I think television is by far the most important educational institution and I do think we waste it too often [1984]. . . .*

GOLDBERG: *It isn't clear if we watch the commercial networks because we actually like what's on or if we watch simply because, like Mount Everest, it's there. What is clear is that the very same questions we asked of television in the beginning, we are still asking today.*

Edward R. Murrow, who, along with William Shirer and others, was a pioneer of radio news broadcasting during World War II, went on to become the "father" of TV news journalism. Goldberg's report showed an old clip of Murrow, saying, "We are impressed with the importance of this medium. We shall hope to learn to use it and not to abuse it. . . . This instrument can entertain, it can inform. Yes, it can even inspire. But it can only do that to the extent that men and women are determined to use it for that purpose. Otherwise, it's just lights and wires in a box."

Fred Friendly, a long-time colleague of Murrow, said, "If Murrow were to look at nightly television . . . the quiz programs and the 'Real People' kind of thing, and the *capsulated news* [my emphasis], I'm afraid that this sainted man would say, 'It's just lights and wires in a box.' "

Friday, September 28: Video Détente

The much media-hyped meeting between President Reagan and Soviet Foreign Minister Gromyko was finally at hand. Depending on which broadcast, or which part of which broadcast one viewed, the meeting was reported to have gone moderately well or moderately not so well. In the end, it seemed a nonevent. The most striking video image of the day was seeing Ronald Reagan squirming with such discomfort in the "photo opportunity" with Gromyko in the White House preceding their meeting that he looked as though he would have given back all the jelly beans he had ever eaten to avoid being in this situation. Whether he was in control of his persona (which seemed likely, given the stakes) or not, this image Reagan projected was probably to his advantage. Voters concerned about the threat of nuclear holocaust were reassured by the very fact of seeing Reagan and Gromyko together. Voters concerned about the threat of the Soviets were reassured by Reagan's discomfort in the presence of the emissary from the "evil empire."

This nonevent was in many ways one of the most important events of the campaign. Whether it would ever yield real results in terms of the message it was sending to the electorate was another matter. But the message to the electorate was obviously the concern at hand. President Reagan's weakest area in terms of public opinion was concern about the nuclear arms race. With this meeting, and all the media attention that preceded it, he was able to change his image appropriately.

Consider these opening lines of the network evening news reports on September 11, the day Reagan announced the meeting with Gromyko.

CHRIS WALLACE *(NBC): It was a big diplomatic and political move. The President announcing that after almost four years in office, he'll meet for the first time with a top Soviet official. . . . Reagan advisers see the president's bad relations with the Soviets as his biggest political weakness. And they see the Gromyko meeting as helping take away that issue. And so this life-long anti-communist may get an election-year boost from his old foes.*
LESLIE STAHL *(CBS): The September surprise. Ronald Reagan was handed a plum by the Soviet Union that could offset criticism that he has plunged U.S.-Soviet relations into the deep freeze. . . . Republicans were ecstatic. They say this will show the president is flexible toward the Soviets.*
SAM DONALDSON *(ABC): The Kremlin seemed to sign on to the Reagan reelection campaign today. . . .*

It was not a good day for Walter Mondale's campaign. Leslie Stahl described the effect of the Reagan-Gromyko meeting announcement on the Mondale campaign, saying, "The announcement sent the Democrats reeling. . . . Walter Mondale got a big lesson today in incumbency politics." NBC's Tom Brokaw stated, "The Reagan-Gromyko meeting deflates one of Walter Mondale's charges, that Reagan hadn't met with the Soviets during three and a half years in office." ABC's Britt Hume reported, "Seldom have the difficulties of being the challenger been more evident than they were to Walter Mondale today. While Mr. Reagan was at the White House announcing an unexpected step forward in his dealings with the Soviets, Mondale was in Chicago trying to make a complicated economic point about the relationship between the budget and trade deficits. Then at a news conference before departing for Wisconsin, Mondale wanted to reemphasize his point, but the questions centered on Reagan and Gromyko."

Not only did the Reagan-Gromyko story deflect attention from the deficit issue, which the Reagan campaign clearly did not want attention focused on, but in terms of another issue, a potential political powder keg for the president, the meeting itself could not, as it turned out, have been better timed. The bombing of the American embassy annex in Beirut was clearly a result of extraordinary security lapses, particularly in view of the previous embassy and marine barracks bombings. The evidence was quickly mounting and pointing to extreme negligence on the part of the administration. This was compounded by some rather strange comments by Reagan seeming to blame former President Carter for the problem, as a result of impeding the CIA intelligence-gathering capacity. In fact, the personnel changes Reagan seemed to allude to had occurred under President Ford, and CIA funding had risen under Carter. Reagan said that his remarks had been "distorted" and spokesman Larry Speakes claimed that the president had not meant to blame Carter. But NBC's John Chancellor reported that one of Reagan's aides confirmed that Reagan was referring to Carter. Reagan was forced to call Carter to apologize. In addition, it appeared that ample intelligence warning existed, but more important, the most obvious security precautions had not been taken. Reagan had dumped gasoline on this fire by an offhand remark (explaining why his aides were keeping him away from the press), describing the security problems as similar to a homeowner having their "kitchen redecorated. . . . It never gets done as soon as you wish it would." All of this made the Reagan administration look weak and inept in foreign policy, and began to resurrect the entire Lebanon policy debacle, a loss Reagan had attempted to cut some months before with the removal from Beirut of the American "peace-keeping force," which in reality was supporting the right-wing Christians against the majority Moslems in a civil war. All of this was coming to a head, and would have undoubtedly dominated the news even more than it already was. But during this entire week there had been the various events building up to the Reagan-Gromyko meeting: Reagan's speech at the United Nations, Chernenko's emerging from seclusion to respond in Moscow, Gromyko's speech before the United Nations. And then, the Reagan-Gromyko meeting itself, at the White House. This helped tremendously in taking the news "momentum" away from the Lebanon issue.

In addition, Mondale's best speech of the campaign gave him some positive video visibility, but in this week of building to the Reagan-Gromyko meeting climax, this plus didn't count for much. Mondale's only other opportunity in the spotlight was his own meeting with Gromyko the day before Reagan's, where he walked the politically perilous line of saying he urged Gromyko to negotiate with Reagan now, and tried to take some credit no matter how things turned out by saying, "I did my best," implying that success or failure was now up to Reagan. But however this played, it was clearly a mere warmup for the main act at the White House. It seemed all Mondale could do was tilt at the shadow cast by the giant he was challenging.

The Reagan-Gromyko meeting was, of course, another perfect opportunity for responsible broadcast journalism to cover the issue of arms control and defense policy. ABC and CBS both had reports related to these issues, but essentially devoid of information. During the entire week, which should have focused attention on these issues, there was only one other related report, on CBS, which also was a typical network report, filled with one-liners and no followup. The one noteworthy aspect of the Monday CBS report by Susan Spencer was that for only the second, and last time, during the campaign, on any of the nightly news programs, Mondale's proposed moratorium on nuclear and antisatellite testing was mentioned. Spencer had reported it the first time, as well. In this second report, she said that the Reagan administration considered the idea "reprehensible." This was the extent of the discussion and debate of this issue for the entire campaign. There were other important issues also never heard about. Reagan was saying that the military "balance" had been restored and that negotiations could now begin. In fact, a look at the strategic forces of the United States and the Soviet Union showed that nothing substantial had changed since he took office. If anything, the Soviets were possibly a bit stronger than they had been. Of course, Reagan's famed "window of vulnerability," like Kennedy's "missile gap," had turned out to be simply election year rhetoric, which Reagan's own commission on the MX missile had concluded. No American military official was willing to trade the U.S. strategic forces, which relied on the diversified "triad" of land-based missiles, bombers, and submarines, with the Soviet forces which relied heavily on land-based numerical superiority. The new weapons systems, such as the MX, Trident II, the Pershing and Cruise missile deployments in Europe, were raising serious questions of stability. The potential for missiles to be launched and accurately hit Moscow in ten minutes, and reciprocal potentials being threatened by the Soviets, raised the launch-on-warning-by-computer scenario, and brought to mind the computer failures of recent years. The "Star Wars" defense proposed by Reagan could not, according to the most optimistic projections, keep enough missiles from getting through to still annihilate the nation. Yet the idea of having to deal with "Star Wars" seemed to be bringing the Soviets back to the table (or at least, at this point, to the Reagan-Gromyko meeting), the administration could argue. And the increased defense spending and NATO deployment of Pershings and

Cruises had reaped psychological benefits in terms of U.S. and Western alliance resolve, sending the Soviets an important message, according to the Reagan White House. Whether or not this had been necessary or was worth the cost and risks involved were the pertinent questions. Some saw both the massive defense increase and European missile deployment as dangerous and unnecessary. Some had a mixed view. There were a good number of political, military, and arms-control experts who agreed, for instance, that the European deployment was necessary, but who were concerned by the administration's emphasis on arms buildup rather than serious arms negotiations. There was also the question of compliance with previous treaties. Various Reagan administration officials were accusing the Soviets of multiple violations. Yet when pressed on why arms-control should be pursued in the face of such evidence, the same officials generally stated that the violations were minor. Both the United States and the Soviets had raised compliance questions regularly over the years that had generally been addressed to the satisfaction of both sides over time. These were issues that the voters ought to have deliberated on after a substantive debate. These subjects, among others related to them, should have been thoroughly examined on the nightly news programs and in news-produced election specials.

MacNeil/Lehrer did examine some of these issues, and more than once during the campaign. On this day, the entire one-hour report dealt with various aspects of the arms-control debate and U.S.-Soviet relations. One segment pitted Mondale foreign policy adviser and former National Security staff member David Aaron against the deputy director of the State Department's Bureau of Political and Military Affairs, Robert Dean. The moderator was Robert MacNeil. Here is the entire exchange.

MacNeil: *Mr. Aaron, of the differences between you and President Reagan on arms control, what is the most significant one? What does it boil down to in your view?*
Aaron: *I think it boils down to a genuine commitment to really halt the arms race. Right now we have a situation in which there have been no talks . . . and in which we are moving so swiftly into the area of space weapons without any real negotiations going on between the two sides, that these deployments will undermine existing treaties, such as the ABM treaty, and they will make impossible the deep reductions that Mr. Reagan has asked for. In other words, the space-weapons issue is a very fundamental one between the two sides because of its devastating impact on the hope to control arms.*
MacNeil: *Mr. Dean, from the administration's point of view, what is the fundamental difference between you and Mr. Mondale on arms control?*
Dean: *. . . I think the issue before this nation is and has been for the last*

years the preservation of the nuclear balance between the two superpowers. That preservation can only be found in a combination of force modernization, which any administration would be duty bound to undertake, and a policy of serious arms-control proposals designed to channel the so-called arms race into more constructive, less destabilizing directions. It's a policy that we regard in the mutual interest of both the United States and the Soviet Union.

MacNEIL: *Mr. Aaron, a voter listening to this, very interested in the subject but perhaps a bit bewildered by the detail, might ask himself, "Well, they're both talking about making some kind of good deal with the Russians about arms control. Maybe Mr. Reagan wasn't, but he is now. They're both talking about that. What's the difference?"*

AARON: *I think the difference lies first of all in the history. Mr. Reagan has opposed every arms-control agreement put forward by every president since Eisenhower. He was against the limited Test Ban Treaty, and if he had his way we'd still have strontium 90 in our milk. He was against the non-proliferation treaty, he was against SALT I, SALT II, the ABM treaty, and so forth. So there's a record here and there's a history. The second issue comes down to a question of what do you want to do with the arms race? Do you want to stop it, do you want to curb systems that now coming on board could be devastating in their consequences for the very nuclear stability that Mr. Dean is talking about? Or do you want to legalize this? Now, as far as we can tell, it's the proposition of the Reagan administration that space weapons should be legalized and controlled and somehow brought on board for both sides. This is a very dangerous philosophy.*

MacNEIL: *Let me put the question the other way around to you, Mr. Dean. Why shouldn't a voter say, "Well, Mr. Reagan's talking about getting a deal now, but he hasn't been for a long time. Why shouldn't we let Mr. Mondale try?"*

DEAN: *We have sat with the Soviets for over two years in negotiations on both medium-range nuclear systems and strategic systems. We have presented to them, in complex detail, two intrinsically logical proposals that would result in reductions of nuclear weapons on both accounts. The fact is that the Soviet Union walked away from the table, in our view, for political reasons having to do with the deployment of new American systems in Europe—a deployment we regard as a victory for the Atlantic alliance and the cohesion of that alliance. We have been in an unusually politicized situation with respect to arms control over the last three years.*

MacNEIL: *That boils down to the Russians haven't wanted an agreement now for one reason or another. Why would Mr. Mondale do any better than Mr. Reagan at getting one?*

AARON: *The issue is, how do you challenge the Soviets to negotiate seriously? You never know if they are going to negotiate seriously. They always negotiate toughly. Now, it's pretty clear that when the administration waits more than a year to get back on the negotiating track after it entered office, about European missiles and about strategic missiles, and when it does so, it finally comes forward, it makes a proposal, and then it brags that it was a propaganda proposal—the famous zero option that was put forward—we open ourselves up for political manipulation by the Soviet Union because we undermine our own credibility. It's very important that our proposals be serious and complete. And I think that many keen observers of this situation, including our allies, looking at the proposals we put on the table, feel that we opened ourselves up to this kind of political warfare by the Soviet Union.*

MacNeil: *You're saying that the reason there aren't any talks is the Reagan administration's fault? Is that what you're saying?*

Aaron: *I believe that is correct. I think it takes two, however. First of all, there's no excuse for the Soviets walking away from the table. No excuse for that. And the purpose of Mr. Mondale's meeting with Mr. Gromyko yesterday was to make precisely that point. But on the other hand, it is also very dangerous to treat these negotiations in a political manner. They have to be dealt with in a substantively solid way, and up until now that hasn't been the case.*

MacNeil: *Excuse me. If there's no excuse for the Russians walking away from the table, then is it still the Reagan administration's fault that they did?*

Aaron: *I think there's blame on both sides.*

MacNeil: *. . . Mr. Dean?*

Dean: *There are some who advocate making concessions to the Soviet Union to bring them back to the table, which in our view would be rewarding them for walking away and for their intransigence. It's not a course that we consider prudent or sound. We think that, in future, the Soviet Union will reconcile itself to the fact that both sides have to engage in serious negotiations on nuclear-armaments reductions.*

MacNeil: *But Mr. Gromyko said the other day in his speech at the United Nations that the Reagan administration would have to remove the obstacles that it placed in the way of further arms talks before the talks could resume.*

Dean: *. . . We could engage in a criminological examination of what that phrase meant. There are some who see some change in the formulations that Mr. Gromyko chose and some progress in and of itself in those changes. I think we simply have to wait and see. We would rather take stock of what he says to us privately before we can assess the prospects.*

MacNeil: *Is this a fundamental difference, Mr. Aaron, that the Mondale camp believes that something must be offered or a gesture made to the Russians to get them back to the talks, and the Reagan administration believes they should just hold firm and not do anything and let the Russians come back when they want to? Is that putting it fairly?*

AARON: *No, I don't think that is putting it fairly. I think, if I may put it unfairly from our point of view, the Reagan strategy has been that we're going to build up and we're going to conduct an arms race, and that's going to drive the Soviets to the table and make a good deal. We've now seen an arms race does not produce an agreement; an arms race produces an arms race. Our view, Mr. Mondale's view, is that we need to take the initiative in our own interest to make concrete and serious proposals that are in our interest and put them vigorously to the Soviets. If we do that, if we do that in all seriousness and we do that effectively, we believe that we can move forward.*

MACNEIL: *But isn't that what Mr. Dean says that the Reagan administration has done?"*

AARON: *Well, it comes down to a question of whether their proposals are serious, and we can discuss that. All I can tell you is that their proposal for the European missiles, the so-called zero option, was widely heralded by the administration as a propaganda victory. That's not serious negotiating.*

MACNEIL: *Is that what the administration regarded that offer as, that proposal as?*

DEAN: *I think it's important for the audience to realize that that proposal was a going-in position. We, in a matter of months, altered our position and told the Soviets that we would accept an equal level of missiles on both sides, that in fact they could choose the number of those missiles with a view to their own security, only recognize that NATO and the United States have legitimate interests as well.*

AARON: *May I make a point about this? I also think it is important to recognize that when a proposal was developed by Mr. Reagan's own chief arms negotiator and the head of the Arms Control and Disarmament Agency for an equal-number deal, he fired the arms-control agency chief and he reprimanded his negotiator. So the history of this is very tangled. It's not flattering to the administration, and I think that the problem that they face today is this whole question of credibility. Are they seriously interested, is there anything in their history that shows that they're interested, and is there a possibility of real success? I hope . . . the meeting will produce something.*

That hope was shared by many. The meeting certainly produced one thing: good video of Reagan and Gromyko at the White House on the nightly news.

Monday, October 1:
The One-Minute Report

The beginning of week five, heading into the stretch, with the first debate between Reagan and Mondale, only a few days away. Even "Entertainment Tonight" covered the upcoming debate as its top story at the top of the week. The Presidential Election Show hadn't been getting the best ratings so far, but if it was ever going to get hot, now was the time.

"NBC Nightly News" definitely decided that the campaign was not hot and won the all-time award for brevity, covering both Mondale's and Reagan's day in *sixty-four seconds,* including Tom Brokaw's narrative. Adding insult to injury, the "story" wasn't run until well into the second half of the program, after some newsworthy reports and several others insignificant enough to raise serious questions about the journalistic perspective of the program director and producer. Some of the stories NBC considered more important than the campaign were on a mafia informer, the U.S. Navy getting a court order in regard to a ship under repair, a Panamanian crew ship falling from its drydocks, and umpires going on strike during the playoffs. And as if this sixty-four-second blip on the radar of a campaign report wasn't unbelievable enough, Tom Brokaw's words came across as if the report should not only have been of some length, but at the top of the news. Here is the entire report.

BROKAW: *President Reagan and Walter Mondale today made one of the* sharpest *attacks [my emphasis] of their campaigns. Mondale focused on what he called Reagan's incompetence, zeroing in on his misstatements about nuclear weapons.*

MONDALE: *You can dream all you want. But if you believe that nuclear missiles can be recalled after they've launched, as Mr. Reagan did, you won't lead toward a safer world. If you don't learn that most Soviet missiles are land based, as Mr. Reagan did not bother to learn, then your efforts at arms control are doomed.*

BROKAW: *And for his part, Reagan said Mondale would lead this country back to economic despair.*

REAGAN: *There are two things we do know that are not a matter of prediction. First, my opponent is committed to a large spending increase and a tax increase equivalent to $1,800 per household. The second, those policies, which he has supported all his political life, gave America an economic hangover that we must never suffer through again.*

Too bad neither of them said anything interesting, provocative, questionable, or concerned with crucial issues, anything that was worth covering for more than sixty-four seconds! How could Brokaw describe these statements as among the "sharpest attacks of the campaign" and then with a straight face give the story only sixty-four seconds, over halfway through the broadcast? Besides putting these remarks at the top of the news and covering the candidates remarks for longer than these grotesquely short clips, any serious news program would have followed up with some at least brief analysis. Unfortunately, NBC was not the only place where serious news was hard to find. But ABC and CBS, if nothing else, had the usual approximately three minutes of reporting on the candidates, an insult one had grown accustomed to. In addition, the CBS report immediately followed the top story on all the networks, which was the indictment of Labor Secretary Raymond Donovan for grand larceny, falsifying documents, and false statements. He was the first sitting member of a cabinet to ever be indicted, and the story obviously had political significance. ABC's report followed this story and one on the Supreme Court, also election related. So at least the CBS and ABC stories were prioritized in some sort of logical manner.

The one interesting moment in these other more extended blips on the radar came on ABC. On the preceding day, Sunday, on ABC's "This Week with David Brinkley," Secretary of State George Schultz had said, when pressed about who was responsible for the security lapse at the American embassy annex, that he would take responsibility, if someone must. It was clear that he didn't think he was responsible, but that the line of questioning was leading directly to Reagan, so Schultz played the good soldier. In the "World News Tonight" report on Reagan, ABC's Sam Donaldson commented, "Reporters tried to ask him [Reagan] about Secretary of State Schultz's Sunday comment that he, Schultz, would if demanded take responsibility for the Beirut bombing." Donaldson was then heard asking Reagan on camera, "Is George Schultz responsible?" Reagan responded "Sam, it's a photo opportunity."

It was a priceless moment in the history of politics and video.

Meanwhile, an annual ritual in the American constitutional system took place this day, which brought to mind another significant issue in the campaign. It was the first Monday in October, which meant that the Supreme Court opened its new session. All the networks had reports, including the political significance. Fred Graham of CBS did the most informative story. The following is an excerpt.

MARIO CUOMO *(Governor of New York): The reelection of Ronald Reagan could have a greater impact on the Supreme Court than on any other branch of government. Mr. Reagan has already made major changes in domestic and foreign policy, and with a few poor appointments, he could set the Supreme Court on a more conservative path for many years to come.*
GRAHAM: *The Supreme Court has generally resisted President Reagan's most conservative legal policies by narrow margins. Four of the justices who have consistently voted against Reagan positions seem vulnerable to the inroads of time. William Bennett is seventy-eight and has had a cancer operation; Thurgood Marshall, seventy-six, has had a series of ailments;*

Harry Blackmun, seventy-five, was operated on for cancer of the prostate; and Lewis Powell, seventy-seven, is said to be considering retirement. Four justices have generally supported President Reagan's policies: Burger, White, Rhenquist, and O'Connor. So, one or two new Reagan appointments could swing the Court to his conservative view on four major issues: restricting women's abortion rights; allowing prayer in public schools; limiting school busing to achieve racial balance; and outlawing racial quotas in affirmative action. This has prompted the Democrats to raise cries of alarm.

MONDALE: *We must ask ourselves what kind of court and country will be fashioned by the man who believes in having government mandate people's religion and morality.*

GRAHAM: *But Reagan strategists see the court as a positive issue on the Republican side.*

LYN NOFZIGER *(Reagan-Bush campaign)*: *I'm perfectly willing, for the president or the Reagan campaign, to take the Democrats on that issue. Do you want the kind of people that, Walter Mondale, say, would appoint to the Supreme Court, or the kind that Ronald Reagan would appoint? I think that's a good issue for us.*

GRAHAM: *President Reagan has at least three staunch conservatives waiting in the wings: Interior Secretary William Clark, Attorney General William French Smith, and U.S. Appeals Court Judge Robert Borg. But liberal justices Brennan, Marshall, and Blackmun have given subtle indications that they have every intention of trying to outlast even a reelected Ronald Reagan. And history shows that Supreme Court justices can be very durable. Oliver Wendell Holmes stayed on the court until he was ninety, a reminder that even the best laid court stacking plans can go awry.*

No one could know, as Fred Graham commented, what would happen in terms of the Court. But reporter Lyle Denniston, who covered the Court for the *Baltimore Sun,* when interviewed on MacNeil/Lehrer, seemed more certain as to the influence of whoever was elected president in 1984: "I would say that the next president, whoever's elected on November 6, will get a minimum of two appointments, and probably as many as five or even six. . . . And that could make the difference for another generation." Given this statement, it was odd that MacNeil/Lehrer chose to concentrate only on the agenda of the Court in 1984 and 1985, rather than the longer-term issue related to the election. However, several days later, on October 9, MacNeil/Lehrer did have a lengthy issue-and-debate segment on this important subject. It would have been more appropriate this day, but one could not fault them too much, as they managed to schedule so many important issues into their programs.

One problem with Fred Graham's report on CBS, and the other network reports as well, was that they had a built-in assumption that Reagan would probably win the election, and the Court issue was looked at in terms of the impact he would have on it. The impact of a Court dominated by Walter Mondale should also have been examined. It was unfortunate that no one really covered this issue in the sense of exploring in detail the potential influence of a future Supreme Court, assuming either Reagan or Mondale would have a chance to appoint enough judges to reflect their philosophies. It was an issue that had the potential for having the most widespread and long-term influence of any domestic policy consideration.

As the campaign headed toward the climactic debates, the question arose as to whether the constantly reported huge Reagan lead in the polls meant that the election was for all practical purposes decided. On the previous day, an article in the Sunday *New York Times* (30 September) reported that pollster Lou Harris showed Reagan with a 13 percent lead over Mondale (a much smaller spread than many other poll results being reported) and quoted Harris as saying, "It hasn't played out yet. The key is if Mondale can bring President Reagan down to his level and chip away on the issues." Harris said Mondale would get his chance in the debates. He also said that his polls showed a number of factors working against the president, including his handling of arms control, the Middle East, and Central America, his perceived closeness to business and the wealthy, his relative unpopularity with women, and religion. Harris said that Reagan's alliance with the Reverend Jerry Falwell on issues of school prayer and abortion bothered voters. The entire tone of the remarks, from one of the foremost polling experts around, was that Mondale was still very much in the game. You wouldn't know it from watching TV, or from most other sources for that matter. The problem with this, and with concentrating on polls and images instead of issues in general, was best summed up by a letter to *Time* magazine (8 October, 1984) which hit the newstands on October 1: "The polls keep reminding us that the President is maintaining the confidence of most Americans. A friend of mine, quite taken by the statistics, told me, 'I am not going to vote against those figures.' That is his right, but I am bothered by what persuaded him."

Thursday, October 4: Blackout on Blacks

"And now, presidential politics . . ." The voice was that of Peter Jennings introducing ABC's in-depth look at the issues likely to be discussed in the Sunday debate between Ronald Reagan and Walter Mondale, right? Wrong. It was the introduction to—guess what?—another story on new poll results, showing Reagan accelerating into a space-warp lead over Mondale. Remember when "going to the polls" meant voting? Now the polls not only come to us, the media constantly bombard us with them. Television news might as well have aired as its campaign reports the equivalent of "Saturday Night Live" reruns with Gilda Radner, as Emily Litella, doing a commentary on the weekend update about the election and concluding with her famous line, "Never mind." That was, in essence, the message we were getting about the relevance of voting.

After running through the lopsided poll results, ABC's Barry Serafin concluded the report saying, ". . . The huge difference in electoral vote outlook at this point indicates that, more than ever, Mondale's prospects for helping himself and other Democratic candidates will depend on his *performance* [my emphasis] in the upcoming presidential debate." Performance was the right word given the context that television nonjournalism had established for the campaign. It wasn't the issues that mattered but the polls, the strategy, the performance. The election was the superbowl, it was late in the third quarter, the Reagan-Bush team was in the lead, 35-0, and people were leaving the stadium. The problem is that the only points that really matter in an election are counted on election day. And the people in the stadium aren't just spectators, they're supposed to be participants. So when they start leaving the stadium it causes problems for the game called democracy.

Peter Jennings then led into another "important" report on the continued theme of the hopeless situation the Mondale-Ferraro team was in.

JENNINGS: *Well, it seems that some of those other Democratic candidates have already decided the debates will come too late. As ABC's Rebecca Chase reports in the South, there are a lot of Democrats trying to get out from under the Mondale-Ferraro umbrella. [Chase then went through various examples of Republicans making the connection between their Democratic opponent and the Mondale-Ferraro ticket and Democrats trying to dodge this connection. She concluded:]*
CHASE: *. . . With increasing frequency, when the top Democrats come to town, the news becomes who stays away. In Mississippi, Governor Bill Allain made headlines with his absence. In Georgia, Governor Joe Frank Harris says he has better things to do.*
HARRIS: *I will not participate in promoting the national candidates at all.*
CHASE: *Of course not all Democrats from the South are snubbing their party's national candidates. But those who are say it's just not worth the risk of being associated with a losing ticket.*

Reports such as this, which impart absolutely nothing useful about the candidate's qualifications for high office or the issues before the nation, are devastating to the candidacy in question. They simply reinforce a perception that in turn causes more fellow politicians to avoid the candidate, not for reasons of principle but of strategy, just as the above examples did. This is where concentrating on polls and strategy leads. It snowballs into an avalanche that buries the democratic process.

In direct contrast to the above story, President Reagan was seen on the TV news this evening surrounded on the White House lawn by 150 Republican incumbents and fifty more would-be incumbents, trying "to stick to Mr. Reagan's coattails," as CBS's Dan Rather put it. Everyone was all smiles, particularly the president. It was another perfectly constructed picture show for the evening news. Rather segued from here into a report on Reagan and television.

RATHER: *It was but one example of a presidency that projects a personality, an image, that even in the view of harsh critics is almost picture perfect in its skillful use of television. But in using the medium, what is the Reagan message? Does it distort the big picture of reality? Leslie Stahl has been looking into it.*

STAHL: *How does Ronald Reagan use television? Brilliantly. He has been criticized as the rich man's president, but the TV pictures say it isn't so. At seventy-three, Mr. Reagan could have an age problem but the TV pictures say it isn't so. Americans want to feel proud of their country again and of the president, and the TV pictures say you can. The orchestration of television coverage absorbs the White house. Their goal—to emphasize the president's greatest asset, which, as they say, is his personality. They provide pictures of him looking like a leader, confident, with his "Marlboro man" walk, a good family man. They also aim to erase the negatives. Mr. Reagan tries to counter the memory of an unpopular issue with a carefully chosen backdrop that actually contradicts the president's policy. Look at the handicapped Olympics, or the opening ceremony of an old-age home. No hint that he tried to cut the budgets for the disabled and for federally subsidized housing for the elderly. Another technique for distancing the president from bad news is to have him disappear, as he did the day he pulled the marines out of Lebanon. He flew off to his California ranch, leaving others to hand out the announcement. There are few visual reminders linking the president to the tragic bombing of the marine headquarters in Beirut; but two days later, the invasion of Grenada succeeded, and the White House offered television a variety of scenes associating the president with the joy and the triumph . . . running the presidency, the White House often prevents reporters from questioning Mr. Reagan. Aides admit that helicopter engines are revved up so the questions can't be heard. At other times, it's aides who interrupt. This tight control has baffled those who think Mr. Reagan is at his best when he's spontaneous. . . . [Reagan is shown at a rally responding*

to the first and only heckler of the campaign who managed to penetrate the screening process.]
REAGAN: *I'll raise his taxes.*
STAHL: *Or in tossing off one-liners.*
REAGAN: *I never get good reviews from TASS.*
STAHL: *He can be masterful at deflecting a hostile question.*
REPORTER: *Did you mean to give a signal to other Republicans that if they don't conform . . . off will go their heads?*
REAGAN: *How can you say that about a sweet fellow like me?*
STAHL: *Time and again, the president, with uncanny skill, shifts the focus from the details of an unpopular issue to a popular subject, himself. Take education. He responds to a briefing about an inner-city school's dilapidated conditions with a personal story.*
REAGAN: *In our high school gymnasium in my day, there were a few places on the floor that you couldn't try for the basket, because the beams holding the ceiling up interfered.*
STAHL: *There is, of course, a sound reason the White House has kept the president under wraps. It's his gaffes. But since he was criticized for being isolated and wrapped in a cocoon, Mr. Reagan has been taking more questions lately, resulting in more mistakes. His explanation of security lapses at the Beirut embassy annex:*
REAGAN: *Anyone that's ever had their kitchen remodeled, will soon see that it never gets done as soon as you wish it was.*
STAHL: *There is a lot of evidence that the American people don't care if Mr. Reagan makes mistakes. They like him anyway.*
DAVID GERGEN *(former Reagan media advisor): He is one of the best people I have ever seen at turning a mistake into a positive, turning on the dime when he makes a mistake. He knows how to cut his losses so fast and so quickly and so effectively that they become positives and people say, "Ahhh."*
STAHL: *President Reagan was accused of running a campaign in which he highlights the images and hides from the issues. But there is no evidence that the charge will hurt him. Because when the people see the president on television, he makes them feel good about America, about themselves, and about him. [The report ended with the scene at the Grand Ole Opry when Reagan, the country-music stars, the band, and the audience sang "God Bless the USA."]*

In the report on the poll results on ABC there was a clip of Geraldine Ferraro saying, "Ronald Reagan has been an actor for forty years; he's good at doing what he does. Look at the amount of money being spent on ads. And if you can keep those ads going over and over and over and over again, it's almost like brainwashing." The television advertising of the

Reagan campaign was truly astounding. As a tactic, it was perfect. The commercials had one purpose only: to evoke emotion. The "It's morning in America" and "It's springtime in America" themes were devoid even of the slightest reference to any issue. The idea was to associate Reagan with everything good in everyday life, with a postcard version of America, everything sparkling and perfect, with family and friends, with America peaceful and prosperous now—and forever—with Reagan reelected. The music was as awesome as the video. The producers undeniably created masterpieces. They also created a precedent that will probably haunt the democratic process. But Ferraro's concern about brainwashing should have been directed to the TV networks for their news coverage. For it was the free advertising on the nightly news that undoubtedly had the greatest impact. It reinforced and energized the paid advertising. Strangely, a report such as the one by Leslie Stahl didn't detract from the impact of the Reagan strategy. Television would observe the phenomenon, then do nothing to address its own role in the process. Even the Stahl report seemed to build to a crescendo with the closing remarks and visuals having exactly the effect that the narrative describes, washing away intellectual concentration in a sea of positive images. In combination with the constant negative images associated with Mondale and Ferraro, the never-ending conducting and reporting of the polls, the decision not to opt for the primacy of issues, television news was raising serious questions about its journalistic ethics.

On the preceding Friday on MacNeil/Lehrer, in what had become a weekly segment, a number of newspaper cartoons were shown. The two described below are a perfect way to end this discussion. The first, with the cartoonist unidentified, deals with a Reagan TV commercial.

Video *(Reagan commercial): The sun is rising, coffee brewing, a pickup truck going down a country road.*
First Viewer: *McDonald's!*
Video: *Puppies in a wagon, chickies in a barnyard, black and white kids playing in a fire hydrant.*
Second Viewer: *Nope, Pepsi!*
Video: *Surprise party for Grandma, small-town Fourth of July parade, ethnically mixed construction workers eating lunch together, laughing.*
First Viewer: *Or maybe Kodak!*
Announcer: *President Reagan. When you care enough to vote the very best.*
First Viewer: *My God! The president's been Hallmarked!*

The second cartoon, by Wasserman of the *Los Angeles Times* Syndicate, shows Mondale and Reagan facing off.

MONDALE: *The deficit, the arms race, and Central America.*
REAGAN: *Flag.*
MONDALE: *Medicare, exports, and the Mideast.*
REAGAN: *Family and faith.*
MONDALE: *Interest rates, hunger, and acid rain.*
REAGAN: *The Olympics . . . Who says I'm afraid to debate?*

An issue that very much needed to be debated was the most significant story of this particular day, October 4: the release of a shocking new study about the incredible widening of the economic gap between whites and blacks between 1981 and 1984. It was a day that should have shamed the sleeping conscience of America into the most serious self-examination, but the medium that could have delivered the message chose not to. Of the commercial networks, only NBC covered the story. The Center on Budget and Policy Priorities released a study, based on government agency statistics, showing that long-term unemployment since 1981 was up 1.5 percent for whites, but an incredible 72 percent for blacks. According to the graph shown on the NBC report, median family income was up $549 to $22,508 for whites and down $2,060 to $15,174 for blacks. The statistics of the Center on Budget and Policy Priorities were from nonpartisan sources, and match similar findings by every organization that had done studies since the onset of the Reagan tax and budget policies. Other studies have pointed to dramatic increases in infant death rates (even as the overall national rate declined), malnutrition, and poverty in general, among both whites and blacks. This particular study was a stark illustration of the fault line that not only continued to separate blacks from whites, but that was getting drastically worse. The lack of response to this reality, in the media and in the campaign, exemplified the sad fact that the majority of Americans didn't see the situation as an urgent priority and were being neither informed nor led in a responsible way.

The politics of solutions to this national obscenity was not the point. People could honestly disagree about that. It seems evident that there are upsides and downsides to be found among both liberal and conservative approaches. The liberal approach had made tremendous inroads in ending the worst aspects of racism and poverty, despite the currently popular notion that the Great Society programs didn't work. The Voting Rights Act made a tremendous difference in black enfranchisement and political participation. The candidacy of Jesse Jackson was in many ways the natural outgrowth of a growing and more politically active black voting population. The food stamp program, women, infant, and children feeding programs, and other social welfare programs all dramatically reduced hunger and infant mortality rates. But liberals have been largely unimaginative in the face of the downside of a permanent welfare state, dependency (although the majority of welfare cases are short term), and the need to create self-sufficiency and economic development as an alternative to poverty. Conservatives have a point when emphasizing the need for the economy as a whole to expand, but the trickle-down theory has never worked without special action to help those at the bottom. And the draconian sink-or-swim budget policy of the Reagan administration has been demonstrably cruel, in statistical contradiction to Reagan's Orwellian cry of demagoguery when the issue is raised. On the other hand, the enterprise-zone proposal of the administration, to provide tax credits for businesses located in ghetto areas, has potential merit. But Reagan has not made it a priority, nor have Republicans or Democrats who support the idea. Whatever one's policy inclinations, there was a deplorable lack of leadership in not making this disgraceful situation a top priority but instead contributing to a mood of national resignation.

A historical perspective on the interrelationship between leadership, prioritizing of issues, and television is of interest here. The argument could be made that public consciousness of the problems of racism and poverty reached its zenith in the late 1960s. Before then, Michael Harrington's book *The Other America* had caught the eye of President Kennedy, which helped bring to public attention the shameful contradiction between the grinding poverty of millions and the historically unmatched economic boom time in the land of plenty. Kennedy's and Lyndon Johnson's War on Poverty resulted. Although the current popular dictum is that throwing money at poverty didn't work, the statistics on hunger and infant mortality contradict this belief. Food stamps, women, infant, and children feeding programs, Aid to Families with Dependent Children, Medicare and Medicaid; and, for the elderly poor, rising Social Security levels—all of these played a role. No study has demonstrated significant levels of fraud in these programs, with the possible exception of Medicare, where the concerns are in the service, not the beneficiary end. To be sure, the proper program must be in place for the money to be useful, which was certainly the case with the various nutrition programs. Yet these programs were cut substantially during Reagan's first term, which demonstrably increased hunger in America, the president's and his right-wing supporter's objections notwithstanding. Many moderate conservative supporters of the president recognized this reality, which was one reason why the proposal in March 1985 by Senator Jesse Helmes to cut food stamps another $3 billion to $5 billion was not taken seriously. Further cuts were on the Reagan administration agenda, however, even though the national study by the Physicians Task Force on Hunger in America released in February 1985 documented, as many previous reports had, the negative impact of the previous nutritional program budget cuts. As Ellen Goodman pointed out (*Boston Globe* reprint, *Seattle Times*, 16 April, 1985), the Congress was behaving as if it were "spiritually malnourished" in response to the resurgence of hunger in America. Nor was there a public outcry, which was predictable given the lack of political leadership or consistent media focus. Goodman wrote: "The odd part of the lack of interest in hunger programs is that these are not programs that failed. The reports of program abuse don't hold up to scrutiny. If ever there was a success in federal aid, it was in food programs."

Other programs may never have been given an adequate test. As the Vietnam War escalated and demanded greater resources, the antipoverty program was scaled down; some analysts believe that the real mistake was that not enough money was "thrown" at the problem. The story of the Office of Economic Opportunity may be a case in point, as its original quite radical approach of funneling funds directly to the grass roots of poverty, encouraging self-help and democratic political action by the local community, was scaled back substantially from what was first envisioned within a few years, and was largely disbanded during the Nixon administration. The success of the community-action-program approach spawned by OEO is documented in Edwin L. Cobb's *No Ceasefires: The War On Poverty In Roanoke Valley,* which examines one of the surviving programs. The other programs that remained and continued to grow, until Reagan's election, have been largely of a maintenance character. In the much discussed book, *Losing Ground: American Social Policy, 1950-1980,* Charles Murray claims that the war on poverty was a dependence-fostering failure and advocates abolishing welfare maintenance altogether. Aside from the obvious Social Darwinism inherent in such an approach, Robert Kuttner persuasively demonstrates (*Washington Post* National Weekly Edition, 17 December 1984) that Murray's argument often depends on misleading and incomplete statistics. Senator Daniel Patrick Moynihan points out (*New York Times,* 7 April 1985) that the poor have suffered increasingly as a result of both tax and welfare policies. A personal exemption for each family member of $600 in 1948 (equivalent to approximately $5,600 today) is presently only slightly above $1,000. In 1948 a family 10 percent above the poverty line was exempt from income tax while today a family considerably below the poverty line is taxed. In addition, the largest welfare program, Aid to Families with Dependent Children, has had payments *reduced* by over 60 percent since 1969 in inflation-adjusted dollars. Nonetheless, Murray makes points that inevitably lead to a recognition shared from many perspectives: that the ultimate solution to much of the poverty in America is employment. How to create employment opportunity for everyone capable of working is another matter. Various approaches to urban and particularly black poverty along the enterprise-zone lines have never received the leadership backing necessary to enact them on a large scale. Although convincingly criticized as an unworkable waste of money by National Federation of Independent Business President John Sloan (*Wall Street Journal*, 26 March 1985), enterprise zones need, in some form, a long-term trial. This point is persuasively made by Dick Cowden of the Sabre Foundation in his effective refutation of Sloan's assertions (*Wall Street Journal*, 10 April 1985). Nor has there been adequate discussion or leadership for government-created employment alternatives to welfare where the private sector leaves off, particularly in areas of social and economic benefit to the nation. And what was the contribution of quality education, or the lack of it, to this entire equation? This is an area that needs the most thorough examination. Another idea that has been heard little of recently, in terms of welfare reform, is the concept of direct payment replacing many support programs, described as a negative income tax or guaranteed annual income, advocated by various conservative and liberal economists. Whether this is desirable or not is debatable, but as with all the above mentioned approaches or areas of concern, discussion and debate is what's called for, as opposed to the present comparative silence in the media and lack of leadership from politicians.

At the same time Harrington's book was receiving wide exposure because of President Kennedy's interest, the issue of racism in America was coming to a climactic moment, beginning with the issue of segregation in the South. Martin Luther King, Jr.'s leadership and charisma brought this issue to the attention of the wider public, more than any other single factor. The grass-roots Gandhian civil-disobedience tactics of the movement were also an integral part of gaining attention, as a result of the cruel reaction of southern racists. As the movement reached to the northern cities, rage born of centuries of oppression and fed by rising expectations exploded into an unprecedented series of urban riots. This, too, brought attention to the issue. In terms of the majority of whites, the riots could be said, in a very general sense, to have created a reaction of fear. The alternative nonviolent route being preached by King appealed more to conscience. But to reach a majority of whites, a white politician of stature was required. Presidents Kennedy and Johnson had provided this to some degree, but Robert Kennedy's role in the 1968 presidential campaign was particularly significant. After President Johnson's withdrawal from the campaign and announcement of a bombing halt and peace talks with the North Vietnamese, Kennedy's major issue became the dispossessed, particularly the black under class. No other major presidential candidate had ever run on such a seemingly sure prescription for defeat. America, to many, seemed on the precarious edge of a race war. Kennedy had the attention of the public because of who he was, and he combined a message of compassion and love with law and order in a uniquely effective way. He defined patriotism as truly creating equal opportunity for everyone, and advocated not only sufficient welfare maintenance, adequate education, stronger civil rights law, and other structural reforms, but economic development by the private sector spurred by tax incentives. In many ways he was a synthesis of Mondale's traditional liberal commitment to government caring for the disadvantaged and Reagan's conservative approach of looking to the private sector for solutions. But whatever one thought of the man or his proposals, the point here is that he provided real leadership by making the issue visible and urgent. As a powerful example of bringing whites and blacks together, he continually had personal contact with the black community and the dispossessed of every color on *their* turf in a way no other politician of his stature had ever done. He shared with Martin Luther King, Jr., an understanding that the white and black communities needed to be brought together to really bring about change and avoid catastrophe. (Kennedy as attorney general had authorized wiretaps on King under pressure from FBI director J. Edgar Hoover, undoubtedly to prove King's innocence from Hoover's Communist-baiting smear tactics and to keep Hoover from going public. Hoover's hatred of King was reported by an aide to be exceeded only by his hatred of Bobby Kennedy. When JFK was president, King had to push the Kennedys for action on civil rights, because although they supported his goals, they were politically cautious. But by 1968 it was clear that both Robert Kennedy and King considered themselves close allies working on parallel paths.) The most extraordinary fact about the 1968 presidential election campaign, often overlooked, is the fact that in the Democratic primaries Kennedy received not only a huge majority of the black vote, but a large majority of the white working-class vote as well, including the votes of many who later voted for Nixon, and even more ironically, independent candidate George Wallace.

This is in telling contrast to trends in voting patterns since then, particularly the results of the 1984 election, in which white and black voters were the most polarized in any election since the onset of the civil rights era. This matches a decreasing national concern with the issues of racism and poverty, which in the author's view began its downward spiral after the assassinations of King and Kennedy, effectively removing both leadership and publicity for these concerns. To be sure, other political leaders and social activists have played major roles in this arena, but none with the widespread appeal of King or Kennedy. The other major force, the pressure from the grass roots, was demoralized by the loss of these and other leaders. The rage born of racism and poverty abated for a time due to a combination of programs and temporary national attention. It began to reemerge in a new guise, the cumulative violence of individual crime, always a problem in black and poor neighborhoods, but now a growing one. It was no longer in vogue in 1984 to examine the environmental causes of this kind of crime. And there was no doubt that, at some point, desperation would again turn to rage on a larger scale, surpassing that seen in the 1960s. In the politics of 1984, the costs of the various poverty assistance and nutrition programs were questionable, even though they were insignificant compared to defense, Social Security, Medicare, and government pensions, not to mention the interest on the federal debt. There was no leadership in offering an alternative to welfare maintenance. The visibility of the new black middle class and political leaders was in a very real sense an illusion for the majority of blacks left behind. Most of white America saw only the illusion.

The importance of television in this situation cannot be overstated. As Robert Kennedy pointed out in one of his most eloquent speeches (Citizen's Union, New York City, December 14, 1967), it cannot help but be torturous for the young ghetto dweller in the TV age, to see the unattainable objects of the consumer society constantly dangled before him on television commercials. Yet television's record of dealing with the problems of the black under class is abysmal, as was demonstrated again on this day of the 1984 presidential campaign, when two of the commercial network evening news programs didn't even report the Center on Budget and Policy Priorities release of the incredible long-term black unemployment figures and other shattering statistics. More important, the issues surrounding the plight of the black under class were never addressed in depth by the commercial network TV news programs during the campaign. As with so many important issues, it is seldom addressed at any time. In 1968, the Kerner Commission on Civil Disorders, initiated by President Johnson after the inner-city riots of 1967, stated: "The media have failed to report accurately on the causes . . . of civil disorders and the underlying problems of race relations. . . . The media have never . . . ever glimpsed at what it is like in a racial ghetto and the reasons for unrest there." Nearly two decades later little has changed. The length and format of the nightly news does not allow it. This is just one example of why an issue without a strong majority constituency cannot be communicated to the public without either the presence of committed political leadership or some kind of social action that affects the majority of the public. Television news will cover the charismatic or controversial leader, or successful politician, a visible media star of some kind. And television news will cover violent unrest and major riots. But what about the root causes? And even more important, what about an ongoing examination of the potential solutions? Why not contribute to a participatory democracy of individuals self-sufficient in pondering issues and collectively choosing priorities, rather than feed dependence on enlightened leadership or catastrophic events to spur action? A well-informed electorate can create enlightened leadership and take action to prevent catastrophic events as well as ongoing suffering and injustice.

In terms of the report released this day, MacNeil/Lehrer did an excellent objective job of covering it as a partisan event, which was appropriate, given the political overtones during a presidential election campaign. One of the interesting aspects of this segment was that the representative for the Reagan administration was a black woman. It was a fascinating example of the impact of image, as the experience of seeing and hearing her was significantly different from the intellectual experience of reading the transcript. The fact that she was black, had a pleasant personality, and self-assured tone, contributed to a *visual* image of credibility on this subject, even though the logic of her remarks was often impossible to follow. Whether or not the decision was a conscious one by the Reagan campaign, the *image* of a black woman was probably more effective in dealing with any Reagan weakness on this issue than whatever words she said or might have said. The advantage of the MacNeil/Lehrer approach, however, is that there is a real possibility that image will wear thin, and substance become the primary focus of the viewer. The segment is worth reviewing.

JIM LEHRER: *A new political indictment concerning black Americans was delivered today against President Reagan. It came from a Washington-based, Democratic-leaning think tank called the Center on Budget and Policy Priorities. The charge: In every key economic area, the gap between being white and being black in this country has widened under the Reagan administration—that blacks are poorer, they pay more taxes, and they are more likely to be out of work now than when Reagan came to office. Using Census Bureau and other data, the center says, for instance, black income fell 5.3 percent, a typical black family loosing $800, while white income increased. Black unemployment increased two percentage points, while the rate among whites went down. . . ."*

ROBERT MACNEIL: *To discuss whether these statistics really reflect what is happening to black Americans and why, we have Robert Greenstein, who was head of the food stamp program in the Carter administration. He's now director of the center which released today's report. Dr. Gloria Toote is vice-chairperson of the President's Advisory Council on Private Sector Initiatives and a member of the Reagan-Bush advisory committee. Mr. Greenstein, your report blames Reagan policies for this apparent decline in black prosperity. How are those policies to blame?*

GREENSTEIN: *The report says that the Reagan policies are the single most important factor. Obviously there are some economic factors as well. But up until the last few years, those economic factors that tended to divide blacks and whites and take them further apart, we had federal policies to* *deal with that. Instead, during the current administration the federal policies have further divided rich and poor and black and white. A few specifics. The Congressional Budget Office, a nonpartisan budget office of the Congress, found in a report issued in April that those households who have incomes below $20,000 a year lose $20 billion in income and benefits over the '83-'85 period solely because of the budget and tax policies, while those over $80,000 gain $35 billion. Now, when we look at the black population, we find that nearly two-thirds of all black families are in that under $20,000 category that has the big losses. Only one-half of 1 percent of the blacks are in the over $80,000 category. There's an Urban Institute study that focused right on the budget cuts themselves. Its finding: The '81 budget cuts, the average black family lost three times as much as the average white family. We've gone to the CBO [Congressional Budget Office] figures and looked at those programs that had the deepest percentage cuts. Without exception . . . we found that those programs with the deepest cuts were those where blacks constituted the largest proportion of the recipients. And a final point in the tax area: The Urban Institute data and many others, the IRS data, clearly shows that the working poor and low-wage working families pay far higher federal taxes today than they did in 1980. There's generally been a tax shift. The Urban Institute says that the bottom 40 percent pays more of its income in taxes than in '80, and the top 40 percent pays less. Once again we've got nearly two-thirds of the blacks in that bottom 40 percent, and I think that's why every key indicator—the census data, what does that show? Highest black poverty rate last year since 1966. What else does it show? It shows that the gap between the bottom and the top of U.S. society in income is now wider than at any point since 1947, and that bottom group, the bottom 40 percent, has three times as many black families as the top 40 percent.*

MACNEIL: *Well, let's give Dr. Toote a chance to comment on this. Dr. Toote, first of all, do you accept these findings published today that show, to put it very simply, blacks worse off than they were when Reagan took office?*

TOOTE: *No, I don't. I've just seen the study this afternoon, so of course it's a peripheral view that I've given it. However, I notice that its documentation was by the poor. [Deciphering the meaning or intent of this statement would be of interest.] First of all, there are no footnotes for me to verify the accuracy of the figures given, and secondly, no consideration whatsoever is given to the fact that indeed the poverty level within this nation—on one page they cite it, I think it's page 17—clearly showed the statement made by the president that the number of blacks who were gaining employment under the recovery, percentage-wise, is indeed better than the number of whites. They cite the report, they give the figures on the table, but they don't refer to it. I think as long as inflation is reduced, as long as interest rates are*

*reduced and kept lower, as long as there's a strong economy, minority
America, as all Americans, must improve. We must bear in mind that
Lyndon Johnson meant great things with his Great Society, spent a considerable amount of money, and was a failure. The failure is because we have
what is called the structurally unemployed. And until we have the kind of
economy where a person who has to work every day and take care of their
children will know that the dollar this earns is going to be a dollar sufficient
to buy the food for their family, then the poor will continue to suffer. But
right now, a mother who secures that dollar can be confident that by the end
of the week, or certainly by Christmas, in projecting what the Christmas
club will bring in, which a lot of people still have, they'll be able to buy the
gifts and toys that are needed. [These curious remarks needed journalistic
attention.] The second thing I'd like to refer to is the fact that a number of
people stated that with the changes in our tax structure, the poor would be
hurt more than others and that massive numbers of minorities in particular
would be on the welfare rolls. If you look at your welfare rolls throughout
the United States, there has not been that drastic increase. Surely no one is
going to say that poor black heads of households are mean to their children,
and rather than apply for welfare, which is something that they or certainly
their family that pay taxes for, would rather have their children starve. The
hypothesis of the report I think is based upon erroneous figures, erroneous
assumptions, and unfortunately I'm sorry to see it released in a climate of
politics. I think that the problems of the poor, the structural unemployment
of minorities in particular, deserve a better study.*

MacNEIL: *Well, you made quite a list of points there, so let's go back to Mr.
Greenstein in Washington. How about this? Let's take, for instance, the
inflation having come down. Does that not benefit blacks, as Dr. Toote
says?*

GREENSTEIN: *I'm just struck listening to Dr. Toote. I can't imagine she's
read the report in much of a sense at all, to the degree that she even missed
the source notes that cite the fact that virtually every piece of data in this
report is from the Census Bureau, the Bureau of Labor Statistics, the
Congressional Budget Office. It's all there. Let's take the inflation. Yes, the
rate of inflation is lower than it was a few years ago, but that's factored into
all of these figures. The Urban Institute report clearly shows and the Census
Bureau data on median income shows as well that even after you factor in
lower inflation and the economic recovery, middle-income blacks and poor
blacks are worse off, they have less disposable income after adjusting for
inflation, and a lower standard of living than in 1980. As for not more
blacks going into welfare, of course not. The welfare program's been
severely cut. But most of all, I'd like to get back to these unemployment
figures. The one thing Dr. Toote and I might agree on is the importance of
long-term structural unemployment, and that's where I think the concern is*

the greatest. The Labor Bureau statistics are very clear. Unemployment was 14.4 percent for blacks when the president took office; it's 16 percent today. White unemployemnt has declined during the recovery 50 percent faster than black unemployment. And finally, the most staggering figure of all: The people hurt the worst are the long-term unemployed—those who've been out of work more than half a year—they are still looking for work and want to find a job. . . . The official Labor Department figures: long-term white unemployment 1.5 percent above January '81. Black long-term unemployment is now 72 percent above January '81 levels. These are the official figures.

TOOTE: *Let me respond to the unemployment figures for the nation as a whole. Now I'm going specifically to the report. Nowhere does the report refer to the fact that we have more Americans employed than ever in the history of this nation. [Populations grow, percentages are what matter.] The more Americans you have employed, the larger the number of those who are seeking jobs. [Interesting math. If the point is based on population growth there is a double standard operative.] We have increased employment in America, and indeed even minority employment has increased. [Again, percentages are the point.] The report at one point refers to the fact that the poor are being more heavily—are paying heavier taxes than at any time in the history of the country. But it does not cite that much of that tax increase is Social Security, which all Americans must pay. [Also true of other taxes. A more regressive income tax and reduction of federal program support made the difference for the poor.] It is the way that the report is slanted that disturbs me, because indeed the problems of black America and the poor are ones that need to be addressed and need to be discussed within the full parameters of all the documentation.*

MACNEIL: *Mr. Greenstein, is it your contention that if Mr. Reagan is re-elected, blacks are going to continue to be worse off?*

GREENSTEIN: *The purpose of the report is not really to participate in the campaign. [It obviously was one of the purposes.] And in fact, our center gets requests from leading Republicans on the Hill as well as Democrats. . . . If I were to say what our main point is in this report . . . it is to get more public attention to the situation black Americans do face, to how the budget and tax policies that both the administration and the Congress have adopted have affected them, so that next year, in '85, when major federal policy decisions are made by Congress, this is taken into greater account.*

MACNEIL: *I must get a final comment from Dr. Toote here. And your position would be what on Mr. Reagan's reelection and the prosperity of blacks?*

TOOTE: *I think that indeed the future for all Americans is very positive, and in particular that of black Americans. I look at the number of black middle-class Americans who lost their jobs because the companies they worked for*

could not borrow money, and as a consequence reduced their work force. I
think that every step taken by Ronald Reagan as president and indeed our
Congress, which enacted the legislation, one House controlled by the Dem-
ocrats, are to bring forth a solid economy for all.

It was unfortunate that the one issue Greenstein and Toote seemed to
have some common ground on, structural unemployment, wasn't pursued
further. Toote simply fell back on a rather ineffective and sometimes
extremely curious presentation of the Reagan campaign's economic
growth and "springtime in America" theme. Greenstein effectively layed
out the impact of cutting the "maintenance" programs, but as his own
statistics showed, and as he acknowledged, the most staggering problem
was long-term unemployment. Why didn't he offer some potential
solutions?

One shortcoming of "The MacNeil/Lehrer NewsHour" is the fact that
often there are interviews with conflicting descriptions of facts that are
never resolved even on the level of objectively factual information. There
are also different sets of facts that can be used as counterpoints in the
sense of changing the subject rather than addressing the facts raised.
These are areas where journalistic intervention is called for; otherwise the
information can be confusing, particularly with television or radio, which
cannot be reviewed like the printed word. In an interview, the journalist
should keep everyone honest, should influence the discussion on the level
of imposing some logical flow. Questions of interpretation and policy
shouldn't and can't be resolved, as that is the purpose of discussion and
debate. The resolution, such as it is, should take place with the viewer.
The report and interview in good journalism should spur the reader,
listener, or viewer to explore issues further on his or her own. But there
are objective facts. And the recitation of these facts, and a format imposing logic upon the discussion, should be the base from which the rest of
the process unfolds.

Friday, October 5:
Polls and Images

Needless to say, the main topic on the election news front on this day was
the upcoming presidential debate on Sunday, in Louisville, Kentucky.

ABC had the distinction of being the only network to cover it as the top
story, a decision undoubtedly based on the fact that Peter Jennings had an
exclusive interview with Walter Mondale. It was an interview in which
Jennings did not distinguish himself. And from a video perspective, there

was a stunning image of an exhausted-looking Walter Mondale. One wondered how this campaign-weary face, which had never been very telegenic to begin with, could possibly compete with a refreshed Ronald Reagan, who had campaigned in vacation style since Labor Day, and who was a master of the video medium.

ABC began with a report from Richard Threlkeld, who immediately trivialized the upcoming debate with an attempt at proving he was "cultured" in his opening: "The Louisville Ballet has coopted the Performing Arts Center for most of this weekend, so they'll have to wait till the last minute to set up for Sunday night's presidential 'pas à deux' here." Threlkeld then accurately pointed out that this debate (like other televised presidential debates thus far) would in no way resemble the Lincoln-Douglas debates of the last century, when the candidates "matched words and wits face to face with no newspersons in the way." (He should have mentioned that Mondale wanted this kind of debate and Reagan refused.) "Even so, this debate is an antidote to campaigning as usual."

Historian J. McGregor Burns was shown saying "There is so much evasion of the issues in these presidential campaigns, and in a debate, if all goes well, there is a direct confrontation and the other guy has to answer, and that's crucial." Threlkeld decided to inform us, as would most of his colleagues, that "Walter Mondale, so far behind in the polls it's unlikely these debates will win the election, but they could turn his campaign around if he comes out slugging." At least he used the word *unlikely*, instead of stating directly that the election might as well be called off.

Peter Jennings continued in the Threlkeld vein by referring to television election coverage's favorite topic in his opening to the Mondale interview, reminding us that as reported on the previous night's ABC broadcast, the latest ABC/*Washington Post* poll showed Mondale being trounced by Reagan. Mondale was then shown saying, "I know we're behind. . . . But I think it's moving." Apparently smelling blood, and unable to forgo following up on the most important "issue" in the election, the polls, Jennings then said, "There are going to be people, I think, watching and listening to this, who are going to say that all the polls have you at sixteen, seventeen, eighteen, some at twenty [points down], and are going to say when you sit here and say that I'm moving, they're not quite going to understand what you mean."

MONDALE: *Most of these polls had me at twenty, twenty five a few weeks ago, and they've got me up four, five, six points. We've got polls showing that we've moved six, seven points the last ten days. Your poll, for example, is ten days old, you started taking it ten days ago. Most of our move has been the last week. . . .*
JENNINGS: *I sometimes get the impression, I think a lot of people who know*

you do, and especially a lot of people who like you, that television is a beast that you've got to keep feeding, that you really don't like it. . . .

MONDALE: *I'm not in love with it, but this is modern America. . . .*

JENNINGS: *You really, then, dislike all this advice about how to be on television.*

MONDALE: *Yes, I do. I would prefer to concentrate on the case. I think leadership begins when assuming the responsibility of understanding problems and speaking to their solution. If you don't do that, you really have a salesman, not a leader. You have a cheerleader and not a quarterback. . . .*

JENNINGS: *Isn't it a bit frightening that after all this time campaigning for the presidency, that so much hinges on these two ninety-minute periods?*

MONDALE: *I think it's always been true, that's why I was for these debates. In other words, so much of what the public hears in a campaign is paid advertising in which each side says what it wants to. These debates pose the one opportunity for Americans to hear us challenged by tough reporters, [except the Mondale and Reagan camps disqualified most reporters from the debates], measure each other's answers, and watch the candidates to make those other judgments about strength, leadership and personality, and the things that you can't quantify, but are very very important. [What Mondale didn't mention, and didn't dare while the campaign was still on, was that more important than paid advertising was TV news coverage, which had been informing people little about issues, but spent so much of its in effect "snapshot" coverage talking about strategy and polls, which Jennings would now demonstrate once again.]*

JENNINGS: *In the polls, even those people who agree with you on issues often prefer President Reagan's quality of leadership.*

MONDALE: *Our polls show that I'm coming up, that people look at me increasingly as a strong leader, that my favorable ratings are improving. . . .*

JENNINGS: *Have you been campaigning too long?*

MONDALE: *You know, I'd like to campaign less, but that's not the way our democracy works.*

JENNINGS: *But you keep saying to me, when the American public sees you and the president side by side in these two debates, their attention is going to be focused. They're going to see the differences. [Apparently what Mondale "kept saying" was edited.] What have you been doing for the past eighteen months?*

MONDALE: *Getting nominated. Now we're running for president. Now the debate is really under way. The debate occurs, the first one is Sunday night. And these issues are starting to be clearly framed for the American people.*

The line of questioning here was totally lacking in journalistic integrity. Mr. Jennings should compare the record of every speech and position paper issued by Mondale (and the other candidates for that matter) over the preceding "eighteen months" with the quality and quantity of ABC's and the other network's coverage of the same, and draw the appropriate conclusions. But Jennings saved his most intellectually empty and insulting remark for last.

JENNINGS: *Any risk . . . that the public is bored with Walter Mondale?*
MONDALE: *I can't answer that, Peter. All I can answer is that I am doing my very best.*

All the network reports explored the strategy of each side in the upcoming debate. NBC's Roger Mudd told us that "the contrast will be sharp. Mondale trying to nail Reagan with a mistake that accentuates his age and isolation, Reagan trying to make Mondale look shrill and frantic by exuding his 'Aw shucks' optimism . . . the best Mondale can hope for is that people see through the Reagan television technique, think seriously about the issues that would stabilize his position, and perhaps he'd then begin to pick up momentum and peak around the second debate. What Reagan hopes to do is make the people concentrate on Mondale's proposal for a tax increase. That will freeze him in place and allow Reagan to continue his rather stately campaign style."

Susan Spencer of CBS reported, "Mondale sees it as a chance to cut through what he calls the arrogance of the Reagan campaign, one, he says, of happy talk, TV images, and distance from the press. For Mr. Reagan, the key is to do just what he did in 1980 when he looked presidential and poised against the steely stares of Jimmy Carter. The key is not to do what Gerald Ford did in 1976 when he made a serious and mystifying mistake." Videotape of the 1976 debate with Jimmy Carter was then shown, with Ford saying, "There is no Soviet domination of Eastern Europe." Spencer went on: "The Mondale campaign is confident its man won't pull a Gerald Ford; hopeful, but not optimistic that the president will. . . . In either case, millions of Americans will be watching this Sunday. Mondale hopes it's the start of the most dramatic political turnaround in American history. But polls show that, barring some serious misstep, most Americans tend to view as the winner of a debate the candidate they liked best in the first place."

In the CBS report, Senator Robert Dole, who debated Mondale in the vice-presidential debate in 1976, was shown saying, "I don't quarrel with Mondale's ability to debate, the knowledge of the issues, but he's there with a master and the master is Ronald Reagan." On MacNeil/Lehrer, in a report by Judy Woodruff, Mondale adviser Richard Leone echoed this sentiment, saying that Reagan was "an actor" and "does this extremely well" and that Mondale would have to win on the issues. David Gergen, a former Reagan aide, said that Mondale's greatest hope was a "Ford" gaffe, but that even if Reagan made mistakes, most of his performance was likely to be "impressive." Robert Squirer, Democratic political analyst, offered that "unless they can figure a clever way to build Mike Deaver [Reagan's media adviser] into the podium," Reagan would make significant mistakes. But former Reagan campaign manager John Sears felt that people were used to Reagan's mistakes, and that Mondale had the harder task, improving his leadership image. Richard Leone said that Mondale was not concerned about "theatrics," but Judy Woodruff noted that some said Mondale should be more concerned about such things. Leone was shown saying, "I don't think that the election will be decided on the angle of the podium, but I could be wrong." Jim Lehrer then interviewed Representative Philip Crane (R.-Ill.) and Senator Alan Cranston (D.-Cal.), who had debated Reagan and Mondale respectively in presidential primary campaigns. Crane expressed the view that Reagan "could get away with about anything" in terms of making mistakes, both because of his overall TV persona and his tremendous lead in the polls. Cranston ventured that after the debate, someone reading the transcript would say that Mondale won, whereas someone watching would say Reagan won. He said that Mondale is a warm, intelligent man, but for some reason it didn't come across on TV, a medium in which debates are won with image and passion, which Reagan's TV acting background lent itself to, as opposed to Mondale, who concentrated on the issues.

George Will, ABC commentator, made some interesting comments that gave ABC's report at least something not to be ashamed of: ". . . Walter Mondale's going to win and he's going to lose, and we already know how in both ways. He's going to win in the sense that any challenger who comes out and stands on the stage as an equal of an incumbent president is elevated by the company he's keeping. On the other hand, Walter Mondale lost, and couldn't help but lose the great debate about the format of the debate. Walter Mondale needs a big break and that means a big Reagan mistake. The Reagan people know it and therefore they insisted on a format so highly structured that it minimizes the chances of anything unexpected occurring. . . . Consider what Richard Threlkeld referred to, the Lincoln-Douglas debates. Those men debated seven times. Each debate itself was three hours long. The first man would start and talk for a full hour. . . . Then the challenger, whoever started second, would talk for ninety minutes. Then the first man would come back and talk for thirty minutes more. The skills tested in a real debate, reasoning at great length, thinking on your feet, really aren't the skills of a president. A president spends most of his time reading memos and trying to stay awake in meetings with stuffy people in stuffy rooms."

Informative observations, with the exception that Will's cynical sounding description of what was and was not a presidential skill seemed a rather transparent defense of President Reagan, particularly the "stay awake" comment. A study of the Lincoln presidency, and some more recent presidencies, not to mention common sense, would indicate that "debating" skills as defined above by Will are indeed invaluable assets for an optimally effective and responsible execution of the duties of the office.

Will continued: "We're not saying that these are essential presidential skills, but if we're going to call these things debates, if we're going to have truth in labeling in politics, we probably ought to have real debates. The key to that is not having journalists there to clutter up the stage. Lincoln and Douglas didn't need journalists to tell them what the issues were."

Debates such as these would be welcome, indeed, but they were not likely to occur while television journalism made it so easy to wage a campaign of images instead of ideas. If TV news formats and reports refused to let the camera be used strategically, instead using the camera to help visualize at length and in depth the issues facing the country, pressure on the candidates to agree to real debates would undoubtedly be substantial. There are a variety of devices by which TV news could invite the candidates to participate in live forums, giving whoever showed up hours of free air time. The "no shows" wouldn't last long. Having the candidates sit together at a table for several lengthy sessions to discuss and debate the issues is an exciting concept, and it would be an invaluable contribution to the political and intellectual cultures in a democracy.

On Saturday night on CNN's "Election Watch" with Charles Bierbauer, guests Ronnie Dugger, author of *On Reagan*, and Vic Kamber, Democratic political consultant, made some interesting observations. Kamber said that the polls were a "chicken and egg" situation because they both tell us what people are thinking and in turn affect how people think. He also said that the country perceives Reagan as the Great Communicator and Mondale as a whiner (or boring, colorless, etc.) because of sixty-second TV coverage on the news. He pointed out that it was easy for Reagan to look good and Mondale to look haggard or not come across as well when Reagan was campaigning for half an hour a day and Mondale for ten hours a day. Dugger observed that there hadn't been a campaign yet because Reagan wasn't campaigning and that Mondale was right to concentrate on the issues. He had strong words for the media, especially TV and particularly the evening news programs, which he said concentrated on the polls and "junk" politics. At the end of this campaign, Dugger said, "National TV has to ask itself what it is doing to democracy." Dugger echoed what Lou Harris had been quoted saying by the *New York Times* a week earlier: Although the polls showed Reagan-Bush far ahead, they also showed voters more in agreement with Mondale-

Ferraro on some very basic issues. For this reason Dugger, like Harris, said he still saw the election as a horse race (i.e., with Mondale-Ferraro still very much in contention) because the issues hadn't yet been focused on, but would now finally get attention because of the debates.

Of course, that depended on the debates themselves, and how the media treated them.

(Opposite page) League of Women Voters sponsored presidential debate, October 7, 1984 in Louisville at the Kentucky Center for the Arts. Moderated by Barbara Walters, ABC News. Panelists, left to right: Fred Barnes, Baltimore Sun; Diane Sawyer, CBS News; James G. Wieghart, Scripps-Howard New Service. (LEAGUE OF WOMEN VOTERS EDUCATION FUND)

CHAPTER FOUR

Campaign on the Nightly News: The Debates

Monday, October 8: Media Shock

Well, there they went again; the prognostications of the experts down the drain, that is.

Walter Mondale had accomplished the one thing that no one dreamed possible in the first presidential debate of 1984: He had outperformed Ronald Reagan on television.

Mondale was relaxed, warm, gracious, humorous, and at the same time strong and dramatic in his presentation, concentrating more on the thematic aspects of issues than the details, while utilizing specifics at strategic moments to hammer away at Reagan's vulnerabilities. The president seemed ill at ease and hesitant at times, and ironically, spent much time spouting "facts and figures" as opposed to his usual effective thematic approach. There were flashes of the famous Reagan charm, but he seemed generally overshadowed by Mondale's personality, a phenomenon the media had told us was an impossibility, a contradiction in terms. Reagan was the Great Communicator, if not too solid on the facts; Mondale was the "boring, whining, whimp," if solid on the issues. It was almost as if the two men had switched roles, each in an attempt to prove wrong the stereotypes about them, self-created and media created, which they and their advisers perceived as their greatest vulnerabilities. To the surprise of everyone, Mondale seemed to get the best of the role reversal. It was a strategic coup for the Mondale camp. Reagan clearly was not prepared for the Mondale persona that showed up at this debate.

And regardless of the ultimate effect on the election, it was a tremendous personal triumph for Walter Mondale, who finally succeeded at being "himself" on television. On ABC, Britt Hume reported that in an interview with ABC news, Mondale had said "his performance last night resulted partly from having his back against the wall." Mondale said: "It kind of forces you to get to bedrock about yourself and I guess how you want to be remembered. And that was my chance last night to be heard, like I've never been heard before in my history. And I knew that it was up to me. No one could take that away from me, if I said it clearly and as strongly as I could." Those who have experienced Mondale in person (the author included) were not unfamiliar with the man America saw during this debate. The larger lesson of the television medium and presidential politics is the impact in terms of "image" when the candidates are given real time, without editing, and with minimal journalistic interference (compared with the nightly news programs), to face each other and express themselves directly to the American people. And despite the cynicism expressed by much of the media before the debates as to the potential for a "real debate" of the issues, there were several flashes of "real debate," even within the limitations of the format.

From a video perspective, the most striking thing was the comparison between how Mondale and Reagan looked. When watching Mondale deliver his acceptance speech at the Democratic Convention, it occurred to me that the image of Reagan and Mondale next to each other might turn out to be very favorable to Mondale. On the eve of the debate, however, I had abandoned all such thoughts. Mondale looked more and more tired from his relentless campaigning, and during the ABC interview with Peter Jennings on Friday he looked downright awful. Reagan, on the other hand, was maintaining a most relaxed schedule in what was as close to a stress-free campaign as one could imagine. But when they walked onto the stage in Louisville, Mondale seemed young, refreshed, and vigorous, whereas Reagan appeared under stress and, quite simply, looked his age. He also stumbled verbally, and seemingly mentally, so badly at one point, that he provided ammunition for the "age" issue. This "message" of the medium would have the most impact of all from this debate.

The first "reviews" on the debate from the media were exemplified by the reports on the "CBS Morning News," which began with the results of a *Newsweek* poll showing that the American public considered Mondale the winner by the overwhelming margin of 54 percent to 35 percent, an ironic reversal of the polls in terms of how people had said they would vote, up to this point. It was also a testament to the extent of Mondale's triumph, since people generally declared whoever they were already supporting the winner of a debate. A potential sea change was in the air. CBS reporter Bruce Morton said that most reporters who witnessed the debate agreed with that *Newsweek* poll, that Mondale had put Reagan on the defensive, and was even able to use humor and turn Reagan's own line against him, an ill-advised repetition of his famous remark during the 1980 debate with Carter, "There you go again." Reagan used it this time as a prelude to saying that Mondale's claim that he (Reagan) would raise taxes after the election wasn't true. Mondale then turned to Reagan, asked him if he remembered the last time he used that line, and, as Reagan looked down at the podium uncomfortably, reminded him it was in response to Carter's claim that Reagan would try to reduce Medicare benefits if elected. Reagan had said Carter's claim wasn't true, then after being elected, noted Mondale, tried to cut approximately $20 billion from Medicare. "People remember this," Mondale stated somewhat wryly in conclusion, emphasizing the word *remember*. He had stolen the show. This clip was run on all the morning news shows, and was featured on all the evening programs as well.

Three journalists discussed the debate on the "CBS Morning News." Al Hunt of the *Wall Street Journal* stated, "It's going to be very hard for anyone to say Walter Mondale is a whimp after that impressive performance last night." Howell Raines of the *New York Times* said that the media, having been "harsh" on Mondale for so long, must now give him his "full due," that he was the "clear winner" of the debate. Raines felt that the fact that Reagan had been an outsider, a critic, all through his career, had made him uncomfortable in the role of incumbent. Jack Nelson of the *Los Angeles Times* noted that Reagan had reaped the results of his own decision to avoid the press in the campaign, that his isolation had made him "rusty." Nelson felt that the debate would help Mondale a little bit, but was not sure how much it would help in the long run. Al Hunt replied, "A long journey starts with one step. . . . [Mondale was] "very impressive . . . aggressive without being abrasive . . . he not only held the upper hand on the issues but he showed a lot of personal charm."

The shock of what Hunt described had shown clearly on the face of ABC's Peter Jennings immediately after the debate. He looked dazed, reticent to say what he felt, which appeared to be, "Did I just see what I think I saw?" George Will, a Reagan partisan, to his credit showed no reticence at all. He stated that he was "astounded" by Reagan's weak conclusion, a rambling recitation of incomprehensible facts, and that Mondale had clearly helped himself. Will was an exception to the general media trend, in that he didn't wait for the polls to confirm Mondale the clear winner before expressing a judgment.

In terms of substance, the debate was largely a recitation of the stands of each candidate, with the tremendous advantage of not being edited into one-liner clips, as on the nightly news.

Reagan held to the view that a growing economy and further spending cuts would cure the deficit problem, although he was not specific about what would be cut. Mondale attacked Reagan on the issue, claiming that taxes would be raised and Social Security and Medicare cut, no matter what Reagan said now. Mondale claimed his tax-and-spending-cut plan would solve the deficit problem without touching Social Security and Medicare. Reagan responded that he would never cut Social Security, but was vague on Medicare.

A great deal of time was spent on the religion-and-politics issue, the questions of religious tests for judges, school prayer, and particularly abortion. Mondale was very specific and seemed to score well on these issues, whereas Reagan was comparatively ineffectual and somewhat defensive. When asked why he didn't attend church regularly or have services at the White House or Camp David as other presidents had done, Reagan began by stating (untruly) that he had gone to church regularly all his life. He then talked only of not going to church at present for security reasons, never answering the question in regard to services at the White House and so on. His conclusion was vintage Reagan: "And I miss going to church but I think the Lord understands."

There was a segment on poverty and minorities during which Reagan rattled off figures showing how many more people were receiving food stamps and student loans, even though he had cut benefits for some who didn't need them, by his definition. His own Agriculture Department statistics proved him wrong, as the actual number, not just percentage, of food stamp recipients had dropped by almost half a million since 1981. There was no reference to how his next budget would affect these and other programs for the disadvantaged. Mondale began and ended his statement with reference to the need to get the deficit down to lower interest rates, decrease the value of the dollar, stimulate exports and create jobs. Who was the liberal and who was the conservative here?

Reagan claimed that there was absolutely no relationship between deficits and interest rates, and that he had brought interest rates and inflation down. Mondale responded that he couldn't believe what he'd heard, that real interest rates, the difference between interest and inflation, which is the actual value cost of borrowing money, had doubled during Reagan's term. This was true for home mortages and consumer loans, but business loans were about the same. Mondale pointed out that Reagan's own economic adviser (about to be ex-adviser), Martin Feldstein, had told him of the relationship of deficits to interest rates. In a television address in 1981, Reagan himself had said interest rates would come down only when deficits came down. Mondale said of Reagan's present economic views that they were once referred to as "voodoo economics," as George Bush had labeled them in 1980. Mondale asked Reagan, "What will you cut? Whose taxes will you raise? Will you finally touch that defense budget? Are you going to go after Social Security and Medicare and student assistance and the handicapped again, as you did last time?" Reagan responded only to Social Security, saying, "I told you never would I do such a thing," and he went on to say, "Now again, to get to whether I have—am depending on magic—I think I have talked in straight economic terms about a program of recovery that was, I was told, wouldn't work; and then after it worked, I was told that lowering taxes would increase inflation, and none of these things happened. It is working and we're going to continue on that same line. As to what we might do, and find in further savings cuts, no, we're not going to starve the hungry." Mondale responded, "Well, we've just finished almost the whole debate and the American people don't have the slightest clue about what President Reagan will do about these deficits."

At another point Reagan stated, in response to a question about his being at a ceremony opening an old-age housing project that his budget proposals had opposed, "Our policy was not to cut subsidies. . . . We are today subsidizing housing for more than 10 million people. . . . We have no thought of throwing people out into the snow, whether because of age or need. We have preserved the safety net for the people with true need in this country, and it has been pure demogoguery that we have in some way shut off all the charitable programs or many of them for the people who have real need. The safety net is there and we're taking care of more people than has ever been taken care of before by any administration in this country." Mondale, stunning everybody as "Mr. Personality," smiled broadly and said, "Well, I guess I'm reminded a little bit of what Will Rogers once said about Hoover. He said it's not what he doesn't know that bothers me, it's what he knows for sure that just ain't so . . . the housing unit for senior citizens that the president dedicated in Buffalo was only made possible through a federal assistance program for senior citizens that the president's budget sought to terminate."

Perhaps Mondale's most effective and charming move of the night was his disarming statement in response to a question by Diane Sawyer of CBS: ". . . What do you think the most outrageous thing is your opponent said in this debate tonight?" Mondale turned to Reagan, smiled, and said, "You want to give me some suggestions?" He then continued, "I'm going to use my time a little differently. I'm going to give the president some credit. I think the president has done some things to raise the sense of spirit and morale, good feeling in this country. And he's entitled to credit for that."

The difference between the closing statements was night and day. Reagan began by saying he was confused when the moderator, Barbara Walters, told him he hadn't been given enough time for rebuttal and could take that time before making his closing statement. Reagan instead began his closing statement. Incredibly, he spent his time talking about GNP figures, incomprehensible poverty statistics, a 600-ship navy and overly expensive military spare parts such as a $500 hammer, saying, "We are the ones who found those." It was a rambling potpourri of numbers with no unifying theme. One's instinct was to change the channel to make certain this was reality, that it was happening on the other networks as well. Mondale stepped into this media-shock vacuum and knocked it out of the park: "I believe that if we ask those questions that bear on our future, not just congratulate ourselves, but challenge ourselves to solve those problems, you'll see that we need new leadership. . . . We can be better if we face our future, rejoice in our strengths, face our problems, and by solving them build a better society for our children."

NBC's Tom Brokaw, John Chancellor, and Roger Mudd discussed the debate both after its conclusion and also the next morning on the "Today" show. Chancellor felt the debate was fairly even for the first hour, but that in the last half hour, Reagan fell apart and Mondale soared. Tom Brokaw was a broken record, both immediately following the debate, and the next morning. He granted that Mondale was impressive, but in the guise of wondering out loud, seemed to be editorializing, declaring that the American people still wouldn't buy his argument about raising taxes. But when Today's Bryant Gumbel asked if Mondale's performance would turn into votes, Roger Mudd said, almost as if surprised to hear himself saying it, "I don't know," but that people would definitely be taking a new look at Walter Mondale. Mudd's tone and expression appeared to be saying, "It seems impossible, but maybe we actually have a contest now."

All the evening news programs made clear, that, for the time being at least, the momentum had shifted to Mondale, and at last his campaign was alive. On MacNeil/Lehrer, former Reagan White House media adviser David Gergen stated that Mondale had presented himself as a viable alternative. Democratic analyst Alan Baron described Mondale's performance as better than Reagan's in 1980 or Kennedy's in 1960. As ABC's Britt Hume put it, "Walter Mondale flew into New York today, but the way he was feeling after last night's debate, he probably didn't need the plane." NBC's Lisa Myers said of the Mondale campaign, ". . . They say that they now have a real chance and after the last few weeks, having a chance is terrific." ABC, NBC, and CBS had virtually identical reports on the Mondale and Reagan campaigns. An ebullient Walter Mondale was shown walking with Geraldine Ferraro in the Columbus Day Parade in New York City, the streets packed with thousands of cheering supporters, tremendous excitement in the air, a sharp contrast to the campaign-opening Labor Day Parade on these same streets exactly five weeks to the day earlier. Vice-President Bush walked in the same parade with his wife, Barbara, but the Reagan-Bush supporters were sparse in comparison to those for Mondale and Ferraro. As for Reagan, ABC's Sam Donaldson reported, "The presidential motorcade rolled slowly and painfully out of Louisville this morning, its occupants well aware that the heavyweight debating champ had stubbed his toe on Walter Mondale." President Reagan was shown in North Carolina speaking to a large, but fairly subdued crowd, matching his own dejected mood. As NBC's Chris Wallace put it, "The seemingly unstoppable Reagan bandwagon hit a bad rock last night and the president seemed to know it." When Reagan spoke to the crowd he sounded different than I had ever heard him. He seemed physically and emotionaly drained, uncertain and very much in need of reassurance as he said, "Whether I won [the debate] or not, I've—I know now that I have won the fruits of victory because I get to be with all of you."

NBC's John Chancellor had an interesting commentary about the debate: "You know, it's hard for mere mortals to understand the pressure on the two men who debated last night in Louisville. Walter Mondale had never faced a bigger challenge in the quarter of a century he's spent in politics. And if Mondale had a lot to gain, President Reagan had even more to lose. Tremendous burdens for both of them. But the way things have been going in the era of televised debates, physical pressure is being added to mental pressure. The Kennedy-Nixon debates in 1960 lasted one hour, not an hour and a half. They had chairs, and while one talked the other sat down. Ford and Carter had chairs in 1976, but wouldn't use them, and last night there were no chairs at all. The debaters were on their feet 100 minutes without a break, an hour and forty minutes. The moderator sat, the panelists sat, the audience sat, but the two people doing the work preferred to stand. And if you don't think that's hard to do, you try standing for 100 minutes with your brain going at top speed. Tough on Mondale, who is fifty-six, even tougher on Reagan, who is seventy-three. This display of stamina was not the fault of the League of Women Voters, which arranged the debate; if the candidates had asked for chairs they would have had them. Or couches, or hammocks. In presidential politics these days, sitting is out. The ideal debate would have had the debaters sitting comfortably behind tables with pots of coffee or tea, and maybe even jars of jelly beans or antacid tablets. After all, the point of the debate is to show how well prepared these people are to be president, but apparently that's not enough in the macho world of presidential image making."

On CBS, Dan Rather discussed the new post-debate campaign situation with correspondents Bob Schieffer and Leslie Stahl.

RATHER: *Bob, along the Mondale campaign plane today, what were they talking about?*

SCHIEFFER: *They were absolutely beside themselves and they were almost just tap dancing down the aisle. You know, this is a campaign that has not had very much to cheer about. They've been behind for a long time and they know it, now they think they've really done something. Congressman Tony Coehlo of California, who is traveling on the plane with them, even said that Mr. Reagan himself may have raised an issue that they haven't quite known how to get at, how to go about raising. And that is the age issue. The way Coehlo saw it, the president looked a little bit out of focus at times last night and they think that the president himself may have raised this age issue and the way they see it, that he, at some times, appeared not quite in control.*

RATHER: *Leslie Stahl, what worries the president's men most now as they launch into what we can call the middle third of this campaign?*

STAHL: *Well, I think they're a little concerned that they may be losing control of the agenda. Up until last night the President managed to keep this campaign focused on the economy, on Mondale's raising taxes. Last night Mondale did a lot about Social Security and the spending cuts, the fairness issue. They want to get back in control and talk about the recovery and the low inflation rate, and I think they're also a little worried about the next debate that's coming up. They figured that the economy was their strong point, they had a lot of good points to make. In foreign policy the President doesn't have that much to boast about. So, they're very worried about what's coming up.*

RATHER: *Yet, their man did score some points last night. Where do they think he did best?*

STAHL: *Well, there was a strategy that said, "We have to prove to the American people that this man is in command of the facts." They crammed him with figures and numbers and little bits of information because they expected Mondale to be what they said was "Fighting Fritz," they thought he'd be aggressive and try to pin the president down on issues to show he wasn't in command. There has been a lot of finger pointing today over the strategy and the strategists who didn't realize that Mondale might be easygoing and respectful. And they think that maybe they were a little off in their preparations by making him focus so much on numbers and statistics.*

RATHER: *Bob Schieffer, very quickly, are the Mondale people now concerned that Geraldine Ferraro may not be able to keep it going against George Bush in the debate on Thursday night?*

SCHIEFER: *They have all said, more than, I'll bet, six of them said to me today, "This really puts the pressure on this next debate." This makes this next debate very, very important. They're all thinking about that a great deal.*

The commercial networks definitely gave Mondale his "full due," as Howell Raines had put it. They gave it on the same terms that had served Reagan so well until this point—imagery, polls, strategy, and momentum. Mondale "looked" like a winner, Reagan like a loser. The Reagan camp, for the first time, was concerned, the Mondale camp for the first time, excited. The positive for all of us, and for the system, regardless of one's partisan position, was the sense of uncertainty, and possibility, in the air.

But still, on this day when the potential for a real campaign, an actual contest, ever so slightly began to stir in the national consciousness, the one thing missing throughout the Presidential Election Show on the TV nightly news thus far continued to be absent: the issues. Only MacNeil/Lehrer spent any time on substance, and even their coverage was rather sparse in this regard. There was literally *nothing* on the commercial network programs about the substance of the presidential debate! *Real* statements more than one or two lines long were made by the candidates, *actual exchanges* occurred between them *on the issues.* Social Security, Medicare, the deficit, interest rates, taxes, abortion, religion and the state, the environment, and more. Never mind that it was not nearly what it could have been with a different format. It was more than many had expected, and most important, it was something.

There may have been nearly as much exploration of issues in that ninety-minute presidential debate as in all the commercial network evening newscasts combined since Labor Day, a point perfectly illustrated by *this* evening's news programs.

Wednesday, October 10: TV Giveth and TV Taketh Away

This day was, in hindsight, the last day of Walter Mondale's brief moment of glory and possibility, following the first presidential debate, although the potential remained for an incredible upset if his "performance" had been even better, and President Reagan's even worse, during the second debate. But Mondale's momentum was slowed somewhat by the vice-presidential debate between George Bush and Geraldine Ferraro. The Mondale-Ferraro ticket almost needed another barn burner in the Ferraro-Bush debate to keep the momentum going at the pace required to win the election. They didn't get it. Both Ferraro and Bush had something to take home from their debate: Ferraro made the historic demonstration that a woman could be president; Bush stopped the Reagan campaign tailspin. But that story is to come.

No one can say what might have happened had the vice-presidential debate not occurred so soon after the first presidential debate cremation of the "Gipper" by Fritz. The media would have then continued to fuel the fire started by the presidential debate. The voting public would have continued to concentrate on Reagan's "not all there" performance and the appealing showing by Mondale. After the election, the Reagan campaign staff admitted that during the first week following the debate their own polls showed Mondale coming up fast, too fast, and they were worried. On this day, CBS released a poll that showed Mondale coming up six points in three days. Although still twenty points down, the rate of gain, and the volatility in the air, made anything possible. ABC showed Mondale fifteen points down. The following week, Harris would show Mondale only nine points away from Reagan. It is useful to remember that Reagan's reelection was not absolutely inevitable.

For three days following the Louisville disaster, the Reagan campaign did resemble an airplane that had lost its engines. Television giveth and television taketh away. A more potent demonstration of TV's influence would be difficult to conjure. Because he stumbled so badly in front of the cameras, and because of Mondale's surprise showing, the medium that his campaign strategy had been based on turned on Reagan with a vengeance. The main focus became the president's age. The impact of the debate can be seen in some of this day's reporting.

ABC's Peter Jennings began" World News Tonight" with: "It was only a few days ago that most political analysts in this country thought Walter Mondale was on the ropes. Then came Sunday's debate, the hard fight on the issues [this phrase raises the eternal question, Why no reporting on those hard-fought issues?], and later the first talk about the president's age." Dan Rather opened the "CBS Evening News" saying, "Indications are tonight that the first impression that Walter Mondale won his show-down Sunday matchup with President Reagan may be making a first concrete dent in President Reagan's huge lead in the polls. . . . it was another rare-up-and-over-the-hurdles day for Walter Mondale; another day of damage control for President Reagan."

CBS's Leslie Stahl reported, "The White House planned a day of hard political punches by a vigorous and robust Ronald Reagan. But he kept running into the age issue and his debate performance."

REAGAN: *No, I wasn't tired. And, uh, with regard to the age issue, and everything, if I had as much makeup on as he did, I'd look younger too. [On ABC Reagan went on to assert he never wore makeup when acting, which was later refuted by previous Hollywood coworkers. No one asked him if he had meant that in his judgment he had worn "less" makeup than Mondale, or none at all, during the debate. Needless to say, he sounded fairly defensive and childish, which demonstrated the impact the debate results were having.]*

STAHL: *At a parochial school just outside of Detroit, the president himself brought up the age issue when a student asked him about teenage alcohol abuse.*

REAGAN: *You only get this piece of machinery once. Take care of it, really take care of it. And I'm prepared to tell you from personal experience, because I've been thirty-nine years old now for about thirty-one odd years. [He was seventy-three when this statement was made.]*

STAHL: *The president's doctor, Daniel Ruge, seemed to make matters worse for the president.*

DR. RUGE: *Well, I think he's tired. He really looks tired.*

REPORTER: *Has he lost any of his stamina over the four years?*

DR. RUGE: *I don't know.*

STAHL: *Today, a show of stamina. The president walking when normally he would take his limousine. Campaigning among ethnic groups, Mr. Reagan tried to regain the offensive, swinging hard at Mondale on taxes and defense. At a loud and enthusiastic college rally, he swung again.*

REAGAN: *Whenever I talk about Franklin Delano Roosevelt or Harry Truman or John F. Kennedy, my opponents start tearing their hair out. They just can't stand it. Well, of course they can't. Because it highlights how far the leadership of the Democratic party have strayed from the strength of the Democratic political tradition.*

This is the consummate illustration of the Reagan ability to use symbols to his advantage without regard to factual reality. What had the Democrats abandoned? What did *he* associate with in this tradition? Roosevelt, Truman, and Kennedy created and expanded the welfare state. Roosevelt believed in accommodation with Stalin, Truman fired MacArthur in Korea to limit the war, Kennedy took the least aggressive option in the Cuban missile crisis and initiated the Test Ban Treaty. Reagan has been the leader and hero of the right wing of the Republican party ever since Barry Goldwater's defeat in 1964. This element in American politics despises Roosevelt, Truman, and Kennedy. Reagan signed on in time to oppose Kennedy on virtually every issue. Although Reagan has moved somewhat to the center in comparative terms, he remains perhaps the most ideological president of the century. In terms of general philosophy and policies while president, Reagan in most cases has stood for the opposite of what Roosevelt, Truman, and Kennedy stood for. And the Democratic party still stands for very much the same philosophy reflected by these presidents. If anything, the 1984 ticket was somewhat more conservative, reflected by Mondale's deficit-reduction plan. Reagan's harsh attacks on Mondale on defense were disinguous, as Mondale was a traditional liberal who believed in increasing defense spending, but at a lower rate than Reagan, and concentrating more on conventional rather than nuclear forces. But, of course, Reagan had called Kennedy "weak" for not attacking the Cuban missile sites, which probably would have led to World War III. So where was the intellectual integrity in Reagan's comments? The strategy, of course, was to identify with Democratic political heroes in order to woo the Democratic vote, to take the focus off the issues, and to put Reagan, in the national consciousness, in the company of these legendary presidents. The entire point was to say something over and over again, persuasively, until it was believed. This "big lie" tactic can succeed because TV and the media do not concentrate on the content but simply supply the medium for delivery.

Leslie Stahl finished her report with, "The first commandment of the president's campaign strategy is: 'Thou shalt let no negative issue fester.' And so, the president's aides made public for the first time today the results of Mr. Reagan's last medical exam, which was done five months ago. It confirms the president is mentally alert and robust. Now Mr. Reagan and his aides wait to see if this and more television pictures of an energetic campaigner are enough to put the age issue behind them."

CBS's Bob Schieffer reported on Mondale's day.

SCHIEFFER: *Walter Mondale was in Pittsburgh, a Democratic stronghold, when he replied to the president's charges; so the huge partisan crowd loved it when he said Mr. Reagan's attempts to link himself to late Democratic heroes amounted to grave robbing. And as for Mr. Reagan's charge that Mondale had better makeup at the debate, Mondale said he'd heard that one before.*

MONDALE: *That's the same answer Nixon gave [in the 1960 debate with Kennedy]. . . . Mr. President, the problem isn't makeup on the face; it's the makeup on those answers that gave you a problem.*

SCHIEFFER: *He also had an answer to the president's challenge yesterday to arm wrestle. [Reagan, in another school-yard response to the age question, said he'd be glad to arm wrestle Mondale any time.]*

MONDALE: *Well, we had a little brain wrestle on Sunday night, didn't we? He'll find that the issue that worries Americans is not arm wrestling, but the need for arms control.*

SCHIEFFER: *But it was the poll findings that put the icing on today's cake for Mondale's people. Last night, CBS News and the* New York Times *called back 515 voters who had been polled before the debate, and the survey was full of good news for Mondale. Sixty-six percent of the people thought Mondale had won it. More voters than ever, 53 percent, agreed with Mondale that taxes must be raised to lower the deficit. By a margin of nearly two to one, Mondale was seen as the candidate most likely to preserve Social Security and Medicare. And almost half the people polled thought the president was not as sharp as he was four years ago. On balance, these last four days have been the best of the Mondale campaign, with the polls finally beginning to show some improvement. The Mondale people are beginning to believe that the Teflon presidency can be scratched, after all.*

On ABC, George Will had some interesting comments about the age issue: "It's fascinating that the age issue has become as hot as horseradish, for two reasons. The last time age was an issue regarding a candidate, the candidate was John Kennedy. He was forty-three and some people said he was too young. Second, in 1980, the one person who relentlessly tried to make an issue of Ronald Reagan's age was George Bush. He did so by jogging all the time and getting his picture taken and stressing his own vitality. But this is an important issue, the health, general prospects of any candidate. Woodrow Wilson, it's well remembered, was just sixty-two when he was incapacitated. Franklin Roosevelt was elected president in 1944. He was sixty-two then. His doctors must have known that he was dying and was very unlikely to finish out his full term. . . . Winston Churchill was eighty when he stepped down for the last time as prime minister, and papers recently released in Britain indicate that he, frankly, was not competent at all times, mentally competent in his later years. On the other hand, de Gaulle served at his full capacity until age seventy-nine. And most interestingly, Konrad Adenauer was Reagan's age, seventy-three, when he began a fourteen-year term ruling Germany."

It goes without saying that there were more important issues than Reagan's age that should have emerged from the first presidential debate. One would have hoped that it would have served, finally, to focus attention on the policy records and proposals of the candidates. MacNeil/Lehrer this day quoted from an editorial in the October 9 Orlando, Florida, *Sentinel*, which read, "If voters were listening as well as watching, the next four weeks will be a two-way race, not a runaway." The problem, of course, was that TV never gave the voters the opportunity to do more than watch. "Listening" on the video medium requires going over the statements about issues more than once, and following with analysis. Reading occurs at the reader's pace, with no visual distractions from idea content. The televised debate, although far superior to the nightly news in terms of both content and length, moves at its own pace as well as demanding visual attention. There are advantages to seeing and hearing the candidate on television, but only if length and depth allow the advantages to be utilized. And then it is crucial for broadcast journalism to provide the equivalent of what the reader can do, which is review the material. When all TV news does after a debate is show a few seconds of clips emphasizing performance and strategy, and concentrate on such themes for days following the event, it actually detracts from whatever thought process had been stimulated in the viewer by watching the entire debate.

On the terms that it operated, it was fascinating to watch the response of TV news and the media to the first debate, over the period of the three days following the actual event. At first, the TV and press reports were very tentative about Reagan's stumbling and Mondale's winning. But as the poll results began coming in, the media commentary became much more solid in terms of a strong Mondale victory and a bad Reagan showing. On MacNeil/Lehrer, media critic Edwin Diamond, director of MIT's Press Study Group, had some interesting comments in an interview by Robert MacNeil.

DIAMOND: *I think it's the press as a reactive system rather than an active system. The poll results came in, the people who watched the debate pronounced their decision, and the press felt more emboldened to report this and not feel that their flank, their left flank so to speak, would be exposed to any criticism of being unfair to Mr. Reagan, because the public was speaking. . . . What happened was that 80 or 90 million people who are not media experts . . . they dialed in on Sunday and they saw this, their leader, looking visibly tired and maybe a little confused. So if you ask who the opinion leader in this matter is, it was the people who voted and told the pollsters that they thought Mondale had won.*

MACNEIL: *Let me ask you about another phenomenon. Television is able nowadays, as it does in sports coverage, to instant replay, and then replay many times in news programs and things, highlights, and they've done that in this debate as they did in others. What is the effect of replaying moments like that, and which moments in this debate do you think the nation is going to remember?*

DIAMOND: *It's reinforcement, and we saw, we've studied, my colleagues and I have studied, the '76 debates and the '80 debates. And in '76 it was Gerald Ford liberating Poland from Eastern European rule, which may have gone by a lot of people, but the press kept replaying the tape and pointing that out, and you could see Ford drop in the polls. I mean, instantly after the debate, Ford seemed to be doing very well in the polls, but with the press talking about the Eastern European gaffe, repeating the mistake, he began dropping. In '80, it was—what do people remember? Reagan saying, 'There you go again' to Jimmy Carter, and Jimmy Carter revealing that he discussed nuclear nonproliferation with Amy. So those bits, or bytes, as you call them, get replayed over and over again and they become fixed in the mind, reinforcement.*

MACNEIL: *This is very interesting, because a lot of people praise the debate because it's an opportunity for many millions of Americans—eighty million it's estimated in this case—to watch and judge for themselves, the first opportunity to see the two candidates side by side for ninety minutes. Is that more what causes the electoral impact, or the impact on public opinion; or this reinforcement process you're describing in the media? Which has the greater impact on how people feel in the end about that?*

DIAMOND: *That's a very good question. I think, you know, the shorthand about the medium being the message, or the media being the message, I don't think so. I think the message is the message. A reality occurred on Sunday night that eighty million people saw, unfiltered and uninterpreted by anybody else. They saw something happening on that screen. Now, Mondale seemed to look better than they thought he would. . . . Reagan seemed to look more tired and more confused than they thought he would. So there was a reality. Now, the press is picking up in its reinforced, in its reactive reinforcement system, it's picking that up and echoing it and reechoing it, and fixing those new images. . . . You know, in the political ads, we get the thirty seconds, the candidate is controlled by his media managers; on newscasts, the commercial newscasts, we get the thirty or forty-five seconds of the candidate as controlled by the producers of the news. At least in the debate—we know they're not really debates—but in these parallel news conferences, we do get the candidates for ninety minutes, and fairly close to election day, when I maintain, and all the voting data I have looked at shows, a lot of Americans have not dialed into the campaign until now. So this is in a way the beginning of the campaign for many people. And that's good, I think.*

True enough, but TV news would do nothing to help keep the electorate "dialed" in. The "what's the strategy, what's the score" type coverage had relentlessly reported from the beginning that this election was no contest. Then on the same terms, surprising nobody more than itself, the medium gave the public a contest for a brief moment. But what TV giveth, it can taketh away very quickly.

Thursday, October 11: Making History

This was a historic day in American political history. For the first time since the founding of the Republic, a major party's candidate for vice-president of the United States, facing off in debate with the opponent, was a woman. The long-term impact of this image on the TV screens of America would undoubtedly prove the most memorable and important legacy of this day.

Unlike the previous Sunday, there was no clear winner or loser in this faceoff. Ferraro seemed quite subdued, speaking in a soft monotone, perhaps overcompensating for a concern that she would come on too strong. She also seemed somewhat tentative, probably as a result of wanting to make certain she committed no major blunders. Bush, on the other hand, tended to come on much too strong, in a somewhat high-strung and overly dramatic manner. Each candidate's approach seemed to play against the other's in a way that highlighted what was missing from both performances. There were some good moments for both candidates, however, and each of them gave effective closing statements. And as moderator, Sander Vanocur of ABC said after the debate, the quality of substance of both debates in this campaign so far had been fairly good compared to TV debates in the past.

The pressure on both candidates was enormous. For Ferraro it was not only the pressure to help keep the favorable momentum going from the first Mondale-Reagan debate, but the aspirations of millions of American women were connected to this moment, and the spotlight of history was on her. For Bush, the pressure was to stop the whirlwind that threatened to unravel the seemingly insurmountable lead he and Reagan had enjoyed, thereby making or breaking his own political future as well.

At the beginning of the debate, Bush seemed so wound up that he might lose control. He sounded as if he were talking through a loudspeaker. He was at his worst when he described Walter Mondale's message, in a shrill voice, with a badly delivered attempt at humor, as "Whine on harvest moon." He hit another low when saying condescendingly to Ferraro, "But let me help you with the difference, Mrs. Ferraro [he refused to call her Congresswoman, as he had agreed before the debate], between Iran and the embassy in Lebanon. Iran—we were held by a foreign government. In Lebanon you had a wanton terrorist action where the government opposed it. We went to Lebanon to give peace a chance. . . . We saw the formation of a government of reconciliation." (Not true, the Lebanese government was a faction in a virtual civil war. Bush's entire comment was in reply to Ferraro pointing out that when the Iranian hostages were returned, President Reagan had said that any future such actions would be met by a swift and immediate response. This did not occur after the bombings of the marine barracks and the embassy in Beirut.)

BUSH: *And for somebody to suggest, as our two opponents have, that these men died in shame—they better not tell the parents of those young marines.*
FERRARO: *Let me just say, first of all, that I almost resent, Vice-President Bush, your patronizing attitude that you have to teach me about foreign policy. [This line brought the loudest burst of applause of the debate from the evenly divided partisan audience.] . . . Secondly, please don't categorize*

my answers either. Leave the interpretation of my answers to the American people who are watching this debate. [This was in response to Bush's comment that he thought Ferraro had said she would do away with all covert CIA activities, which he categorized as having very serious ramifications. His comment was probably effective, if inaccurate. Ferraro had said she did not support the "covert" war in Nicaragua, specifically.] And let me say further that no one has ever said that those young men who were killed through the negligence of this administration and others ever died in shame. No one who has a child who is nineteen or twenty years old, a son, would ever say that at the loss of anybody's child.

This exchange over the deaths of the U.S. marines in Lebanon would echo for a few days after the debate, with Mondale and Ferraro demanding an apology, Reagan sticking by Bush (although refusing to specifically back up his statement), and Bush feverishly, almost obsessively, trying to find quotes to back up his assertion. Failing that, he was reduced to the ridiculous spectacle of brandishing dictionaries and trying to twist the words *in vain* to mean *shame*.

Bush was at his best when responding to Ferraro's statement that she would not impose her religious views on others (in regard to abortion), but if there was a time when she felt she could not both practice her religion and do her job properly, she would resign. Bush said in a manner that seemed entirely sincere that he respected her for saying that. He was also quite effective in the area of foreign policy. On Central America, he made a very strong statement claiming that there was a night-and-day difference between El Salvador and Nicaragua, with the former at least beginning to function as a democracy, and improving its human rights record under President Duarte. Besides the complexities involved in that particular statement, he left himself wide open in regard to the death squads in El Salvador, which not even the critics of the Sandinistas claim has a counterpart in Nicaragua. But Ferraro failed to respond effectively, instead talking about the Contadora negotiating process (an attempted negotiated end to the military conflicts in Nicaragua and El Salvador organized by neighboring Central American countries), which was important, but needed further explanation for the many viewers not familiar with it, just as Bush's remarks needed a direct response. As a result, Bush undoubtedly made his points stick more effectively. He also delivered a tailor-made comment simultaneously dealing with perhaps the two most important issues of the campaign at this point: Reagan's being in control (age, competence) and the nuclear arms race. "Nuclear weapons," Bush said, "should never be fought with, and that's our approach. So therefore, let's encourage the Soviets to come to the table as we did at the Gromyko meeting. I wish everybody could have seen that one—the president giving the facts to Gromyko in all these nuclear meetings—excellent, right on top of that subject matter. And I'll bet you that Gromyko went back to the Soviet Union saying, 'Hey, listen, this president is calling the shots; we'd better move.' " This may have been the most strategically important remark Bush made during the debate and the one that had the most impact.

Ferraro sometimes seemed as if she were an academic debating in a college lecture hall. Bush used television and the limitations of the format more effectively. One of the most distracting aspects of Ferraro's presentation was the fact that she was constantly looking down at her notes. It was bad TV visually, and it created the impression that she was not as good as Bush at thinking on her feet. There were times when her message had dramatic potential, but she delivered it in the flat tone that dominated much of her presentation, instead of with the strength and flair she demonstrated on the campaign trail. In beginning her arms-control comments, for instance, she referred to this day being the hundredth birthday of Eleanor Roosevelt and quoted her as saying, "It is not enough to want peace, you must believe in it. And it is not enough to believe in it, you must work for it." It was an appropriate quote, for the appropriate subject, on the appropriate day, but she didn't give it the power it could have had with some vocal inflection, which usually seemed natural for her. When talking about Mondale's proposal to challenge the Soviets with a test-ban moratorium, she not only delivered the lines in a tone that made the issue seem passé, but incorrectly referred to the initiative as relating to the atmosphere, and then compounded the error by saying that this approach was taken in 1960. The atmospheric Test Ban Treaty was in fact initiated and signed in 1963, and Mondale's proposal was for the remaining legal underground testing.

Toward the end of the debate Ferraro seemed to come alive, and she was particularly good when responding to a loaded question from Robert Boyd, Washington bureau chief for Knight-Ridder newspapers.

BOYD: *Congresswoman Ferraro, you have had little or no experience in military matters and yet you might someday find yourself commander-in-chief of the armed forces. How can you convince the American people and the potential enemy that you would know what to do to protect this nation's security, and do you think in any way that the Soviets might be tempted to take advantage of you simply because you are a woman?*

FERRARO: *Are you saying that I would have to have fought in the war in order to love peace?*

BOYD: *I'm not saying that, I'm asking you—you know what I asked.*

FERRARO: *All right. I think what happens is when you try to equate whether or not I have had military experience, that's the natural conclusion. It's about as valid as saying that you would have to be black in order to despise racism, that you'd have to be female in order to be terribly offended by sexism. And that's just not so. . . . I think that the people of this country can rely on the fact that I will be a leader. I don't think the Soviet Union for one minute can sit down and make a determination on what I will do if I'm ever in a position to have to do something with reference to the Soviet Union. Quite frankly, I'm prepared to do whatever is necessary in order to secure this country and make sure that security is maintained. Secondly, if the Soviet Union were ever to believe that they could challenge the United States with any sort of nuclear forces or otherwise, if I were in a position of leadership in this country, they would be assured that they would be met with swift, concise, and certain retaliation. . . . The most important thing though, I think as a leader that what one has to do is get to the point where you're not in that position. . . . I will not put myself in that position as a leader in this country. I will move immediately toward arms-control negotiations.*

Both Ferraro and Bush had strong concluding statements.

BUSH: *Ronald Reagan and I have put our trust in the American people. We've moved some of the power away from Washington, D.C., and put it back with the people. . . . There's a new opportunity lying out there in the future. . . . And abroad there's new leadership and respect. And Ronald Reagan is clearly the strong leader of the free world. . . . Some of you out there are finishing high school or college and some of you are starting out in the working place. And we want for you America's greatest gift. And that is opportunity. And then peace. . . . It is absolutely essential that we guarantee the young people that they will not know the agony of war. America's gift, opportunity and peace.*

FERRARO: *Being the candidate for vice-president of my party is the greatest honor I have ever had. But it's not only a personal achievement for Geraldine Ferraro, and certainly not only the bond I feel as I go across this country with women throughout the country. I wouldn't be standing here if Fritz Mondale didn't have the courage and my party didn't stand for the values that it does, the values of fairness and equal opportunity. Those values make our country strong, and the future of this country and how strong it will be is what this election is all about.*

Immediately following the debate, the reaction of TV journalists on the different networks was somewhat diverse, with a general consensus that it was a tossup.

On ABC, David Brinkley stated that "they both had something to say and said it well. I didn't see any winner or loser." Peter Jennings felt that

Bush may have had the upper hand on the foreign policy part of the debate, which was his area of expertise. George Will said that what "they were looking for on the Republican side was some spectacular achievement by George Bush that would stop the surge that the Mondale forces have clearly made since Sunday; I don't think that happened. On the other hand, the Democrats may have been worried that Ms. Ferraro couldn't take the heat, or that she would be shrill in some way; clearly she has the manner to play in this league in politics, so I don't think either side gained much or lost anything." Will added that he felt the caliber of the debate was rather poor, that neither of the candidates "coherently presented their positions." Sam Donaldson told us, "Well, I think we've seen a debate between Mr. Emotional and Ms. Cool, and perhaps Ms. Cool scored some points for that, because people did expect that she would be shrill and she wasn't. George Bush was effective at times, clearly on the question of religion, I thought he was very effective in his answer there. But sometimes his emotion got away from him, as in the case when he did . . . fall into sort of a trap that Ms. Ferraro then sprang by saying, 'Don't interpret my answers, and I didn't say anything about shame.' But there might not be any clear winners and losers, but as in the case with a presidential debate, any time someone less well known takes the stand with someone more well known, she, in this case, makes some points."

On ABC's "Nightline," which aired one hour after the end of the debate, a poll had already been taken that showed Bush the winner by 42 percent to 33 percent, with 25 percent calling it a tie. This poll had a margin of error of 4.5 percent. Ironically, the same poll showed a one-point gain by Mondale-Ferraro from 41 percent to 42 percent against Reagan-Bush at 55 percent. "Nightline" reporter Jeff Greenfield, however, like most other journalists heard from this evening, saw the debate as basically a tie, and felt that Ferraro had accomplished her most important task, which was to demonstrate that she was qualified to be vice-president or, if necessary, president. Greenfield said, "Ties in debates usually go to the outsider who can prove that he, or she in this case, can stand toe to toe on a podium and debate. I think she did quite well. I think she made her points in a subdued manner because that is what she had wanted to do, and I think that to that extent she answered some of the more primitive kind of doubts, about, well, can a woman really do that." Greenfield added that the October 21 debate between Mondale and Reagan would be extremely important because the first debate had caused the ground to shift under the feet of the previously smoothly sailing Reagan campaign, and if the next debate went the same way, "the rumbling could turn into an earthquake."

On NBC, Tom Brokaw felt that Ferraro had been too low-key, and John Chancellor made the most definitive statement when he said that

Bush had won the debate. NBC reporter Norma Quarles, who was one of the questioners for the debate, appeared with Brokaw, Chancellor, and Roger Mudd to discuss the outcome. She said, "I thought it was a draw . . . and not only me, but another panelist, Bob Boyd. We thought it was a draw." Roger Mudd said that in terms of expectations, people had thought that Ferraro would come out and "be-bop around" instead of being more subdued. "I thought it was generally boring." John Chancellor concluded with: "Jackie Robinson went on the field for the Brooklyn Dodgers in 1947 on his first day as a black in the major leagues. He was 0 for 3 at bat, he was pretty good at first base, and he made history. A first woman did this tonight, and I think she made history." Tom Brokaw responded, "Well that's true. We've never seen anything quite like this in American politics. . . ."

Dan Rather on CBS described Ferraro's best moment as her remarks on the religion-and-abortion issue and Bush's best moment as the comment on covert action by the CIA, saying that Ferraro apparently opposed it under any circumstances. Reporter Bruce Morton told us that both candidates did a good job and the debate was a tossup. Dan Rather concluded with the observation that who won and who lost would for the first time be influenced by the issue of women in politics.

This was undoubtedly true, and many voters were still not prepared to have a woman one heartbeat away from the presidency. This was one of the reasons George Bush's comments, during and after the debate, which dominated the news the following day, had so little negative impact. In addition to the "shame" comment during the debate, a microphone picked up Bush saying, "We tried to kick a little ass," when referring to the debate as he campaigned the following day. At first he somewhat frantically, and illogically, since the damage had already been done, tried to demand that the microphone be turned off. Subsequently, he took to lame explanations and insisted that he had nothing to apologize for. It seemed a definite gaffe, as it detracted from media coverage of polls showing he was the winner of the debate, although not decisively. However, having the spotlight on something other than the first presidential debate was in itself a positive result for the Reagan-Bush team.

The day following the debate, MacNeil/Lehrer had an interesting segment on viewer reaction, reported by Elizabeth Brackett, who began, "It was a mixed group that gathered in this living room on the North Side of Chicago to watch last night's debate between George Bush and Geraldine Ferraro. Some Republicans, some Democrats, and some still on the fence. When it was over there were no new converts to either side, but there was agreement that both candidates had done what they had to do."

JOANNE CICCHELLI: *He is certainly a known person. We expected him to be well informed on affairs. And he spoke, I think . . . well. But she really, she had to make a show, and I think—show is the wrong word—she had to be impressive and she was.*

BRACKETT: *Did you think that Geraldine Ferraro's understanding of foreign affairs, of nuclear disarmament, was in enough depth to have her become a vice-president or a president?"*

GEORGE THRUSH: *She came across, I should say to me at least, as being somewhat naive on some issues, specifically the disarmament issue, where she suggested that all you needed was a strong-willed administration. And I certainly don't agree.*

KAREN HOWELL: *I was very impressed with the amount of effort she's taken to educate herself on it, and I was impressed with her sincerity.*

TOM HOWELL: *I think she appeared relatively naive, but I wouldn't say that in a way that indicts her or says she's not qualified to be vice-president. She appeared to me to be a very qualified candidate. It seemed to me that on that particular issue I liked George Bush's answer to the question better than hers. [The report then showed the "hottest" exchange between Bush and Ferraro.]*

BUSH: *But let me help you with the difference, Mrs. Ferraro, between Iran and the embassy in Lebanon. Iran, we were held by a foreign government.*

FERRARO: *Let me just say, first of all, that I almost resent, Vice-President Bush, your patronizing attitude that you have to teach me about foreign policy.*

BRACKETT: *You almost got the feeling that she had been waiting for that opportunity.*

THRUSH: *She was going to raise the "Are you condescending to me because I'm a woman or treating me that way?" whether it came up or not.*

CICCHELLI: *I thought that his remark was outrageous and I was extremely pleased that she came back like that. I don't see how anyone could not have.*

BRACKETT: *On the issue of abortion and on the issue of separation of church and state, who do you think made their case the best?*

THRUSH: *On those general principles—and I'm not getting into abortion, I say that I'm talking just the church—I don't think the stands are really appreciably different.*

MARY DISSER: *I think their stands are very different. I think George Bush did a good job tonight of playing down the administration's ideas, and I think that was his role tonight. But I think maybe in that way he did a better job because he sort of neutralized that issue.*

TOM HOWELL: *I am, I think, not too uncommon in tending to like the Republicans' economic platform and the Democrats' social program. I believe strongly that a woman should have the right to have an abortion if she wants to. I had harbored a hope that that's the way George Bush felt in his heart, too, and he said tonight in front of the world that he doesn't.*

BRACKETT: *There was the perception that George Bush would have a very difficult time with this debate with "How do you handle a woman?" How do you think he did on that score?*

THRUSH: *I think he treated her as an equal—*

CICCHELLI: *—and I wasn't sure he would be able to do that, not because of his attitude toward women, just because of his basic personality.*

MIKE GUERRIERI: *Tonight he was wound up. He was well coached, I thought. But I thought that was probably in response to what happened Sunday night when Reagan obviously wasn't, or else something was happening to him while he was speaking.*

BRACKETT: *Did anyone change their ideas significantly tonight about either candidate?*

GUERRIERI: *I thought both were more qualified to be president than I had previously thought.*

THRUSH: *We're not just electing a vice-president. We're electing a potential president—"heartbeat away" is the coined phrase. I don't think to assume the position of president of the United States she does have an adequate depth.*

DISSER: *I think she showed herself to be really in command of the issues and articulate, cool, strong. I was very, very impressed and real pleased to see how she did.*

BRACKETT: *But you were a supporter anyway?*

DISSER: *. . . I was a supporter, but I think there are a lot of people here who aren't her supporters have said the same thing tonight.*

TOM HOWELL: *Well, I agree with that, but in response to your question, I don't think either party won. I'd have to rate it a draw.*

MacNeil/Lehrer then ran a fascinating segment allowing an unusual look behind the scenes of each camp in terms of the preparations for the debate, as well as a unique perspective on the outcome. Reporter Judy Woodruff began: ". . . Two people who played a critical role in the preparations for last night's debate were the standins the candidates rehearsed for the debate with. We are fortunate to have both of them with us tonight. First, Republican Congresswoman Lynn Martin of Illinois, who stood in the role of Ms. Ferraro during Vice-President Bush's debate preparation. . . . And Robert Barnett, a Washington attorney, a Democrat, who stood in the role of Mr. Bush during Ms. Ferraro's rehearsals for the debate. . . . The polls are saying that Mr. Bush won, and yet we're hearing a lot of comments that leads us to believe, from this report we just saw from Chicago, that both candidates really came out doing well. What do you think? Mr. Barnett?"

BARNETT: *It's fascinating, because I've obviously heard about the polls. I talked to a lot of people today, admittedly not a scientific sample, but overwhelmingly . . . people felt, I thought, that Gerry Ferraro won. And I think the greatest evidence was the event today in Madison, Wisconsin, where Fritz Mondale and Gerry Ferraro appeared at the state capitol. I spoke to someone who was there, and apparently you could not see beyond the people. There were anywhere from thirty to forty thousand people there. There is a new enthusiasm in the campaign. The Mondale-Ferraro ticket is generating enthusiasm. . . . The momentum that started last Sunday [the first presidential debate] has continued, and last night really helped it, in our view. [Wishful thinking or public posturing. Ferraro certainly didn't "win" the debate in this sense.]*

WOODRUFF: *Miss Martin, who do you think won?*

MARTIN: *Well, I am going to try to be fairly objective, ex-government teacher here. Both of them won. Gerry Ferraro, because she had to prove that she could stand coolly under pressure, and she did; and Vice-President Bush, because he had to prove not only was he the vice-president but a superb candidate. Now, I'm going to argue that the polls are correct, and I don't think you can judge a rally—a Reagan-Bush rally can pull out a lot of people too—but most of them, frankly, are going to be Reagan-Bush people. Same thing in a Ferraro-Mondale rally. [This reversal of "Mondale-Ferraro" on Martin's part happened at other times during the campaign. It was the downside for Mondale of picking the first woman vice-presidential candidate, who was also full of personality, in contrast to the media image of Mondale as being drab.] I think what happened is that—foreign affairs overall—that George Bush, his experience showed. That doesn't denigrate Representative Ferraro, by the way, and I think she did herself proud. She had to hit—we're using too many sports, I'm starting to feel like the . . . Colosseum and the gladiators—and they're two very good competent people. She had to do even better to dominate the polls because Vice-President Bush is so ahead. And that she did not do. But she did well. Neither side has to be ashamed; frankly, I was quite pleased, and I think the happiness of the Reagan-Bush people is exemplified in the polls. But even if you said George Bush did well, you didn't say Gerry Ferraro blew it. She did not; she did fine too. [This was the most remarkably objective commentary heard from a partisan in this or any other campaign, in my experience.]*

WOODRUFF: *Let me ask you both about style. Lots has been said today about how unusually subdued Ms. Ferraro seemed, that she looked down a lot. Did you expect that from the rehearsal?*

BARNETT: *I heard that too, today. Let me see how I can explain it. I think I can. Most people prior to three, four months ago didn't know much about Gerry Ferraro, may have heard her name but hadn't seen her. Over the past four months they've seen her on the evening news shows, little snippets, five seconds, ten seconds, generally the punch line or the applause line or the criticism of President Reagan. And through this mosaic they've gotten the impression that she somehow is that person. The Gerry Ferraro, the real Gerry Ferraro that you saw last night—thoughtful, intelligent, competent, measured—*

WOODRUFF: *That's the real Gerry Ferraro.*

BARNETT: *That's the real Gerry Ferraro—*

WOODRUFF: *Not the more fired up—*

BARNETT: *There's also a sense of humor and there's also an ability to say what she thinks and to fight back when it's required and be tough, but I think people were so surprised because what they saw last night was different than those little snippets, but, as I think all of us know, those little snippets are not representative. . . .*

MARTIN: *Well, I just would comment, I've worked with Gerry, and I think they slowed her down a little too much. As a Republican I'm pleased. I think she does have a nice sense of humor, and I think there's a liveliness to what had been an incredibly bland, dull Mondale campaign. [This is either politicking or an example of the power of media image. Mondale's campaign had not been bland, but the media coverage and image of it was.] I think it [Ferraro's liveliness] was slowed down. But I also was told, and I don't know if this is true, that she debated once yesterday in the morning. Boy, that's an awful lot to ask of a person to, you know, get the emotions up twice. . . .*

BARNETT: *I don't know who told her that, but it's wrong. . . .*

MARTIN: *Oh, good.*

WOODRUFF: *How much were you all, as standins, able to really anticipate what the other guy was going to say last night?*

BARNETT: *From my point of view it was very easy. We were amazed. I put together a George Bush briefing book based on his statements, his speeches, the Republican Campaign Committee materials and all, and I was—*

WOODRUFF: *Did you watch tapes of him?*

BARNETT: *I watched tapes of him, put together transcripts of that. And I would say 90 percent of what he did last night came right out of the Republican National Committee. . . . Not many surprises from our point of view. He basically took the Reagan line.*

WOODRUFF: *What do you do when you're a standin? Do you, I mean do you actually use some of his phrases? Do you try to sound like him? . . .*

BARNETT: *I tried to resist becoming the Rich Little of American politics. I wasn't doing an impersonation. I was simply saying what I thought he would say. George Bush really has a style, and that style, I think you saw in the debate last night, sometimes it was a little overwhelming, for my taste anyway. But we tried to duplicate it. We tried to let Congresswoman Ferraro see what she was going to see. And I think we succeeded.*

WOODRUFF: *Ms. Martin, how did you get ready? How did Mr. Bush get in the right frame of mind? I guess so many people were looking at him to see how he was going to deal with a woman. How conscious were you all going into the debate of that, and what advice did you give him in that?*

MARTIN: *I really didn't give him advice. We had debated a number of times, and so if there had been a problem—and, frankly, I never noticed it— it certainly would have been over. I don't think, you know, I didn't try to put on a Queens accent, and I don't know if my counterpart had this, but once in a while last night I even found that I was expecting Gerry to say something, and not in the sense of rooting, but okay, here's, you know, here's the way to go through it. . . . I think it's an interesting thing to do because you identify with both candidates. I think what Vice-President Bush did was debate an opponent, and being a man or woman didn't enter.*

BARNETT: *Congresswoman Martin, you'll be interested to know I had the same experience.*

MARTIN: *Really. Isn't it just amazing?*

WOODRUFF: *. . . Did she [Ferraro] rehearse the line when he started to tell her about the Middle East. . . ?*

BARNETT: *. . . I can stand here and tell you honestly and truthfully that was not rehearsed. That was truthful. It came right out of her. She felt that he was being patronizing and she said so. That was not rehearsed.*

MARTIN: *I believe that, but I have to tell you that I used the same line on the vice-president because I thought it would come up during the debate.*

WOODRUFF: *All right. That's wonderful. Thank you . . . Congresswoman Martin and Robert Barnett for being with us.*

As usual, none of the commercial network evening news programs covered any of the issues discussed during the debate. Only Mac-Neil/Lehrer did this, with an extensive segment on Central America, which will be examined in the following chapter. "ABC World News Tonight" didn't even headline the historic debate, but ran it second after a lengthy report on the unsuccessful bombing attempt on British Prime Minister Thatcher's life. Although this was an important story, ABC apparently forgot that it was the *American* Broadcasting Company. NBC and CBS ran the debate story as their leads.

ABC, however, did have an interesting commentary by George Will: "It's been an utterly changed week. . . . It's a week that demonstrates the old axiom that in American politics overnight is a long time and a week is forever. It's a week that ends with the president in Ohio and it confirms for the Republicans what I would call the Ohio-in-1895 principle. In Ohio in 1895 it is said there were just two automobiles and they collided, which means if something can go wrong it will. The president's debate went wrong. As a result we've had a third debate this week, a fierce and public debate among the president's aides about who's to blame for inadequately briefing him. Now the various Bushes, George and Barbara, have said some indiscreet things [George, the "shame" comment during the debate and the "kick ass" comment afterward; Barbara, calling Ferraro something that rhymes with "witch," as she put it], one of which has started a fourth debate between Walter Mondale and George Bush. [Mondale demanding that Bush apologize for the "shame" comment.] Look how things have changed . . . in one week. Last Friday, Ronald Reagan, to the extent that he was running at all, was running against Jimmy Carter in a kind of lethargic way. Walter Mondale couldn't get Ronald Reagan to pay any attention to him, so he seemed to be running against Jerry Falwell. It was widely said that Ms. Ferraro was running for the Senate in 1986 and George Bush was running against, or perhaps away from, the Internal Revenue Service. [He had resisted disclosing his tax return to the public, and when he finally did, it turned out he had a dispute with the IRS as to how much his bill should be.] Now, as a result of the various debates, all four of them, we have a clearly concentrated race between the tops of the ticket. . . . I think Ms. Ferraro scored a point today in Madison when she said . . . that the Republicans are feeling the heat. This is the behavior of people who, frankly, seem quite rattled."

This commentary is particulary interesting in the hindsight context of one of the great landslides in American history that was about to occur. It reemphasizes a point already made. The results of this election were not inevitable. Volatility was the name of the game after the first Mondale-Reagan debate. The momentum toward Mondale-Ferraro was slowed by the vice- presidential debate. In lieu of a decisive Ferraro win, the media attention on the Reagan debacle in the first debate abating was in itself a great help to the Republicans, as the feeling in the air for the first three days after the presidential debate was akin to a dam about to break. In retrospect, Ferraro probably could not have done much better. She was playing point at a historic moment, and it would take society a while to catch up. In addition, George Bush did what he had to. Even so, the outside potential for an upset in the election remained. It depended entirely on the outcome of the second, and last, presidential debate between Ronald Reagan and Walter Mondale. This was true because the media said it was, and the media said it was for the wrong reasons, which nonetheless established the context in which the electorate would come to judgment. It was set up, as the others were, as indeed the entire campaign was, as a strategic contest, not a discussion of issues. The outcome, our video monitors told us, would depend almost entirely on whether Ronald Reagan appeared charming or senile. After the disastrous first debate, the question was, Would he drop the other shoe? If not, the election was still easily his.

The most significant aspect of these observations is the question of what the outcome of the election might have been had the media, predominantly television news, taken an entirely different approach to the campaign than what we have already seen, what was to come, and the alternative journalistic options available. These options, already referred to, will be discussed more thoroughly in the concluding chapters of this book. But it can be said with some confidence, in the author's opinion, that the election would at least have been much closer, and that the winner, whoever it was, would have been in a better position to lead in terms of the serious questions facing the nation, had TV news left the images on the video equivalent of the cutting room floor, and communicated substance, at length and in depth, to the American public.

Monday, October 15: The Story Behind The Picture

The scene was deeply moving. In the small town of La Palma in El Salvador, tens of thousands of Salvadorans lined the roads, waving small white flags, expressing their yearning for peace. The catalyst was a meeting initiated by El Salvador's President José Napolean Duarte with the rebel leaders fighting a civil war against the government. This emotional scene was projected into America's living rooms this evening on the television news.

For background, it is useful to turn to a report on Central America the previous Friday on MacNeil/Lehrer, the only television news report to follow up on the substance of the Bush-Ferraro debate.

JIM LEHRER: *On matters of substance, there were many differences on display last night, few more so than on the issue of Central America policy.*
BUSH *(from the debate)*: *We don't like it, frankly, when Nicaragua exports its revolution or serves as a conduit for supplies coming in from such democracies [apparently this is sarcasm] as North Korea, Bulgaria, the Soviet Union, or Cuba, to try to destabilize El Salvador. Yes, we're concerned about that because we want to see this trend toward democracy continue. There have been something like thirteen countries since we've come in move toward the democratic route.*

This last statement needed to be a subject of exploration by itself. Were the Reagan policies responsible, or the human rights policies of Jimmy Carter, or was it a natural indigenous process, or a combination? In Latin America, the move toward democracy had its roots before the Reagan presidency, and this taking of credit by Bush begged for journalistic challenge.

FERRARO *(from the debate): Quite frankly, now what is being done by this administration is an Americanizing of a regional conflict. This administration seems almost befuddled by the fact that Nicaragua is moving to participate in the Contadora process, and El Salvador, through its President Duarte, is reaching out to the guerrillas in order to negotiate a peace. What Fritz Mondale and I feel about the situation down there is that what you do is you deal first through negotiation, that force is not a first resort. It's certainly a last resort in any instance.*

MACNEIL: *That exchange between the vice-presidential candidates echoes a similar debate that's run almost throughout the first Reagan term. It's pitted the White House against congressional Democrats over U.S. military aid to El Salvador, covert support for the* contras *[counterrevolutionaries] in Nicaragua, and U.S. policy toward Central America in general. We turn now to what we call an issue-and-debate segment, part of our extended coverage of the political race. We begin with a background report by correspondent Charles Krause.*

KRAUSE: *From the very beginning, the Reagan administration viewed political violence in Central America as part of the larger East-West global conflict. The administration's basic assumptions and policy goals have changed very little in the four years President Reagan's been in office. The policy is to stop what the administration views as Communist aggression in El Salvador and to put an end to Cuban and Soviet influence in Nicaragua.*

REAGAN *(May 9, 1984): What we see in El Salvador is an attempt to destabilize the entire region and eventually move chaos and anarchy toward the American border. As the national bipartisan commission on Central America chaired by Henry Kissinger agreed, if we do nothing, if we continue to provide too little help, our choice will be a Communist Central America with additional Communist military bases on the mainland of this hemisphere and Communist subversion spreading southward and northward. This Communist subversion poses a threat that 100 million people from Panama to the open border of our South could come under the control of pro-Soviet regimes.*

The Kissinger commission referred primarily to economic aid. There has never been a successful "Communist" insurgency outside the context of massive and long-standing economic injustice. Remember Reagan's Caribbean basin initiative? What happened to leadership on this front? In addition, the constant use of the word *"Communist"* raises many questions, not the least of which is, don't we seem to have managed to work with the Chinese Communists as quasi allies, after years when they were characterized as a menace? There has been ample evidence over the years that the Cubans, for good economic and strategic reason, have been less than thrilled with dependence on Moscow. Although Castro began turning to the Soviets even before the Bay of Pigs, American reaction to the revolution was essentially hostile from the start. Given the American connection to the Batista dictatorship overthrown by Castro, a positive response to the revolution without attempts to dictate or threaten would more likely have served the strategic interests of the United States. Nicaragua presented a similar challenge when the Sandinistas overthrew the American-backed Somoza dictatorship in 1979. Although the Carter administration had suspended aid to Somoza when the Sandinista revolution succeeded, heavy-handed American attempts to influence the new government predictably backfired. Substantial economic aid was sent to Nicaragua for a brief period, but only after a lengthy struggle in Congress rendered the aid untimely. After the election of Reagan in 1980, relations deteriorated rapidly. The new administration increasingly described Nicaragua as a pawn of the Soviet Union and Cuba. Clifford Krauss and Robert Greenberger reported in the *Wall Street Journal* (3 April 1985), however, that the evidence showed that this was not the case, and that even a classified U.S. intelligence report indicated that the Nicaraguan military buildup was defensive in nature. The report indicated that this was a direct result of the CIA-sponsored campaign of the *contras* to topple the Sandinista regime. The one thing accomplished by the United States support of the *contras* (consisting mainly of field commanders formerly in the National Guard of the Somoza dictatorship) was helping the Sandinistas maintain a degree of popular support while they moved increasingly in an undemocratic direction. But the impact of American support of oppressive regimes and both covert and direct military intervention throughout Latin America over the decades continues to take a toll that few North Americans seemed to comprehend. There are reasons why the nations "from Panama to the open border of our South" oppose Reagan policy in Central America, pushing instead for a serious attempt at negotiation, the so-called Contadora process (named after the island where the concerned nations, Mexico, Panama, Venezuela, and Columbia, first met in 1983.) They have other ideas about what would cause or prevent "communism" or chaos in their countries, which it would seem they might be better equipped to determine than outsiders. All these issues needed further examination by broadcast journalists.

The Krause report continued: "To counter the appeal of armed revolution the Reagan administration has promoted elections in Central America. For the United States perhaps the most important vote was held earlier this year in El Salvador, where a moderate, José Napolean Duarte, was elected president. The administration hailed the election as proof that

U.S. policy is to encourage peaceful, democratic change. But since 1981, the Reagan administration has also greatly expanded U.S. military aid and activity to further its policies in Central America. In El Salvador, direct U.S. military support for the army has climbed from $35 million four years ago to $196 million this year. U.S. military advisers play an important and at times controversial role in training Salvadoran troops. From the beginning the Reagan administration has claimed that El Salvador's guerrillas receive their arms from Cuba and the Soviet Union through Nicaragua. In Honduras, where there is no guerrilla threat, U.S. troops built airstrips and other military installations, part of ongoing U.S. military maneuvers. Some of these installations are also reportedly used by U.S.-backed guerrillas at war with Nicaragua's Sandinista government. President Reagan calls the guerrillas freedom fighters. The Sandinistas call them counter-revolutionaries or *contras*. Whatever they're called, they've attacked Nicaraguan ports and mined the country's harbors as part of a campaign to destroy Nicaragua's economy."

There are basic facts missing from this "background" report. The history of the *contras*: their roots with the national guard of the overthrown dictator Somoza, although eventually moving beyond this base; the CIA role in their creation and its lack of support for the efforts of the separate guerrilla force led by ex-Sandinista hero of the 1979 revolution Eden Pastora, who resisted pressure to unite with the larger *contra* group because of its ties with former Somoza soldiers; and the opposition to the *contras* within Nicaragua by most of the vocal opponents of the Sandinista regime. Also, the international outcry, including strong condemnation from U.S. NATO allies, of the CIA's mining of Nicaragua's ports should have been mentioned. The archetypal anti-Communist, Senator Barry Goldwater, read the riot act to CIA director William Casey, because this was a direct act of war under international law.

KRAUSE: *Critics, including Democratic presidential candidate Walter Mondale, charge that President Reagan's policies have heightened tensions in Central America, that the president has downplayed diplomacy and increased the possibility of a direct U.S. military intervention.*
MONDALE *(May 15, 1984): I predict that if Mr. Reagan is reelected, he will present the American people with a December surprise.*

There was no "December" surprise, but the inference of some immediate catasrophe following the election made for what Mondale must have thought was good dramatic political rhetoric. In the end, it's intellectually empty and counterproductive. When politicians make statements like this, journalists should probe their meaning and demand specifics.

MONDALE: *His [Reagan's] policies will continue to fail, and at some point after the election, American boys could well be fighting and dying in Central America.*

KRAUSE: *President Reagan denies any plans for a Grenada-style invasion of Central America.*

REAGAN *(May 9, 1984): "The issue is our effort to promote democracy and economic well-being in the face of a Cuban and Nicaraguan aggression aided and abetted by the Soviet Union. It is definitely not about plans to send American troops into combat in Central America.*

KRAUSE: *On the campaign trail this year both Reagan and Mondale have, for the most part, left Central America to their running mates. Geraldine Ferraro accuses President Reagan of being reckless and trigger happy. Central America is part of what the Democrats call their "war and peace" issue.*

FERRARO *(September 16, 1984): They just don't see the whole picture. They see the Soviets and the Cubans as do we all, but not the centuries of poverty, oppression, and militarism. They see what's wrong with guerrilla sabotage, but not what's wrong with CIA mining. They see the need for aid to Central America, but not the need to tie that aid to improvements in human rights conditions. We have now had almost four years of Ronald Reagan's policies in that region and cannot ignore the threat that Soviet and Cuban forces pose to our security, and we cannot look the other way while any government threatens its own people. But we cannot succeed by force alone. We must be willing to fight if necessary, but we must be willing to negotiate if possible. The marines should be our last choice, not our only option.*

At the beginning of this statement, Ferraro makes comprehensible points concerning different perspectives on these issues. But in the end, she was saying exactly the same thing the Reagan administration would say. Did she truly believe that they thought of the marines as their only option? Obviously they wanted to avoid that, even if they seemed willing to use them more readily than Mondale or Ferraro would. The question was what policies could best avoid such an eventuality, which her original comments began to address. The concluding remark was rhetorical excess, to say the least.

In early 1985, the Reagan administration would begin to demonstrate even more clearly its willingness to use force to remove the Sandinista regime. But they obviously preferred to rely on the *contras* before sending in the marines. The question Ferraro did not raise was, Under what circumstances did the United States or any government have the right to forcefully overthrow another government? If the United States was taking upon itself the role of democratic liberator, why had it supplied Somoza with military aid? What about South Africa, South Korea, the Philippines,

Chile, and so on? Would the United States use force to install democratic regimes in those nations? And what about the Soviet Union and Eastern Europe? Presumably an updated and aggressively interpreted version of the Monroe Doctrine was more likely to be pursued than actions that would lead directly to World War III. But U.S. actions in Nicaragua were raising serious questions that the American people needed to examine. The Reagan administration's refusal to remain under the jurisdiction of the World Court and international law was an unprecedented U.S. action. These issues required much more significant coverage by broadcast journalists than they received.

KRAUSE: *Vice-President Bush accuses the Democrats of being weak and naive.*
BUSH *(September 6, 1984): They voted to cut off aid to Nicaraguan freedom fighters. They don't even acknowledge that there is a threat from Marxist-Leninists down there. Now you can't see this, but there is a commemorative stamp from Nicaragua. That is the Communist Manifesto. These are stamps of Karl Marx. Ortega, the head of Marxist Nicaragua, says, "Without Marxism-Leninism there is no Sandinismo." If you walk like a duck and you quack like a duck and you say you're a duck, you're a duck. They are Marxist-Leninists. They're not liberals, as Mondale says.*

This brilliant polemic, "the duck analogy," will undoubtedly take its place among memorable political commentary in American history. But Bush's claim about Mondale calling the Sandinistas "liberals" was an untrue and irresponsible smear. It seemed in this report that the vice-presidential candidates were waging a contest in this regard. Also, is there any record of Bush or Reagan referring to Eden Pastora as a freedom fighter in 1979 when, as the Sandinista "Commandante Zero," he helped lead probably the most popular insurrection of the century in overthrowing the ghastly Somoza dictatorship?

Charles Krause concluded, "The outcome of this year's election in the United States will have a direct and important impact on what happens next in Central America. If Mondale is elected, he promises to remove all U.S. troops from Honduras, end U.S. support for the *contras*, and enter into serious negotiations with Nicaragua's revolutionary government. In El Salvador, Mondale would condition U.S. military aid to respect for human rights and would encourage a dialogue between the government and the guerrillas. If President Reagan is reelected, he would press Congress for a resumption of U.S. aid to the *contras*. He has also warned the Sandinistas not to introduce MIG jet fighter planes into Nicaragua as planned. Otherwise, the president is expected to continue what the administration now views as a successful policy in Central America."

Robert MacNeil and Jim Lehrer then interviewed Ambassador Otto Reich, the State Department's coordinator of public policy for Latin America and the Caribbean, and Congressman James Shannon, Democrat of Massachusetts.

MacNeil: *The neighboring states, the Contadora group, have drafted a peace treaty with United States encouragement. Now Nicaragua suddenly says that it will sign the treaty, and now the United States has reservations about that. Why is that Ambassador Reich?*
Reich: *Well, first of all, Nicaragua said two weeks ago that it would sign a draft treaty at that time without any further changes. We find it very interesting that they do not want the process to continue, a process that, by its own definition, hasn't finished. In fact, comments from the other members of Contadora are not due until next Monday, and yet Nicaragua felt, we believe for public relations purposes, that it had become so isolated internationally and had become so unpopular domestically that it had to try to take the public relations initiative and that's why it decided, we believe, to make that announcement. Now, the process is not finished, and we're not the only country, by the way, that has expressed reservations. As you know, a number of other countries have said that that process of Contadora is not yet complete.*

The comment about Nicaragua's isolation was most curious. The United States was considerably more isolated internationally in terms of its policy toward Nicaragua. Because of its increasingly antidemocratic actions, the Sandinista government was undoubtedly encountering growing opposition. But it was illusion to discount popular support for the Sandinistas after decades of the Somozas, broadly increased health care, literacy and nutrition, and the impact of the "Yankees" in effect invading the country once again. The same illusions had led to the Bay of Pigs.

MacNeil: *Congressman Shannon, what's your version of that?*
Shannon: *Well, I think it's this kind of doubletalk that makes me worried about the future, if we have another four years of a Reagan administration. We've been hearing the administration talk so much about this Contadora process and the fact that they were drafting a treaty. And they come up with a draft treaty which the Nicaraguans say that they will accept, and all of a sudden the United States backs off and tries to get our allies . . . in the region to reject that treaty. I think that this is an issue that has to be resolved by the people of Central America. The Contadora process is designed to bring about that kind of agreement. The United States, it seems to me, and the Reagan administration is serving as an obstacle to that kind of agreement.*

Shannon, unfortunately, does not pursue the obvious, which is explaining the motivation for the purported obstruction, just as Reich failed to explain what the United States required in the process beyond the draft treaty. These are situations where journalistic intervention should take place as a matter of course, otherwise the viewer will hear only sweeping generalities.

LEHRER: *Mr. Ambassador, how has the Reagan administration policy worked in Central America?*
REICH: *If you look at the situation today compared to what it was four years ago, you have to say that without the administration's policy, which, I have to admit, has been distorted in some of the statements by a lot of critics, as some of the tape we saw here a few minutes ago, which does not recognize, for example, the support for social and economic reforms [in El Salvador], some of the most radical economic reforms ever undertaken in this hemisphere. Without those policies, those reforms and the policies, the situation in Central America would be much worse, similar perhaps, to what it was four years ago.*

Reich later referred specifically to land reform, the most significant of the "radical" reforms he mentioned. In the first place, these reforms, as well as democratic elections, were initiated during the Carter administration. Second, land reform had been all but abandoned in a slow but steady process during the Reagan years. This was at the heart of the Salvadoran conflict, the Third World scourge of hungry, landless peasants that will be examined in later pages. As usual, this crucial factor was neglected in the increasing media optimism concerning El Salvador in 1985. The one major accomplishment was a dramatic decline in death-squad murders, although the Reagan administration had opposed the human rights and land reform progress stipulations to aid by Congress. George Bush had personally told Salvadoran military and business leaders that unless the human rights situation improved, it would be politically impossible to continue aid. At the same time, however, Roberto D'Aubisson, the extremist right-wing Salvadoran leader who had achieved power in part by lying to the peasants about supporting land reform, and widely believed to be involved with the death squads, was finally issued a U.S. visa with the help of Senator Jesse Helms, after being denied entry to the United States previously. This action sent an unsavory symbolic message. Only time would tell what the human rights situation in El Salvador would be over the long run. But the civil war was clearly escalating, with the rebels growing in strength and the army receiving increasing U.S. aid and training. The election of Duarte, a Christian Democrat who believed in reform and dialogue with the rebels, was perhaps Salvador's last thin hope. But all depended on what the military would allow, which depended in turn, to a significant extent, on U.S. policy. These were issues that should have been explored. One unfortunate aspect of the October 15 report on MacNeil/Lehrer was that even with its one-hour length, it tried to cover too much ground. This happened at other times as well. But journalistic intervention and focusing would make a tremendous difference, which in turn demands a first-rate research staff.

REICH: *Take the case of El Salvador. On Monday, President Duarte is scheduled to meet with the guerrillas of El Salvador. That probably would have been unheard of if he did not have the political legitimacy which has been provided for him by the free elections the country's had in the last four years, the international support that he's obtained—*
LEHRER: *In other words, your position is that the La Palma meeting grows directly out of Reagan administration foreign policy in Central America?*
REICH: *I'm saying that without the support of the administration for the political reforms, the elections, the improvement in human rights, the support that the government of El Salvador has received from the broad center of the population—the administration has helped to isolate the violent extremes in El Salvador. But without that this meeting may not have been possible.*
LEHRER: *Is he wrong, Congressman?*
SHANNON: *I think he's dead wrong. I think it's much more likely that the La Palma meeting is taking place because Duarte feels that after the election, at a less politically opportune moment, it'll be more difficult to get the Reagan administration to go along with such a meeting with the guerrillas. It's been clear for the last several years that they don't want these kinds of meetings to take place, and I think it's very courageous of President Duarte not only from the viewpoint of his own internal political situation, but from the viewpoint of dealing with the Reagan administration in the future should the president be reelected, to go ahead with this move.*

On the day Duarte's "move" was made, some of Shannon's remarks were given credence from a more objective source on "NBC Nightly News." After the opening story showing the emotional scene in La Palma, Tom Brokaw reported, "And publicly today the Reagan administration had high praise for the Salvador summit, but Marvin Kalb has learned the administration privately expects this war to continue.

KALB: *The president praised the meeting, his top aides portraying it as a vindication of his controversial policy in Central America.*
REAGAN: *President Duarte is participating at great personal risk. But it is a*

risk worth taking in the cause of peace; and the president has our prayers for success in this historic endeavor.

KALB: *When Secretary of State Schultz conferred with Duarte last week, they agreed there would be no power sharing of any kind, no deal before the rebels put down their guns and joined the electoral process—a prospect considered very remote.*

JOHN HUGHES *(State Department spokesman): President Duarte has made very clear the basis on which he goes into these discussions with them; and President Reagan has very vigorously endorsed that position, so there's no change in policy. . . .*

KALB: *Meaning, the administration still thinks a military solution is more likely in the short term than a political one. The Salvador military . . . is seen as getting stronger and doing better and, after the American election, able to take the offensive against the rebels and hit them badly if the talks fail to produce a breakthrough. And, Tom, no official I've talked to believes that a breakthrough is imminent, or even likely.*

BROKAW: *But, Marvin, why are we getting all this upbeat talk from the Reagan administration today?*

KALB: *Well, there's not really much conviction behind all that upbeat talk. There's no sense among many officials here that something truly historic is happening in Central America. Besides, it is very much in the political interest of the administration a few weeks before the presidential election to make it seem as if the president's very controversial policy in Central America is being seen as triumphant.*

BROKAW: *But Duarte has surprised the State Department in the past. Why don't they think there that something may, in fact, emerge from these talks?*

KALB: *Well, Tom, anything is possible. But it seems, from many of the conversations that I've had, that many officials in this administration believe that there can be no real compromise, no real negotiation with the Communists in Central America; in fact, that eventually, if not this year, then next year, the United States will have to use its muscle in that region and get rid of the problem.*

This last remark by Kalb was a shocker and begged the obvious question: Did using muscle mean the use of American forces? It was difficult to conclude otherwise. Although Kalb and NBC deserved credit for airing this report, it was outrageous to end it with such an inference and no followup. American forces trying to "get rid of the problem" in a Central American war? This would be no Grenada. Public opinion had consistently opposed such a move. This kind of information should not have been offered as a concluding one-liner, but as the jump-off point for more thorough reporting. It should have been the headline story, pursued vigorously and reported in all respects in terms of its implications.

As for the other networks, none of this crucial information was covered at all. Only the pictures of Duarte going to La Palma, the thousands of Salvadorans waving their white flags and begging for peace. And the pictures of Reagan, praising Duarte for his courage. But pictures are only images, which can mean many things. It's the story behind the picture that responsible journalism should tell.

Friday, October 19: Self-Fulfilling Prophecy

'Twas the day before the last debate, and all through the TV news, once more they would restate, the election was Reagan's to lose.

This was basically the theme on every network on this last broadcast evening before the final presidential debate between President Reagan and Walter Mondale. If there was to be any contesting of this election, Mondale would not only have to do very well, but Reagan would have to do quite badly, matching or surpassing his flop performance in Louisville. As Democratic analyst Alan Baron said on MacNeil/Lehrer, "Well, I think that Ronald Reagan's got to do it, or undo it, so to speak, and I would say the odds against that are fairly heavy."

On MacNeil/Lehrer, there was a brief examination of the one reason the election probably would have been Reagan's to lose under most any circumstances: the state of the economy. In an interview with correspondent Charlayne Hunter Gault, Wall Street analyst David Jones made the following comment: "The Republican National Committee could not have written a better script for this economy at least through the end of the year." But he went on to say, "It looks like the economy can continue at a 3 to 4 percent growth rate in the early part of next year, but as we move toward the latter part of the year we still have problems. For example, interest rates are still much too high to be sure that we can sustain growth. The federal deficit is much too large, and young couples have to compete effectively with the government when they want to go out and get a mortgage, particularly on these adjustable-rate mortgages. They're nose to nose with excessively heavy government borrowing. So we still have on the horizon, maybe late 1985 or 1986, some problems that could exist."

There seems little doubt that people's pocketbooks have come first over the years. But one of the great failures of television journalism and the media at large has been the lack of education provided in regard to economic issues. To be sure, there are few areas where more disagreement and unsuccessful prophesying can be found. However, there are basic facts and patterns from which the average voter can learn and be better positioned to demand real discussion from politicians as opposed to simplistic rhetoric. It is damning testimony that voters generally support a president, Republican or Democrat, if the economy happens to look good on election day, and otherwise throw him out, regardless of the actual effect of his policies on the functioning of the economy. It is a grossly shortsighted and simplistic practice. Television news reports tend generally to report simply that either the economy looks good, which is good for the current occupant of the White House, or the economy looks bad, which is bad for the current occupant of the White House. It is the same old image reinforcement instead of in-depth informational process.

Walter Mondale's only source of encouragement in this regard, other than the fact that historical precedents are made to be broken, was that there had been one exception to the good economy-bad economy rule of presidential elections in modern times. That was Gerald Ford's defeat by Jimmy Carter in 1976. This was predominantly because of the continuing aftershock of Watergate, and Ford's unpopular pardoning of Richard Nixon. In addition, Jimmy Carter waged a more skillful media campaign, particularly on television, and Ford managed to forget, in a nationally televised debate, that Poland was a Warsaw Pact nation. Still, Ford came close. Mondale's hope now rested entirely on the second and last debate with Reagan. He needed Reagan to confirm lingering fears about the nuclear arms race, and most important, he needed Reagan to pull a "Poland" and worse. Reagan needed to stumble badly, to add fuel to the fire of the age and competency questions raised by the first debate. This clearly should not have been the basis for deciding an election, but the media and video screens kept saying it was so, and therefore, it was.

The good news for Mondale was that there was even a slight hint of a question still present in the media projection of the election's outcome. On the "CBS Evening News," Dan Rather reported, "President Reagan and Walter Mondale put in more prep time today for their second and last side-by-side joint question-and-answer session, the presidential candidates forum in Kansas City this Sunday. The subject: defense and foreign policy. Object: a chance to score points, be perceived as winner of the match, and hope it will translate to winning on election day. [Yes, that is the object, since you've defined it that way, as a sporting event, with the lack of intelligence and civic-mindedness so characteristic of TV's shallow "journalism."] For the moment, the latest CBS News/*New York Times* poll out tonight indicates this: the twenty-six point lead the Reagan-Bush ticket had over the Mondale-Ferraro ticket earlier this month now may be whittled in half to thirteen points. Indications too, of a shift among voters under thirty. They still support President Reagan by a large margin, but not by the gaping gap the poll indicated earlier. The Reagan lead shrunk among men. The Reagan lead among women has shrunk. Mondale has gained in every region of the country, gained most in the South. [Considering the final outcome, this says a great deal about the impact of the first debate.] Still, the Reagan-Bush ticket leads in every region of the country and in every age group. Bruce Morton looks tonight at the foreign policy mood of Americans, found by the latest poll, as the nation prepares to watch this Sunday's clash of two candidates whose world views are worlds apart.

MORTON: *Ronald Reagan and Walter Mondale see the world very differently.*

REAGAN: *In the four years before we took office, country after country fell under the Soviet yoke. Since January 20, 1981, not one inch of soil has fallen to the Communists.*

MONDALE: *The four years of Ronald Reagan has made this world more dangerous. Four more will take us closer to the brink.*

MORTON: *But voters in today's* CBS/New York Times *poll thought the American situation in the world was better now than it was four years ago. . . . Nowhere are the differences between presidential candidates sharper than on arms control. Mr. Reagan stresses strength, Mr. Mondale, negotiations.*

REAGAN: *Weakness invites trouble and strength deters it.*

MONDALE: *My opponent has opposed every arms-control effort over the last twenty years.*

MORTON: *Our poll sample thought the United States should do more to reach arms-control agreements with Moscow. Mr. Mondale is for a bilateral verifiable freeze on nuclear weapons. Mr. Reagan opposes the freeze, saying it would leave the Soviets with arms superiority. The two candidates also disagree sharply over plans for antimissile weapons in space. The so-called "Star Wars" technology.*

MONDALE: *He has conducted an arms race on earth, and now he wants to extend it to the heavens.*

REAGAN: *Now, some are calling this "Star Wars." Well, I call it prudent policy and common sense.*

MORTON: *Both candidates would increase defense spending. Mr. Mondale by about 4 percent per year and Mr. Reagan by about 7 percent. Voters in our poll would keep the defense spending where it is. Both candidates are for the Trident II submarine, the Stealth bomber, and the mobile landbased Midgetman missile. Mr. Reagan is also for the B-1 bomber and the MX missile. Mr. Mondale is not. The president would continue aid to the antigovernment guerrillas in Nicaragua. Mr. Mondale would not. But Mondale has talked about quarantining Nicaragua without saying whose troops and ships would do that. On the Middle East, Mr. Mondale attacks what he calls poor security precautions in Beirut.*

MONDALE: *This time it is inexcusable. These terrorist threats were publicly known.*
MORTON: *Our sample agrees, the United States should have done more. The president talks about the hostages in Iran during the Carter administration.*
REAGAN: *After the hostages were taken in Iran, my opponent said it would be a temporary problem.*
MORTON: *But more than on specific issues, the debate is likely to turn on who seems knowledgeable and strong in foreign affairs. Mr. Mondale may label Mr. Reagan uninformed, reminding viewers that the president once said that submarine-launched ballistic missiles, once launched, could be recalled. They can't. Mr. Reagan is likely to say often, that with him in charge, America is standing tall again.*

Morton's concluding statement was the same old self-fulfilling prophecy, relegating "specific issues" to an invisible back seat. The report itself was one more example of everything wrong with TV news reporting on the campaign. It brought up important issues and trivialized them with one-liners from the candidates that raised nothing but questions. It would have been useful, for instance, to be illuminated as to which "country after country fell under the Soviet yoke" during the Carter-Mondale administration, according to Reagan. And how about some followup to the Mondale talk of quarantining Nicaragua: What exactly did he say? What would the consequences be? What is the point of bringing up issues without examining them? In addition, the characterization of the poll results made it impossible to understand exactly what those results were. What were the specific questions asked? This was shoddy journalism, and a common practice in these kinds of reports.

The most disconcerting fact, however, was the concentration, once more, on polls as the central story of the campaign. Given the "game," it was always good news to hear the "losing" side was making a "comeback," so that the "fans" would maintain enough interest to perhaps vote on election day. But the approach was shameful. Instead of reporting on what people think about the issues, broadcast journalists should be reporting about the issues, giving people something to think about.

But this assault by the image makers on the intellectual integrity of the nation was about to end, in terms of the 1984 presidential election campaign. For the "last hurrah" was at hand.

Monday, October 22: The Last Hurrah

Today, two weeks and a day before election day, the media officially declared the campaign over. The very declaration, hammered home on every TV news show following the second and final presidential debate on Sunday, and setting the tone for all the coverage for the remainder of the campaign, was itself undoubtedly a major contribution toward the "inevitable" Reagan victory. Further examination of this issue will come in the following chapter.

The Kansas City presidential debate on foreign policy was declared a draw by the media, which by television standards, it was. But as both TV and print journalists told us again and again, a draw was a victory for Ronald Reagan. As *Time* magazine headlined it, "A Tie Goes to the Gipper." This was true despite broad agreement that Walter Mondale had won the debate on points, because, as we had been told for days in advance by the media, Walter Mondale needed a "knockout" in order to have a chance in this election. And a knockout meant that Reagan had to drool or fall over from exhaustion during the debate. Since, instead, he improved his television demeanor compared to the Louisville disaster, the election was now declared over. We had come, in this TV-magnified and largely media-created expectation game, full circle, back to the pre-Louisville inevitability in which the nightly news had contextualized the Presidential Election Show since Labor Day, and before.

There was no question that President Reagan's performance was an improvement over the Louisville debate. His most effective moment was probably his comment in defusing the "age" issue, when he jokingly said that he would not make an issue of Mondale's "youth and inexperience." Walter Mondale, on the other hand, was not as effective as he had been in Louisville. First of all, he looked as if someone had carved circles under his eyes with a knife. Whether this was due to lighting, makeup, or lack of adequate rest before the debate, the comparison with his appearance during the first debate was striking and to his detriment. A Harris poll after the debate indicated that by a two-to-one margin, viewers thought Reagan looked better than Mondale. More important, Mondale seemed somewhat formal and tight, less spontaneous and aggressive than he had appeared earlier. He made the tactical error of being too concerned about tactics, of being too self-conscious, instead of simply being himself, as he had done so effectively in the first debate. As a result, he seemed to hold back at times, when his natural instinct might have been to go after Reagan more aggressively, which could have changed the entire tenor of the event. Reagan offered his jugular to Mondale several times, but Mondale's responses, although often to the point, seemed muted, as if he had memorized a game plan from which he would not stray. Objectively speaking, winning a debate on points should suffice. But Mondale knew in advance that this would not be enough, given the post-Louisville expectations of a TV-oriented campaign. He needed to make sparks fly, to unnerve Reagan through aggressive confrontation. Whether or not the game as defined by the media was either fair or good for democracy was not the point at this juncture. It was the only game in town.

The debate began with the newly publicized issue concerning the CIA manual for the *contras* in Nicaragua, which clearly indicated terrorist acts, including "neutralization," widely regarded as a euphemism for political assassination. Mondale was particularly effective on this issue, and at the beginning of the debate it appeared he might have Reagan on the run.

MONDALE: *This brings up the whole question of what presidential leadership is all about. I think the lesson in Central America, this recent embarrassment in Nicaragua where we are giving instructions for hired assassins, hiring criminals and the rest—all of this has strengthened our opponent. . . . Strength requires knowledge, command. We've seen in the Nicaraguan example a policy that has actually hurt us, strengthened our opposition and undermined the moral authority of our country in that region.*

REAGAN: *I have ordered an investigation; I know that the CIA is already going forward with one. We have a gentleman down in Nicaragua who is on contract to the CIA, advising, supposedly on military tactics, the* contras. *And he drew up this manual. It was turned over to the agency head of the CIA in Nicaragua to be printed, and a number of pages were excised by that agency head there, the man in charge, and he sent it on up here to the CIA, where more pages were excised before it was printed. But some way or other there were twelve of the original copies that got down there and were not submitted for this printing process by the CIA. . . . So I can only tell you, about the manual, that we're not in the habit of assigning guilt before there has been proper evidence produced in proof of that guilt; but if guilt is established, whoever is guilty, we will treat with that situation then and they will be removed.*

GEORGIE ANNE GEYER *(panelist)*: *Well, Mr. President, you are implying then that the CIA in Nicaragua is directing the* contras *there. I'd also like to ask whether having the CIA investigate its own manual in such a sensitive area is not sort of like sending the fox into the chicken coop a second time.*

REAGAN: *I'm afraid I misspoke when I said a CIA head in Nicaragua. There's not someone there directing all this activity. . . .*

In addition to this major blooper and subsequent embarrassing denial, a confirmation of the CIA "covert" role that everyone in the world was aware of, the following day Senate Intelligence Committee member Sam Nunn challenged the president's remarks on deletions from the manual, stating that though some deletions were made, the term "neutralization" was in all the documents. Reagan never answered Geyer's question about the "investigation."

Mondale responded, "What is a president charged with doing when he takes his oath of office? He raises his right hand and takes an . . . oath of office to take care, to faithfully execute, the laws of the land. Presidents can't know everything, but a president has to know those things that are essential to his leadership and the enforcement of our laws. This manual, several thousands of which were produced, was distributed, ordering political assassination, hiring of criminals, and other forms of terrorism. Some of it was excised, but the part dealing with political terrorism was continued."

The subject changed to U.S.-Soviet relations, and Reagan recaptured the high ground with his response to the following question from NBC correspondent Marvin Kalb: "Mr. President, you have often described the Soviet Union as a powerful evil empire intent on world domination. But this year you have said, and I quote, 'If they want to keep their Mickey Mouse system, that's okay with me.' Which is it, Mr. President? Do you want to contain them within their present borders and perhaps try to reestablish détente or what goes for détente, or do you really want to roll back their empire?"

Reagan responded, "I have said, on a number of occasions, exactly what I believe about the Soviet Union. I retract nothing that I have said. I believe that many of the things that they have done are evil in any concept of morality that we have. But I also recognize that, as the two great superpowers in the world, we have to live with each other. And I told Mr. Gromyko, we don't like their system. They don't like ours. And we're not gonna change their system and they sure better not try to change ours. But, between us, we can either destroy the world or we can save it. And I suggested that certainly it was to their common interest, along with ours, to avoid a conflict and to attempt to save the world and remove the nuclear weapons. And I think that perhaps we established a little better understanding."

This statement was, in the author's opinion, the first of two steps that insured Reagan's reelection. He went on to make the highly questionable assertion that the Soviets were engaged in the biggest military buildup in the history of the world. His own CIA report had shown that the Soviets were increasing defense spending at a considerably lower rate than the United States. He also engaged in an unfair smear by saying that Mondale had supported unilateral disarmament. Reagan had used the same tactic when referring to the nuclear freeze movement in the past. But TV journalists seldom pick up on statements like these and correct the record, so the president's very effective opening statement carried him through.

Marvin Kalb then turned his questioning to Mondale, who was also effective in responding.

KALB: *Mr. Mondale, you have described the Soviet leaders as, and I'm quoting, cynical, ruthless, and dangerous, suggesting an almost total lack of trust in them. In that case, what makes you think that the annual summit meetings with them that you've proposed will result in agreements that would satisfy the interests of this country?*

MONDALE: *Because the only type of agreements to reach with the Soviet Union are the types that are specifically defined, so we know exactly what they must do, subject to full verification. . . . I have no illusions about the Soviet Union leadership or the nature of that state. They are a tough and ruthless adversary, and we must be prepared to meet that challenge. And I would. Where I part with the president is that, despite all those differences, we must, as past presidents before this one have done, meet on the common ground of survival. And that's where the president has opposed practically every arms-control agreement by every president of both political parties since the bomb went off. And now he completes this term with no progress toward arms control at all, but with a very dangerous arms race under way instead. . . . There will be no unilateral disarmament under my administration. I will keep this nation strong. . . . To do that, a president must know what is essential to command and to leadership and to strength. And that's where the president's failure to master, in my opinion, the essential elements of arms control, has cost us dearly.*

In an interesting role reversal in terms of image, Reagan reaffirmed his proposal to share the Strategic Defense Initiative ("Star Wars") technology with the Soviets, and Mondale, who opposed the development of "Star Wars," said he "sharply" disagreed with the idea of sharing it with the Soviets. Reagan looked visionary, Mondale seemed to be going for political points. In fact, politics was involved in both cases. The impact of Reagan's Strategic Defense Initiative would likely have little to do with vision, and the "sharing it with the Soviets" line had an unrealistic ring to it. Mondale was obviously concerned with proving his toughness. In terms of image, Reagan got the better of it. Reagan followed by saying that he didn't know what the Strategic Defense Initiative would consist of in terms of weapons or where they would be deployed (even though the essence of the concept clearly would be a space-based system), and Mondale responded with one of his best lines of the night: "Well, that's what a president is supposed to know—where those weapons are going to be. If they're space weapons, I assume they'll be in space. If they're antisatellite weapons, I assume they're going to be armed against any satellite."

Mondale's answer on the nuclear freeze was less effective. He kept saying, under hard questioning, that only verifiable agreements would be signed. But he could have been more specific, saying that testing and deployment are readily verifiable and are certainly the most important aspects of the issue. Research and production present verification problems, but they are less important in terms of the intent of the freeze. He could have mentioned the many experts who, as former CIA director William Colby described it, believe the freeze is not "simplistic but simple" and an effective first step to halt the arms race. Mondale's own testing-moratorium proposal was the most important aspect of the freeze, but he never mentioned it in the debate, or the historical precedent set by President Kennedy.

During a discussion of immigration reform, Mondale made a complex point concerning the impact of the federal debt on interest rates, the ensuing difficulty Third World countries had servicing their debts, increased poverty, and therefore increased immigration pressure. Reagan smiled, either because he didn't understand it, or knew no one else would, and effectively responded that he'd heard the national debt blamed for a lot of things, but never immigration problems. Given the format of the debate and the nature of TV news coverage, Mondale attempted an impossible intellectual exercise and Reagan took advantage of it.

There was an extremely important and fascinating exchange over human rights and the support of "friendly dictators," which following chapters will examine at length.

For much of the debate there was a considerable amount of bantering back and forth on arms control, policy in Lebanon, and the marine and embassy bombings. Reagan did an effective job of avoiding specific answers to the questions raised by shaping his responses to fit his themes, even though he made several assertions that were misleading in terms of the facts. For instance, he claimed that the marines in Beirut had only defended themselves, when in fact, they had shelled Druze positions in support of the Lebanese government troops. But reading transcripts is an entirely different experience than video viewing.

When a question about his age was asked, Reagan gave the "performance" line of the evening: "I will not make age an issue in this campaign. I am not going to exploit for political purposes my opponent's youth and inexperience."

This line, delivered with the endearing Reagan smile, got the crowd response of the night, and even Mondale was forced to smile. From this moment, the tension and drama left the debate. Reagan would not drop the other shoe. The campaign was over. Mondale had opportunities to revive, particularly on the "Star Wars" issue, which will be examined at length shortly. But he seemed emotionally not quite up to par from this moment on. His conclusion was good, but lacked passion. Reagan's conclusion took the opposite tack from Louisville, eschewing facts for symbols, taking us on a rather strange and rambling ride down the coast of California. He was cut off before he finished, as he had exceeded his time limit.

The "CBS Morning News" convened the same panel of journalists featured after the first debate: Howell Raines (*New York Times*), Jack Nelson (*Los Angeles Times*), and Al Hunt (*Wall Street Journal*).

RAINES: *If you wanted to score this in factual debating points, I suppose you could say Walter Mondale won. But this was a political contest, and in political terms, President Reagan was the candidate who got what he had to have. What we saw in political terms was not so much Reagan versus Mondale as it was Reagan versus Father Time, and I think the president succeeded in confronting the age issue, and although he stumbled and faltered a few times, I think he probably put it behind him. . . . I was a little surprised that Walter Mondale did not try in a tactical sense to throw the president off balance more, because Walter Mondale had to have more than a draw.*

NELSON: *I think that one of the keys to Mr. Reagan's coming out as well as he did in this debate was that he was aggressive and he provided the only light moment [the "age" joke]. . . . Other than that, it was a sort of grim debate and lacked some of the spark of that first debate, and I don't think that helped Mr. Mondale any.*

HUNT: *I don't think Reagan did nearly as well as has just been suggested. I think some people whose views are much closer to Reagan's than Mondale's, such as former Undersecretary of State Joseph Cisco, were saying after the debate that Mondale won. Reagan did start out with a series of gaffes . . . on missiles and CIA involvement in Nicaragua, he seemed to visibly tire at the end, and I thought for Reagan his closing statement was very very weak. But Reagan—I suppose Howell's right—is running against time, or age, and compared with that very mediocre performance in Louisville, he did much better last night, especially in the middle, where he was sharp and crisp and attacking Mondale's defense record, and he came up with that marvelous, I'm sure carefully scripted, but nonetheless very effective answer on the question of age, where he said he would not make an issue of Mondale's youth and inexperience.*

On NBC's "Today," the nightly news crew of Tom Brokaw, John Chancellor, and Roger Mudd shared their thoughts.

BROKAW: *I think that he [Mondale] did have to have a knockout last night, to use that boxer's term that we've been using throughout this campaign [Yes, you have, but why?], that he had to have the kind of night that he did in Louisville. [Yes, because you kept saying so.] I thought Walter Mondale did very well last night, but the president did a lot better than he did in Louisville, obviously, and I think that that probably checked any erosion he had going on in this country.*

CHANCELLOR: *You know this is the only contest in America where they change the score after the game is over. And you'll have to wait and see what the reaction is in the public, and that depends a great deal on what television does and what clips from the debate are shown today, tonight, and tomorrow on television programs. So, I'm not certain how it's going to come out, although I don't think Mondale knocked anybody out last night.*

MUDD: *I think really that Reagan did well enough last night, that the issue is no longer his ability to debate the fine points on a live television show. I think the debate still is his record over the last four years. [In which case, why don't you cover it in detail on the nightly news?] I think that the stakes were so high last night that neither candidate wanted to swing from the floor and try for a knockout punch for fear of missing and falling on his face. So, therefore, they were a little more cautious.*

CHANCELLOR: *I tend to agree. I think also that both of them, having watched the tapes of the Louisville debate, backed off a little bit from too many facts and figures. I think they were talking themes and policies more than they were specific responses to one another. I also found them not very responsive to each other last night.*

BROKAW: *I think the difference between last night and Louisville is that in Louisville, you kind of saw the president coming apart before your eyes, and that added to a lot of the tension that evening. . . . Last night, it was curious that he [Reagan] did what he often does [then why was it curious?]: He goes back to, if you will, a story out of his past or a fable or an anecdote of some kind. It was that amiable Ronald Reagan. I do think that there may be lurking in the minds of some people after these two performances the question of whether or not he is healthy and strong enough to lead on a day-to-day basis . . . the question that Henry Trewhitt raised last night: "What would you do in a crisis, would you be able to see it through?" Because at the end of ninety minutes of debate last night he didn't seem to have the energy that he had at the beginning, and therefore, we saw that summation that was kind of wandering.*

MUDD: *You know, if Reagan wins, and I think that everybody sort of thinks that he probably will win [a somewhat humorous example of contorted hedging], there are those two videotapes left for the world to see, and you've got a president for the next four years, who in a public forum, doesn't do very well with his command of facts and subjects. [This last statement by Mudd would seem to contradict, at least in part, his initial observations.]*

On the "CBS Evening News," Dan Rather began the coverage with these words: "The defense and foreign policy forum of the presidential candidates, the day after. First question: Who won? First, though not necessarily last, or lasting perceptions of a CBS News/*New York Times* poll overnight indicate this: Ronald Reagan and Walter Mondale may have battled to a draw. So far, the poll indicates no big winner or loser has been perceived in last night's contest. Also, no indication that many minds may have been changed." On ABC's "World News Tonight," Peter Jennings began in much the same vein: "This evening, the political debates, as we now know, have a way of continuing when the candidates get off television. President Reagan and Mr. Mondale have certainly kept theirs going today. Mr. Reagan said he felt good about the debate last night in Kansas City. Mr. Mondale said he'd been the winner and predicted he would pick up more support in the remaining two weeks before the election. Our own ABC News poll showed that *you* [my emphasis] thought Mr. Reagan had done slightly better, but 25 percent of the people we talked to thought it was a tie."

ABC's Sam Donaldson reported, "Age. The president seemed to sweep away that issue last night with a joke." A clip of Reagan's clever remark about not making Mondale's youth a campaign issue was then shown, including the audience responding with laughter.

DONALDSON: *But no one was laughing with the question of competency, with Mondale accusing Mr. Reagan of saying erroneously that submarine-based missiles once launched could be recalled, and the president insisting indignantly that only the submarines themselves could be recalled, a dispute that continued today full force.*
REAGAN: *How . . . any reasonable human being could think that you could turn a missile around and bring it home, I think that that shows a lack of intelligence on their part if they believe that.*
REPORTER: *But that's what you said.*
REAGAN: *No, I didn't.*
DONALDSON: *This is what the president said at a May 1982 press conference. He pointed out that land-based missiles could not be recalled, then went on to other missiles.*
REAGAN: *Those that are carried in bombers, those that are carried in ships of one kind or another, or submersibles, you are dealing there with a conventional type of weapon or instrument, and those instruments can be intercepted, they can be recalled if there has been a miscalculation. And so they don't have the same, I think, effect that the presence of those other ones that, once launched, that's it. [Clearly the president's only defense, which he declined to take, was that what he said was not what he meant. The use of the world* conventional *seems to indicate this possibility.]*
DONALDSON: *This afternoon it was bombers, not submarines, on the president's mind as he toured the Rockwell B-1 bomber plant in California and hit at Mondale's pledge to kill the B-1.*

REAGAN: *If it were up to my opponent, I'm afraid Rockwell might still be building the B-25. That is, if he were building anything at all.*
DONALDSON: *And later at a rally in San Diego:*
REAGAN: *My opponent, Mr. Mondale, offers a government of pessimism, fear, and limits, compared to ours of hope, confidence, and growth.*
DONALDSON: *The confidence of the president's managers has clearly been restored. They believe Mr. Reagan passed the test of age and vitality last night in Kansas City. And though Mondale will be able to narrow the gap, he will not be able to close it.*

Britt Hume then covered Mondale's day, beginning, "Maybe Walter Mondale didn't get the big lift last night he got from the Louisville debate, but the word from the Mondale camp today was that he got something just as good: new ammunition to fire at the president." (Wishful thinking, given the style of media coverage.)

MONDALE: *In one sense, he [Reagan] didn't do as poorly as he did last time, but on the central questions of command, of knowledge, of taking responsibility, I think he did worse.*
HUME: *Yes, Mondale aides acknowledged, the lighting or something had made their man look haggard. And, no, he hadn't shown the ease and humor of his Louisville performance. But the president, they said, had falsely denied his own words about recalling missiles, blamed others for trouble in Lebanon and Central America, and shown ignorance about his proposed "Star Wars" space weapons plan.*
REAGAN *(from the debate): I never suggested where the weapons should be or what kind. I'm not a scientist.*
MONDALE *(from the debate): Well, that's what a president's supposed to know —where those weapons are going to be. If they're space weapons, I assume they'll be in space.*
HUME: *On the stump today in Philadelphia, Mondale had a new speech full of that new ammunition.*
MONDALE: *Last night we got into the "Star Wars" question. And what did he say? First, he said he didn't know where these weapons would be located. Second, he came up with the idea of demonstration shots of "Star Wars"—he wants to call the Soviets in for a little nuclear skeet shooting. Last night, the American people saw with their own eyes what the problem is. They saw a president who cannot discuss any major issue without making a major mistake.*
HUME: *Mondale's closing arguments in this contest will rest heavily on the record of the debates, which he thinks is full of evidence the president is a weak leader who doesn't know his stuff. Mr. Reagan will rely more on the record of the last four years, which one way or another have brought no*

wars and a strong economic recovery. The outcome, it seems, will depend on which way the voters find more compelling. [That might have been true, if the voters had encountered the opportunity through television news to truly examine the record.]

The network reports were all similar, attempting balance by reporting both Reagan's one-liner coup on the "age" issue, as well as some of his shakier moments on issues, particularly the question of recalling launched missiles. But the psychological bottom line of the reports, as with other examples already seen, is illustrated by the following.

BRUCE MORTON (CBS): *Candidates and staffs and just plain fans will argue for the next couple of days over just who did just how well here. But Walter Mondale probably needed to leave with a big win, and most people think he didn't get one.*
SUSAN SPENCER (CBS): *He [Mondale] is trailing virtually everywhere, and he has just two weeks.*
DAVID GERGEN (MacNeil/Lehrer): *Reagan sealed his victory.*

As to the debate itself, in keeping with tradition, TV news coverage managed to almost entirely avoid that most dreaded and boring of subjects, the issues.

All the networks mentioned some issues raised in the debates, *slightly* more so than after the first debate, as witnessed by the above ABC reports. The president's "missile recall" misstatements were universally covered. CBS reported on the State Department's scramble to back off from Reagan's statement limiting the U.S. policy choice in the Philippines to either supporting dictator Ferdinand Marcos or seeing the country go Communist, and also covered the president's misstatements concerning the CIA manual's use of the word *neutralize*. MacNeil/Lehrer offered a discussion on "Star Wars" between Mondale adviser Richard Leone and Reagan campaign manager Ed Rollins. Some of these issues, and others raised in the debate, along with a closer look at the implications of what was and was not covered by TV news, will be examined in greater detail in the following pages. But the commercial network reports were woefully inadequate in covering the important issues raised in this debate. And although Reagan made himself much more vulnerable than Mondale on issues, this didn't explain why the network's only references to issues were related to Reagan gaffes. Mondale's rather garbled explanation of the possibility of quarantining Nicaragua under the terms of the Rio Pact, for instance, raised many questions. But most important, both candidates staked out different positions on problems deserving in-depth coverage.

Nothing resembling this occurred. Even MacNeil/Lehrer was less issue oriented than usual.

And the implications of perhaps the most significant policy statement made by a president of the United States in the nuclear era seemed to be missed by everyone, with the exception of the journalist who asked the pertinent question during the debate, Henry Trewhitt, diplomatic correspondent for the *Baltimore Sun.*

In the last question before the summations, Trewhitt asked, "Mr. President, could I take you back to something you said earlier? And if I'm misquoting you, please correct me. But I understood you to say that if the development of space military technology was successful, you might give the Soviets a demonstration and say, 'Here it is,' which sounds to me as if you might be trying to gain the sort of advantage that would enable you to dictate terms, and which I would then suggest to you might mean scrapping a generation of nuclear strategy called mutual deterrence, in which we in effect hold each other hostage. Is that your intention?"

Reagan responded, "Well, I can't say that I have round-tabled that and sat down with the chiefs of staff, but I have said that it seems to me that this could be a logical step in what is my ultimate goal, my ultimate dream. And that, the elimination of nuclear weapons in the world. And it seems to me that this could be an adjunct, or certainly a great assisting agent in getting this done. I am not going to roll over, as Mr. Mondale suggests, and give them something that could turn around and be used against us. But I think it's a very interesting proposal to see if we can find first of all something that renders those weapons obsolete, incapable of their mission. But Mr. Mondale seems to approve MAD—MAD is Mutual Assured Destruction, meaning if you use nuclear weapons on us, the only thing we have to keep you from doing it is that we'll kill as many people of yours as as you will kill of ours. I think that to do everything we can to find, as I say, something that would destroy weapons and not humans is a great step forward in human rights."

One had to hear the disbelief in Henry Trewhitt's voice when he asked Reagan if he really meant to imply "scrapping a generation of nuclear strategy called nuclear deterrence" to fully comprehend the degree to which Trewhitt understood the importance of his question. Reagan, in effect, answered yes, that was exactly what he meant to do, which should have made headlines indefinitely. The print media, and MacNeil/Lehrer to some degree, picked up some of the many questions raised by this Reagan response, but not even the likes of *Time* magazine's Strobe Talbott responded to the larger issue raised by Trewhitt's question. Talbott, although quoted by Mondale in the debate, has opposed the nuclear freeze and supported the deployment of Pershing and Cruise missiles in Europe, and is one of the most informed mainstream arms-control experts in the country. Along with virtually everyone else in the field, he has expressed concern regarding the Reagan administration's radical departure from the arms-control policies of every other president since World War II, Republican and Democrat alike. Writing about the debate (*Time*, 29 October 1984), Talbott pointed out, "One extremely contentious issue concerns Star Wars, the President's grandiose scheme for erecting a comprehensive defensive umbrella over the U.S. The twin dangers in the plan, as Mondale pointed out, are (a) that it won't work and (b) that it will provoke Soviet countermeasures, both in offensive and defensive weaponry, and thus a double helix in the arms race. On what could become the single most important and controversial national security issue of the next year and even the next decade, Reagan provided, in one throwaway line Sunday night, a disturbing hint of his inclinations: he said he wanted to develop a space-based missile killer in order to prove to the Soviets the U.S. had such a thing. Then, said the President, 'we'll give 'em a demonstration.'

Besides the fact that even the Reagan State Department, as Talbott further points out, interpets such a course as meaning the violation and abrogation of a number of arms-control treaties, the bottom line, indicated in Henry Trewhitt's question, is much more significant: the jettisoning, unilaterally, by the United States of the strategic understanding with the Soviets, called mutual deterrence, a corollary of which is the doctrine of Mutual Assured Destruction (MAD), upon which the entire arms-control concept has been built, and both nuclear and conventional war avoided. The point of MAD is that neither the United States nor Soviets would start a war because it would mean the total destruction of both nations and, indeed, very possibly all life on the planet (as opposed to the tamer-sounding equivalent killing on both sides that Reagan described in his answer). It was, and is, not so much a conscious strategy as a recognition of reality in the nuclear world. A related military doctrine has been the targeting of cities, and both sides have military target strategies as well, which developed in recent years into theoretical flirtation with the concept of limited nuclear war. An escalation would seem difficult, if not impossible to avoid. And the newly publicized scientific findings on a nuclear winter indicate that Mother Nature will keep MAD intact in an even more threatening sense as long as there are nuclear arsenals on the planet. The conscious element in this "doctrine" has been the mutual U.S.-Soviet understanding that an essential balance of strategic capability is required to insure a mutual-deterrent effect. The purpose of arms control has been largely to maintain this balance, at more stable and lower levels of weapons than would otherwise be the case. The next step, theoretically, would be agreements to reduce the number of weapons substantially and prevent the development of new and more dangerous ones, all within the context of deterrence. No one is comfortable with deterrence, particularly at present armament levels, which is one of the driving forces behind the nuclear freeze movement. But for either the United States or the Soviets to unilaterally abandon the concept in favor of a strategy of winning a nuclear conflict (whether by offensive or defensive means is of no significance) is a potential prescription for World War III, by design or accident.

If the "Star Wars" system was viable and about to be deployed, the pressure on the Soviets to launch a first strike would be incalculable. It should be kept in mind that many of the most strident defenders of "Star Wars" also insist that Soviet military doctrine includes the option of a first strike. The alternative would be the "double helix" arms race described by Talbott, creating greater instability and the increased likelihood of miscalculation or malfunction as we move farther into the technological maze. And, of course, even the most strident defenders of "Star Wars" admit it would probably be 90 percent effective at best, allowing enough Soviet missiles through at present arms levels to incinerate the United States and probably ecologically destroy the planet, which obviously means that the system has no value in terms of the president's "dream." And the Soviets would obviously greatly escalate missile production and deployment in the face of such a defense. Even if one's imagination could be stretched to envisioning a strategic defense 100 percent foolproof, the accomplishment would surely be fleeting. It takes no more than a functioning mind to know that in the real world there will be no permanent technical advantages to insure survival from nuclear weapons or whatever new means of mass destruction are created in the future. These concerns, though utilized in part by Mondale politically, went beyond partisanship and were shared by many Republicans and other supporters of the president, as well as American allies in Europe. It would have been a much more useful contribution to the national discussion and debate if the Reagan administration had made the case for the Strategic Defense Initiative wihtout selling pie-in-the-sky illusion. The argument would more intelligently have been made on the basis of honestly describing "Star Wars" as an effort to temporarily establish a leg up on the Soviets, with the purpose of creating political advantages for the United States, and a potential bargaining chip for nuclear arms reduction. Another issue never mentioned in the debate or explored by the media was Soviet research along "Star Wars" lines. After the election, the administration would assert that the Soviets were outspending and perhaps ahead of us in this arena. Yet outside observers, including most "Star Wars" supporters, considered the United States technologically superior in this field, as in others (although the Soviets had a history of catching up fast). If the Soviets really were first out of the blocks in a serious commitment to "Star

Wars," or ahead of us in any way in this area, it seems obvious that the president would have used this as the primary rationale for going forward with his Strategic Defense Initiative. But nothing of the sort was heard during the debate or the campaign. None of these issues were examined on the commercial networks.

But most important, the unilateral abandonment of the strategy of mutual deterrence would, by itself, create a vacuum dangerous beyond overstatement, as Henry Trewhitt clearly understood. For this reason, no American president, at least publicly, had ever indicated even the possibility that deterrence would be abandoned. Indeed, President Reagan had justified his military buildup in the name of deterrence. Furthermore, administration officials for the previous two years, including, prominently, Defense Secretary Caspar Weinberger and Reagan's negotiator with the Soviets on Strategic Arms Reduction Talks (START), General Edward Rowney, had publicly defended the strategy of mutual deterrence and its successful record of avoiding war, stating (arguably) that the nuclear freeze would weaken this strategy. Of course, behind the scenes, beginning during the Carter administration, a partial departure from MAD had begun, with strategic options for more "limited" nuclear war being explored. This dangerous fantasizing about limited nuclear war was at first given more credence under Reagan, and even talk of winnable nuclear was was heard, until the nuclear freeze movement and general public anxiety forced the administration to at least publicly reject such notions. But all this was small potatoes compared to the implications of the president's "Star Wars" speech in 1983, which thanks to Henry Trewhitt's question, became more clearly defined during the debate in Kansas City. Without, unfortunately, stating it more directly, Strobe Talbott seemed to indicate an understanding of the significance of Reagan's position by inference when he declared that his debate statements had initiated "what could become the single most important and controversial national security issue of the next year and even the next decade."

During the debate, Reagan effectively turned Trewhitt's question around by using the acronym for deterrence, MAD, and suggesting that this approach was "mad" (thereby contradicting many previous policy statements of his own administration). Mutual Assured Destruction doesn't have a very pleasant ring to it (which is exactly the point), and Reagan both sugarcoated and belied the actual impact of his proposed radical policy changes by saying, "Something that would destroy weapons and not humans is a great step forward in human rights."

If Reagan had thought there was any chance television news would follow up in depth on this issue, he might have approached it differently. As it was, Mondale seemed to respond defensively when Trewhitt asked him if he believed in MAD, saying he believed in a "sensible arms-control approach. . . . And in the meantime we have to be strong enough to make certain that the Soviet Union never attempts this." He went on to describe, fairly effectively, the serious questions raised by Reagan's approach to arms control and "Star Wars," but he had lost a much more significant opportunity. This was a perfect example of the candidate having his destiny in his own hands, in spite of the media handicaps. If Mondale had turned to Reagan and said, "You just made the most incredible statement an American president has made in the postwar era, and here's why," he almost certainly could have shaken Reagan, and at the least he would have started a real discussion and debate in the media.

It was beyond understanding that the story was missed in any event, except as one more indication, a most jarring one, of the shallowness of TV news reporting, and much of the print media as well. But TV is where the audience is, as Peter Teeley, George Bush's press secretary, made clear in a statement after the Bush-Ferraro debate. *Time* (5 November 1984) quoted him as saying, "You can say anything you want during a debate and 80 million people hear it [and if the press focuses on a mistake] . . . so what? Maybe 200 people read it, or 2,000 or 20,000." He was obviously referring to the print media. Only TV news can point out with real impact a mistake made in a televised debate. Teeley's obvious inference is that the candidates live under no great fear that such an eventuality will come to pass.

George Will made some rather curious remarks on ABC the night after the Kansas City debate, reflecting on all three debates of this campaign: "It may be possible that all these debates diminish our estimation of all our leaders for the following reasons. We do not have a political culture that places a great stress on rhetorical gifts. Therefore, when they get up and they're not talking as they do on television [news] in what we call, rather indicatively, thirty-or forty-second sound bites, when they're asked to talk for longer than that, they somehow, all of them I think, lose stature."

Find the logic here, if you can, but apparently the American public is supposed to ask nothing more of its presidential and vice-presidential candidates than a few seconds of one-liners on the TV news in order to save them a loss of "stature." What an ingenious formula for encouraging quality leadership and promoting an informed citizenry. In addition, Will was dead wrong. The only possible example of a candidate losing stature in the debates was President Reagan in Louisville, which he largely made up for in Kansas City, in terms of image. Walter Mondale enhanced his stature greatly in Louisville by demonstrating how much more engaging he was than the evening news "thirty- or forty-second sound bites" had ever shown. George Bush, under enormous pressure to prevent any further damage after Reagan's performance in Louisville, successfully displayed his debating ability. And most significant historically, Geraldine Ferraro demonstrated, to those in need of conclusive evidence, that a woman was intellectually and emotionally capable of being vice-president, and by inference, president.

Peter Jennings asked George Will, "Haven't they [the debates] given people an opportunity at least to concentrate on the issues, despite what you said?" Will responded, "Well, they have concentrated on the issues a bit, but what have they [the public] heard that they haven't heard more effectively and coherently presented throughout the campaign?"

Apparently George Will needs to spend a bit more time on the other side of the TV screen. Where and when does he suppose this effective and coherent presentation of issues occurred, and through what medium was it communicated to the public? He would have done well to listen to his ABC colleague, Sander Vanocur, moderator of the Ferraro-Bush debate, who was interviewed this same night on CNN's "Election Watch." Vanocur said he thought the debates "had some real substance. . . . I think it's better than the snippets we offer up—whether CNN or the three commercial networks."

CHAPTER FIVE

After the Election: Looking Back, Looking Forward

The snippets offered up on the nightly news from the day after the final presidential debate to election day had one basic message: The only remaining question about this election was how big Reagan's winning margin would be. Mondale was given credit for campaigning bravely and well, but his obviously heartfelt message urging an America of "compassion over selfishness" couldn't be heard above the ever-rising background noise of the coming landslide being predicted on the nightly news. The Reagan camp was so confident that the president was pulled off the campaign trail for a couple of days.

Howell Raines wrote in the *New York Times*, the Sunday before the election, "Some commentators insist that opinion polls and the dominance of television have conspired to make this election a footnote to a process that has already declared Mr. Reagan a winner. But *no one* [my emphasis] who has spent a lot of time talking to voters is likely to buy such arguments. . . . Often, the choice can have as much to do with *feelings* [my emphasis] and with emerging demographic trends as with *issues*" [my emphasis].

What are *feelings* based on in an age of TV *images*, where *issues* are only lightly touched on? One is not required to be an expert of any kind to determine the answer to that question. But for those of us who have worked in the film and video media, from advertising to public affairs, the answer comes from experience as well as simple logic. And as far as the "no one" remark is concerned, many "commentators," as the reader has seen, who have spent a great deal of time talking to voters, and/or who have some expertise on the impact of television, have arrived at very different conclusions, for reasons evidenced in these pages. The evidence weighs heavily against Raines's comment, and the logic of his own wording, as demonstrated above, can be used to refute his conclusion. Even more telling are the final words of the same article: "The nation may well have seen the last contest in which a major party will nominate a candidate like Mr. Mondale, with self-acknowledged faults as a television candidate." This statement was in keeping with the same observation Raines had made in other articles, that television had been utilized as never before by the Reagan campaign to create a whole new style of electioneering, which would make campaigns based on issues a relic of the past. One cannot describe the impact of television on the electoral process on one line and then deny its impact on another. As noted in the opening chapter of this book, Raines had a tendency on this subject to make rather contradictory observations. Ironically, in a separate article by Raines, also in the *New York Times* on the Sunday preceding the election, he gives the most telling evidence of the impact of television on the campaign process and the electorate that one could possibly find, through, in effect, objective scientific method. A Reagan campaign official (not named) was quoted as saying, "By being off the road for a couple of days, we were also off the *evening news.* That began to show (in the polls). Now he's [Reagan's] back on the road, and we're beginning to climb."

On Saturday, November 3, on CNN's "Election Watch," Carl Leubsdorf, reporter for the *Dallas Morning News*, observed, "Mondale has tried to work various issues and there's been no response from President Reagan, except in the debates—it's been the only time there's been a real dialogue between the two campaigns. The Reagan White House has totally ignored what Mondale is saying. If you ask what they're going to do in the second term, about all you've gotten out of this Republican campaign is, 'You ain't seen nothing yet.' " *Washington Post* reporter Martin Schram, a journalist who had not only talked with voters throughout the campaign, but had watched election-related television with them as well, responded, "You know why I really think this [Mondale's attempt to raise issues] doesn't cut in the end, I think it's because of this medium, largely, that we're doing right now. I watched the past week's worth of television all at once, all the political coverage from all the networks, and in presenting the news, it really *pushes* the news. Every standup virtually on every network would start off with:—'Mondale hopelessly behind, no chance to come up'. . . and say what the latest poll showed."

In this context, it was perplexing, to say the least, to read Hugh Sidey's description (*Time* 19 November 1984) of "the network commentators, gamely trying to disguise their preference for Mondale." Which commentators? ABC's George Will, who made no effort to conceal his support of

Reagan? NBC's John Chancellor, if a Mondale supporter, was more than "gamely trying," in fact, was quite successful. CBS's Bill Moyers, seldom heard from, might have fit the bill. No one on MacNeil/Lehrer qualified. And CNN's large number of commentators were fairly evenly balanced, with possibly a conservative tilt. Perhaps Sidey meant to include the anchors and reporters, in which case his grounds become, if possible, even shakier. But he misses the essential point, in any event. Whether the TV journalists are conservative or liberal is obviously not a significant factor when the horse race is the focus of coverage. If it was a factor, the argument that there was a pro-Reagan bias could be much more easily defended than Sidey's premise, for TV coverage from the start focused on the Mondale campaign as a hopeless cause, and the Reagan campaign as a perfectly run and invincible juggernaut. Periodic criticism of the image-over-substance approach didn't alter these fundamental messages. Issues were discussed secondarily, briefly, and ineffectually. Sidey's own disdain for the "issues" was apparent in his attempt to define them as the exclusive domain of "the group of inbred Democrats who have controlled the thought and mechanics of official Washington for so long," defining "issues" as "encyclopedic knowledge of programs and laws." Such a narrow definition would offend most Democrats, Republicans, independents, and indeed thinking people. Is Sidey truly unaware of the degree to which many of Ronald Reagan's supporters are "issue" oriented? Does he not understand the concept of issues in a stage of evolution preceding "programs and laws," or is he merely accusing this "elite" group of missing such a distinction? He goes on to say that this "group of inbred Democrats" who are concerned about "issues" (and his article makes clear by inference that this "group" is representative of "a sizable segment of the pundits, academics and campaign theorists, as well as the press") has "limited sensitivity to the intangibles of leadership, like boldness and enthusiasm, that cannot be written into bills and dropped in a legislative hopper." It would seem that "leadership," not "issues," is his concern, as he gives us no positive example, from his perspective, of how issues might be defined in a manner worth discussion. As was pointed out in the opening chapter, the separation of leadership and intellectual ability contributes to less capable leadership.

But given his emphasis on the intangibles of leadership over the specifics of issues, Sidey should have noticed that television news hardly concentrated on anything except the "images" of leadership, and given "credit" where it was due. In addition, he scolds the print media by quoting James Reston, who wrote, "Not since the days of H. L. Mencken have so many reporters written so much or so well about the shortcomings of the President and influenced so few voters." Accepting this statement as fact, for the sake of argument, intellectual integrity would demand from the open-eyed the balancing acknowledgment that the same could be said of Walter Mondale's treatment by much of the press, with more effective impact on the voters. But the main game in media is TV. And when Sidey says that the "media heavyweights were . . . wrong . . . [and] out of touch," referring to the above Reston quote, one can only reply that he is not concentrating on the real heavyweights, and to the degree that he does include the TV networks (without giving a scrap of evidence), he is the one who is clearly out of touch. He not only overlooks or misunderstands the actual impact of the TV news approach, but seems to indicate that Mondale should have been the beneficiary, except the voters weren't buying the message. Apparently he did not watch the various network evening news programs throughout the campaign to any significant degree.

Finally, Sidey claims that for years "voters had been praised and pumped up by overpaid TV commentators and underpaid instructors of political science as the most informed and best educated and therefore the wisest electorate in the world." Examples of both this position and its opposite have always been available from both conservative and liberal perspectives, but a somewhat less extreme view is more commonly found among both TV commentators and academics, in my experience. To hear such views as described by Sidey coming from TV commentators would be difficult to stomach (as would any complaints regarding a lack of voter wisdom, which Sidey implies is the new position of the "commentators" due to Ronald Reagan's success with the voters), not because of their political views, which, unlike Sidey's stereotype, vary from commentator to commentator, but because of the abysmal job television does informing the electorate. There is some additional ironic humor to be found in the title of this article, "When the Elite Loses Touch." As any reader of Sidey knows, his column, "The Presidency," has long since allowed him to carve out his niche in the upper echelons of the media "elite." Sidey is often an engaging writer, but in this article he misses entirely the essence of media coverage of the 1984 campaign, coming across himself as a partisan elitist, expressing one ideological version of the mythology of the monolithic press.

In his "Newswatch" column (*Time*, 12 November 1984), Thomas Griffith also argued that the press had lost its influence in the 1984 presidential campaign, not because the public was paying no attention to its supposed "views," but for exactly the opposite reason, because it had become a timid "echo" of public opinion. "If it has been an unsatisfactory election campaign," writes Griffith, "with issues sloganized more than argued, the melancholy state of affairs says something about the decline of the power of the press. It has been much less effective this time as the self-appointed monitor of political campaigns, stirring up the issues, keeping each side honest and the facts straight . . . the Reagan Administration had effec-

tively excluded the press. The President stopped holding press conferences that might embarrass him; so did George Bush. But outcries from
the press against such high-handedness were muted by the discovery that
the public seemed not much concerned. It is this constant sensitivity to
public reactions—endemic in an institution now all too often corporately
managed rather than run by opinionated old press lords—that mocks the
idea of an all-powerful media." Griffith makes legitimate points, but he
seems to miss the larger impact of his observations. The media can be
timid and shallow and extremely powerful all at once. Scrambling to
reflect the majority attitudes, ignoring important issues, guarantees a
vicious circle of ignorance. The media may be increasingly abandoning the
traditional role of the press, but this does not diminish its powerful
impact, in this case clearly negative.

The real media elitism in the 1984 campaign, particularly in television,
was the continuing assumption, in effect, that the American people
wanted only to be entertained in the fashion of the Roman masses at the
games, and that political coverage should therefore not venture too far
from the *People* magazine approach. A corollary to this has been the
assumption that the public either (a) already is fully informed on the issues
(from what source, God knows), or (b) is too stupid or apathetic (certainly
not inherently, but perhaps functionally, thanks to mindless media coverage) or both to benefit from an in-depth, issue-oriented approach to
reporting. Although to an entirely different purpose, Hugh Sidey referred
in his article to a George Orwell quote that is applicable here: "One has to
belong to the intelligentsia to believe things like that: no ordinary man
could be such a fool."

People become conditioned to expect what they get. That expectation
clearly has not added to participation in the democratic process quantitatively. The effect on the quality of participation, and indeed the quality of
our political leadership, cannot be truly tested until television journalism
is radically altered to emphasize information on issues as even-handedly as
humanly possible. Specific recommendations in regard to such an
approach are forthcoming. My belief is that, given the opportunity, realistically assuming that the transition will be difficult, the American people
will ultimately respond to a new definition of television journalism as to
water in the desert.

The alternative is not a promising one, as it will be more of the same.
As columnist Tom Wicker pointed out on election night on ABC, the 1984
election had seen the "full flowering" of TV in presidential election politics: "Television has become *the* instrument that dominates our national
politics, and that's true, I think, beyond parties and beyond *issues*."
Wicker later said that the first thing the Democratic party must do to
become competitive in the next presidential election is to find a "televi-

sion candidate." Barbara Walters responded that this sounded "so cynical." Wicker replied that it wasn't cynicism, it was reality.

On ABC's "This Week with David Brinkley" the Sunday preceding the election, George Will stated that the effect of exit polling and network projections in terms of influencing voter turnout on election day was insignificant compared to the "depressant" effect of news coverage constantly emphasizing the polls throughout the campaign. This was a rare instance of hearing a reference on television to the potential negative impact on voter registration and turnout of the media's obsession with polls. And in terms of those who do vote, in an impressive moment of candor for a pollster, Barry Sussman, director of polling for the *Washington Post*, wrote (*Washington Post* National Weekly Edition, 12 November 1984): ". . . poll findings that show large numbers of Democrats or young people supporting Reagan could well prompt other Democrats and young people to vote for Reagan when they otherwise would not. That would be only one way in which polls might have an effect on the election. There are others." Although a May 1985 *Washington Post*—ABC News poll indicated that pre-election polls had little impact, even this scientifically limited survey showed Reagan gaining half a million votes through the poll's influence. A study by University of Alabama political science professor William Kimmelman showed that in the South, black turnout was only 41 percent compared to a 62 percent white turnout, in part because "voters may have been discouraged by the Democrats' seemingly impossible job of ousting President Reagan" (Scripps-Howard News Service, 10 February 1985).

But the most significant problem was pointed out on election eve on CBS's "Nightwatch" by University of Virginia political science professor Larry Sabato: "You know, when you look at the amount of time and effort we're spending on polling in the campaign process, it's obvious that something's getting squeezed out, and what's getting squeezed out is discussion of policy issues. There's only so much time on the evening news every evening to devote to politics. More so this year than ever before, more time has been devoted to horse race, who's ahead, who's behind, who's gaining—well, that doesn't matter, *what matters is where the candidates stand on the issues.*"

In the *Washington Post* National Weekly Edition (5 November 1984), a Herblock cartoon showed a distraught man, rising from his chair in front of the TV, opening the door to a campaign worker holding in her hand a reminder to "Vote November 6." He looks at it and says, "You mean after all those primaries and polls and scoring of debates, there's going to be an election too?"

The Presidential Election Show in 1984 was a flop by any standard of journalistic integrity. It was in fact a "show" and hardly journalism at all.

It was almost certainly a negative influence in terms of participatory democracy, which neither the nation nor the planet can afford at this juncture in history. These comments apply particularly to CBS, ABC, NBC, and CNN (which was not covered in this book, but which during its prime-time evening news programs was essentially indistinguishable from the others). "The MacNeil/Lehrer NewsHour" was in a league apart, far superior in some ways, but also sharing some of the defects of the commercial network programs. And it must also be stated plainly that to a significant degree, the print media demonstrated many of the same failings of television. But television is where the real action is in terms of audience, and by definition of the characteristics of the medium, its impact is unique. The following summation of the failures of television coverage of the presidential campaign illustrate a format and approach that must be radically altered if television is to rescue its honor and its right to apply the term "journalism" to its news programming.

Theodore White, in his book *America in Search of Itself*, noted that the weekend before election day in 1980 was the one-year anniversary of the Iranian hostage crisis, and all the networks aired special reports, reminding the electorate of the Americans still held captive by the Iranians. Throughout the weekend, the constant images of impotence and humiliation flooded America's TV screens. What had been a close race turned to a route, the polls showing major movement toward Reagan in the forty-eight hours before the polls opened. By running its nightly update on "America Held Hostage" (the forerunner of "Nightline"), ABC was perhaps the single greatest influence in the defeat of Jimmy Carter. The operative words here are *image* and *repetition*. By creating an image and repeating it over and over again, television has an immeasurable impact. The Iranian hostage crisis was certainly not the single most important issue before this country every day for over a year, but the image created by television made it seem so, which, politically, made it so. ABC News didn't care whether or not it was good journalism, because it was a good "show," bringing good ratings and good money. ABC's "Nightline" has been highly touted as a showcase example of how TV and good journalism can come together, but isn't this a classic case of "compared to what?" Listen to Ted Koppel announce, "This is 'Nightline'" every evening as if he were announcing the Second Coming and then ask whether showmanship or journalism is the primary concern of this kind of programming. Examine the format, and notice the often seemingly conscious attempt to create fireworks between adversaries in brief "interviews," rather than contribute to some real understanding of a subject by narrowing it, following a logical progression of thought, and expanding the discussion if necessary over concurrent nights. The stories are often worthwhile, but too often they are absurd, as on the opening day of the campaign. In March, 1985, Koppel and "Nightline" gave the consummate demonstration of what broadcast journalism *could* accomplish with the extraordinary programs from South Africa. With Koppel's talents unleashed on the same story for an entire week, a truly informative process took place. But why was this approach never utilized to cover issues during the presidential election campaign? And how often did "Nightline" cover campaign-related stories? Wouldn't one expect at least half of the reports between Labor Day and election day to do so? Divide by four and you will be closer. And when there were election-related stories, they seldom concentrated in depth on issues. This was also true of the weekly CBS election report with Dan Rather, which was not much more than a weekly recap of the evening news highlights. The greatest contribution by CBS's "60 Minutes" to democracy during the campaign (September 16, 1984) was by Andy Rooney in one of his supposedly folksy, wise, humorous comments. He informed us "that the presidential election is too long. If it was a television show it would be canceled after four weeks." He neglected to observe that it was a television show, a very bad one precisely because of the shallowness of the video-noninformation pushers such as himself. In a stunning display of his intellectual depth and commitment to democracy, he told us that everyone knew how the vote would turn out, so we should get it over with. NBC didn't even bother with special programming, which was just as well, all things considered. CNN's various programs, although sometimes filled with interesting observations from diverse perspectives, did not cover issues in depth. The network and PBS weekend programs mentioned in the introduction to this book all had the tendency of TV news programming as a whole, which was to deal with issues only in terms of their strategic impact (according to the commentators, polls, etc.) on the campaign. MacNeil/Lehrer, because of both its one-hour length and format, was the only program that even approached the kind of in-depth study of issues that journalistic integrity should demand.

Every night on the nightly news programs, image and repetition was the operative approach. Ronald Reagan was the Great Communicator and his reelection was inevitable. Walter Mondale was "boring" and his challenge was impossible. To think that the constant repetition of these images does not have an enormous impact on the electorate would be to have one's head in the sand. This cannot be confirmed by a poll, of course. How can one ask the conscious mind how the unconscious mind has been affected by such a bombardment? The first thing TV news must do is examine its descriptive language, its assumptions, its preoccupation with strategy and polls. Was Ronald Reagan such a great communicator during the debates, or anytime without a prepared script and proper staging? Was Walter Mondale that bad on TV, or not bad at all when the commentators and evening news editors got out of the way, as during the first debate? How many times during the year was the volatility of the polls demonstrated? So why keep talking about them, analyzing them, worshiping them, reinforcing them, and so on? After the first debate, Reagan's own polls showed Mondale picking up ten points in a week, a momentum, if continued, that would have resulted in a Mondale landslide! What caused this and the other wild swings after the Democratic Convention and after the second debate? As we have seen, TV images had much to do with it in all cases. It is a vicious circle. It is impossible to decipher precisely the entanglements of this TV-image, repetitious, poll-taking, poll-reporting monster that feeds on itself. But it is easy to recommend what to do with this entire intellectually empty approach: Throw it into the junkyard of video political history. We don't need the media labels pinned on the candidates for us, defining for us who they are. We don't need to be told again and again who will win the political "superbowl," or the statistics that prove by reinforcing until fact. Concentrate on the issues and let the American people do the rest.

Investigative journalism has a time-honored niche in press coverage of politics, and the contradictions and failures in this regard in 1984 are difficult to fathom. They all revolve around Geraldine Ferraro. The media tore her apart on the questions surrounding her family finances, which she initiated by her own mistakes, then handled admirably by her accessibility to the press and success in alleviating any suspicion of real wrongdoing. But the toll on the Mondale-Ferraro campaign was perhaps, in hindsight, fatal, which gives added weight to the following. NBC reported, on September 21, that the Reagan campaign was behind the Washington Legal Foundation's suit brought before the House Ethics Committee concerning Ferraro, as part of a larger effort to discredit her. The "undercover operation," in which the Reagan campaign denied involvement, also included criticism by conservative Catholic bishops and heckling of Ferraro by antiabortion demonstrators. The sources were top Republicans involved in the campaign, independently corroborated a few days later by Dr. John Wolkee, president of the National Right-to-Life Committee. ABC and the *Wall Street Journal* had related reports within the same week. Then the story disappeared altogether for the remainder of the campaign. This series of events has caused the author bewilderment beyond adequate description.

On December 5, 1984, C-SPAN aired a forum on the media and the campaign at the American University. Lyn Nofziger, Reagan-Bush campaign consultant, made several interesting comments. He began by acknowledging that it was difficult after carrying forty-nine of fifty states in the election to find anything to complain about in terms of media coverage. Nonetheless, he had a short list, and a strange one. He brought up the heckling of the Mondale-Ferraro campaign and alleged Reagan-Bush campaign involvement as an example of one-sided reporting. In view of the facts of this reporting as reviewed in these pages, this was an incredibly brash statement, and raised again the real question: What happened to the journalistic followup on that story? This was the man who refused to comment to NBC when the story was first reported, and now he was saying, unchallenged, that the media coverage of this story, which had subsequently been dropped, had been one-sided! Nofziger then delivered an even stranger criticism of the media, an intellectual lapse that seemed difficult to comprehend. He noted that, after the first debate, the TV network and other media commentators did not declare Reagan's performance a disaster until a day later. This, he asserted, was evidence that the media commentators were trying to influence voters and he credited them with success, stating that he had never seen public opinion change so fast. (This was a telling indication of how worried the Reagan campaign was after the first debate, at least momentarily.) The obvious logical question was how did Nofziger conclude that the media delay in pronouncing a verdict indicated attempted voter influencing? It would seem obvious that, if that was the intent, there would have been no delay. And there was the additional evidence, available to him and everyone else who watched TV the night of the debate or read a newspaper the following morning, of the original media hesitation to declare a definitive winner. Another member of the panel, Jim Lehrer of "The McNeil/Lehrer News-Hour," set the record straight on this bizarre Nofziger comment. In fact, Lehrer stated, the media had bent over backward trying to be evenhanded immediately following the debate, even though it was apparent to everyone that it was a Reagan disaster, which explained why, as Nofziger had pointed out, the media took an extra day to come in with a verdict. In reality, the media had followed public opinion, not led it; the network nightly news programs and then the newspapers described the debate as a clear Mondale win and Reagan loss only *after* the polls confirmed this was the opinion of the viewers. If anything, it was an example of media timidity, particularly that of television news, which covered the event live. Lehrer described watching the event with partisans of both camps, and by the latter part of the debate they were all looking at each other in disbelief, with everyone acknowledging the obvious, that it was a shocking debacle for Reagan. Yet when they went on the air for postdebate analysis, everyone resumed their professional role, and in effect went through a facade instead of expressing what they had mutually experienced.

Given his choice of "complaints" about media coverage, it almost seemed as if Nofziger was looking for stinking corpses to bring to the inaugural ball. He was to be credited, however, for his forthrightness about the Reagan campaign's using the media, particularly television. He stated clearly that the function of the campaign apparatus was not to please the press, but to win the election. He was absolutely correct. It is the responsibility of the press, primarily television, not to allow itself to be used, to establish a context in which imagery is difficult to pull off and substance hard to avoid.

A major failure of TV and the media at large during this campaign was the extraordinarily weak response to the Reagan campaign's unprecedented shutting out of the press. There were periodic strenuous objections, but nothing compared to what was called for under the circumstances. TV continued to provide the Reagan campaign a forum for its image strategy on the nightly news. Instead, the dangerous precedent being set by the undemocratic treatment of the press by the Reagan campaign should have been the lead story nightly, covered at length, until the president became regularly accessible to press questioning.

For a further description of atrocities committed by TV against the American electorate, consider these words by *Newsday* media critic Tom Collins (*Los Angeles Times* Syndicate; *Seattle Times*, 19 November 1984): "Other candidates have tried to use TV as a propaganda instrument, but none with Reagan's success. He was the first to impose total control over his campaign appearances, with the result that they had the verisimilitude of commercials. And with their balloons and music and colorful backdrops, along with careful crowd selection and the neutralization of the press, his campaign stops were superior to commercials because they had the verisimilitude of reality . . . so he [Reagan] changed the rules and the role of the media in a campaign. There was no obligation to explain anything, not so long as the balloons were working . . . What we have witnessed in modified form was the application of totalitarian principles of propaganda to the furthest extent possible in a nontotalitarian country. And as Reagan himself has often said: 'You ain't seen nothin' yet.' "

Television did not have to cooperate. One solution would be to turn off the cameras and issue verbal reports of the candidate's "day," then move on to cover the issues that were or were not being discussed. The candidates could be offered all the time on camera they wished, as long as it was an interview or press conference. To the degree that campaign appearances are stage-managed, the camera can be a powerful tool for behind-the-scenes expose' instead of the medium for delivering the center-stage polished act. Shortly before the election, PBS's "Frontline" series aired a superb two-hour documentary on Gary Hart's primary campaign. It made clear that the candidates not only try to manipulate TV, but are indeed slaves to the nightly news, their entire campaign schedules built around these programs. A segment of the documentary showed the advance team "setting up" a scene where Hart would meet with a group of farmers and other local people in a sort of minirally. The scene was ludicrous, people being moved around like cattle, all to create a few seconds on the nightly news of "spontaneity" and "political passion." It is a business of grotesque lies, and TV makes it all possible, even necessary from the candidate's perspective. To eliminate this theatrical nonsense, to demonstrate the basics of journalistic integrity, all television news has to do is turn the cameras on the preparations and skip the stage-managed sham.

In Suzanne Garment's "Capital Chronicle" column in the *Wall Street Journal*, (28 September 1984), she reported on the conservative viewpoint on partisan bias in TV news reporting during the election campaign up to that point. She wrote that Michael Robinson, a political scientist at George Washington University and the American Enterprise Institute, and his associate Maura Clancey had been "tracking" network coverage and had found "just about no liberal bias in network coverage." (This "tracker" would agree, adding that there was little conservative bias, in a direct partisan sense, to be found either. However, there can be no doubt as to which partisans were left smiling by the impact of the TV news approach in this campaign.) Garment's article continued, "Far more striking than simple partisanship are other qualities he [Robinson] finds in network campaign news. It is overwhelmingly negative and almost invariably suggests that our political system is bad or getting worse . . . [My experience has not been so much hearing this on network reports, as seeing the networks create such an outcome by their journalistic irresponsibility, which Garment, reporting Robinson's findings, accurately describes in the following.] . . . It treats the leading candidate as cynically manipulative, the trailing candidate as an incompetent. It likes to deal with 'horse race' issues, those concerned with technical campaign strategy, rather than policy issues."

In the December/January 1985 edition of the American Enterprise Institute's magazine, *Public Opinion*, Robinson and Clancey reported their findings in full. Their methods of measurement in a study presented as if scientific were referred to but revealed only in part. In a distinctly different tone from that expressed in the *Wall Street Journal* article, they concluded that Reagan-Bush had received considerably worse press coverage by NBC, CBS, and ABC than Mondale-Ferraro, thereby giving cannon fodder to the conservative audience they were writing for. Robinson and Clancey are not right-wing zealots, however, as they take issue with the view of Senator Jesse Helms and others that network television news has a liberal bias. They argued in the *Public Opinion* article that the results of their study were not a function of liberal bias but of other factors, such as the natural tendency of the press to be harder on the incumbent, citing the fact that in 1980, Jimmy Carter fared much worse than Ronald Reagan. They had a point here, but their conclusion that

Mondale-Ferraro got the better of TV news coverage in 1984 is incomprehensible. Interestingly, when one sifts through the "facts" offered in this study and adds what is missing, a quite different interpretation emerges.

At the outset, Robinson and Clancey state that there may be some questions about the validity of their measure, but there can be no question about the "lopsidedness" of their results. Having been thus alerted that logic has been thrown to the wind proves useful in the attempt to decipher this "study." First of all, a finding reported, but not emphasized, should have been the headline. Robinson and Clancey found that 74 percent of the campaign stories on network TV news had no clear bias, or "spin" as they called it. While acknowledging that their analysis was based only on the remaining 26 percent, the tone of the entire study and stated conclusions are expressed in terms implying the totality of TV news reporting on the campaign. In addition, it becomes clear that these statistics are based on limited, and to a large degree, undisclosed criteria. It would have been useful to examine a variety of stories in detail, to determine how their conclusions were arrived at.

Robinson and Clancey divided the stories they analyzed into two categories: *campaign* issues, as opposed to *policy* issues, and *horse race*. The highest ranking in the campaign issues category was given to the Beirut bombing, which was covered as a campaign issue seventeen times according to this study, with particular focus on Reagan's comments blaming the bombing on former President Carter and his comparison of the security lapse to an unfinished kitchen remodeling job. Aside from the fact that Reagan so clearly brought this on himself, it would be interesting to discern how the campaign and policy aspects of this issue were separated. The same applies to the CIA assassination manual story, which the study says was covered eleven times as a campaign issue. Another top-billed campaign issue, according to the study, was George Bush's attempt to define the word shame from several dictionaries, which even Robinson and Clancey called "feeble." Only one of the top ten was a bad news story for the Democrats, which was the controversy surrounding Ferraro and the Catholic Church over abortion. The question occurs, where are the numerous references to Mondale as boring, ineffective as a communicator, or lacking in leadership qualities factored in? Also omitted was the tidal wave of media coverage before Labor Day on the Ferraro-Zaccaro financial controversy, the Bert Lance fiasco, and Mondale's problems with Jesse Jackson. And oddly, though the article mentions the Reagan-Gromyko meeting as an example of favorable press for Reagan, and the networks ran several stories before and after the event, it does not make the study's top twenty stories list, even though some on the list had only three related reports. In any event, some examples given of Reagan's "bad press" included NBC's John Chancellor blaming Reagan for the security lapses in Lebanon, CBS's Bob Simon's report on the failure of Reagan's Lebanon policy, and ABC's George Will complaining about Reagan's injection of religion into politics. (It would be interesting to know when this occurred, as Will's first commentary on religion and politics was nondescript and would hardly qualify.) Also mentioned were ABC's Sam Donaldson, CBS's Leslie Stahl, and NBC's Chris Wallace for stories on Reagan's TV-image-over-substance campaign strategy.

In addition to the fact that Robinson and Clancey admit that this *was* Reagan's strategy, and state that none of the above reporting was inaccurate or irresponsible, this brings up one of the most important missing elements in this study, the factor which overwhelmed these reporter comments and which was so central to the entire TV news impact on the campaign. In notes at the conclusion of the text, Robinson and Clancey inform us that they have excluded the "performance" of the candidates on camera from their analysis, claiming their emphasis was on "journalism," as opposed to the comprehensive "message." It does not take a professional to realize that the impact of video cannot be measured in out-of-context parts, but must be looked at as a whole. And to define broadcast journalism as separate from the choices of what the camera shows; what events, visual background, and one-liners by the candidates are chosen to be aired, is quite obviously, to miss the heart of the matter.

Turning to horse race coverage, Robinson and Clancey state that compared with past campaigns, this type of reporting was secondary in 1984 to stories on campaign issues (again, as opposed to policy issues.) Based on the fleeting glance given to examples in the article, it seems probable that some of the stories categorized as concentrating on *campaign* issues would just as appropriately have been labeled *policy* issues or *horse race* reports, depending upon whether a policy issue or strategy impact was emphasized. Indeed, the very distinction between campaign and policy issues implies that the former is emphasizing not substance, but impact on the horse race. At the least, this kind of categorization is a highly ambiguous area. And since the study addresses *stories* as the measurable category, the question is raised as to how segments and comments within stories were addressed, such as horse race comments within campaign issue stories, of which there were countless examples. The answer apparently is that these factors were not considered. Robinson and Clancey state that in what they call the "spin variable," their term for measuring a reporter's positive or negative comments, tone and gestures in campaign stories, they have "excluded" all references to the horse race.

Surprisingly, even in terms of the reports this study analyzes, the graphs shown in the article contradict the text, as they show considerably more time spent on horse race stories than on campaign issue stories. This makes the following conclusion even more perplexing than it already is on its face. For while acknowledging that Mondale-Ferraro came out solidly on the negative end of the horse race reporting, Robinson and Clancey state that in something called the "cosmic index," an unexplained methodology for taking both kinds of reporting analyzed into consideration, Reagan-Bush still come out with more than twice as much negative press as Mondale-Ferraro. This index is aptly named, as the manner in which this curious conclusion is reached is as mysterious as the cosmos itself. Of course, speaking of mysteries, leaving out the visual aspect of TV news reporting in terms of candidate performance, production, and editing choices, as well as horse race comments by reporters, no doubt assisted in making this leap of the imagination. But even within the context of the "evidence" offered, the mystery goes unsolved. Because the graphs *in the study* indicate the opposite of the so-called cosmic index finding. They show Regan-Bush with slightly more negative TV news time, but also with significantly more positive time percentage-wise, faring better than Mondale-Ferraro overall. This more closely coincides with reality. It is no easy task to imagine how someone could watch TV news reporting throughout the campaign and fail to see how broadcast journalism allowed itself to be successfully utilized by the Reagan campaign or the network nightly news role in contextualizing the election as a sports contest, and the probable impact of these realities on the viewers. To read instead, in the second part of the Robinson and Clancey report, analysis of how and why the electorate had opted overwhelmingly for Reagan in spite of media bias *against* his campaign, was an almost halucinatory experience.

Besides the stupifying internal contradictions and lack of information as to methodology, this study was lacking in at least three basic ways. First, no study of the media and politics dare call itself such when from the outset the impact of video image—production choices ranging from what is covered to camera work to editing—in terms of presenting the "performance" of candidates, is ignored and artificially separated from other journalistic choices. Second, the qualitative and quantitative difference between many different campaign issue stories and the constantly reinforced horse race themes of the unbeatable Reagan-Bush campaign and the hopeless Mondale-Ferraro campaign is overlooked or unrecognized. In terms of reporter comments, the horse race emphasis is consciously excluded. And finally, mimicking the TV news programs supposedly being studied, the reporting, or lack of, on *policy* issues, and the impact on the campaign and the democratic process, is not remarked upon at all.

In the Garment article, Robinson and Clancey observed that TV news treated the leading candidate (Reagan) as "cynically manipulative" and the trailing candidate (Mondale) as "incompetent." This was in many cases an accurate observation. But it should be pointed out that when people are given a choice between the image of "cynically manipulative" or "incompetent," as unpleasant as the choice may be, logic rules out the latter. Thus, even in the negative images game, Reagan came out the winner. And more importantly, in reports measured in seconds on the nightly news, the visual images and well-delivered, catchy one-liners by the candidate, simply outweighed any one line critique by the reporter. The reports are so fast, with the reporter attempting to cram so much into them, the circuits of the viewer are overloaded, and he or she learns not to give much credence to narratives that constantly raise more questions than give answers. For the viewer it is a somewhat irritating blur. In the author's opinion, the shallowness of the nightly news format causes the viewer to "turn off" the reporter on one level, retaining only the visual images, and to some degree, the words of the candidate. If the images and the reporter's words are not contradictory, the narrative will have impact. Thus when Mondale and Ferraro were shown being heckled at "real" campaign appearances, or when the turnout at the factory is poor because the candidate arrives too late, or the microphones don't work, and so on, and the reporter says that this candidacy has no real chance, it does double damage to that campaign. But when the images of Reagan singing "God Bless America" at the Grand Ole Opry with revered country musicians, a hand picked adoring crowd, and visual background "made in Hollywood," are challenged by the reporter calling this "stage-managed," the reporter is discounted. This is a logical reaction. Why, the viewer might ask, if unconsciously, is the image being shown on the "news" if it is really just a commercial, as the reporter's narrative sometimes implies?

In addition, if the image is powerful enough, it will be more convincing than the reporter's words. Writing in the *New York Times* magazine ("The President and the Press: The Art of Controlled Access," 14 October 1984) the Time's chief White House correspondent Stephen Weisman noted: "The Reagan aides have learned very well how to take advantage of media opportunities. 'TV has changed everything so much,' Mr. Deaver (Reagan aide Michael Deaver) commented. 'The visual image becomes all important.' He offered an example: A presidential announcement about housing. 'It's a lot better,' Mr. Deaver said, 'to have the president stand at a construction site so you can see him.' Then, even if the President's remarks are summed up by a broadcaster, the footage of the President in the background will show his concern. 'You need that visual to get something across,' Mr. Deaver said." Consider this observation by Al Hunt, writing about the impact of television (*Wall Street Journal*, "Politics 84," 2 November 1984): "Even a tough CBS report seemed drowned out by the marvelous visuals the Reagan campaign produces." In the previously quoted Tom Collins article, Collins referred to "comments by a Reagan campaign official that it did not matter what television correspondents reported; the only thing that counted was the positive pictures." Former White House press secretary Jody Powell summed it up best (*Los Angeles Times* Syndicate; *Seattle Times*, 21 November 1984): "The President's men had a plan, and they were open and unapologetic about what they were up to. They spent an unprecedented amount of time on both long-range strategy and short-term tactics necessary to get what they wanted on the evening news each day. Their approach was to make the boss, as one of his strategists later described it, '*visible but not vulnerable.*' Shield him from cross-examination while presenting him in an astounding array of skillfully staged scenarios that are irresistible to the cameras."

The "visible but not vulnerable" strategy cannot succeed without the cooperation of TV news. And the ultimate casualty in all this, as we have seen, is the discussion of issues.

George Will wrote in *Newsweek* (19 November 1984): "The Democrats' thesis is that Reagan's victory was 'merely personal'—whatever that means. Presumably the voters stood with their hands hovering over their ballots and thought: 'Mondale is right on the issues. Reagan is going to impoverish me and then incinerate me. But, shucks, he is sweet and will do it sincerely.'" Of course, the soothing supposition on the part of some Democrats that Reagan's victory was "merely personal" is nonsense. Of course, people vote on the fundamental issues that affect them, *to the degree they understand them* and, just as important, to the degree they are informed concerning the *relationship of the candidates' positions and records* to these issues. Will had already demonstrated his sense of commitment to the notion of the people deserving a serious discussion of issues by his comments after the final presidential debate: that the candidates should be spared, for the sake of their "stature," anything more strenuous than their few seconds of exposure on the nightly news. Words befitting a "royalist manifesto."

It is not meant to be implied here that, had the issues been truly the centerpiece of the campaign, Walter Mondale would necessarily have been the beneficiary. Such a campaign dynamic would have changed the approach of both candidates, but particularly of Ronald Reagan, who otherwise would have encountered serious difficulty. As pollster Barry Sussman noted (*Washington Post* National Weekly Edition, 7 January 1985), the public was moving away from Reagan on key issues. It seems likely that a truly issue-oriented campaign, in terms of TV news emphasis, would have resulted in a very close election. As the incumbent with a good economy on his side, Reagan still would certainly have had the advantage. And he may well have surprised those who believe he was not capable of running a campaign on specific issues. But it would have demanded a radical change of style in terms of staking out specific positions and accurately defending his record. Mondale, although already far more specific than Reagan, would also have been forced to acknowledge the hard choices as opposed to just attempting to make political hay on certain issues. A campaign that had involved serious in-depth discussion of policy choices would have had unpredictable results, with the nation making a truly informed choice, regardless of the outcome. As the post-election confusion over what Reagan's "mandate" represented illustrates, there are important reasons in a democracy for the serious debate of policy issues being the essence of our presidential campaigns.

In 1984, we did not get the "ideological election" that columnists Richard Reeves, David Broder, and others had predicted: a real national debate as to whether to continue the conservative "Reagan revolution" or to preserve, at least to some degree, the liberal-activist approach to government. Throughout his political career and right up to a few months before the election, Ronald Reagan's most famous battle cry had been: "Government is not the solution to our problems. Government is the problem." And yet, as David Broder pointed out (*Washington Post National Weekly Edition*, 26 November 1984), ". . . When the campaign began in earnest, that kind of wholehearted anti-Washington rhetoric was toned down. Reagan got kind of squishy soft on government. His favorite sources switched from Calvin Coolidge and Friedrich von Hayek to Franklin D. Roosevelt, the inventor of Big Government, and John F. Kennedy, the exponent of energetic governmental intervention." In addition, Reagan bent over backwards to defend the sacredness of Social Security, adopted (in effect) the deficit-spending, economic-stimulus theories with an impact far surpassing the policies he had always damned the Democrats for in the past, and came on like a champion of nuclear arms control during the campaign. So what was the mandate for?

One thing the mandate seemed to be for was to not raise taxes. One of the great ironies of the campaign, as David Broder pointed out in the above article, was that "Walter F. Mondale helped blunt the edge of the 'sharp choice' election by offering his tax-increase proposal, not as a straightforward necessity for financing the welfare state but for the traditionally conservative purpose of reducing the federal deficit. Even then, Reagan used it as a way to whip middle-class voters back into line." And for good political reason, as George Will accurately pointed out in the *Newsweek* article previously referred to. He stated, with obvious jesting pointedness, that should the Democrats have found the perfect media candidate, such as Robert Redford, Walter Cronkite, or Lawrence Olivier, "put him on a podium in San Francisco and have him say in the most polished way, 'Mr. Reagan will raise taxes. So will I. He won't tell you. I just did.' The nation will say: 'That handsome fellow sure talks well.' Then the nation will give that fellow's opponent about forty-nine states."

The impact of television in terms of image is too powerful, in ways already examined, to accept this statement by Will as an absolute. But to the degree that it is true, it serves as a potent example of television's greatest failing, and how deep this failure runs. Walter Mondale made what will inevitably turn out to be an accurate observation in his acceptance speech in San Francisco. Anyone who thought taxes wouldn't be raised, under whatever guise, before the end of Reagan's second term, should at least have been aware of the various consequences, all terrifying, of such an outcome. The necessity for increased taxes was well documented by conservative economist Martin Feldstein, former chairman of the Council of Economic Advisors in the Reagan adminstration (he was finally hounded out for persistently telling the truth). But it was the kiss of death for Mondale to simply state the obvious. It was a major political plus for Reagan to promise pie-in-the-sky economic miracles that many politicians in his own party were disturbed by. This was possible because the economy was robust and the inclination of people unless faced with a crisis they can feel here and now is to prefer believing in fairy tales. The problem with such an approach historically is that the price ultimately paid is so much more horrendous than it needs to be. The single greatest failing of the media in general, and television in particular, has been the lack of continuing education on policy issues for the public, to enable citizens to discern the fact that both self-interest and the national interest depend on seeing beyond the end of one's nose. Ironically, the chickens began coming home to roost with remarkable speed immediately following the election. Within days of the end of the campaign, economic indicators pointed to a slowdown in the economy, and the administration announced that deficit projections for fiscal 1985 had "suddenly" grown by almost $30 billion, to a record $210 billion or more.

Richard Reeves reported in his syndicated column (*Seattle Times*, 25 February 1985) that Walter Mondale, in his first commentary on the campaign since the day after the election, had told an AFL-CIO meeting that TV image caused his defeat. "What a fool," wrote Reeves of Mondale. Echoing George Will, Reeves stated, "Americans judged Reagan not as a performer but as president, and they decided, on balance, that he deserved another term. They didn't want Mondale or what he stood for. . . . Politics, in the end, is about ideas. Even if Mondale had looked like Redford and sounded like Cronkite last year, he would still be unemployed this year." Just as Reeves had been dead wrong in predicting an "ideological election" at the beginning of the campaign, he was dead wrong in this facile and unsubstantiated postelection analysis. He showed himself to be the fool, not Mondale. One of the ironies that Reeves failed to ponder or comment on was the fact that public opinion polls showed a majority of Americans in agreement with more of what Mondale "stood for" than what Reagan did. But Reagan campaigned on the basis of those polls, often sounding liberal themes, to the degree he sounded any, as has already been pointed out (and as Reeves himself noted in his revision of the ideological election forecast in the *New York Times* magazine, 4 November 1984). Television provided the medium for this "performance" and broadcast journalism fell on its face in terms of providing a credibility check. Like a handful of other observers quoted here, Reeves assumed that the American people were thoroughly informed on the issues, the records and positions of the candidates. This begs the question: When, where, and how did this supposed process take place? If it had, Reagan's God-and-country campaign for the TV cameras strategy would never have succeeded on the same scale, even with an economy peaking on election day. The outcome may have been different, and it certainly would have been closer, had TV news pulled the cameras from the show-biz rallys, stopped declaring Reagan invincible and Mondale hopeless, and truly examined the issues. Politics, in the end, *should be* about ideas, but anyone who thinks this is reality in late-twentieth-century America doesn't watch television.

Consider just a few of the issues that were either covered so briefly as to be meaningless or missed entirely by TV "journalism."

After the first presidential debate, on CNN's "Crossfire," Jody Powell observed that Reagan was being disingenuous about taxes and Mondale disingenuous about Social Security and Medicare, in both cases because the deficit had become a crisis that could leave no one's sacred cows untouched. The one thing that must be said for Mondale is that, whereas his political use of Social Security resulted in Reagan following suit, Reagan's political use of the tax issue did not result in Mondale's abandoning his politically "losing" position. On the other hand, it must also be said that Mondale, far behind in the polls, was playing political poker, gambling that the American people would face reality and see him as a "leader" for taking a "courageous" and honest stand. But the television coverage of these issues was almost always focused on the political rather than the policy implications, contributing to the freezing of responses on the issues by the campaigns in outworn political modes, instead of contributing to a focus on the need for rethinking positions in the face of new realities.

Responsible issue-oriented news coverage requires including historical background as a prelude to discussing present policy options. For example, where during the campaign did we see a lengthy and thorough report on the history of Social Security? How many Americans know that the massive program it has become bears little resemblance to the concept originally proposed by Franklin Roosevelt? How many Americans know that from 1960 to 1984 the percentage of gross national product spent on

Social Security and Medicare jumped from 2.3 percent to 6.6 percent? And where during the campaign did we see a detailed examination of the economic realities and options for Social Security and Medicare over the next several decades, and how these factors influence present potential policy decisions? All of this is to say nothing of the larger issue of the crisis of government spending in general. It was easy politically for Mondale to challenge Reagan on never cutting these programs, but how realistically would he have dealt with the black-hole economics involved?

Consider another aspect of this crisis: defense spending. Reagan periodically attacked Mondale as being weak on defense, but the fact was, both candidates favored increasing the defense budget substantially, although Reagan wanted a rate of increase approximately twice the size of Mondale's. The defense budget had approximately doubled in four years, the fastest rate of growth in peacetime by far in American history. Where did we see an in-depth analysis of the impact of defense spending in terms of specific weapons systems, military strategy, economic impact on jobs and the deficit, particularly since the accelerated Reagan buildup began in 1981? And what about the future cost of a full-blown "Star Wars" program? As former Republican Senate Foreign Relations Chairman Charles Percy said on CBS "Nightwatch" (10 April 1985), the cost of developing and deploying "Star Wars" would be unprecedented, running into the "trillions." Even a tentative start down this path should have required the most thorough public debate. There was also the question of the cost that would be involved in a transition from NATO reliance on the American nuclear umbrella to matching Soviet conventional strength. As numerous military reformers and strategists have pointed out (most recently, defense consultant Edward Luttwak in his book, *The Pentagon and the Art of War*), perhaps the greatest danger of nuclear war lies in U.S. dependence on nuclear weapons to deter a Soviet invasion of Western Europe. Would the American people be willing to meet the economic and/or political cost of a massive conventional buildup and perhaps reestablishment of the draft? If military strategy and spending priorities were changed, deemphasizing the strategic nuclear component, and abandoning the unrealistic planning to wage war simultaneously on several fronts, would increased expenditures be necessary, or would there be net savings? What should be the role of the NATO allies? These were the kind of difficult and crucial issues that should have been discussed and debated before the American electorate, with the media leading the way in the examination process.

An issue that was all but invisible during the election was the environment. In the first presidential debate, the candidates made the following statements.

MONDALE: *The American people want this environment protected. They know that these toxic waste dumps should have been cleaned up a long time ago, and they know that people's lives and health are being risked because we've had an administration that has been totally insensitive to the law and the demand for the protection of the environment.*

REAGAN: *The environment, yes, I feel as strongly as anyone about the preservation of the environment. When we took office we found that the national parks were so dirty and contained so many hazards, lack of safety features, that we stopped buying additional parkland until we had rectified this with what was to be a five-year program, but is just about finished already, a billion dollars, and now we're going back to budgeting for additional lands for our parks. We have added millions of acres to the wilderness lands, to the game refuges.*

What was learned from these statements? Walter Mondale was raising the critical questions, but he was sometimes criticized by environmental groups for not being specific enough about what he would do, for example, on the acid rain question. Ronald Reagan didn't even seem to be in the game. The environment to him meant going camping. There were environmental pollution problems of staggering proportions confronting the nation, probably the greatest public health crisis ever facing this society. It was incredible that, as the evidence continued to mount on environmental causes of cancer and other diseases, this issue was barely mentioned during the campaign. It could certainly never be covered in all its crucial aspects and complexity in short clips on the evening news, even if it was made a top story. When some kind of catastrophe or near catastrophe occurred, the cameras were there. But what of all the "little" catastrophes destroying the health of individual lives? And what of the many larger catastrophes waiting to happen? This was an area that demanded unrelenting investigation and coverage, of the kind that TV news in its present format could never provide. During the campaign there was hardly an attempt made.

In the area of foreign policy, the Soviet invasion of Afghanistan was never discussed during the campaign by either Reagan or Mondale. Covert CIA assistance to the *Mujaheddin* guerrillas was being supplied. But why not supply substantial support, in the open, to these embattled freedom fighters? If the Reagan administration was willing to expend so much effort to obtain support for the so-called freedom fighters, the *contras*, against a supposed Soviet surrogate in Nicaragua, why was there not an even greater effort to support unambiguous freedom fighters against actual Soviet aggression? Why was Mondale never heard from on this issue? Television news has done a fair number of reports on Afghanistan since the Soviet invasion, but these policy issues were not pinpointed during the campaign when such coverage would have been the most useful in terms of public debate.

During the second presidential debate, Walter Mondale repeatedly attacked President Reagan for his mishandling of the security arrangements for the American embassy annex in Beirut, and it would seem, justifiably so. But Mondale was silent when it came to the far more significant issue, of which the marine and embassy bombings were merely a symptom: U.S. foreign policy objectives in Lebanon. How would his policy have differed from Reagan's? On CBS's "Nightwatch" (December 28, 1984), the mother of marine sergeant Michael Mercer asked why her son was killed. It was a poignant moment and the only answer to her question was an awful silence. It was the kind of moment that should have been broadcast on the nightly news during the election over and over again until someone answered the question. American problems in Lebanon began with the Israeli invasion in 1982 and were explosively exacerbated by the transformation of the U.S. military presence from a neutral peace-keeping force to virtual combatants choosing sides in a civil war. The Gemayel government represented an attempt by a Christian minority to maintain its power over a Moslem majority through the questionable implemention of an outmoded constitution that legitimized their privileged position. Israel, then the United States, supported this attempt, supposing that Gemayel would be their best bet as a potential ally. It was not surprising that Mondale had nothing to say in this regard, since, given his original support of the American mission and his uncritical and consistent support of Israel, it would be difficult to imagine what he would have done differently. As a result, the extremely important issue of blundering U.S. policy in Lebanon was never really addressed, although a thoroughly predictable series of tragedies and failures of policy had occurred. Reagan was not taken to task for one of the most serious U.S. foreign policy debacles in the postwar era. His "America standing tall again" rhetoric turned into "America retreating fast" in reality. The stated goals of his policy in Lebanon, after the peace-keeping fiction was abandoned, were to restrain Syrian, and therefore Soviet, influence in the region. It is universally recognized that his policy achieved precisely what it was supposed to prevent. Mondale was not taken to task for his failure to explain what he would have done, attempting instead to brazenly use the disaster politically by attempting to outmacho Reagan on the issue of retaliating against the "terrorists." The political, social, and religious complexities fostering this terrorism and, more significantly, contributing to the inevitable failure of U.S. policy in Lebanon were the basic issues the American people needed information about. They wouldn't find it on the commercial TV networks. As is all too often the case, there were a handful of short overviews, a comment here, a comment there, the best of which, edited and taken together over the course of the campaign, might have served as a useful introduction to what should have been a series of lengthy examinations on every network.

And while on the subject of terrorism, what of the issue of human rights, and the impact of Reagan's statements and policies regarding "friendly" dictators? Reagan's argument had been that the human rights policies of Jimmy Carter were ineffective and counterproductive, "needlessly antagonizing our old friends," as he said in 1980. Yet how many Americans were aware of the fact that Jimmy Carter, in the midst of the 1984 campaign, was welcomed as a "hero" by millions of South Americans (Jack Epstein and James Evans, *Seattle Times*, 21 November 1984), including "presidents, governors, archbishops, and leading journalists"? He was responsible, in their view, for saving countless lives in countries such as Chile and Paraguay and the resurgence of democracy in Peru, Argentina, and Brazil. How successful had the "quiet diplomacy" approach of the Reagan administration been? Shortly after the election, a large group of Republican members of Congress sent a letter to Reagan calling for an end to quiet diplomacy on the issue of apartheid in South Africa. In the wake of this event and his meeting under pressure with Nobel Peace Prize-winning South African Bishop Desmond Tutu, President Reagan for the first time spoke out in public condemning apartheid. Where was TV journalism's examination of these issues to be found during the campaign?

These examples are only a few among many. It is impossible, and indeed useless, to discuss issues without expressing a viewpoint. But the primary point here is not the author's perspective on these issues, but the lack of TV news coverage of the issues themselves. It is the job of responsible journalism to present both point and counterpoint as fairly as possible. But first must come the commitment to really examine at length the major policy questions of our time.

As has been previously stated, only "The MacNeil/Lehrer NewsHour" approaches such subjects with any depth. To ascend from the abyss to the plane the medium is capable of, and the American electorate in need of, the commercial networks and MacNeil/Lehrer as well must first eliminate the horse-race and image-making approaches already described here. Then the commercial networks must take the obvious step of extending their news programs to one hour and adopting a format similar to that of MacNeil/Lehrer, mixing in-depth visual and voice-over reports with pertinent interviews, with greater emphasis on "reporting" on the issues, laying out the basic facts and different sides of policy arguments. Interviews are excellent supplements, but by their nature cannot impart information with the same effectiveness as a good report. Even if the commercial newscasts remain at their present length, they should at least devote the majority of time to the campaign, incorporating the above recommendations. During a presidential campaign, there should be additional special programming, taking the same approach just described, preferably every evening. On the commercial networks, it is conceivable that public financing in terms of "buying time" could play a role, in effect creating "islands" of public television on the commercial networks during the campaign. It is even theoretically possible for the Federal Communications Commission or the Congress to mandate the public use of air time in this regard. But the implementation of the journalistic reforms recommended here will likely ultimately occur only if the networks opt for integrity over dollars, at least for a few months every four years. Enlightened self-interest could potentially lead to a marriage of integrity and profit in broadcast journalism, which will be explored further. The historical record does not make one overly optimistic, but I believe in the possibility of salvation.

The dean of broadcast journalism, Walter Cronkite, has made a radical recommendation to transform television into an effective agent of participatory democracy during presidential campaigns. The following are his words before members of Congress (March 14, 1985) at an event sponsored by the Congressional Clearinghouse on the Future.

"I think one of the great disappointments of our time, quite honestly, is our Presidential political campaigns. We face these vast and great issues, those that directly affect us, those for tomorrow, those for next year, those for a decade hence. . . . We need desperately a national debate on these issues. We need to go to the people every once in a while—and four years is a good time—with these issues clearly enunciated and clearly approached with solutions provided, or attacks on the problem at least suggested, by the candidates. We are finding that the campaigns get slicker in the media sense, and that candidates do not face the issues as they should. If they do, they don't get listened to, which happens on occasion as well. I think that this is a problem for media, but mostly it is a problem for the political structure itself. It seems to me that we should legislate, if that's possible, and if it's not possible, we should find a way to get around the impossibility, so that we can legislate Presidential debate. There's no reason why in this modern age we cannot use television the way it could be used for a great national platform and put on a series of debates, let's say six, over six of the principal, the major, issues facing the nation to be decided in that campaign. Make those debates formal, Oxonian debates . . . resolved that, the proposition is put and it is opposed, with formal debate rules, no panels, no phony questions, but a straight-out debate on, say, the six principal issues. Maybe if we found this worked, we could expand it to fifteen of them. That could be the principal campaign. That could be the entire campaign. Whistle stops are ridiculous these days in a Presidential campaign, it seems to me. The whistle stop campaign was to let people see the candidate. Well, they see the candidate every night on television. They don't have to see him being met in Ohio, or Topeka. We don't have to see him traveling the country every day, getting off an airplane, getting on an airplane—no substance at all in the darn thing. The debate is the way to do it."

Cronkite's suggestion has great merit. But whether such an approach is ever legislated or not, TV news itself could help bring about such an outcome by reporting and format choices. If the candidates knew that there would be no horse race coverage, that the cameras wouldn't be there for the whistle stop charade or rose garden campaign, but were available for interview and debate appearances only, American presidential politics would take an evolutionary step in the direction of fulfilling the democratic promise. To complete the process of democratic reform in television, Cronkite suggested that Congress ban the thirty-second and sixty-second spot for political campaign advertising, allowing only commercials three minutes or longer with only the candidate appearing in them. If this was done in conjunction with equal-spending and equal-time guarantees, and combined with the even more crucially needed reforms in television news outlined here, then democracy would not only survive the video age, it would flourish in it. If these reforms, particularly in broadcast journalism, are not implemented, then the legacy of 1984 to American democracy will be the video images of Ronald Reagan, surrounded by Hollywood props, smiling but silent, and of Geraldine Ferraro, after the election, drawing the conclusion that Diet-Pepsi TV commercials are the stepping stone to the political future.

Real journalistic integrity on the part of television demands continuing programming that will explore honestly and in depth the public-policy questions of our time as the essential definition of "news." This cannot happen just during a presidential election campaign, but must be an ongoing process. Of course it may require, at first, dragging some viewers kicking and screaming to the "classroom." That is the price of addicting people to junk. And the networks will have to start by kicking the habit themselves.

CHAPTER SIX

TV's Invisible Issues, An Example: World Hunger And U.S. Foreign Policy

Theoretically, given the particular form of our participatory democracy, a presidential election campaign should provide the opportunity for the electorate to examine the major issues confronting the nation, in an especially focused manner. It should be the time for the citizens of the Republic to make decisions on these issues, reflected in the views of the candidates. But this is not likely to occur in any fundamental sense, if the only time most citizens pay attention to issues and participate in the democratic process is every two or four years. (And even then, with only half participating, and even fewer concentrating on issues.) Under these conditions, politicians are less accountable, more prone to rhetoric, and citizens more likely to accept this, or be alienated from the system entirely.

It follows that television's impact on a presidential election campaign goes far beyond the time frame of the campaign itself. It is, in fact, continuous. The information TV does or does not provide is constantly influencing public opinion and political choices. To do its job properly, television news must go beyond just cleaning up its act during the presidential election season. Even if TV news eliminated all the negative aspects of campaign coverage that have been seen in these pages and concentrated in depth on the issues, no one is capable of either disseminating or assimilating all the relevant information on a number of major issues in the period of a few weeks. Additionally, the very nature of human experience, of learning, is a continuous process. Unfortunately, as even the most casual observer knows, television's contribution to this ongoing process is as dismal as its contribution to the democratic process during a presidential campaign.

What follows is one example of that failing, and its cost.

In the opening pages of this book, I described my experience with the White House press corps at the initial meeting of the Presidential Commission on World Hunger in 1978. During the 1984 presidential campaign, the issue of world hunger, after being virtually invisible on television news for a decade, came suddenly back to our TV screens with a fury, as we witnessed the heartrending and agonizing pictures of starving Ethiopians. But the ongoing tragedy of world hunger, the worst holocaust in human history every year, and the role of the United States was never discussed during the campaign. There are many reasons, humanitarian and in the national interest, why it should have been. But to understand the implications of this cycle of appearance and disappearance of the world hunger issue on TV news, we must back up.

My own involvement in both documentary film production and the issue of world hunger was directly related to the role of television news during its last "period of concern" during the Sahel drought in Africa in the early 1970s. The situation largely resembled the present African drought, with TV viewers momentarily horrified by the grotesque pictures of starving thousands. The only time between 1975 and 1984 that there was a similar reaction was during the famine in Cambodia in the aftermath of the barbarism of the Khmer Rouge. But that was treated as a famine resulting from political evil, whereas the African droughts fit more neatly under the media perception of the banner of world hunger. It is a major failing of most of the media, particularly television, that world hunger is always narrowly defined as meaning famine. This definition leaves out the 13 to 18 million who die every year, famine or not, mostly infants and children, from hunger and malnutrition related or complicated disease. It leaves out the millions, indeed billions, whose quality and length of life is cut drastically by this monster. It leaves out the ironic fueling of the population explosion that hunger causes, as parents conceive as many children as possible to fight the high infant death rate. It leaves out the fact that U.S. food and development aid has generally been at the low end of the list of western donor nations in terms of GNP. It leaves out the impact of our foreign aid, both in terms of its meagerness and its concentration, like much of the private loans to the Third World as well, on useless industrial and "infrastructure" development, when most of the population is composed of impoverished peasants in the countryside, in need of land, credit, appropriate technology, health care, and so on. It leaves out the cry of half a billion peasants for land reform, to be able to feed themselves instead of their landlord, and their eventual despairing turn to violence, and to whoever supplies the guns, in revolutions that often involve U.S. foreign policy and perhaps U.S. troops.

Upon returning to the United States after months of traveling in Third World countries and seeing the realities of world hunger first-hand in 1974, I was at first encouraged by the TV news coverage of the Sahel drought in Africa and then perplexed by the limited definition of world hunger I was seeing presented. Of even greater concern was the hopelessness about never-ending world hunger that emanated from the TV screen. The appeal to compassion was blunted by the underlying message that, in the end, world hunger would always be with us. I was reminded that the same had been said of slavery.

So I made the decision to produce a film on world hunger. The director of the film, Stephen Codling, did the editing in the basement of my home. The footage we were able to beg from various sources was meager, and the film was technically primitive. But it was substance, not image, we were after. The result, in 1976 was *The Hungry Planet*. The bottom line message of the film was that hunger on earth could be ended in two decades, by increased but manageable expenditures, but, most important, by focusing on foreign aid and foreign-policy decisions that addressed the root problems. Through the initiative of former Oberlin College president Robert Fuller, singer John Denver saw the film, and he in turn facilitated showings to several U.S. senators, U.N. Ambassador Andrew Young, and Chip Carter (the president's son), all of whom agreed that the film should be seen by newly inaugurated President Carter. In June 1977, the entire Carter family watched *The Hungry Planet* in the family theater in the White House. At the next cabinet meeting, Carter announced that he had seen the film and that he wanted to do something on the issue. As Andrew Young later told me, the "right to eat" became a cornerstone of Carter's human rights concerns. Carter instructed Dr. Peter Bourne to coordinate a White House Hunger Working Group to formulate policy recommendations. Eventually, Bourne would organize the formation of the Presidential Commission on World Hunger.

One of the people appearing in *The Hungry Planet* was the late singer Harry Chapin, founder of World Hunger Year. During production, I had seen Chapin on the "Tonight" show with Johnny Carson, spending the entire time passionately talking about world hunger. I contacted him the next day, and we maintained a working relationship until his tragic death in 1981. In one of the most incredible citizen-lobbying jobs of all time, Harry Chapin was almost single-handedly responsible for getting the resolution to set up the Presidential Commission on World Hunger through Congress. He was also, as a member of that commission, a major catalyst, along with his staff support from Marty Rogol of the Food Policy Center, (currently Executive Director of USA for Africa), in producing a commission report that ended up being something worthwhile. The other members of the commission were: Sol Linowitz, chairman, conegotiator of the Panama Canal treaties and Middle East special negotiator; Dr. Jean Mayer, vice-chairman, Tufts University president and chairman of the 1969 White House Conference on Food, Nutrition and Health; Dr. Stephen Muller, vice-chairman, John Hopkins University president, former director of the Center for International Studies; Dr. Norman Borlaug, "Green Revolution" initiator and 1970 Nobel Peace Prize Winner; D. W. Brooks, who served on agricultural advisory commissions under Truman, Eisenhower, Kennedy, Johnson, and Ford; John Denver, popular singer/songwriter and executive producer of a film about world and domestic hunger, *I Want to Live* (coproduced, codirected, and written by the author); Senator Robert Dole (R.-Kan.), ranking member of the Agriculture Committee, currently majority leader; Dr. Walter Falcon, director of the Stanford University Food Research Institute; Orville Freeman, former U.S. secretary of agriculture; Congressman Benjamin Gilman (R.-N.Y.), International Relations Committee member; Senator Patrick Leahy (D.-Ver.), Agriculture, Nutrition and Forestry Committee member; Bess Myerson, former commissioner of Consumer Affairs, New York City; Congressman Richard Nolan (D.-Minn.), Chairman of the Subcommittee on Family Farms, Rural Development and Special Studies; Dr. Howard Schneider, former director, Institute of Nutrition, Consolidated University of North Carolina; Dr. Adele Smith Simmons, president, Hampshire College; Raymond Singletary, president, Blakely Peanut Company; Dr. Eugene Stockwell, associate general secretary, Division of Overseas Ministries, National Council of Churches; Dr. Clifton Wharton, chancellor, State University of New York; Thomas Wyman, vice-chairman, the Pillsbury Company, currently chairman of CBS.

The fact that this diverse group agreed on solid recommendations was both a tribute to them individually and to the process of input the commission experienced for over a year and a half. Another book would be required to detail the degree to which Carter's original initiative was devoured by Washington's bureaucracy and politics. Dr. Peter Bourne told me after his resignation that, in hindsight, study groups and commissions should have been avoided and the problem should have been attacked head on, which was Carter's first instinct. This would have required going to war with various agencies and their allies in Congress, however, and the political "imperative" against such a course prevailed. But even so, the commission ended up serving a valuable purpose by fashioning a consensus report, released in 1980, that was well documented and covered the essential bases, and could be sold to the Congress and the American people.

Unfortunately, the commission's report ended up doing exactly what

Chairman Sol Linowitz said would never happen to it: "gathering dust." He also said, on that October day in 1978 in the White House, in response to a network TV reporter's question that was never aired, world hunger could be ended if the political will was summoned to do it. The commission's report is gathering dust and the political will has not yet been summoned because television news, first and foremost among the media, never reported the story at all. (The print media did a somewhat better job.) It was an ongoing story that in its many aspects should have been concentrated on by broadcast journalism for years. If it had, public opinion and the momentum to act would probably have superseded the disinterest in the issue of the new president, Ronald Reagan. Indeed, it might have altered his perspective, just as it certainly would have altered the public's in general, if the nightly news had consistently been presenting the facts of world hunger, before, during, and after the presidential commission's report. Perhaps then it would not have required a letter from Nobel Peace Prize winner Mother Teresa during the 1984 campaign to motivate Reagan, according to White House aides, to act on the Ethiopian crisis, without regard to the politics of Ethiopia's Marxist regime (*Newsweek,* 24 December 1984). Perhaps it would have led, finally, to a more intelligent response to the revolts of hungry peasants than simplistic anticommunism, such as a bipartisan economic and policy commitment to a democratic alternative, beyond rhetoric and partway measures. Television had shown, by its very coverage of the Ethiopian disaster, what an incredible impact it could have. The outpouring of generosity from the American public was overwhelming. Why was television news blind to the larger unending holocaust and its implications for American foreign policy?

A perfect example of TV journalism's failure to even keep the record straight, much less substantially examine these issues, is illustrated by the following Reagan comment during the second 1984 presidential debate regarding the "reforms" carried out by the late shah of Iran: "The shah, whatever he might have done, was building low-cost housing, had taken away land from the mullahs, and was distributing it to the peasants so they could be landowners, things of that kind."

Reagan was referring to the shah's so-called White Revolution, the linchpin of which was land reform. This program did have an ambitious launching, but was all but abandoned years before the shah's downfall, its main accomplishment having been to arouse the expectations, then the anger, of the landless peasantry. It was the sons and daughters of landless peasants who by the hundreds of thousands crowded the streets of Tehran demonstrating against the shah and America. Ironically, Khomeini and the mullahs were angered because some of their land was confiscated. If the shah had followed through with his reforms, it isn't likely that peasants with land and food would have chosen to follow their "religious" leaders. Typically, TV news had never understood or communicated these facts, just as it never corrected Reagan's gross error.

President Reagan didn't mention land reform when, after the "shah misstatement," he voiced support of the Marcos dictatorship in the Philippines because the only alternative was communism, an assertion the State Department hastily denied the following day. But how many Americans know that the New People's Army (NPA), the Communist guerrilla movement in the Philippines, is the direct descendant of an earlier rebel army, the Hukbalahops (the "Huks"), who had fought the Japanese alongside U.S. troops and then led a peasant uprising against the landlord-controlled Philippine government? They were at the outskirts of Manila in 1950 when a newly appointed defense secretary, Ramon Magsaysay, blunted the rebellion with promises of land reform and amnesty. He began to make good on those promises, was elected president in 1954, but was killed in a plane crash in 1957, and the feudal system stayed intact. How many Americans know that when Marcos declared martial law, he promised that he would finally carry out land reform? But he didn't, and the peasants are back in the hills, joining the NPA in growing numbers, as they had joined the Huks a generation before. How many Americans know that General Douglas MacArthur had said during the Huk rebellion that if he were a Philippine peasant he too would be a Huk? (From *American Caesar* by William Manchester.) When MacArthur carried out a land-reform program in Japan more radical than anything Mao did in China, the State Department warned him at the time that dismantling the power structure of the emperor and the feudal aristocracy would lead to communism! How many Americans were aware of that ironic bit of history, in the context of President Reagan's statement about the Philippines?

The importance of land reform in Third World countries, where the majority of people, or the single largest "group," are tenant farmers and landless peasants, cannot be overstated. The tenant farmer will not make even simple labor-intensive improvements, leading to greater food production, if the land is owned by someone else. The landlord will just increase the rent. If the value of the land is increased by the tenant's labor, it may be taken from him and sold or given to a landlord's relative. Peasants who own the land they work are motivated to organize cooperatives, seek credit to finance improved irrigation, purchase fertilizer, high-yield seeds, and other technical support that increases food production further. This has been accomplished successfully on plots of an acre or less. The peasant owner-operator can adequately feed the family. Because their children will now live, parents don't need so many "insurance" births and become open to contraception. A healthy peasant economy stimulates the entire economy, creating additional employment and sustainable economic development that results in stable Third World trading partners rather than economic black holes contributing to the international debt crisis. The alternative is a hungry peasantry, paying much of their crop to the landlords, and ripe for revolution.

Fully half of the world's poorest billion people live on the Indian subcontinent, which consists of India, Pakistan, and Bangladesh. Unless there is a war, religious violence, or assassination, the nightly news doesn't venture to these parts, even though India is the largest democracy in the world and Pakistan, a dictatorship, is a U.S. ally. When Indira Gandhi was assassinated, toward the end of the 1984 U.S. presidential campaign, there were lengthy segments on India for the first time in memory. But as usual, the fundamental realities were missed. In the film *Gandhi,* there is a scene showing the great independence leader Mohandas K. "Mahatma" Gandhi going to a village where hungry, landless peasants are struggling with the local landlord. This scene was a microcosm of the great majority of India as a whole, then and now. Although every American schoolchild knows (or used to) that the American Revolution was ended by Lord Cornwallis's surrender at Yorktown to George Washington, how many Americans know that this same Lord Cornwallis created a system under British colonialism in India that was responsible for many of that country's ongoing difficulties? In 1793, Lord Cornwallis imposed the "Permanent Settlement" by which the British destroyed the communal land-tenure system and created a favored class of landlords called "Zamindars" who would collect and then turn over taxes to the colonial masters. This hated feudal system, the Zamindari system, was the object of peasant revolts that grew in number and tenacity over the years. Gandhi's roots were in support of the peasants. He believed that true independence, as well as an end to Hindu-Moslem antagonism, required economic self-sufficiency in the villages of India. But after Gandhi's assassination, the Congress party, under Nehru and later his daughter, Indira, pursued a policy geared to industrial development. The villages, where 80 percent of the population lives, were given lip service only.

However, one of the most interesting Third World success stories is to be found in India. In 1967, the French filmmaker Louis Malle took his cameras to India to produce a seven-hour documentary series for the BBC, "Phantom India." One of the best documentaries ever made, it is a stunning example of what television can accomplish. One of the segments followed events that were then unfolding in the state of Kerala, on the southwest coast of India. As his cameras followed a huge demonstration by thousands of peasants demanding land reform in Kerala's capital city, Trivandrum, Malle commented that it appeared possible there would soon be a Maoist-type revolution there. He was right, but the revolution was carried out with ballots instead of bullets. A Marxist-led coalition of parties democratically elected in 1968 (and democratically turned out later) initiated the land reform act of 1969, which simply abolished tenancy, automatically making one-third of the population small-farm owner-operators (mostly on one to two-acre plots) instead of the virtual serfs they had previously been. Their increased income led to better wages for the landless laborers, which made up another third of the population. A third of these laborers were also given small "garden" plots. Basic health care was extended to the entire population. Education, already widespread, was made universal for boys and girls. Kerala had previously been one of the most malnourished areas in India, with one of the highest infant death and birth rates and the greatest population density in the country. Within a few years, food production had increased, infant death rates and birth rates had dropped dramatically and life expectancy had jumped. Hunger and the population rate had been dramatically reduced. The standard economic models were exploded, as Kerala continued to have a very low per-capita income, but with the above results proving that distribution of income was the key. Kerala also has the greatest religious mix in India, with Hindus, Moslems, and Catholics generally living peacefully together. There were no angry peasants in the streets of Trivandrum when I visited Kerala a decade after Louis Malle had been there with his cameras.

But there are hungry and angry peasants in many other places, which is why the Kerala example is so important for India, for the rest of the Third World, and for U.S. foreign aid and foreign policy. The conditions of Kerala in 1967 can be found today among U.S. allies such as Pakistan and the Philippines, with the latter coming rapidly to the boiling point. These conditions had existed in Russia, Mexico, China, Cuba, Vietnam, Ethiopia, Peru, Iran, Nicaragua, and El Salvador as a prelude to violent upheaval. And the list could go on. Too many times, U.S. support of one evil has helped create another, which its policy was ironically designed to prevent. Ethiopia may have starved its way to the TV screen in late 1984, but the whole story has never been seen on television. The Ethiopian revolution overthrowing U.S. ally Emperor Haile Selassie in 1974 was catalyzed by the famine that was the last straw for the hungry, serflike majority. It was no accident that land reform was at the top of the agenda for the Ethiopian military revolutionaries (much as it was for the military reformers who engineered the coup in El Salvador in 1979). Approximately 80 percent of the Ethiopian population lives in the countryside. If the United States had turned a swift and generous helping hand to Ethiopia in 1974, when in spite of understandable anti-American feeling there was a window of opportunity, the bloody Mengistu regime may not have found a foothold, and the land reform begun then may have stayed on course, complemented by small-farmer technical support, credit, irrigation, and fair prices, instead of being abandoned for the bankrupt policy of Soviet-style collectivization. And of course, even more to the point, there had been years of U.S. aid to Ethiopia before 1974, while nothing in the barbaric feudal system changed. More recently, in Nicaragua, after the 1979 revolution supported even by the upper class because of the Somoza dictatorship's inhumanity, the Sandinista government was at first promisingly pluralistic. Those Nicaraguans wanting it to remain so came to Washington asking for generous aid to carry out reforms and rebuild the country. After lengthy Congressional haggling that ended up, understandably, being insulting to the Nicaraguans, the aid sent, though generous by previous standards, was too little and too late. As the Sandinistas increasingly censored dissent, many major opposition leaders, some very conservative, asked the Reagan administration to stop playing into Sandinista hands by its aggressive policy. It seemed that the *Norte-Americanos* could not get it through their heads that the impact of their imposing the murderous Somozas and their feudal czardom on the poor, landless peasants of Nicaragua for decades went very deep.

In El Salvador, U.S. aid had been contingent on progress in land reform until the Reagan administration successfully pressed Congress to remove the requirement. In reality, the letter of the law had been flaunted all along. Land reform in El Salvador had a promising start, but quickly came to a standstill, opposed by extremes on the right and left. The largest peasant union, *Union Communal Salvadorena* (UCS), which did not support the rebels, regularly sent representatives to Washington to impress the point that without U.S. pressure, the military would not truly support the reform process, and the peasants would abandon hope of democratic reform and join the rebels. The land reform not only ceased going forward, but began to be reversed, and U.S. aid kept flowing. Whether the April 1985 election giving the Christian Democrats a majority in the national assembly would sufficiently strengthen the reform-minded president, José Napolean Duarte, to salvage the situation, remained to be seen.

It was a pattern that repeated itself in American foreign policy. It was a pattern that was sometimes questioned, sometimes reinforced, by different presidents, to varying degrees. But it was a pattern that had never truly been debated on a national scale, because the information was not communicated to the public—again, particularly by TV news—except in a periodic, disconnected, insufficient manner. As a result, U.S. foreign policy seemed generally to be applied only in geopolitical terms, while self-defeatingly missing the details that dictated those terms. Journalist I. F. Stone's description of the inevitability of American defeat in Vietnam was that wars aren't won in peasant countries on the side of the landlords.

Amazingly, years of intense television coverage in Vietnam had hardly touched on land reform, though lack of it was demonstrably the central issue promoting Viet Cong recruiting. When in El Salvador a U.S. foreign policy consensus developed around the need for land reform (at least rhetorically), commercial TV news made periodic references to the issue, but never examined it in depth.

Much of Africa is currently suffering from perhaps the worst famine of the century. Television news brought us the horrendous images of starvation, but what about the root causes, the long-term problems and solutions? Television news along with the media at large gave tremendous publicity to the inspiring effort of many popular music stars, United Support of Artists (USA) for Africa, in producing the song, *We Are the World*. But how many broadcast journalists read the inside jacket of the album cover that called for concentration on the causes of hunger and the need for self-sufficiency, not just the immediate tragedy—the result of overlooking these issues in the past? Billions of dollars of development aid from the West (and a considerably smaller amount from the Soviet Union and the Eastern bloc) poured into Africa during the 1970s. But instead of helping, this aid largely contributed to the present nightmare, as it reinforced the colonial legacy of cash-crop dependence instead of aiding food self-sufficiency, sometimes contributed to soil erosion, and worked against the interests of the peasant small farmers. The measure of failure is that during the 1970s sub-Saharan African food production fell 14 percent, while food imports increased by 9.5 percent each year. Although small steps toward multilateral aid agency reform are starting to be made, the Reagan administration is slashing multilateral aid and concentrating on bilateral aid, emphasizing free-market economics and U.S. strategic interests. Since 1981, U.S. military aid to Africa has expanded from nineteen to thirty-six countries. The Reagan administration is ending all U.S. funding for the World Bank's International Development Association and the International Planned Parenthood Federation. The former is the multilateral loan agency for development projects. The latter funds family planning projects, one of Africa's most crucial needs. In terms of development projects the administration plans a bilateral aid program as a substitute, but whether cash crops or food self-sufficiency will be emphasized is unclear. In examining these and other facts ("When Foreign Aid Fails," *Atlantic Monthly,* April 1985), Jack Sheperd makes the point that only policies that promote food self-sufficiency, by both aid donors and the Africans themselves, will end the African tragedy.

One of the reasons that the reporting from the examples cited has been so lacking is that the reporters themselves often do not speak the language of the country they are in, or venture out of the capital city (other than short excursions) to engage in real research. The information sources for the reporter are therefore extremely limited. This situation is similar to the problems that have haunted AID (Agency for International Development), the administrator of American bilateral foreign aid. It is something that broadcast journalists should be reporting about, not mimicking. The ultimate decision is one of resource allocation and directives from news producers that determines the quality of research and air time concerned with these life-and-death issues, affecting not only the Third World, where the largest segment of the world's population lives, but the economy and national security of the United States as well.

One of the most senior State Department officials of the Carter years told me in 1977 that the "spear carriers" don't make revolutions, that the grievances of hungry, landless peasants were not a concern in that sense. Only great leaders and superpowers could create such happenings, in his view. When I pointed out that without the "spear carriers," as he put it, revolutions couldn't happen, it fell on deaf ears.

The Presidential Commission on World Hunger made very clear what conclusions it had reached on the issue of "spear carriers" when it stated that ending world hunger should be at the top of the U.S. national security agenda. Whatever one's views on such issues, it could hardly be argued that a thorough national discussion and debate of U.S. foreign policy in the Third World is long overdue. A presidential election campaign certainly should have included more than a few peripheral references to this important issue. However, as with other major issues, a presidential election campaign is not where the debate should start, but where it should culminate.

The specific issue of world hunger has been elaborated on here as an example of the necessity in a democracy for in-depth information to be continuously provided to the public. Only over time can people absorb enough information to understand any major issue in its complexity. In terms of world hunger, there are numerous historical and present-day examples of successful reforms and unsuccessful facades by governments on the right, on the left, and of every political stripe. For instance, a Marxist-led government in Kerala and a rightist dictatorship in Taiwan successfully carried out similar reforms, which greatly reduced both hunger and population growth and economically benefited the majority of their people. In the face of the monster of world hunger, intellectual integrity quickly leads to the generally healthy realization that no political ideology has all the answers. That, of course, is the ultimate rationale behind true democracy. The option for change and experimentation in achieving goals is always maintained. But without information, the option that is democracy can hardly be exercised.

A final example, in terms of the issue of world hunger, of what kind of information is deemed important by television "journalism" illustrates both the lack of TV news integrity and the intellectual emptiness of its approach to important issues.

On March 7, 1980, shortly after the Presidential Commission on World Hunger had released its preliminary report, I received a phone call from the producer of an upcoming special segment on" NBC Nightly News." The subject the producer was interested in was an organization called the Hunger Project. This organization had been initiated in 1977 by Werner Erhard after he had seen the film I had produced on world hunger. Erhard was the founder of est, Erhard Seminars Training, the preeminent self-exploration vehicle of the "me decade," as Tom Wolfe labeled the 1970s (which must make the 1980s the "super me decade"). Primarily because this organization was visibly afflicted with devotee syndrome, Erhard was a somewhat controversial figure. The producer of the special segment stated flatly her concern about cults and seemed to associate Erhard with Jim Jones of Guyana massacre infamy in our conversation. I told her that, based on my knowledge, this association took a rather substantial leap of the imagination. In addition, the Hunger Project as an organization was originally criticized by some long-time hunger activists for being overly consumed with enrollment and organizational expansion and lacking hard issues and programmatic focus; but its reputation seemed to evolve positively over the years. It is primarily an educational organization, but has also helped raise money for Cambodian and African famine relief, and has become involved in development projects.

The producer of the special segment clearly intended to present a highly negative report on both Erhard and the Hunger Project. She asked me to appear on the program if I would say anything critical of the individual or the organization. I had mentioned that I was working on a book about hunger, and she promised to mention the book and help make it a "best-seller," if I would come on the program and say something negative. I was appalled at her unethical tactics, but even more so at the fact that NBC was willing to waste air time on something so comparatively insignificant, when the Presidential Commission on World Hunger had just released its preliminary report! I attempted to explain this to her, but she was obsessed by her search for controversy. "If you are concerned about hunger," I told her, "if you want to do an important story, do it on the presidential commission." I found out later that other hunger activists had told her the same thing. But it was to no avail.

When the segment aired, it began with a clip from a film on hunger I had coproduced with Lowell Norman for singer John Denver, who was a Hunger Project board member. Clearly, permission to use it had not been obtained by an honest representation of the purpose of the story. Reporter James Polk described it as a "film at the beginning of the Hunger Project." After this incomprehensible statement, the report only got worse. The producer had failed to find anything truly controversial, so controversy was mimicked by intonation and technique. Though acknowledging that the Hunger Project was an educational organization and represented itself as such, the report illogically attacked it for not directly feeding hungry people. It was a textbook case of the unethical use of image-creating techniques.

But the infinitely more important point is this: During the segment Polk said, "The Presidential Commission on Hunger says that world hunger is getting worse rather than better, because not enough is being done about it." Hearing these words in this report could only elicit outrage. It was possible that this was the only time that the presidential commission was even mentioned on network TV!

Once again, a crucial issue was buried by the controversy-over-substance sickness infecting broadcast journalism. Not enough was being done about world hunger because, thanks to television news, it was invisible to the public. According to the presidential commission's final report, world hunger could realistically be ended by the end of the century, given the political will. Is this not a proposition worth serious national discussion? Is this not an issue that should be addressed in a presidential campaign by the candidates? A presidential commission spent the taxpayer's money to arrive at this momentous conclusion, but the taxpayers were left largely uninformed because of a television news blackout.

In terms of both American democracy and the millions who have died and billions of our suffering fellow humans, television news has much to haunt its conscience, if it can find it.

Add to this the fact that this is just one example of the vacuousness of broadcast journalism, in terms of putting important issues before the public eye. How can a participatory democracy be expected to function properly without an informed citizenry? If television news does not provide basic factual information on the crucial issues and policy choices facing both the nation and the planet, not to mention more substantial ongoing examination of these concerns, how likely is the prospect of an informed citizenry in the video age?

(Opposite page) March 25, 1984—Reporters fill the press briefing room at the White House for President Reagan's new conference. (AP/WIDE WORLD PHOTOS)

CHAPTER SEVEN

Reagan and the Media

On January 9, 1985, eleven days before his inauguration for a second term, President Reagan held his first press conference in six months. The preceding day in Geneva, Secretary of State George Schultz had reached an agreement with Soviet Foreign Minister Andrei Gromyko to reopen negotiations on strategic, intermediate, and defensive weapons. The press had treated this Geneva meeting, something that in the past would have been regarded as routine, as if a historic agreement was at hand. This "talk about talks" was given unprecedented media attention precisely because U.S.-Soviet relations had sunk to their lowest level in over twenty years. Dan Rather, Tom Brokaw, and Peter Jennings all anchored the evening news from Geneva. Once again, one pondered the logic of TV news. If an issue was so important as to merit this high profile, why was the in-depth coverage of the many factors that had led to this moment so lacking in the previous four years and before, not to mention during the presidential campaign?

In his press conference, Reagan managed to totally contradict himself on the issue of "Star Wars" as a negotiable item. In responding to UPI's Helen Thomas, he declared both that everything was on the table for negotiation, but that "Star Wars" was not a bargaining chip. In answering a followup question by NBC's Chris Wallace, he made clear that since the idea was only in the research stage, the testing or deployment of a hypothetical system couldn't be negotiated at present. This approach, which was not the logical absolute Reagan presented it as, would bring the entire reason for negotiations into question. Reagan himself strangely pointed

217

this out indirectly when responding to a question from the *Christian Science Monitor's* Charlotte Saikowski, explaining that the basis of these new negotiations would be tradeoffs between the superpowers vis-à-vis their various strengths. As anyone who read the front page of a newspaper understood, that meant, first and foremost, the United States trading "Star Wars" for deep cuts in the Soviet's large number of land-based strategic missiles. In addition, the president confirmed every charge Walter Mondale leveled in the campaign about his not being competent on the arms-control issue. In an almost childlike way, Reagan acknowledged that once he understood that the Soviets weren't too keen on reducing their strategic stockpile for nothing substantial in return, he switched to the "tradeoff" approach. In other words, he was finally conceptualizing actual negotiation. From the beginning of the original START proposal, anyone barely literate in arms control realized that the U.S. negotiating position could mean only two things: Either the Reagan administration didn't want an agreement, but a public relations effort masking an arms buildup, or it was frighteningly out of touch with the most basic strategic realities. There was no question that the administration did not want a comprehensive test ban treaty, even though bipartisan support for it was strong, exemplified by the call for negotiating such a treaty from former Presidents Ford and Carter in April 1985. Where was broadcast journalism's thorough examination of these issues during the election campaign?

Then there were the domestic issues touched on in the press conference, which were also echoes from the campaign. Reagan did a transparent softshoe backslide on the Social Security issue. He made it clear that *he* wouldn't break his campaign promise, but if a bipartisan congressional mandate were put in front of him to freeze cost-of-living allowances (COLA's,) he just might go along with it. It was obvious that he planned on just such a development. Walter Mondale had predicted Reagan would do this. But the issue had never been debated on its merits because Mondale and Reagan were too busy stumbling all over each other saying that any kind of Social Security benefit cut was out of the question, now and forever, amen. Television's shallow approach to campaign reporting let them get away with this. Most nonpartisan observers (and a remarkably large number of partisans on each side, as well) agreed that the deficit would require cuts in defense, government pensions, and Medicare, at least temporary limits on Social Security, and raising taxes for a fiscal crisis to be averted. The only chance for any real deficit reduction required, in political terms, not only going where the big dollars were, but leaving no one's sacred cows untouched. Mondale bravely bit one of these bullets, taxes, but dodged the rest. Even on the defense issue, he wasn't making much noise about cuts, although he did favor a smaller increase than Reagan. The president, on the other hand, took the politics-as-usual route on all the above issues. His solution was to count on the economy booming along ad infinitum, an illusion that magically dissipated within days after the election, and in terms of budget cuts, to further impoverish the poorest of the poor, to decimate what remained of the infamous "safety net," as well as to slash such programs as student loans and farm subsidies (making his campaign farm subsidy action appear all the more cynical), all of which would hardly dent the deficit. When asked at the press conference if he would be willing to let the Congress also "mandate" tax increases and defense cuts, Reagan got tough, proving once again that consistency and politics were usually incompatible. It is these kinds of inconsistencies that television news should hammer away at, not in fleeting one-liners but at length, in special reports, in lengthier news programs, in more regularly scheduled news specials. Otherwise a pretty face, a reassuring voice, and a presidential seal will guarantee every time that the inconsistencies go unnoticed.

But there is another duty of television and the media that this press conference brought to mind.

This was the first formal news conference held by President Reagan in nearly six months. The last was on July 24, 1984. There had been a brief minisession on November 7 in Los Angeles the day after the election. On December 6, a scheduled news conference had been canceled. Reagan held the all-time record in the television age for the least number of presidential news conferences, twenty-eight in all, during his first term. He barely edged out Richard Nixon for this dubious honor, whose fear and loathing of the press is legendary, but who managed thirty press conferences in his first term. Eisenhower held ninety-nine in his first term, Carter fifty-nine. In an article titled "Phantom of the White House" (*Washington Post* National Weekly Edition, 24 December 1984), White House correspondent Lou Cannon subtitled his column: "Before you can hold a news conference, poof!, he's gone." This reference was to the sudden cancellation of the December 6 news conference. The reason for the cancellation was given in a quote in the article from then White House deputy chief of staff Michael Deaver, also Reagan's chief media adviser: "*We* [my emphasis] had not made the decision on the budget or the tax plan. . . . We really didn't feel a great sense of pressure to hold a news conference. The time to *put* [my emphasis] him out there would be after the holidays, when people begin focusing on policy." (Deaver gives ample ammunition here to those who say that Reagan is not in control of his own presidency, but is taking his cues from others, as he was trained to do in his Hollywood career.) Cannon then wrote, "This comment contains an implied—and deserved—rebuke for those of us in the White House press corps, who have not been as insistent as we should be in calling for news conferences. . . . Other presidents, such as Franklin D. Roosevelt and

Eisenhower, recognized that news conferences serve a national purpose even after landslide victories. In terms of responsible governance, a claim to which Reagan ought to be responsive, news conferences serve the purpose of making the president accountable and accessible. Beyond the civics books arguments and the obvious interest of the media in more frequent news conferences, Reagan's advisers ought to show a little more respect for the president they claim to serve . . . it is in the interest of the country for Reagan to come out of hiding. A case could be made that it is also in the interest of the president."

This last comment is interesting and, in the author's opinion, reflects back on the election coverage by TV news. Reagan squandered a great deal of time after the election in terms of visibility and the opportunity to rally the country around his agenda. But as Michael Deaver's comment made clear, Reagan still had no set agenda, just as he did not during the campaign, other then getting reelected. As a result, the "mandate" he received in his landslide victory went no further than his personality and a general sense in the country that "things were good." In fact, Reagan's few campaign statements and actions, on Social Security and arms control for instance, played more to the old Democratic coalition and new widespread concern about nuclear war than to his conservative base. He didn't campaign on an agenda, he had no mandate for an agenda, and he wasn't holding press conferences after the election because he still didn't have an agenda. On the crucial issue of the budget, the White House had canceled release dates for their budget three times since the election, and for the first time in modern memory the Senate was taking the lead as a result of the executive branch not doing its job. This set of facts would inevitably weaken Reagan's ability to implement whatever agenda and priorities he ultimately arrived at. If TV news had, by the nature of its coverage, discouraged the "photo opportunity" approach to campaigning, and instead, encouraged a real debate of the issues, then in the end, if he had still won, even if he had won by a smaller margin, Ronald Reagan would have been in a much better position to govern and to lead.

During the campaign, in an appearance on the PBS program "Washington Week in Review" (September 21, 1984), *Los Angeles Times* reporter Jack Nelson made the following observation about President Reagan: "I would say he's the most isolated president I've ever seen, more isolated than Richard Nixon."

James Reston wrote in the *New York Times* (20 January 1985): "He breaks almost every rule in the political book and gets away with it. For example, he has almost wrecked the presidential news conference that the papers built up over 50 years, and he makes no effort to be evenhanded in his partiality toward television, but this hasn't hurt him either."

On CBS's "Nightwatch" (December 13, 1984), Charlie Rose interviewed veteran UPI White House correspondent Helen Thomas, who had just won the National Press Club's Fourth Estate Award. (Thomas has covered the White House beat since the Eisenhower years.)

ROSE: *You know when you read stories about us as an institution, the press. . . . particularly it seems recently, there's been a series of stories about our image, our own accountability and our sense of respect and credibility with the American public. When you read those stories what do you think?*

THOMAS: *I think I'll stack up our credibility against presidents any day, or press officers. The issue is that the public wants to kill the messenger who brings the bad news. . . . The people should believe in the president and they should believe in public officials until proved otherwise. But our job is to make sure, to keep the constant spotlight on them, to lessen the possibility of corruption, as Justice Brandeis said. . . .*

ROSE: *Has it changed in terms of the accessibility of the president, in terms of your capacity to get to people, the sources you need to analyze and write . . . ?*

THOMAS: *You can still get to sources, but you can't quite get to the president anymore. . . . I don't think the president's accessible enough. I think there's nothing like hearing the answer from the president himself, no matter how many spokesmen he has or how many times you can get it from anonymous sources who insist on their anonymity. . . . He [Reagan] made these little miniappearances heading for a helicopter. Above the roar you'd have to try to speak to him. After we put a lot of pressure on, saying the president's being shielded, they're hiding him, he's not responsive, and so forth, then they started to produce a little [referring to the above], but that cannot replace a legitimate news conference. . . . During the campaign he did not take any questions on any major issues.*

Speaking of issues and news conferences, Reagan's remarks at the January 9 press conference made clear that "the decision on the budget or the tax plan" had still not been made. Given Michael Deaver's comment quoted in Lou Cannon's article, it was likely that the only reason a news conference was held at this time was that the Geneva talks offered an excellent public relations opportunity, which would take the focus off these other pressing and unsettled issues. But more to the point, it certainly was not held because of pressure from the media, particularly television.

TV news was so oddly unconscious of this fundamental free press and democracy issue, that on the second day of the presidential campaign,

September 4, when the Reagan campaign said there would be no press conferences during the campaign because of equal-time requirements, an absolutely untrue assertion and blatant attempt at finding something to hide behind, only Tom Brokaw of "NBC Nightly News" reported it. This failure of broadcast journalism was impossible to comprehend. As the campaign progressed, Reagan's lack of accessibility increased, as Judy Woodruff's report on MacNeil/Lehrer (September 21) examined so well. But this was about the extent of TV news discussion of this issue, other than periodic references by the reporters on the campaign trail. As Thomas Griffith pointed out in remarks quoted earlier, this lack of concern on the part of the press is essentially cowardice. If the public wasn't screaming, then the press wasn't going to, for fear of losing the audience. There were several journalists in the print media who pulled no punches on this issue and understood that the role of journalism is not to please but to inform the public. Television led the pack in terms of avoidance of this basic concern in a democracy. As stated previously, the appropriate course, in terms of journalistic integrity, would have been for Dan Rather, Tom Brokaw, Peter Jennings, Robert MacNeil, Jim Lehrer, and so on to hammer Reagan nightly and up front on his refusal to talk to the press, until he began to do so. This is not partisan politics, but the essence of journalistic responsibility in a free society. At the beginning of his second term, Reagan's White House indicated that press conferences would be held more often than during the first term and for the first few months this was the case. Under the circumstances, however, more often could still translate into a meager number. But the most significant fact was what had already been accomplished. It was an entirely different matter to be more forthcoming with the media during a second term, when there would be no accountability to the electorate.

Showing his lack of gratitude for media cooperation in his reelection campaign, at the beginning of his second term President Reagan appointed Patrick J. Buchanan as his White House director of communications. This was nearly akin to declaring war on the press, which was an odd switch in the previously successful Reagan White House strategy of massaging the media instead of confronting it, as James Dickenson of the *Washington Post* (6 February 1985) described it. Buchanan, a speechwriter in the Nixon White House, was the primary author of the vitriolic attacks on the press by Vice-President Spiro Agnew in 1969. During the 1984 campaign, he declared that the "big media" was liberal, Democratic, and strongly pro-Mondale. Although cohost of CNN's "Crossfire," he apparently never watched television news. His views seemed to be in the same category as Republican Senator Jesse Helm's attempt to have right-wingers buy enough stock to take over CBS and fire Dan Rather for his purported liberal, anti-Reagan bias and that of the "CBS Evening News."

The same kind of intellectually blind selective viewing could easily demonstrate that the nightly news programs were conservative, Republican, anti-Mondale, and strongly pro-Reagan. In terms of actual impact, because of the nature of TV news coverage, as we have seen, Buchanan and Helms should have been thankful for the approach of broadcast journalism during the campaign. These kinds of ludicrous statements had always periodically come from the fringes of the Right or the Left. (In the case of the Left, for instance, the media were sometimes labeled conscious tools of the military-industrial complex, which controlled the political system.) But to have such narrow views represented in the White House communications office by the man who had led the Nixon administration assault on the press did not auger well for a civilized or democratic climate for government-press relations, in an administration already remote in terms of press accessibility.

There is concern that the right wing perspective on the media of many in the Reagan administration (including Reagan himself, demonstrated by his remarks at his March 1985 press conference) is having a negative impact on funding for PBS. Many right wingers consider PBS public affairs programming too liberal. As Arthur Unger pointer out (*Christian Science Monitor* reprint; *Seattle Times*, 20 November 1984), "Two weeks before the election, President Reagan vetoed a public broadcasting authorization bill for the second time in three months, although it had overwhelming bipartisan support; the bill, a compromise sponsored by Senator Barry Goldwater, passed the Senate unanimously and passed the House by 308–86."

A fascinating exchange on the issue of partisan bias in the media took place on ABC's "Viewpoint" (April 17, 1985), the program that periodically replaces "Nightline," focussing in-depth on various issues with a panel and audience, hosted by Ted Koppel. The issue discussed this night was supposed to be patriotism and the media. Because of the composition of the panel, however, it predictably turned into a debate on "liberal-bias" in the media, with *National Review* publisher William Rusher leading the charge against the purported liberal control of the media. Hodding Carter III, former State Department spokesman in the Carter administration and current columnist and TV commentator remarked, "If you take any reading you want of the press in this country—the publishers association membership, the editors association membership, the corporate ownership of the major networks in this country, if you want to see endorsements in political campaigns—if you want to take any objective measure of where the people who control the media in this country come down—it is not on the liberal side of anything. [Based on other remarks and tone it was clear he was speaking idiomatically and meant—in general—not every specific issue]. That has not happened in my lifetime or yours, and to say otherwise flies in the face of history." Carter also brought up a specific example of a narrow study (the Lichter-Rothman study in 1980) that had interviewed only a small minority of Washington D.C. journalists and concluded that the politics of the majority of them were liberal. Even in this narrowly defined study, Carter noted that one of the authors had stated, "whatever their liberal bias may be, it is in no way demonstrable that it influences the way they handle the news." Without addressing Carter's remarks concerning the various media associations or categories of measuring the politics of journalists, Rusher responded that he had spoken with one of the authors of the study Carter referred to and that, "He tells me that it is inaccurate to say that he has passed judgement one way or the other." Since Rusher *had* passed judgement, this bit of evidence could only prompt a surprised Carter to say, "Thank you, thank you." Apparently referring to the same study, Rusher exclaimed that over 80 percent of the mysterious media elite (200-plus unnamed Washington, D.C.-based journalists out of thousands in the nation's capital) had voted for Jimmy Carter. *Newsweek* correspondent Eleanor Clift noted that this "fact" was extraordinarily ironic, given the mauling by the press that Jimmy Carter took, and the comparatively positive media coverage Ronald Reagan had received.

An audience member offered a purported example of liberal media bias—the coverage of the report of the Physicians Task Force on Hunger in America. The report was described as inaccurate. In fact, its findings were consistent with many other studies, including those by various government agencies. It was asserted that the media covered the report extensively. While it was widely reported, there was no follow up, and those concerned with the issue would consider media coverage of this particular report, and the issue in general, to be sorely lacking. One of the examples given by William Rusher of liberal bias was that the media had blown out of all proportion the controversy surrounding President Reagan's decision not to visit a concentration camp site (a decision reversed by public pressure), but to visit a German military cemetery where some of Hitler's genocide squad, the SS, were buried, on a trip to West Germany commemorating the fortieth anniversary of the end of the Second World War. ABC's Sam Donaldson reminded Rusher that it was not reporters, but the reaction of Jewish organizations, that "liberal" organization—the American Legion, and the general public that had created the controversy. Rusher's choice of examples was almost anti-semitic sounding in its insensitivity. Unlike Rusher and many of his supporters in the audience, there were a growing number of conservatives, evidenced by Congressional pressure on President Reagan over apartheid in South Africa, who were anxious to end the historic conservative surrender to liberals of the moral high ground on issues such as these.

Although Rusher's remarks, along with his continuous tactic of interrupting other speakers and brusquely disrupting their remarks (even moderator Ted Koppel couldn't stop him), undoubtedly gained his ideas few converts among the viewers, the irony of a program focusing on purported liberal media bias is that it gave the left ammunition in claiming the opposite. The subject of the program was supposed to be patriotism and the media. The composition of the panel guaranteed that the subject would be patriotism and the alleged *liberal* media. The panel consisted of Rusher, Carter, Donaldson, Clift, former Interior Secretary James Watt, and Representative Philip Crane (R.-Ill.). Crane is one of the activists of the so-called Fairness in Media group which was involved in Senator Jesse Helm's campaign to take over CBS. (Another group of similar political persuasion, Accuracy in Media, was represented in the audience.) The studio audience seemed stacked very much in favor of the right-wing panelists. Question after transparently prepared question was delivered to William Rusher as a setup for stating his views. Ted Koppel finally put a halt to it, appropriately describing the process as "one hand washing another." The question is: Why wasn't the panel evenly divided, so that both liberal and conservative (or perceived to be) journalists, and media critics, could discuss both liberal and conservative media bias—and beyond simplistic labels—the role of the media in a democracy? The likes of George Will, Jesse Jackson, and the publisher of *Mother Jones*, for example, were needed, in addition to a more pluralistic audience. Philip Crane called this program an example of media fairness, yet liberals and left-wingers would undoubtedly have seen it as a gross example of conservative bias. NBC's "Today" and CBS's "Nightwatch" also ran programs emphasizing liberal media bias during the same time period. Why wasn't the Left getting equal time in terms of programs focusing on conservative media bias? As Thomas Griffith pointed out (*Time,* 22 April 1985) the constant repetition of a "loose charge" gives it credibility. From the perspective of the Left, conservative media bias was every bit as insidious as the right perceived liberal bias to be. From this perspective, the government line on the Vietnam War was not challenged by the media until late in the game. If it weren't for two persistent reporters, the media at large would have slept through Watergate. Anything even mildly left of mainstream liberalism was often described as radical. In the eighties, "moderate" usually meant "establishment conservative." It all depends on point of view, which is why simplistic media-bias labeling from the right or the left is so absurd. A 1982-83 Indiana University School of Journalism national poll (*The American Journalist,* David Weaver, Cleve Wilhoit) of journalists showed that the majority were politically middle-of-the-road, with the remainder equally divided between left and right. A 1985 Roper poll showed most Americans view TV news as objective.

The supposed subject of the "Viewpoint" program, patriotism and the media, was addressed at one point by Hodding Carter in response to a question. A woman in the audience asked, since "We are the good guys, and the Soviets are the bad guys," why did the media spend so much time being negative on America and why weren't the evils of the Soviets examined more often? While disagreeing that the media was overly rough on America or soft on the Soviets, Carter pointed out that if the media didn't examine the faults of government and society, it would be no different than the press in the Soviet Union. As a former government spokesperson, he stated that official statements from government officials are worthless pap, and unless the press searched elsewhere for the facts, it would simply be playing the same role that *Pravda* does in Soviet society.

From the beginning, the Reagan administration's relationship to openness with the press and related First Amendment issues had raised serious questions. During Reagan's first term, there were more stringent attempts at censorship of government employees than at any time in the postwar era and perhaps before. There was the unprecedented barring of reporters from the invasion of Grenada. There was the controversy surrounding the January 23, 1985, space shuttle flight carrying a military payload. And there was the United States withdrawal from UNESCO, the United Nations Educational, Scientific and Cultural Organization.

Starting with the UNESCO issue, *Newsday* media columnist Tom Collins wrote the following (*Los Angeles Times* Syndicate, *Seattle Times*, 9 January 1985): "While the American Press has no reason to weep over the decision of the United States to withdraw from the United Nations Educational, Scientific and Cultural Organization, it may not have any cause to rejoice, either. . . . Some press groups, including the American Newspaper Publishers Association, had thought it wiser for the United States to remain within the organization and continue to fight against any global restrictions on the press. . . . Leonard R. Sussman, executive director of Freedom House, which monitors civil and political liberties around the world, also said he thought it would have been better for the United States to stay and fight rather than pull out, since 'it is harder to fight from the outside.' He said he had been encouraged in recent months, in an exchange of letters with Amadou Makhtar M'Bow, the controversial director of UNESCO, to see that M'Bow was backing away from the issue of governmental licensing of reporters and was putting more emphasis on the practical issue of helping Third World countries develop better communications techniques. But obviously, that was too little and too late, and besides, the Reagan administration has a host of other complaints about M'Bow, ranging from lousy budget management to anti-western propagandizing. The free press issue only made the administration's decision to withdraw that much easier, which is ironic. Ronald Reagan is hardly a champion of free access to government information, and in fact would seem to share in principle and spirit the attitudes of some Third World countries that prefer the public to get its information through government-controlled channels. The press issue, however, gave the administration a chance to appear concerned about an issue it couldn't care less about."

As Collins's article suggests, a case can be made that the Reagan administration's withdrawal from UNESCO will assist in advancing the very press restrictions around the world that it insists is the reason for withdrawal. The action more closely resembles a minor victory for the extreme Right, exemplified by its long-time slogan "United States out of the United Nations." The author's main concern, however, is that whatever the arguments of the case, they were never heard on TV news programs, in spite of the fact that the issue and the many nuances and ironies described by Collins were so directly related to the very essence of news journalism.

Even closer to home was the Reagan administration's efforts to plug leaks of classified information. Lie-detector tests of U.S. employees had become routine. But in terms of the press, the most potentially far-reaching move was the attempted application of the Espionage Act of 1917 to nonespionage-related government leaks. The Nixon administration had attempted to utilize this law in going after Daniel Ellsberg in the Pentagon Papers case, but because of prosecution misconduct, a court test never occurred. The new test case was against Naval Intelligence Support Center employee Samuel Morison, who purportedly gave a U.S. satellite photograph of a Soviet aircraft carrier to the British magazine *Jane's Defence Weekly*. The potential pandora's box opened by this Reagan administration attempt, if successful, could involve journalists being tried as spies for refusing to reveal sources. In addition, there was the ongoing question about what should and should not be properly classified as secret in a democratic society, and what safeguards against government manipulation were to exist in this regard. In remarks at an event sponsored by the Congressional Clearinghouse on the Future (14 March 1985), Walter Cronkite commented: "We find pressure today from this administration against the Freedom of Information Act. There has probably never been any piece of legislation that has been so supportive of people's right to know as the Freedom of Information Act, and it has worked superbly up until the last two or three years when new pressures are coming from the Justice Department to put a clamp on FOI access." These were serious questions that should have been thoroughly examined by broadcast journalists.

The American military action in Grenada represented an unhappy and ominous milestone in the history our "free" press. David Schoenbrun was a pioneer in both radio and television news broadcasting and a colleague of Ed Murrow, William Shirer, Eric Sevaraid, Howard K. Smith, Charles Collingwood, and others. For many years he was CBS's chief correspondent in Paris and then Washington, and is now a news analyst for the Independent News Network. His words (December 20, 1984) on PBS's first-rate program "Latenight America," hosted by Dennis Wholey, in response to a question from a viewer, most eloquently express the concerns raised by the Grenada experience: "As a war correspondent, in twelve wars, I've never once been prevented from covering the wars and telling you, the American people, what was happening. And I thought that the blackout, the boycott of the newsmen on Grenada, was absolutely uncalled for. Who in the world is going to report as objectively as possible to the American people—the reporter, or the general? Is the general going to get up on the air and say to you, 'Boy, I made a big mistake today, a lot of American boys were killed'? If you want to find out what's going on, you're going to find out from an independent reporter. And not taking reporters is in effect not boycotting us, it's boycotting you, the American public. You were kept out of Grenada along with us."

Schoenbrun went on to make clear that security was not the issue, because, as he said, "In a war we [the press] accept censorship." The press could have been taken along on any terms the military required, but it was inexcusable that they were not allowed at all. Those are the methods of totalitarian states. Although, as Schoenbrun pointed out, the American public was the ultimate loser, the public support for the invasion was so strong that initial press complaints fell on unconcerned ears, and the media soon dropped the subject. This was, again, a particular failing of TV news. The issue could have and should have remained on the front burner. It certainly should have been examined thoroughly during the campaign, and the one-year anniversary of the invasion offered the additional opportunity for such a focus. But although there was some focus on Grenada, this clear-cut issue of the people's right to know (compared to the larger and more complex issue of the invasion itself, which also needed closer examination) was not given its due. Because the media were following public sentiment instead of paying attention to basic principles, would only a future military catastrophe, where cameras and note pads were again barred, jar the public into understanding what was at stake when the press is forbidden to cover military actions?

Former CBS News producer and president Fred Friendly criticized both himself and CBS for not covering President Johnson's Tonkin Gulf speech in 1964 with in-depth analysis (in *The Mass Media Book*, Holmgren and Norton, editors). He believed that without taking a position, but simply by reporting the facts, broadcast journalism could possibly have prevented this sham on Johnson's part from turning into the tragedy of full-scale

U.S. involvement in Vietnam. According to Donna Woolfolk Cross in her book *Media-Speak*, Friendly later resigned from CBS because the network decided to air "I Love Lucy" reruns instead of broadcasting the congressional hearings on Vietnam. Two decades after the Tonkin Gulf "incident," the media were barred from even accompanying U.S. troops into action, but press protest and coverage of this issue were short-lived, seemingly out of fear that no one was listening, which of course guaranteed that the public would never concentrate on its importance in terms of the functioning of a free society.

If anything, the media acted as if they had something to prove to the government in the aftermath of the Grenada invasion, that they could be trusted to be taken along next time. This statement is based on the incident surrounding the space shuttle's first major military mission in January 1985. *Newsweek* (31 December 1984) reported that air force spokesman Brigadier General Richard Abel "threatened to investigate if the press even speculated" about the significance of the shuttle's mission, and that Defense Secretary Caspar Weinberger and CIA Director William Casey, along with other Pentagon officials, talked NBC, CBS, the Associated Press, and *Newsweek* out of reporting what they knew about the mission. When the *Washington Post* bucked the tide and ran a story stating what was obvious to everyone, that a new spy satellite would be launched, Weinberger harshly attacked the newspaper for "giving aid and comfort to the enemy."

This ludicrous charge was fortunately discredited by Senate Intelligence Committee Vice-Chairman Daniel Moynihan, who stated: "In my judgment and in [committee Chairman] Barry Goldwater's judgment, there is nothing in that story that was not already public knowledge." But the very attempt by the Pentagon, as in Grenada, to impose a news embargo for no legitimate reason was disconcerting to say the least. And the language used by Weinberger, precisely because it was so totally without foundation, was reminiscent of Senator Joseph McCarthy at his worst. This kind of smear-tactic attack on the press was cause for alarm. That so much of the media was so cooperative, given the facts of this incident as well as the history of Reagan administration actions regarding the press, was also a cause for concern.

In response to another even more disturbing outburst by a Reagan administration official, NBC's Tom Brokaw demonstrated how a free press should function under such circumstances. The following is Brokaw's commentary on NBC Radio (7 March 1985): "The president's science adviser, George Keyworth says the press in America is drawn from the fringe element, that it wants to tear down America. You may know a lot about science, Dr. Keyworth, but I have a thing or two to tell you about the men and women who work in the American news business. . . .

Dr. George Keyworth is the White House Science Adviser. He's an expert on military weapons. He spent much of his career at the Los Alamos Weapons Laboratory, and in his current job, he's an outspoken promoter of the Strategic Defense Initiative and the MX Missile—two of the most controversial weapons proposals to come along in years. The MX and the Strategic Defense Initiative, so-called Star Wars, are expensive and may be destabilizing. That is, instead of preventing nuclear war, many experts believe the MX and "Star Wars" may make a nuclear exchange more likely. So these systems have received a lot of press attention, for and against. I tell you this because it may help explain why Dr. Keyworth unloaded on the press recently, saying it is drawn from the fringe elements of society, the far left; that it is trying to tear down America; that it deliberately distorts science and technological issues. Pardon me, Dr. Keyworth, but that is an outrageously irresponsible statement for any government official to make, especially the president's Science Adviser, who should have a far greater regard for the facts. I know of no journalist in any position of responsibility in any of our major newspapers, news magazines, networks, who can be described as representing some kind of fringe element, or who is interested in tearing down America. My guess is that I know a good many more of these journalists than Dr. Keyworth. Dr. Keyworth also accuses the press of attacking anything that resembles the establishment. Come on, Dr. Keyworth. In most cases, the press in America is part of the establishment. What's especially shocking about these charges is that they come from the president's own science adviser." As Walter Cronkite said (Congressional Clearinghouse on the Future, March 14, 1985): "I sort of want to say, 'Spiro Agnew, where are you?' I have a terrible feeling that—here we go again!"

Tom Brokaw deserved tremendous credit for this necessary and forceful response to the incredible frontal attack on freedom of the press represented by this example. But there was a catch that could not go unnoticed or unmentioned. Brokaw's commentary was for radio only. It was never seen on TV.

Before, during and after the 1984 presidential election campaign, the Reagan administration's disdain for real freedom of the press was made unmistakably clear. But the responsiblity for this not becoming an issue of concern to the American public lay with the news media themselves, pariculary television as it was the medium most effectively used by the Reagan White House, and is the single greatest source of information by far for the largest number of people. In television's infancy, with McCarthyism tearing apart the fabric of our democracy, the most effective act against this threat was from a broadcast journalist, Edward R. Murrow. His confrontation with Senator Joseph McCarthy's Communist-baiting smear tactics and lies was the beginning of the end of the infamous senator's stranglehold on American politics. He did not let considerations of being accused of partisanship, concerns about public opinion, or even the very real potential for personal persecution mitigate his sense of journalistic integrity and commitment to democracy.

The point is not to equate the Reagan administration as a whole with Joe McCarthy. The point is that government and the press in a free society must, by definition, be adversaries, with more at stake at some moments in history than others. The point is that the public in a free society depends on the press for information. And the point is that television news needs to be haunted by the likes of Edward R. Murrow, for the sake of both democracy and its own future.

CHAPTER EIGHT

An Appeal to Conscience

On Wednesday evening, February 6, 1985, President Ronald Reagan delivered the annual State of the Union address to a joint session of Congress and to the American people in their living rooms through television. It was a masterful performance, with a heart-pounding, tear-jerking Hollywood finale, as he introduced as "American heroes" a young Vietnamese woman, Jean Nguyen, who had fled Vietnam ten years earlier and was about to graduate from West Point, and an elderly black woman, "Mother" Clara Hale, who cared for the babies of heroin junkies in Harlem. They were indeed American heroes, but the incongruity of these symbols in terms of Reagan administration policies was undoubtedly lost on most viewers. The show was the thing, and no one puts them on quite like the "Gipper." As Johnny Carson put it in a humorous reference to the event in his "Tonight" show monologue the following night, "It [Reagan's speech] was upbeat, but I thought having the solid-gold dancers behind him was a little much." Ronald Reagan was not only president of the United States. He was the undisputed king of video wizardry. But as CNN's Daniel Schorr astutely pointed out in postspeech analysis, there were "issues as opposed to great theater" about which the president's speech raised questions. There was a particularly telling scene from this February 6 evening that would ultimately have more impact on Reagan's historical reputation than perhaps anything else. During his speech, the president delivered his standard line about economic growth being the answer to the deficit crisis, which received moderate applause. Among those *not* applauding were Senators Robert Dole and Alan Simpson, the top Republican leaders in the Senate. They knew that long-term economic growth or disaster, the future of the Republican party and their own careers, and most ironically, Ronald Reagan's place in history, all depended on their ability to forge a more realistic consensus in Congress to bring down the exponentially escalating national debt. They knew there was a frightening downside to the politics of optimistic video imagery.

However, this was the politics television had created, not by definition, but by news programming's approach. And the Democrats proved that they would not be outdone in intellectual mediocrity by their videotaped "response" to Reagan's address. The concept of loyal opposition, so essential in some form to the health of any democracy, was thrown to the wind, and the Democrats engaged instead in a stampede of what CBS's Bruce Morton accurately described as "me too politics" in a reaction to Reagan's landslide election victory. The Democratic videotape was prerecorded, and therefore was not an actual response to the president's remarks, which is how their time should have been utilized. In terms of imagery, the Democrats' video show was geared to the baby-boom generation, which would be the key to the future of American politics. As a production, it had "attempted slickness" written all over it and failed badly. The producers should have studied the Reagan campaign commercials. But in the end, adopting the Reagan approach could only be suicidal for the Democrats, as it would always be a cheap substitute for the real thing. It certainly did nothing for democracy. It did demonstrate, however, what TV was doing to democracy.

ABC proved beyond dispute on this evening that democracy was irrelevant to its executives. In the most sickening display of greed intoxication and civic irresponsibility in memory, ABC decided to run its trash sensation "Dynasty" instead of the Democrats' response to Reagan's address. It was a conscious cut-throat decision by people whose only ethos was dollars, no matter what the cost to society. The other networks were running both the Democrats' response and extensive analysis of the president's speech, and ABC decided to increase its ratings through this unprecedented tactic, as it was "sweeps month," during which ratings determine advertising rates. There was little doubt that "Dynasty" would draw many viewers away from the political coverage, as the networks for years had conditioned the audience to choose the drug of increasingly vapid entertainment programs over any kind of reality. This was a prime reason why both politics and the news coverage of it had become increasingly packaged in a sports-and-entertainment style for television consumption.

NBC deserved tremendous credit on this night for running two hours of prime-time coverage beginning with Reagan's State of the Union address, followed by the Democratic videotape, and analyis of both. But the question arose: Why was there never such prime-time coverage during the campaign? There wasn't this much analysis even after the debates. What purpose was served by analyzing policy choices at such length at this point, as opposed to before the election? It was certainly appropriate to cover the State of the Union event in depth, and in fact, as has been amply pointed out, there is a need for much more extensive ongoing public-affairs programming. But where was it during the campaign, when it was needed most?

On this night, when the State of the Union was the topic at hand, the various images flickering across the video screen reinforced deep concern for the state of American democracy in the television age.

It is worth keeping in mind that there never was a golden age of television news to which one can urge returning. The first news broadcasts, begining on CBS in 1948, were only fifteen minutes in length and consisted of an anchorman (although the term was not used then) reading short reports in front of a camera. According to Barbara Matusow in her book *The Evening Stars,* Edward R. Murrow and many of his fellow "scholar-reporters" of radio and World War II experience were condescending toward and skeptical about the idea of news on television. Some from this background, however, such as Eric Sevaraid, Howard K. Smith, and David Schoenbrun, would end up playing a significant role in TV news. Murrow, to the end, refused to have anything to do with it. According to Matusow, he once stated his overall concern about the mix of TV and journalism by saying that television was more interested in the picture of the atom bomb than the horror of it. As Fred Friendly, his long-time producer, stated in the CBS report highlighted here during the 1984 campaign, Murrow would have even greater reason to make such a statement today. But part of Murrow's and his colleagues' skepticism about news on television was related to its early inaccessiblity compared to that of radio, which obviously is no longer the case. If the power of the "picture" is used to underline, not overwhelm, the substance, through lengthier reports and interviews, through the use of graphics that please the eye but reinforce instead of distract from the point at hand; if the techniques of TV are used with intelligence and integrity, then there can be a golden age of television yet to come.

Murrow's contribution to broadcast journalism came in the form of longer documentaries for TV and a standard of journalism. The documentary approach is in essence what television news could aspire to with longer programming and/or concentrating on fewer stories per evening, much as MacNeil/Lehrer does. In terms of a standard of journalism, it should be remembered that Murrow's famous 1953 rebuke of Senator McCarthy on his program "See It Now" was in spite of CBS standards that did not allow such an "opinionated" approach. According to

Matusow, these standards were established in 1937 not for journalistic reasons, but because CBS president William Paley wanted to avoid the controversy that had occurred over earlier statements of strong opinion on CBS radio programming. Murrow's action, taken at the risk of losing his job, was a classic case of individual integrity winning out over the institution. Because he was popular and because the overwhelming majority of Americans responded positively to his "opinion," today recognized as historical truth, he was able to get away with it, although funding for his program was cut back within a couple of years. This may, ostensibly, have been because of ratings, which were never excellent for "See It Now," but ratings played a lesser role in network decisions then, particularly in terms of public-affairs programming, which is the proper approach. It should be stated, however, that "See It Now," always widely acclaimed critically, did have a substantial audience and that this was television in its infancy. An indirect descendent of "See It Now" is "60 Minutes," which is a huge ratings success.

The role of the reporter, according to David Schoenbrun ("Latenight America," December 20, 1984), is that of a teacher. A good teacher, of course, attempts to impart the facts as objectively as possible, while realizing that facts need interpretation to be comprehensible. The very act of interpreting facts is by definition subjective opinion. To the degree that broadcast journalism presents the facts in depth as objectively as possible, then offers varying interpretations of these facts, offering a "marketplace of ideas" to the viewing public, it is doing its job. To this definition must be added a caveat for national broadcasting: The network television news programs should concern themselves with news of national and international significance, as they are the communications common ground for the public in a national sense. The great national and international issues should be examined and argued in this forum.

During the week of the historic ABC "Nightline" broadcasts from South Africa, Ted Koppel was interviewed by Barbara Howar on "Entertainment Tonight" (19 March 1985). Explaining why he was spending an entire week broadcasting from and about South Africa, Koppel stated that every once and a while a story comes along that hasn't been told properly. He went on to say, "Maybe once in a while we in journalism need to do a story before it becomes a crisis. . . . We tend both in government and journalism to be crisis-oriented." Koppel ventured that maybe the Iran crisis, for instance, could have been avoided if "we" focussed on it before the explosion. His point is right on the mark. But the quality of journalism demonstrated by "Nightline" during the week of programs from South Africa is not something needed once in a while. It is needed continuously.

As has been said already, to accomplish this goal the commercial network nightly news programs must abandon their present half-hour length and adopt a one-hour format similar to "The MacNeil/Lehrer News-Hour" on PBS. There is no question that in the short run this would require an economically venturous spirit and scheduling changes in affiliates' news programs and network prime-time programs, all of which would be resisted. But in the long run I believe it would pay off. There may be a place for more in-depth reporting and less interviewing than MacNeil/Lehrer if the commercial networks were to move to a one-hour length. Interviews are a most useful approach, as we have seen, but a lengthy report has different and equally useful attributes. MacNeil/Lehrer produces lengthy special reports periodically, which are first rate and highly informative. The former excellent one-hour news program "NBC Overnight" often utilized lengthy reports from the BBC and other foreign sources, as well as lengthy interviews with NBC reporters. The results were exciting. Although not providing nearly the same impact, significant improvement could be made even within the present half-hour format by avoiding superfluous stories and concentrating on a few important ones. "NBC Nightly News" gave us a glimpse of what was possible when late in the presidential campaign it ran lengthy segments of the BBC documentary on the Ethiopian famine. It must be emphasized that program length is not the only issue, as CNN has amply proven, with its constant news updates, which are merely an extended version of the facile approach of the NBC, ABC, and CBS nightly news programs. Program length is a means to an end, the end being quality reporting on the major issues of our times. This should also be accomplished by regularly scheduled documentary and news specials, during prime time, to a substantially greater degree than now occurs. In the 1960s, the networks each produced approximately forty prime-time documentaries a year. Today, the number is only a quarter of that rate. ABC displayed its schizophrenia in terms of network civic responsibility in the State of the Union/"Dynasty" decision, and provided an inspiring example of what was possible on June 6, 1985. ABC took what *Newsweek* (10 June 1985) described as "the prime-time high road for three hours" in the documentary, *The Fire Unleashed,* covering the history of nuclear weapons and energy. This decision to devote the entire prime-time schedule to public affairs deserves both applause and emulation. Another potentially positive move would be the abandoning of the anchorperson "star" system in favor of less personality-oriented news reporting, with multiple and rotating anchors, such as employed by the BBC and other European television news programs, which tends to foster a greater emphasis on the news itself. ABC deserves credit for attempting to move in this direction on "World News Tonight," but abandoned the experiment too early. However, there are potentially positive aspects of the "personality" news delivery, if that personality is highly intelligent, well informed, and not afraid to be creative. "NBC Overnight" proved that both the above approaches have an advantage, as different reporters often alternated as anchors with Linda Ellerbee, Lou Dobbs or Bill Schectner, bringing their varied personalities and styles with them, as opposed to each mimicking the stale, homogeneous, staged-personality approach seen in so many anchors, seemingly learned at the same broadcasting school. It may turn out that personalities are useful, particularly at the beginning stages of the kind of news-programming transition I am advocating, in terms of creating audience interest.

In addition, broadcast journalism must be the first line of defense on the issue of freedom of speech and the public's right to know. The recent rash of libel cases brought against the media—Westmoreland, Sharon, Mobil Oil—demonstrate both the responsibility for accuracy and the constantly endangered terrain on which a free press operates. These difficulties are part of the job description and should not inhibit, but spur on a free press in exercising its rights and responsibilities. Related is the fact that the job of a journalist in a democracy is not to be a reflection of public opinion any more than it is to be a reflection of government opinion. The public may want the reporter to be a cheerleader, as David Schoenbrun asserts. But the job of the reporter is to tell the truth, to the best of his or her ability to do so objectively, while honestly relating an interpretation at the same time. The job of producers and directors is to see that the "opinions" are varied. But the starting point is that much-abused and most fallible word *truth*. Its fallibility cannot be an excuse for journalism to shrink from it, even if it often means a "kill the messenger" response from the public. This response will likely at first turn into an uproar from some in the audience if anything close to the recommendations of this book are ever implemented. That is the normal process of withdrawal from a drug. Not until the process is over does one appreciate where one is in relationship to where one was. However, the transition would not be entirely difficult, as some aspects of the public's current distaste for the media could be immediately ameliorated. The perception that TV news and all news dwells too much on the "negative" is largely based on the fleeting reports of problem after problem without the time to focus on problems in the context of possible solutions. Hard choices presented in the context of workable solutions, perhaps different workable solutions with different tradeoffs, are still hard choices, but they offer the option of optimism over despair. And no matter how difficult the choices or limited the options, does not the public need to know in a democracy? David Schoenbrun used the following example on "Latenight America" (December 20, 1984) as an allegory for the journalist's role in a democracy and how the public should perceive that role. Speaking of his wife, he said, "If she were feeling poorly and had aches and pains, I'd take her to my doctor, and I'd say, 'Doctor, I love this woman. Find out what's wrong with her.' Would I say to the doctor, 'Hey, wait a minute now. I love her. Don't you dare tell me anything bad about her'? Oh, no, I'd say, 'You find out what's wrong with this woman, please sir, and cure her.' And I love my country. And my job is to find out what's wrong with my country, because if you don't know what's wrong, you can't correct it."

This is not to say that we should not hear what is right about our country. Both in pragmatic and spiritual terms, this too is necessary. But healthy adults should be secure enough not to need to indulge in constant back slapping. In fact, human nature seems to require that we spend the majority of our time meeting new challenges to find fulfillment. And in the end, while the potential for destroying our planet exists, while millions starve, while the economic future of the next generation is threatened, as long as these and other human holocausts or perils face us, what option do we have but to face these issues and find solutions? It is the job of broadcast journalism, through the most revolutionary communications medium ever known to humanity, to inform people about the full range of choices inherent in these challenges, and those yet to come.

So we arrive at the ultimate question this book raises. How can we expect or hope for the commercial television networks to make the kinds of radical changes that have been indicated in these pages? Some simply require exercising intellectual integrity within the present framework. Others are more difficult to accomplish.

This question, to truly be given its due, would need to be the subject of another book. But the short answer, the conclusions I have reached, are these.

First, one must ask why the networks take the approach they do.

The national media as well as local media in this country are largely in the hands of a few corporate powers. It is difficult to have a marketplace of ideas when there is so little competition in the marketplace. In his book *The Media Monopoly*, Ben Bagdikian suggests ways in which legal and licensing actions could be taken to change this trend. It would, no doubt, be a healthy development. It is difficult to say, however, what the likelihood of such action is, given the political and/or popular will that would be required. A potential "free market" influence is the proliferation of cable television, the possibility of an infusion of new players and the resulting new, and one hopes creative and diverse, programming. But this will take many years to unfold. And as indicated in the introduction, the evidence so far suggests, at least on a national scale, that in public-affairs and news programming, as in entertainment, the networks will remain dominant.

In her book *Media-Speak*, Donna Woolfolk Cross states that one of the reasons the network news is noncontroversial and lacks substance, particularly on government and politics, is that "Big Brother" in the form of the Federal Communications Commission, is watching. Cross offers quotes of television news executives claiming that their stories are "bland" because of fear of FCC harassment. This is certainly an area that should be examined in depth, and again, one would hope that the political will to pressure Congress to make certain that the FCC is not inhibiting freedom of speech could be mobilized. But political will depends on the public being informed, so the ball is back in the network executive's court. The FCC harassment line, though perhaps credible, is in the end just another excuse used by broadcast journalists. If they won't stand up for their own rights, no one else is likely to.

Taken to the extreme, the monopoly or government control "views" of the media equation have always added up to an establishment "conspiracy" in the eyes of some on both the right and left of the political spectrum. It has always been ironic and mildly entertaining to observe the degree to which they see the same thing, with completely different labels for the supposed politics of the "establishment." In my own view, these approaches, even at their most sophisticated, while sometimes articulating important half truths, are ultimately simplistic and a dead end. We still have one of the more functional, if imperfect and constantly endangered, democracies in the world. Establishments and alliances certainly exist in the United States, but fortunately they have a way of changing, of not being monolithic, of being penetrable, because of changing economic, social, political, and even personal factors. This last consideration is worth focusing on. In the end, institutions cannot exist or functon without the consent of the individual, if he or she is willing to pay any price to affirm that truth. In this century, both Gandhi and Nuremberg affirmed this principle. So it is with the individual that my hope lies, even within the context of institutions as they now exist.

In terms of the institution of network television as it now exists, the dominating force is money (which the recent ABC and CBS takeover activity has made abundantly clear). This is natural enough, as it is a business. But this is almost certainly the main reason for the lack of journalistic integrity in television news. News programming is in many ways a public service bone thrown to the FCC, in theory, to us, the public, for allowing them to do business on the airwaves. Unfortunately, perhaps inevitably, the competition between even the network news programs, which at one time had a more professional journalistic edge to it, has now come down to dollars. Advertising dollars to be precise and, therefore, who has the best ratings. The network executives have read the studies showing how fast the channel can be changed when the news belabors a serious issue. The image, the technical razzle-dazzle, has more and more invaded the newsroom for this reason. The anchorperson has taken on the glamor (and pay) of a movie star. Pictures stories are more entertaining than substance stories. Substance turned into controversy and sports rhetoric is entertaining. Substance dwelt on at length is boring. This is the likely rationale behind the results we see on the nightly news. But there are two essential factors missing from this analysis by the network moguls. And if they ever come to understand these factors, they may be willing to risk change, for they will realize that they can have their dollars and their integrity both, if they're willing to take a chance, to lose money for a while as an investment in the future, for the sake of honorable journalism.

These two essential factors are intertwined. They are, first, that the ratings tell us only that people are addicted to the escapist junk television has given them, and that, second, there are intellectual, emotional, and spiritual needs—the basic human needs to know, to learn, and to grow—that television could cater to, and still prosper. As we saw in Bernard Goldberg's report on the "CBS Evening News" during the campaign, "Television: A Nation Hooked," there are network executives who understand this. The next step, for them, is the courage to act. Every quantum leap in every field of human endeavor requires a certain vision that will sustain the people involved through the difficulty of transition. There is no question that it is easier to maintain the status quo, to not look beyond one's nose, in every aspect of human life. Change is always difficult, particularly when millions of dollars are at stake as well. But without change and risk, there is no creativity, no life. The changes in TV news broadcasting that I have described will cost millions of dollars and probably take many years of perseverance to pay off. There are those who would argue that the evidence suggests it would never pay off. The answer to that assertion is that television hasn't existed long enough, whatever examples one may come up with, to draw such a conclusion. In addition, as I have stated, any such evidence is tainted by the self-fulfilling-prophecy orientation of a ratings system that measures the degree to which people expect and are addicted to what they have always been given. It will take years of commitment to broadcasting the kind of journalism described here to create the objective environment in which comparative ratings can be examined with any degree of validity. The same theory can be applied to television as a whole, in terms of the kind of entertainment programming it broadcasts. If PBS and the corporate sponsors of "The MacNeil/Lehrer NewsHour" stay committed to their pioneer effort for the years it will take to adequately refine the program and become a permanent fixture of broadcast journalism, I believe the public will respond very positively within the confines of PBS's reach, which of course is less extensive than that of the commercial networks. The future of "The MacNeil/Lehrer NewsHour" is still precarious. Commercialism has slowly crept into the PBS system and many of the affiliate program managers have demonstrated the vision of intellectual midgets by their expressed preference for MacNeil/Lehrer to return to a thirty-minute format, as James Traub pointed out in the *Columbia Journalism Review* (January/February 1985.) The discontinuation of this evolutionary program would signify a step back into the dark ages for broadcast journalism. "The MacNeil/Lehrer NewsHour" has been a milestone, defining anew the possibilities for TV news in America. An optimal public response to a new definition of broadcast journalism would probably not be seen until all the major networks were committed to such an approach over a long period of time. But it has to begin somewhere. Someone has to decide to make history. Whoever it is, in my opinion, will be displaying enlightened self-interest, will ultimately be rewarded both financially and in spirit. I am confident that in the long run the American public, the viewing audience, would respond with excitement to this new opportunity to learn and to participate in their country's democracy and their planet's future.

On May 28, 1985 Phil Donahue commented on his syndicated TV program to his guests, NBC's Tom Brokaw and ABC's Peter Jennings: "MacNeil/Lehrer News Hour is in my judgment *very* strong. We should also say that it is an hour, and that neither you (NBC and ABC) or CBS is." Tom Brokaw responded that the local stations control the half-hour between the national news and prime-time and didn't want to give it up. He went on to say, however, that the local stations could justifiably say to the networks, "You guys want an hour news program? You've got three hours between 8:00 and 11:00 every night. Put an hour in there somewhere. Why take it out of our time? So that's the complication. . . . We would like to have an hour at some point in the schedule on a daily basis . . . because I think that everyday we develop, metaphorically speaking, a hundred pounds of information—we still only have a ten pound bag in which to put it—and that's the problem." Peter Jennings remarked," I don't know any reporter, any producer, any editor, any news executive, who would not like ideally to have an hour-long news broadcast at 10:00 every night when at least the day is over and you've had some time to digest it. . . . the former president of CBS was asked this [Why not a one-hour newscast?] . . . and his answer was, 'Perhaps you [the audience] wouldn't watch it, we would certainly do it.' " Brokaw commented, "I think they would watch." The *Donahue* audience whole-heartedly agreed, with strong applause, and comment after comment asking for a one-hour news program during prime-time (most mentioned 8:00 P.M.) when it would be more convenient to watch. But Jennings mentioned the impediment: "I think the three commercial networks are just not very bold."

The main purpose of this book has been to examine the quality and impact of television's nightly news programs on American democracy during a presidential election campaign, which leads by definition to an examination of broadcast journalism overall. Taping and studying all the nationally broadcast nightly news programs throughout the 1984 campaign led me to the conclusion that commercial network television news has a seriously damaging effect on the democratic process and, to a large extent, has no right to be called journalism at all. Any change must start with this realization.

This can and will, I believe, change for the better. Whether through vision or the lessons of cataclysm, the TV medium will ultimately live up to its promise, unless history is brought to an abrupt end. But a price is paid for every moment of delay.

As one who believes in the necessity of vision in any age, and particularly in an age when cataclysms can mean the end of life on earth, I conclude this book with an appeal to conscience. To all those who work in broadcast journalism, to all the viewers in the audience: Every individual can make a difference. The viewer who changes the channel, turns off the TV, writes to advertisers, contributes to their PBS affiliate in support of "The MacNeil/Lehrer NewsHour," writes to the network—this viewer can make a difference. News and information must also be sought from other sources, such as newspapers, magazines, periodicals and books. The quality of thought stimulated by reading can never be replaced by video. At the same time, the video experience has its own valuable qualities. Television viewing and reading should compliment each other, and the responsible viewer will make certain that they do.

But primarily my appeal to conscience goes to the people who make up the institution called network television. Every individual—cameraperson, researcher, editor, reporter, director, producer, anchor, executive—who puts integrity first will make a tremendous difference. Some may make a historic difference.

Americans are all citizens of a nation called the last best hope of humankind. If that promise is to be fulfilled, there is no time to lose. The American people need all the information and diversity of opinion they can get, so that democracy, in full flower, can then deliver on the promise.

The Televised Presidential and Vice-Presidential Debates

Transcript of Louisville Debate Between Reagan and Mondale, October 7, 1984

DOROTHY S. RIDINGS: *Good evening from the Kentucky Center for the Arts in Louisville, Kentucky. I'm Dorothy Ridings, president of the League of Women Voters, the sponsor of tonight's first presidential debate between Republican Ronald Reagan and Democrat Walter Mondale.*

Tonight's debate marks the third consecutive presidential election in which the league is presenting the candidates for the nation's highest office in face-to-face debate.

Our panelists are James Wieghart, national political correspondent for Scripps-Howard News Service; Diane Sawyer, correspondent for the CBS program "60 Minutes," and Fred Barnes, national political correspondent for the Baltimore Sun.

Barbara Walters of ABC News, who is appearing in her fourth presidential debate, is our moderator. Barbara:

MODERATOR: *A few words as we begin tonight's debate, about the format. The position of the candidates, that is, who answers questions first, and who gives the last statement was determined by a toss of the coin between the two candidates. Mr. Mondale won. And that means that he chose to give the final closing statement. It means, too, that the president will answer the first question first. I hope that's clear. If it isn't, it will become clear as the debate goes on.*

Further, the candidates will be addressed as they each wanted and will therefore be called Mr. President and Mr. Mondale. Since there will also be a second debate between the two presidential candidates tonight will focus primarily on the economy and other domestic issues.

The debate itself is built around questions from the panel. In each of its segments a reporter will ask the candidates the same general question. Then—and this is important—each candidate will have the chance to rebut what the other has said. In the final segment of the debate will be the closing segment and the candidates will each have four minutes for their closing statement. And as I have said, Mr. Mondale will be the last person on the program to speak.

And now I would like to add a personal note, if I may. As Dorothy Riding's pointed out, I have been involved now in four presidential debates, either as a moderator or as a panelist. In the past there was no problem in selecting panelists. Tonight, however, there were to have been four panelists participating in this debate. The candidates were given a list of almost 100 qualified journalists from all the media and could agree on only these three fine journalists.

As moderator and on behalf of my fellow journalists I very much regret as does the League of Women Voters that this situation has occurred. And now let us begin the debate with the first question from James Wieghart. Mr. Wieghart.

Deficit, the Budget, and the Economy

Q: *Mr. President, in, 1980, you promised the American people, in your campaign, a balanced budget by 1983. We've now had more and bigger deficits in the four years you've been in office. Mr. President, do you have a secret plan to balance the budget some time in the second term, and if so, would you lay out that plan for us tonight?*

REAGAN: *I have a plan. Not a secret plan. As a matter of fact, it is the economic recovery program that we presented when I took office in 1981. It is true that earlier, working with some very prominent economists, I had come up, during the campaign, with an economic program that I thought could rectify the great problems confronting us: the double-digit inflation, the high tax rates that I think were hurting the economy, the stagflation that we were undergoing. Before even the election day, something that none of those economists had even predicted had happened, that the economy was so worsened that I was openly saying that what we had thought the basis of our plan could have brought a balanced budget; that was no longer possible.*

So the plan that we have had and that we're following, is a plan that is *based on growth in the economy, recovery without inflation, and reducing the share of the, that the government is taking from the gross national product, which has become a drag on the economy. Already we have a recovery that has been going on for about twenty-one months, to the point that we can now call it an expansion. Under that, this year, we have seen a $21 billion reduction in the deficit from last year, based mainly on the increased revenues the government is getting without raising tax rates.*

Our tax cut, we think, was very instrumental in bringing about this economic recovery. We have reduced inflation to about a third of what it was. The interest rates have come down about nine or ten points, and we think must come down further. In the last twenty-one months, more than 6 million people have gotten jobs. There have been created new jobs for those people to where there are now 105 million civilians working where there were only 99 million before, 107 if you count the military.

So we believe that as we continue to reduce the level of government spending, the increase, rate of increase in government spending, which has come down from 17 to 6 percent, and at the same time as the growth in the economy increases the revenues the government gets without raising taxes, those two lines will meet. And when they meet, that is a balanced budget.

Q: *Mr. President, the Congressional Budget Office has some bad news. The lines aren't about to meet according to their projection; they project that the budget deficit will continue to climb. In the year 1989 they project a budget deficit of $273 billion. In view of that and in view of the economic recovery we are now enjoying, would it make sense to propose a tax increase or take some other fiscal measures to reduce that deficit now when times are relatively good?*

REAGAN: *The deficit is a result, it is a result of excessive government spending. I do not, and very frankly, take seriously the Congressional Budget Office projections because they have been wrong on virtually all of them, including the fact that our recovery wasn't going to take place to begin with. But it has taken place. But as I said we have the rate of increase in government spending down to 6 percent. If the rate of increase in government spending can be held to 5 percent—we're not far from there—by 1989 that would have reduced the budget deficits down to a $30 billion or $40 billion level. At the same time, if we can have a 4 percent recovery continue through that same period of time, that will mean without an increase in tax rates, that will mean $400 billion more in government revenues. And so I think that the lines can meet. Actually, in constant dollars, in the domestic side of the budget there has been no spending increase in the four years that we have been here.*

Q: *Mr. Mondale, the Carter-Mondale administration didn't come close to balancing the budget in its four years in office either, despite the fact that President Carter did promise a balanced budget during his term. You have* *proposed a plan combining tax increases and budgetary cuts and other changes in the administration of the government that would reduce the projected budget deficit by two-thirds to approximately $87 billion in 1989. That still is an enormous deficit that we'll be running for these four years. What other steps do you think should be taken to reduce this deficit and position the country for economic growth?*

MONDALE: *One of the key tests of leadership is whether one sees clearly the nature of the problem confronted by our nation. And perhaps the dominant domestic issue of our times is what do we do about these enormous deficit.*

I respect the president. I respect the presidency and I think he knows that.

But the fact of it is every estimate by this administration about the size of the deficit has been off by billions and billions of dollars. As a matter of fact, over four years, they've missed the mark by nearly $600 billion. We were told we would have a balanced budget in 1983. It was $200 billion deficit instead. And now we have a major question facing the American people as to whether we'll deal with this deficit and get it down for the sake of a healthy recovery. Virtually every economic analysis that I've head of, including the distinguished Congressional Budget Office, which is respected by, I think, almost everyone, says that even with historically high levels of economic growth, we will suffer a $263 billion deficit. In other words, it doesn't converge, as the president suggests. It gets larger, even with growth.

What that means is that we will continue to have devastating problems with foreign trade. This is the worst trade year in American history, by far. Our rural and farm friends will have continued devastation. Real interest rates, the real cost of interest, will remain very very high. And many economists are predicting that we're moving into a period of very slow growth because the economy is tapering off and may be a recession.

I get it down to a level below 2 percent of gross national product with a policy that's fair. I've stood up and told the American people that I think it's a real problem, that it can destroy long-term economic growth, and I've told you what I think should be done.

I think this is a test of leadership and I think the American people know the difference.

Q: *Mr. Mondale, one other way to attack the deficit is further reductions in spending. The president has submitted a number of proposals to Congress to do just that, and in many instances the House, controlled by the Democrats, has opposed them.*

Isn't it one aspect of leadership for prominent Democrats such as yourself to encourage responsible reductions in spending and thereby reduce the deficit?

MONDALE: *Absolutely. And I have proposed over $100 billion in cuts in federal spending over four years. But I am not going to cut it out of Social Security and Medicare and student assistance and things that people need.*

These people depend upon all of us for the little security that they have. And I'm not going to do it that way. The rate of defense spending increase can be slowed; certainly we can find a coffeepot that costs something less than $7,000.

And there are other ways of squeezing this budget without constantly picking on our senior citizens and the most vulnerable in American life.

And that's why the Congress, including the Republicans, have not gone along with the president's recommendations.

MODERATOR: *I would like to ask the audience please to refrain from applauding either side. It just takes away from the time for your candidates. And now it is time for the rebuttal, Mr. President: one minute of rebuttal.*

REAGAN: *Yes, I don't believe that Mr. Mondale has a plan for balancing the budget. He has a plan for raising taxes. As a matter of fact, the biggest single tax increase in the nation's history took place in 1977, and for the five years previous to our taking office, taxes doubled in the United States and the budget's increased $318 billion, so there is no ratio between taxing and balancing a budget. Whether you borrow the money or whether you simply tax it away from the people, you're taking the same amount of money out of the private sector unless and until you bring down government's share of what it is taking.*

With regard to Social Security I hope there'll be more time than just this win it—minute—to mention that, but I will say this: A president should never say never. But I'm going to violate that rule and say "never." I will never stand for a reduction of the Social Security benefits to the people that are now getting them.

MODERATOR: *Mr. Mondale.*

MONDALE: *That's exactly the commitment that was made to the American people in 1980. He would never reduce benefits. And of course what happens right after the election is they proposed to cut Social Security benefits by 25 percent, reducing the adjustment for inflation, cutting our minimum benefits for the poorest on Social Security, removing educational benefits for dependents whose widows were trying, with widows trying to get them through college. Everybody remembers that. People know what happened. There's a difference. I have fought for Social Security and Medicare and for things to help people who are vulnerable all my life, and I will do it as president of the United States.*

Presidential Leadership

MODERATOR: *Thank you very much. We will now begin with segment Number two with my colleague Diane Sawyer. Miss Sawyer.*

Q: *Mr. President, Mr. Mondale. The public opinion polls do suggest that the American people are most concerned about the personal leadership characteristics of the two candidates, and each of you has questioned the other's leadership ability. Mr. President, you have said that Mr. Mondale's leadership would take the country down the path of defeatism and despair and Vice-President Bush has called him whining and hoping for bad news. And Mr. Mondale, you have said that President Reagan offers showmanship, not leadership, that he has not mastered what he must know to command his government. I'd like to ask each of you to substantiate your claims. Mr. Mondale first. Give us specifics to support your claim that President Reagan is a showman not a leader, has not mastered what he must know to be President after four years, and then second, tell us what personal leadership characteristics you have that he does not.*

MONDALE: *Well first of all, I think the first answer this evening suggests exactly what I'm saying. There is no question that we face this massive deficit. And almost everybody agrees we get it down the chances for long-term healthy growth are nil. And it's also unfair to dump these tremendous bills on our children. The president says it will disappear overnight because of some reason; no one else believes that's the case. I do and I'm standing up to the issue with an answer that's fair. I think that's what leadership is all about.*

There's a difference between being a quarterback and a cheerleader and when there's a real problem, a president must confront it. What I was referring to, of course, in the comment that you referred to, was the situation in Lebanon. Now, for three occassions, one after another, our embassies were assaulted in the same way by a truck with demolition. The first time, and I did not criticize the president because these things can happen once, and sometimes twice, the second time the barracks in Lebanon were assaulted as we all remember. There was two or three commission reports, recommendations by the CIA, the State Department, and the others, and the third time there was even a warning from the terrorists themselves.

Now I believe that a president must command that White House and those who work for him. It's the toughest job on earth. And you must master the facts and insist that things must be done, are done. I believe the way in which I will approach the presidency is what's needed. Because all my life that has been the way in which I have sought to lead. And that's why in this campaign I am telling you exactly what I want to do; I am answering your questions; I am trying to provide leadership now before the election so that the American people can participate in that decision.

Q: *You have said, Mr. Mondale, that the polls have given you lower ratings on leadership than President Reagan because your message has failed to get through. Given that you have been in public office for so many years, what accounts for the failure of your message to get through.*

MONDALE: *Well, I think we're getting better all the time, and I think tonight, as we contrast for the first time our different approach to government, to values, to the leadership in this country, I think as this debate goes forward, the American people will have, for the first time, a chance to weigh the two of us against each other. And I think as a process, as a part of that process, what I am trying to say will come across. And that is that we must lead, we must command we must direct, and a president must see it like it is. He must stand for the values of decency that the American people stand for, and he must use the power of the White House to try to control these nuclear weapons and lead this world toward a safe world.*

Q: *Mr. President, the issue is leadership in personal terms. First, do you think as Vice-President Bush said, that Mr. Mondale's campaign is one of whining and hoping for bad news. And, second, what leadership characteristics do you possess that Mr. Mondale does not?*

REAGAN: *Well, whether he does or not, let me suggest my own idea about the leadership factor, and since you've asked it. And incidentally, I might say that with regard to the 25 percent cuts of Social Security before I get to the answer of your question the only 25 percent cut that I know of was accompanying that huge 1977 tax increase was a cut of 25 percent in the benefits for every American who was born after 1916.*

Now, leadership. First of all, I think you must have some principles you believe in. In mine, I happen to believe in the people and believe that the people are supposed to be dominant in our society. That they, not government, are to have control of their own affairs to the greatest extent possible with an orderly society.

Now, having that, I think also that in leadership, well, I believe that you find the people—positions such as I'm in—who have the talent and ability to do the things that are needed in the various departments of government.

I don't believe that a leader should be spending his time in the Oval Office deciding who's going to play tennis on the White House court. And you let those people go with the guidelines of overall policy, and not looking over their shoulder and nitpicking the manner in which they go at the job. You are ultimately responsible, however, for that job.

But I also believe something else about that. I believe that—and when I became governor of California I started this and I continue it in this office—that any issue that comes before me I have instructed cabinet members and staff they are not to bring up any of the political ramifications that might surround the issue. I don't want to hear them. I want to hear only arguments as to whether it is good or bad for the people. Is it morally right.

And on that basis, and that basis alone, we make a decision on every issue.

Now, with regard to my feeling about why I though that his record bespoke his possible taking us back to the same things that we knew under the previous administration, his record is that he spoke in praise of deficits several times. Said they weren't to be abhorred. That as a matter of fact he at one time said he wished the deficit could be doubled because they stimulate the economy and help reduce unemployment.

Q: *As a followup, let me draw in another specific if I could, a specific that the Democrats have claimed about your campaign; that it is essentially based on imagery. And one specific that they allege is that, for instance, that recently you showed up at the opening ceremony of a Buffalo old age housing project when in fact your policy was to cut federal housing subsidies for the elderly, yet you where there to have your picture taken with them.*

REAGAN: *Our policy was not to cut subsidies. We have believed in partnership and that was an example of a partnership between not only local government and the federal government but also between the private sector that built that particular structure. And this is what we've been trying to do is involve the federal government in such partnerships. We are today subsidizing housing for more than 10 million people, and we're going to continue along that line. We have no thought of throwing people out into the snow, whether because of age or need. We have preserved the safety net for the people with true need in this country and it has been pure demagoguery that we have in some way shut off all the charitable programs or many of them for the people who have real need. The safety net is there and we're taking care of more people than has ever been taken care of before by any administration in this country.*

MODERATOR: *Mr. Mondale—an opportunity for you to rebut.*

MONDALE: *Well, I guess I'm reminded a little bit of what Will Rogers once said about Hoover. He said it's not what he doesn't know that bothers me, it's what he knows for sure just ain't so. The fact of it is, the fact of it is, the president's budget sought to cut Social Security by 25 percent. It's not an opinion, it's a fact, and when the president was asked the other day, "What do you want to cut in the budget?" he said, "Cut those things I asked for but didn't get." That's Social Security and Medicare.*

The second fact is that the housing unit for senior citizens that the President dedicated in Buffalo was only made possible through a federal assistance program for senior citizens that the president's budget sought to terminate. So if he'd had his way, there wouldn't have been any housing project there at all. This administration has taken a meat cleaver out in terms of federal-assisted housing, and the record is there. We have to see the facts before we can draw conclusions.

REAGAN: *Well, let me just respond with regard to Social Security.*

When we took office we discovered that the program that the Carter-Mondale administration had said would solve the fiscal problems of Social Security for the next fifty years, wouldn't solve them for five. Social Security was due to go bankrupt before 1983. Any proposals that I made at that time were at the request of the chairman, a Democrat, of one of the leading committees, who said we have to do something before the program goes broke and the checks bounce.

And so we made a proposal. And then in 1982 they used that proposal in a demagogic fashion for the 1982 campaign. And three days after the election in 1982 they came to us and said, Social Security, we know, is broke. Indeed, we had to borrow $17 billion to pay the checks.

And then I asked for a bipartisan commission, which I'd asked for from the beginning, to sit down and work out a solution, and so the whole matter of what to do with Social Security has been resolved by bipartisan legislation and it is on a sound basis now for as far as you can see into the next century.

Religion and Politics

MODERATOR: *We begin segment Number three with Fred Barnes.*

Q: *Mr. President, would you describe your religious beliefs, noting particularly whether you consider yourself a born-again Christian and explain how these beliefs affect your presidential decisions?*

REAGAN: *Well, I was raised to have faith and a belief and have been a member of a church since I was a small boy. In our particular church we didn't use that term born-again so I don't know whether I would fit that—that particular term.*

But I have, thanks to my mother, God rest her soul, the firmest possible belief and faith in God. And I don't believe—I believe, I should say, as Lincoln once said, that I could not—I would be the most stupid man in the world if I thought I could confront the duties of the office I hold if I could not turn to someone who was stronger and greater than all others; and I do resort to prayer.

At the same time, however, I have not believed that prayer could be introduced into an election or be a part of a political campaign, or religion a part of that campaign. As a matter of fact I think religion became a part of this campaign when Mr. Mondale's running mate said I wasn't a good Christian. So, it does play a part in my life. I have no hesitancy in saying so. And as I say, I don't believe that I could carry on unless I had belief in a higher authority and a belief that prayers are answered.

Q: *Given those beliefs, Mr. President, why don't you attend services regularly, either by going to church or by inviting a minister to the White House, as President Nixon used to do, or someone to Camp David, as President Carter used to do.*

REAGAN: *The answer to your question is very simple—about why I don't go to church. I start—I have gone to church regularly all my life. And I started to here in Washington. And now, in the position I hold and in the world in which we live, where embassies do get blown up in Beirut, we're supposed to talk about that in the—on the debate the twenty-first, I understand.*

But I pose a threat to several hundred people if I go to church. I know the threats that are made against me. We all know the possibility of terrorism. We have seen the barricades that have been built around the White House.

And therefore, I don't feel—and my minister knows this and supports me in this position. I don't feel that I have a right to go to church, knowing that my being there could cause something of the kind that we have seen in other places; in Beirut, for example.

And I miss going to church but I think the Lord understands.

MODERATOR: *May I ask the audience please to refrain from applause. Can we have your second question?*

Q: *Mr. Mondale, would you describe your religious beliefs and mention whether you consider yourself a born-again Christian and explain how those beliefs would affect your decisions as president.*

MONDALE: *First of all, I accept President Reagan's affirmation of faith. I'm sure that we all accept and admire his commitment to his faith and we are strengthened all of us by that fact.*

I am a son of a Methodist minister, my wife is the daughter of a Presbyterian minister, and I don't know if I've been born again, but I know I was born into a Christian family, and I believe I've sung at more weddings and more funerals than anybody ever to seek the presidency. Whether that helps or not I don't know. I have a deep religious faith, our family does, it is fundamental, it's probably the reason I'm in politics. I think our faith tells us, instructs us about the moral life that we should lead, and I think we're all together on that.

What bothers me is this growing tendency to try to use one's own personal interpretation of faith politically, to question others' faith, and to try to use instrumentalities of government to impose those views on others. All history tells us that that's a mistake.

When the Republican platform says that from here on out we're going to have a religious test for judges before they're selected for the federal court and then Jerry Falwell announces that that means they get at least two justices of the Supreme Court, I think that's an abuse of faith in our country. This nation is the most religious nation on earth. More people go to church and synagogues than any other nation on earth, and it's because we kept the politicians and the state out of the personal exercise of our faith. That's why faith in the United States is pure and unpolluted by the interven-

tion of politicians, and I think if we want to continue as I do to have a religious nation, let's keep that line and never cross it.

MODERATOR: *Thank you. Mr. Barnes, a question? We have time for rebuttal now.*

Q: *I think I have a followup.*

MODERATOR: *Yes, I asked you if you did. I'm sorry I thought you waived it.*

Q: *Yes, Mr. Mondale, you've complained just now about Jerry Falwell, and you've complained other times about other fundamentalists in politics. Correct me if I'm wrong, but I don't recall your ever complaining about ministers who are involved in the civil rights movement, in the anti-Vietnam War demonstrations or about black preachers who've been so involved in American politics. is it only conservative ministers that you object to?*

MONDALE: *No. What I object to—what I object to—what I object to is someone seeking to use his faith to question the faith of another or to use that faith and seek to use the power of government to impose it on others. A minister who is in civil rights or in the conservative movement because he believes his faith instructs him to do that, I admire. The fact that the faith speaks to us and that we are moral people hopefully, I accept and rejoice in. It's when you try to use that to undermine the integrity of private political—or private religious faith and the use of the state is where for the most personal decisions in American life—that's where I draw the line.*

MODERATOR: *Thank you. Now, Mr. President. Rebuttal.*

REAGAN: *Yes, it's very difficult to rebut, because I find myself in so much agreement with Mr. Mondale. I, too, want that wall that is in the Constitution, separation of church and state, to remain there. The only attacks I have made are on people who apparently would break away at that wall from the government side using the government, using the power of the courts and so forth, to hinder that part of the Constitution that says the government shall not only not establish a religion, it shall not inhibit the practice of religion, and they have been using these things to have government, through court orders, inhibit the practice of religion.*

A child wants to say grace in a school cafeteria, and a court rules that they can't do it. And because it's school property.

These are the types of things that I think have been happening in a kind of secular way that have been erroding that separation, and I am opposed to that. With regard to a platform in the Supreme Court, I can only say one thing about that. I don't—I have appointed one member of the Supreme Court, Sandra Day O'Connor, I'll stand on my record on that, and if I have the opportunity to appoint any more. I'll do it in the same manner that I did in selecting her.

MODERATOR: *Mr. Mondale, your rebuttal, please.*

MONDALE: *The platform to which the president refers in fact calls for a religious test in the selection of judges. And Jerry Falwell says that means we get two or three judges. And it would involve a religious test for the first time in American life.*

Let's take the example that the president cites. I believe in prayer. My family prays. We've never had any difficulty finding time to pray. But do we want a constitutional amendment adopted of the kind proposed by the President that gets the local politicians into the business of selecting prayers that our children must either recite in school or be embarrassed and ask to excuse themselves? Who would write the prayer? What would it say? How would it be resolved when those disputes occurred?

It seems to me that a moment's reflection tells you why the United States Senate turned that amendment down. Because it will undermine the practice of honest faith in our country by politicizing it. We don't want that.

Political Parties and the Electorate

MODERATOR: *Thank you, Mr. Mondale. Time is up for this round; we go into the second round of our questioning—begin again with Jim Wieghart. Jim.*

Q: *After that discussion, this may be like going from the sublime to the ridiculous, but here goes: I have a political question for you, Mr. Mondale. Polls indicate a massive change in the electorate, away from the coalition that has long made the Democratic party a majority. Blue-collar workers, young professionals, their children, and much of the middle class now regard themselves as independents or Republican instead of Democrats. And the gap, the edge the Democrats had in party registration, seems to be narrowing.*

I'd like to ask you, Mr. Mondale, what is causing this? Is the Democratic party out of synch with the majority of Americans? And will it soon be replaced as the majority party by the Republicans? What do you think needs to be done about as a Democrat?

MONDALE: *My answer is that this campaign isn't over yet. And when people vote, I think you're going to see a very strong verdict by the American people that they favor the approach that I'm talking about.*

The American people want arms control; they don't want this arms race. And they don't want this deadly new effort to bring weapons into the heavens. And they want an American foreign policy that leads toward a safer world.

The American people see this debt, and they know it's got to come down. And if it won't come down, the economy's going to slow down, maybe go into a recession. They see this tremendous influx and swamping of cheap foreign imports in this country that has cost over three million jobs, given farmers the worst year in American history.

And they know this debt must come down, as well, because it's unfair to our children.

The American people want this environment protected. They know that these toxic waste dumps should have been cleaned up a long time ago. And they know that people's lives and health are being risked because we've had an administration that has been totally insensitive to the law and the demands for the protection of the environment.

The American people want their children educated; they want to get our edge back in science, and they want a policy, headed by the president, that helps close this gap that's widening between the United States and Europe and Japan.

The American people want to keep opening doors. They want those civil rights laws enforced; they want the equal rights amendment ratified; they want equal pay for comparable effort for women. And they want it because they've understood from the beginning that when we open doors, we're all stronger. Just as we were at the Olympics.

I think as you make the case, the American people will increasingly come to our cause.

Q: *Mr. Mondale, isn't it possible that the American people have heard your message and they are listening but they are rejecting it?*

MONDALE: *Well, tonight we had the first debate over the deficit. The president says it will disappear automatically. I've said it's going to take some work. I think the American people will draw their own conclusions. Secondly, I've said that I will not support the cuts in Social Security and Medicare and the rest that the president's proposed. The president answers that it didn't happen or if it did, it was resolved later in a commission. As the record develops I think it's going to become increasingly clear that what I am saying and where I want to take this country is exactly where the country wants to go, and the comparison of approaches is such that I think will lead to further strength.*

Q: *Mr. President, you and your party are benefiting from what appears to be an erosion of the old Democratic coalition, but you have not laid out a specific agenda to take this shift beyond November 6. What is your program for America for the next decade, with some specificity?*

REAGAN: *Well, again, I am running on the record. I think sometimes Mr. Mondale's running away from his, but I'm running on the record of what we have asked for, will continue to try and get things that we didn't get in the program that has already brought the rate of spending of government down from 17 percent to 6.1 percent, a program of returning authority and autonomy to the local and state governments that has been unjustly seized by the federal government and you might find those words in the Demo-*

cratic platform of some years ago. I know because I was a Democrat at that time. And I left the party eventually because I could no longer follow the turn in the Democratic leadership that took us down an entirely different path, a path of centralizing authority in the federal government, lacking trust in the American people.

I promised when we took office that we would reduce inflation. We have to one-third of what it was. I promised that we would reduce taxes. We did 25 percent across the board. That barely held even with—if it did that much—with the gigantic tax increase imposed in 1977. But at least it took that burden away from them. I said that we would create jobs for our people, and we did, 6 million in the last twenty or twenty-one months. I said that we would become respected in the world once again and that we would refurbish our national defense to the place that we could deal on the world scene and then seek disarmaments, reduction of arms, and hopefully an elimination of nuclear weapons. We have done that.

All of the things that I said we would do, from inflation being down, interest rates being down, unemployment falling—all of those things we have done. And I think this is something the American people see. I think they also know that we have.

We had a commission that came in a year ago with a recommendation on education, on excellence in education, and today without the federal government being involved other than passing on to them, the school districts, the words from that commission, we find thirty-five states with task forces now dealing with their educational problems, we find that schools are extending the curriculum to now have forced teaching of mathematics and science and so forth. All of these things have brought an improvement in the college entrance exams for the first time in some twenty years. So I think that many Democrats are seeing the same thing this Democrat saw. The leadership isn't taking us where we want to go.

Q: Mr. President, there's a—much of what you said affects the quality of life of many Americans—their income, the way they live and so forth. But there's an aspect to quality of life that lies beyond the private sector which has to do with our neighborhoods, with our cities, our streets, our parks, our environment. In those areas I have a difficulty seeing what your program is and what you feel the federal responsibility is in these areas of the quality of life in the public sector that affects everybody. And even enormous wealth by one individual can't create the kind of environment that he might like.

REAGAN: *There are tasks that government legitimately should enforce and tasks that government performs well, and you've named some of them. Crime has come down the last two years for the first time in many, many decades that it has come down or, since we kept records, two consecutive years, and last year it came down—the biggest drop in crime that we've had.*

I think that we've had something to do with that, just as we have with the drug problem nationwide.

The environment, yes, I feel as strongly as anyone about the preservation of the environment. When we took office we found that the national parks were so dirty and contained so many hazards, lack of safety features that we stopped buying additional parkland until we had rectified this with what was to be a five-year program, but it's just about finished already—a billion dollars—and now we're going back to budgeting for additional lands for our parks.

We have added millions of acres to the wilderness lands, to the game refuges, I think that we're out in front of most, and I see that the red light is blinking so I can't continue, but I got more.

MODERATOR: *Well, you'll have a chance when your rebuttal time comes up perhaps, Mr. President. Mr. Mondale, now it's your turn for rebuttal.*

MONDALE: *The president says that when the Democratic party made its turn he left it. The year that he decided we had lost our way was the year that John F. Kennedy was running against Richard Nixon. I was chairman of Minnesotans for Kennedy. Reagan was chairman of a thing called Democrats for Nixon. Now maybe we made a wrong turn with Kennedy, but I'll be proud of supporting him all of our life—all of my life. And I'm very happy that John Kennedy was elected, because John Kennedy looked at the future with courage, saw what needed to be done, and understood his own government.*

The president just said that his government is shrinking. It's not. It's now the largest peacetime government ever in terms of the take from the total economy and instead of retreating, instead of being strong where we should be strong, he wants to make it strong and intervene in the most private and personal questions in American life. That's where government should not be.

MODERATOR: *Mr. President.*

REAGAN: *Before I campaigned as a Democrat for a Republican candidate for president, I had already voted for Dwight Eisenhower to be president of the United States so my change had come earlier than that. I hadn't gotten around to reregistering as yet. I found that was rather difficult to do but I finally did it.*

There are some other things that have been said here, back—and you said that I might be able to dredge them up. Mr. Mondale referred to the farmer's worst year. The farmers are not the victims of anything this administration has done. The farmers were the victims of the double-digit inflation and the 21½ percent interest rates of the Carter-Mondale administration and the grain embargo which destroyed our reliability nationwide as a supplier.

All of these things are presently being rectified and I think that we are going to salvage the farmers—as a matter of fact, the—there has been less than one-quarter of 1 percent of foreclosures of the 270,000 loans from government the farmers have.

Positions on Abortion

MODERATOR: *Thank you, Mr. President. We'll now turn to Diane Sawyer for her round of questions. Diane.*

Q: *I'd like to turn to an area that I think few people enjoy discussing. But that we probably should tonight, because the positions of the two candidates are so clearly different and lead to very different policy consequences. And that is abortion and right to life. I'm exploring for your personal views of abortion. And specifically how you would want them applied as public policy.*

First, Mr. President, do you consider abortion murder or a sin? And second, how hard would you work, what kind of priority would you give in your second term legislation to make abortion illegal? And specifically, would you make certain, as your party platform urges, that federal justices that you appoint be prolife?

REAGAN: *I have believed that, in the appointment of judges, that all that was specified in the party platform was that they have a, they respect the sanctity of human life. Now that, I would want to see in any judge, and with regard to any issue having to do with human life.*

But with regard to abortion, and I have a feeling that this is, there's been some reference, without naming it here in remarks of Mr. Mondale, tied to injecting religion into government.

With me, abortion is not a problem of religion. It's a problem of the Constitution. I believe that until and unless someone can establish that the unborn child is not a living human being, then that child is already protected by the Constitution, which guarantees life, liberty, and the pursuit of happiness to all of us.

And I think that this is—what we should concentrate on, is trying—I know there was weeks and weeks of testimony before a Senate committee. There were medical authorities, there were religious, there were clerics there, everyone talking about this matter, of pro-life. And at the end of all of that, not one shred of evidence was introduced that the unborn child was not alive. We have seen premature births that are now grown up happy people going around.

Also there is a strange dichotomy in this whole position about our court's ruling that abortion is not the taking of a human life.

In California, some time ago, a man beat a woman so savagely that her unborn child was born dead with a fractured skull. And the California state legislature unanimously passed a law that was signed by the then Democratic governor, signed a law that said that any man who so abuses a pregnant woman that he causes the death of her unborn child shall be charged with murder. Now isn't it strange that that same woman could have taken the life of her unborn child and it was abortion and not murder, but if somebody else does it, that's murder. And it recognizes, it used the term death of the unborn child.

So this has been my feeling about abortion, that we have a problem now to determine. And all the evidence so far comes down on the side of the unborn child being a living human being.

Q: *A two-part followup. Do I take it from what you've said about the platform, then, that you don't regard the language and don't regard in your own appointment's abortion position a test of any kind for justices that it should be? And also, if abortion is made illegal, how would you want it enforced? Who would be the policing units that would investigate? And would you want the women who have abortions to be prosecuted?*

REAGAN: *The laws regarding that always were state laws. It was only when the Supreme Court handed down a decision that the federal government intervened in what had always been a state policy. Our laws against murder are state laws. So I would think this would be the point of enforcement on this.*

I, as I say, I feel that we have a problem here to resolve, and no one has approached it from that matter. It does not happen that the church I belong to had that as part of its dogma; I know that some churches do.

Now, it is a sin if you're taking a human life. On the same time in our Judeo-Christian tradition, we recognize the right of taking a human life in self-defense. And therefore I've always believed that a mother, if medically it is determined that her life is at risk if she goes through with the pregnancy, she has a right then to take the life of even her own unborn child in defense of her own.

Q: *Mr. Mondale, to turn to you, do you consider abortion a murder or a sin? And bridging from what President Reagan said, he has written that if society doesn't know whether life does—human life—in fact does begin at conception, as long as there is a doubt, that the unborn child should at least be given the benefit of the doubt and that there should be protection for that unborn child.*

MONDALE: *This is one of the most emotional and difficult issues that could possibly be debated. I think your questions, however, underscore the fact there is probably no way that government should, or could, answer this question in every individual case and in the private lives of the American people.*

The constitutional amendment proposed by President Reagan would make it a crime for a woman to have an abortion if she had been raped or suffered from incest.

Is it really the view of the American people, however you feel on the question of abortion, that government ought to be reaching into your living-rooms and making choices like this?

I think it cannot work, won't work, and will lead to all kinds of cynical evasions of the law. Those who can afford to have them will continue to have them. The disadvantaged will go out in the back alley as they used to do.

I think these questions are inherently personal and moral. And every individual instance is different. Every American should be aware of the seriousness of the step, but there are some things that government can do and some things they cannot do.

Now the example that the president cites has nothing to do with abortion. Somebody went to a woman and nearly killed her. That's always been a serious crime and always should be a serious crime. But how does that compare with the problem of a woman who is raped? Do we really want those decisions made by judges who've been picked because they will agree to find the person guilty? I don't think so and I think it's going in exactly the wrong direction.

In America, on basic moral questions we have always let the people decide in their own personal lives. We haven't felt so insecure that we've reached for the club of state to have our point of view. It's been a good instinct and we're the most religious people on earth.

One final point: President Reagan, as governor of California, signed a bill which is perhaps the most liberal pro-abortion bill of any state in the Union.

Q: *But if I can get you back for a moment on my point, which was the question of when human life begins, a two-part followup. First of all, at what point do you believe that human life begins in the growth of a fetus? And second of all, you said that government shouldn't be involved in the decision, yet there are those who would say that government is involved and the consequence of the involvement was 1.5 million abortions in 1980. And how do you feel about that?*

MONDALE: *The basic decision of the Supreme Court is that each person has to make this judgment in her own life, and that's the way it's been done. And it's a personal and private moral judgment. I don't know the answer to when life begins.*

And it's not that simple either. You've got another life involved. And if it's rape, how do you draw moral judgments on that? If it's incest, how do you draw moral judgments on that? Does every woman in America have to present herself before some judge picked by Jerry Falwell to clear her personal judgment? It won't work.

MODERATOR: *I'm sorry to do this but I really must talk to the audience. You're all invited guests. I know I'm wasting time in talking to you but it really is very unfair of you to applaud sometimes louder, less loud, and I ask you as people who were invited here and polite people to refrain. We have our time now for rebuttal. Mr. President.*

REAGAN: *Yes. But with regard to this being a personal choice, isn't that what a murderer is insisting on? His or her right to kill someone because of whatever fault they think justifies that. Now, I'm not capable and I don't think you are, any of us, to make this determination that must be made with regard to human life. I am simply saying that I believe that that's where the effort should be directed to make that determination. I don't think that any of us should be called upon here to stand and make a decision as to what other things might come under the self-defense tradition. that, too, would have to be worked out then when you once recognize that we're talking about a life. But in this great society of ours wouldn't it make a lot more sense, in this gentle and kind society, if we had a program that made it possible for when incidents come along which someone feels they must do away with that unborn child, that instead we make it available to the adoption, there are a million and a half people out there standing in line waiting to adopt children who can't have them any other way.*

MODERATOR: *Mr. Mondale?*

MONDALE: *I agree with that, and that's why I was a principal sponsor of a liberal adoption law so that more of these children could come to term so that the young mothers were educated, so we found an option, an alternative. I'm all for that. But the question is whether this other option proposed by the president should be pursued, and I don't agree with it. Since I've got about twenty seconds, let me just say one thing.*

The question of agriculture came up a minute ago, and that farm income is off 50 percent in the last three years, and every farmer knows it, and the effect of these economic policies is like a massive grain embargo which has caused farm exports to drop 20 percent. It's been a big failure. I opposed the grain embargo in my administration; I'm opposed to these policies as well.

MODERATOR: *I'm sitting here like the great school teacher letting you both get away with things. Because one did it, the other one did it. May I ask in the future that the rebuttals stick to what the rebuttal is and also, foreign policy will be the next debate. Stop dragging it in by its ear into this one. Now have admonished you, I would like to say to the panel, you are allowed one question and one followup. Would you try as best you could not to ask two and three. I know it's something we all want to do, two or three questions as part one, and two and three as part two. Having said that, Fred, it's yours.*

Tax Policy

Q: *Thank you. Mr. Mondale, let me ask you about middle-class Americans and the taxes they pay. I'm talking about—not about the rich or the poor. I know your views on their taxes. But about families earning $25,000 to $45,000 a year. Do you think that those families are overtaxed or undertaxed by the federal government.*

MONDALE: *In my opinion as we deal with this deficit, people from about $70,000 a year on down have to be dealt with very, very carefully because they are the ones who didn't get any relief the first time around. Under the 1981 tax bill people making $200,000 a year got $60,000 in tax relief over three years while people making $30,000 a year, all taxes considered, got no relief at all or their taxes actually went up. That's why my proposal protects everybody from $25,000 a year or less against any tax increases and treats those $70,000 and under in a way that is more beneficial than the way the president proposes with a sales tax or a flat tax.*

What does this mean in real life? Well, the other day Vice-President Bush disclosed his tax returns to the American people. He's one of the wealthiest Americans and he's our vice-president. In 1981 I think he paid about 40 percent in taxes. In 1983 as a result of these tax preferences he paid a little over 12 percent, 12.8 percent in taxes. That meant that he paid a lower percent in taxes than the janitor who cleaned up his office or the chauffeur who drives him to work.

I believe we need some fairness, and that's why I propose what I think is a fair and responsible proposal that helps protect these people who've already gotten no relief or actually got a tax increase.

Q: *It sounds as if you were saying you think a group of taxpayers making $25,000 to $45,000 a year is already overtaxed, yet your tax proposal would increase their taxes. I think your agent said those earning about $25 to $35,000, their tax rate would go up and their tax bill would go up $100, and from $35,000 to $45,000 more than that, several hundred dollars. Wouldn't that stifle their incentive to work and invest and so on, and also hurt the recovery?*

MONDALE: *The first thing is everybody $25,000 or under would have no tax increase. Mr. Reagan after the election is going to have to propose a tax increase. And you will have to compare what he proposes, and his secretary of the treasury said he's studying a sales tax or a value-added tax; they're the same thing to hit middle- and moderate-income Americans and leave wealthy Americans largely untouched. Up until about $70,000, as you go up the ladder, my proposals will be far more beneficial. As soon as we get the economy on a sound ground, as well, I would like to see the total repeal of indexing. I don't think we can do that for a few years but at some point we want to do that as well.*

Q: *Mr. President, let me try this on you. Do you think middle-income Americans are overtaxed or undertaxed?*

REAGAN: *You know, I wasn't going to say this at all, but I can't help it: There you go again. I don't have a plan to tax or increase taxes; I'm not going to increase taxes. I can understand why you are, Mr. Mondale, because as a senator you voted sixteen times to increase taxes. Now, I believe that our problem has not been that anybody in our country is undertaxed, it's that government is overfed. And I think that most of our people—this is why we had a 25 percent tax cut across the board which maintained the same progressivity of our tax structure in the—the brackets on up.*

And as a matter of fact, it just so happens that in the quirks of administering these taxes, those above $50,000 actually did not get quite as big a tax cut percentage-wise, as did those from $50,000 down. From $50,000 down those people paid two-thirds of the taxes and those people got two-thirds of the tax cut.

Now the Social Security tax of '77—this, indeed, was a tax that hit people in the lower brackets the hardest. It had two features: It had several tax increases phased in over a period of time; there are two more yet to come between now and 1989. At the same time, every year it increased the amount of money—virtually every year, there may have been one or two that we're skipping there—that was subject to that tax. Today it is up to about $38,000 of earnings that is subject to the payroll tax for Social Security. And that tax, there are no deductions, so a person making anywhere from $10, $15, $20, they're paying that tax on the full gross earnings that they have after they have already paid an income tax on that same amount of money.

Now I don't think that to try and say that we were taxing the rich and not the other way around, it just doesn't work out that way. The system is still where it was with regard to the progressivity, as I've said, and that has not been changed. But if you take it in numbers of dollars, instead of percentage, yes you can say, well that person got ten times as much as this other person. yes, but he paid ten times as much also. But if you take it in percentages then you find out that it is fair and equitable across the board.

Q: *I thought I caught, Mr. President, a glimmer of a stronger statement there in your answer than you've made before. I think the operative position you had before was that you would only raise taxes in a second term as a last resort, and I thought you said flatly that "I'm not going to raise taxes." Is that what you meant to say, that you will not—that you will flatly not raise taxes in your second term as president?*

REAGAN: *Yes, I had used—last resort would always be with me. If you got the government down to the lowest level that you yourself could say it could not go any lower and still perform the services for the people. And if the recovery was so complete that you knew you were getting the ultimate amount of revenues that you could get through that growth, and there was still some slight difference there between those two lines, then I had said once that, yes, you would have to then look to see if taxes should not be adjusted. I don't forsee those things happening. So I say with great confidence, I'm not going to—I'm not going to go for a tax.*

With regard to assailing Mr. Bush about his tax problems and the difference from the tax he once paid and then the later tax he paid, I think if you looked at the deductions, there were great legal expenses in there. It had to do possibly with the sale of his home and they had to do with his setting up of a blind trust. All of those are legally deductions—the deductible in computing your tax. And it was a one-year thing with him.

MODERATOR: *Mr. Mondale, here we go again; this time for rebuttal.*

MONDALE: *Well, first of all, I gave him the benefit of the doubt on the House deal. I'm just talking about the 12.8 percent that he paid—and that's what's happening all over this country with wealthy Americans. They've got so many loopholes, they don't have to pay much in taxes.*

Now, Mr. President, you said, "There you go again." Right. Remember the last time you said that?

REAGAN: *Um hmm.*

MONDALE: *You said it when President Carter said that you were going cut Medicare. And you said, "Oh, no, there you go again, Mr. President." And what did you do right after the election? You went out and tried to cut $20 billion out of Medicare.*

And so when you say, "There you go again," people remember this, you know. And people will remember that you signed the biggest tax increase in the history of California, and the biggest tax increase in the history of the United States.

And what are you going to do? You've got $260 billion deficit. You can't wash it away. You won't slow defense spending; you refuse to do that.

MODERATOR: *Mr. Mondale, I'm afraid your time is up.*

MONDALE: *Sorry.*

MODERATOR: *Mr. President.*

REGAN: *Yes. With regard to Medicare, no. but it's time for us to say that Medicare is in pretty much the same condition that Social Security was, and something is going to have to be done in the next several years to make it fiscally sound.*

And, no, I never proposed any $20 billion should come out of Medicare. I have proposed that the program—we must treat with that particular problem.

And maybe part of that problem is because during the four years of the Carter-Mondale administration, medical costs in this country went up 87 percent.

Poverty Programs

MODERATOR: *We can't keep going back for other rebuttals. There'll be time later. We now go to our final round. The way things stand now we have time for only two sets of questions and by lot it will, be Jim and Diane and we'll start with Jim.*

Q: *Mr. President, the economic recovery is real but uneven. The Census Bureau just a month ago reported that there are more people living under poverty now—a million more people—than when you took office. There have been a number of studies, including studies by the Urban Institute and other nonpolitical organizations, that say that the impact of the tax and budget cuts in your economic policies have impacted severely on certain classes of Americans—working mothers, head of households, minority groups, elderly poor. In fact, they're saying the rich are getting richer and the poor are getting poorer under your policies. What relief can you offer to the working poor, to the minorities and to the women heads of households who have borne the brunt of these economic programs. What can you offer them in the future in your next term?*

REAGAN: *Some of those facts and figures just don't stand up. Yes, there has been an increase in poverty, but it is a lower rate of increase than it was in the preceding years before we got here. It has begun to decline, but it is still going up. On the other hand, women heads of household, single women, heads of household, have for the first time—there's been a turn down in the rate of poverty for them. We have found also in our studies that in this increase in poverty it all had to do with their private earnings. It has nothing to do with the transfer payments from government, by way of many programs. We are spending now 37 percent more on food for the hungry in all the various types of programs than was spent in 1980. We're spending a third more on all the programs of human service. We have more people receiving food stamps than were ever receiving them before—2,300,000 more are receiving them even though we took 850,000 off the food stamp rolls because they were making an income that was above anything that warranted their fellow citizens having to support them. We found people making 185 percent of the poverty level were getting government benefits. We have set a line at 130 percent so that we can direct that aid down to the truly needy.*

Some time ago Mr. Mondale said something about education and college students and help of that kind—half, one out of two of full-time college students in the United States are receiving some form of federal aid, but there again we found people that there were—under the previous administration—families that had no limit to income were still eligible for low-interest college loans. We didn't think that was right. And so we have set a standard that those loans and those grants are directed to the people who otherwise could not go to college, their family incomes were so low.

So there are a host of other figures that reveal that the grant programs are greater than they have ever been, taking care of more people than they ever have—7.7 million elderly citizens who were living in the lowest 20 percent of earnings 7.7 million have moved up into another bracket since our administration took over, leaving only 5 million of the elderly in that bracket when there had been more than 13 million.

Q: *Mr. President, in a visit to Texas, in Brownsville, I believe it was, in the Rio Grande Valley, you did observe that the economic recovery was uneven. In that particular area of Texas unemployment was over 14 percent, whereas statewide it was the lowest in the country, I believe 5.6 percent. And you made the comment that, however, that man does not live by bread alone. What did you mean by that comment and, if I interpret it correctly, it would be a comment more addressed to the affluent who, who obviously can look beyond just the bread they need to sustain them with their wherewithal.*

REAGAN: *That had nothing to do with the other thing of talking about their needs or anything. I remember distinctly I was segueing into another subject. I was talking about the things that have been accomplished and that was referring to the revival of patriotism and optimism, the new spirit that we're finding all over America. And it is a wonderful thing to see when you get out there among the people. So that was the only place that that was used.*

I did avoid, I'm afraid, in my previous answer also, the idea of uneven, yes, there is no way that the recovery is, even across the country, just as in the depths of the recession there were some parts of the country that were worse off but some that didn't even feel the pain of the recession.

We're not going to rest, and not going to be happy, until every person in this country who wants a job can have one, until the recovery is complete across the country.

Q: *Mr. Mondale, as you can gather from the question of the president the celebrated war on poverty obviously didn't end the problem of poverty, although it may have dented it. The poor and the homeless and the disadvantaged are still with us. What should the federal government's role be to turn back the growth in the number of people living below the poverty level, which is now 35 million in the United States and to help deal with the structural unemployment problems that the President was referring to in an uneven recovery?*

MONDALE: *Number 1, we've got to get the debt down, to get the interest rates down so the economy will grow and people will be employed. Number 2, we have to work with cities and others to help generate economic growth in those communities—to the Urban Development Action Grant program. I don't mind those enterprise zones, let's try them, but not as a substitute for the others. Certainly education and training is crucial. If these young Americans don't have the skills that make them attractive to employees, they're not going to get jobs.*

The next thing is to try to get more entrepreneurship in business within the reach of minorities so that these businesses are located in the communities in which they're found. The other thing is we need the business community as well as government heavily involved in these communities to try to get economic growth. There is no question that the poor are worse off. I think the president genuinely believes that they're better off. But the figures show that about 8 million more people are below the poverty line than four years ago. How you can cut school lunches, how you can cut student assistance, how you can cut housing, how you can cut disability benefits, how you can do all of these things and then the people receiving them—for example the disabled who have no alternative, how they're going to do better, I don't know. Now we need a tight budget, but there's no question that this administration has singled out things that affect the most vulnerable in American life, and they're hurting.

One final point if I might. There's another part of the lopsided economy that we're in today, and that is that these heavy deficits have killed exports and are swamping the nation with cheap imports. We are now $120 billion of imports, 3 million jobs lost and farmers are having their worst year. That's another reason to get the deficit down.

Q: *Mr Mondale, is it possible that the vast majority of Americans who appear to be prosperous have lost interest in the kinds of programs you're discussing to help those less privileged than they are?*

MONDALE: *I think the American people want to make certain that that dollar is wisely spent. I think they stand for civil rights. I know they're all for education in science and training, which I strongly support.*

They want these young people to have a chance to get jobs and the rest. I think the business community wants to get involved. I think they're asking for new and creative ways to try to reach it, and with everyone involved. I think that's part of it.

I think also that the American people want a balanced program that gives us long-term growth, so that they're not having to take money that's desperate to themselves and their families and give it to someone else. I'm opposed to that, too.

MODERATOR: *And now it is time for our rebuttal for this period. Mr. President.*

REAGAN: *Yes, the connection that's been made again between the deficit and the interest rates—there is no connection between them. There is a connection between interest rates and inflation.*

But I would call to your attention that in 1981, while we were operating still on the Carter-Mondale budget that we inherited, that the interest rates came down from 21½ toward the 12 or 13 figure and while they were coming down, the deficits had started their great increase: they were going up.

Now, if there was a connection, I think that there would be a different parallel between deficit getting larger and interest rates going down.

The interest rates are based on inflation. and right now, I have to tell you, I don't think there is any excuse for the interest rates being as high as they are, because we have brought inflation down so low. I think it can only be that they're anticipating or hope—expecting, not hoping—that maybe we don't have a control of inflation and it's going to go back up again.

Well, it isn't going to back up. We're going to see that it doesn't.

MODERATOR: *Mr. President.*

REAGAN: *And I haven't got time to answer with regard to—*

MODERATOR: *Thank you Mr. President. Mr. Mondale?*

MONDALE: *Mr. President, if I heard you correctly, you said that these deficits don't have anything to do with interest rates. I will grant you that interest rates were too high in 1980 and we can have another debate as to why—energy prices and so on. There's no way of glossing around that. But when these huge deficits went in place in 1981, what's called the real interest rates, the spread between inflation and what a loan costs you, doubled. And that's still the case today, and the result is interest costs that have never been seen before in terms of real charges and it's attributable to the deficit.*

Everybody every economist, every businessman, believes that. Your own Council of Economic Advisers, Mr. Feldstein in his report, told you that. Every chairman of the Finance and Ways and Means committees, Republican leaders in the Senate and the House, are telling you that. That deficit is ruining the long-term hopes for this economy. It's causing high interest rates, it's ruining us in trade, it's given us the highest small-business failure in fifty years, the economy is starting downhill, with housing . . .

MODERATOR: *Thank you Mr. Mondale.*

View of the Other Candidate

MODERATOR: *You're both very obedient, I have to give you credit for that. We now start our final round of questions. We do want to have time for your rebuttal and we start with Diane: Diane Sawyer.*

Q: *Since we are reaching the end of the question period, and since in every presidential campaign the candidates tend to complain that the opposition candidate is not held accountable for what he or she says, let me give you the chance to do that. Mr. Mondale, beginning with you, what do you think the most outrageous thing is your opponent said in this debate tonight?*

MONDALE: *You want to give me some suggestions? I'm going to use my time a little differently. I'm going to give the president some credit. I think the president has done some things to raise the sense of spirit and morale, good feeling, in this country. And he's entitled to credit for that.*

What I think we need, however, is not just that but to move forward not just congratulating ourselves, but challenging ourselves to get on with the business of dealing with America's problems.

I think in education, when he lectured the country about the importance of discipline, I didn't like it at first but I think it helped a little bit.

But now we need both that kind of discipline and the resources and the consistent leadership that allows this country to catch up in education and science and training.

I like President Reagan and—this is not personal—there are deep differences about our future and that's the basis of my campaign.

Q: *Follow up in a similar vein then. What remaining question would you most like to see your opponent forced to answer?*

MONDALE: *Without any doubt, I've stood up and told the American people that the $263 billion deficit must come down. and I've done what no candidate for president's ever done, I told you before the election what I'd do.*

Mr. Reagan, as you saw tonight, President Reagan takes the position it will disappear by magic. It was once called voodoo economics. I wish the President would say, yes, the CBO is right. Yes, we have a $263 billion deficit. This is how I'm going to get it done. Don't talk about growth because even though we need growth, that's not helping, it's going to go in the other direction as they've estimated. And give us a plan.

What will you cut? Whose taxes will you raise? Will you finally touch that defense budget? Are you going to go after Social Security and Medicare and student assistance and the handicapped again, as you did last time?

If you'd just tell us what you're going to do, then the American people could compare my plan for the future with your plan. and that's the way it should be. The American people would be in charge.

Q: *Mr. president, the most outrageous thing your opponent has said in the debate tonight?*

REAGAN: *Well, now, I have to start with a smile since his kind words to me. I'll tell you what I think has been the most outrageous thing in political dialogue both in this campaign and the one in '82, and that is the continued discussion and claim that somehow I am the villain who is going to pull the Social Security checks out from those people who are dependent on them. And why I think it is outrageous; first of all, it isn't true. But why it is outrageous is because for political advantage, every time they do that, they scare millions of senior citizens who are totally dependent on Social Security, have no place to turn, and they have to live and go to bed at night thinking is it true: is someone going to take our check away from us and leave us destitute? and I don't think that that should be a part of political dialogue. Now, to—I just have a minute here?*

Q: *You have more time. You can keep going.*

REAGAN: *O.K. All right. Now, Social Security, let's lay it to rest once and for all. I told you never would I do such a thing. But I tell you also now Social Security has nothing to do with the deficit. Social Security is totally funded by the payroll tax levied on employer and employee. If you reduce the outgo of Social Security, that money would not go into the general fund to reduce a deficit. It would go into the Social Security Trust Fund. So Social Security has nothing to do with balancing a budget or erasing or lowering the deficit.*

Now, again to get to whether I have—am depending on Magic—I think I have talked in straight economic terms about a program of recovery that was—I was told wouldn't work and then after it worked, I was told that lowering taxes would increase inflation and none of these things happened. It is working and we're going to continue on that same line. As to what we might do and find in further savings cuts, no, we're not going to starve the hungry. But we have 2.478 specific recommendations from a commission of more than 2,000 business people in this country through the Grace Commission, that we're studying right now and we've already implemented 17 percent of them that are recommendations as to how to make government more efficient, more economic.

Q: *And to keep it even. What remaining question would you most like to see your opponent forced to answer?*

REAGAN: *The deficits are so much of a problem for him now, but that in 1976 when the deficit was $52 billion and everyone was panicking about that, he said, no, that he thought it ought to be bigger because a bigger deficit would stimulate the economy and would help do away with unemployment. In 1979 he made similar statements, the same effect, that the deficits—there was nothing wrong with having deficits. Remember there was a trillion dollars in debt before we got here. That's got to be paid by our children, and grandchildren too, if we don't do it. And I'm hoping we can start some payments on it before we get through here. That's why I want another four years.*

MODERATOR: *Well, we have time now, if you'd like to answer the president's question or whatever rebuttal.*

MONDALE: *Well, we've just finished almost the whole debate and the American people don't have the slightest clue about what President Reagan will do about these deficits. And yet that's the most important single issue of our time. I did support the '76 measure that he told about, because we were in a deep recession and we need some stimulation. But I will say, as a Democrat I was a real piker, Mr. President. In 1979 we ran a $29 billion deficit, all*

year. This administration seems to run that every morning, and the result is exactly what we see: This economy is starting to run downhill. Housing is off, last report on new purchases is the lowest since 1982, our growth is a little over 3 percent now, many people are predicting a recession, and the flow of imports into this country is swamping the American people. We've got to deal with this problem, and those of us who want to be your president should tell you now what we're going to do so you can make a judgment.
MODERATOR: *Thank you very much. We must stop now. I want to give you time for your closing statements. It's indeed time for that from each of you. We will begin with President Reagan.*

Concluding Statements

MODERATOR: *I'm sorry. Mr. Reagan you had your rebuttal and I've just cut you off because our time was going. You have a chance now for rebuttal before your closing statement. Is that correct?*
REAGAN: *No, I might as well just go with . . .*
MODERATOR: *Do you want to go with—*
REAGAN: *I don't think so.*
MODERATOR: *Do you want to wait?*
REAGAN: *I'm all confused now.*
MODERATOR: *Technically, you did. I have little voices that come in my ear. You don't get those same voices, I'm not hearing it from here, I'm hearing it from here. You have waived your rebuttal. You can go with your closing statement.*
REAGAN: *Well, we'll include it in that.*

Four years ago in similar circumstances to this I asked you, the American people, a question. I asked, are you better off than you were four years before. The answer to that obviously was no, and as a result I was elected to this office and promised a new beginning. Now, maybe I'm expected to ask that same question again. I'm not going to because I think that all of you or, not everyone, those people that have—are in those pockets of poverty and haven't caught up, they couldn't answer the way I would want them to. But I think that most of the people in this country would say, yes, they are better off than they were four years ago.

The question I think should be enlarged. Is America better off than it was four years ago? And I believe the answer to that has to also be yes.

I promised a new beginning. So far it is only a beginning. If the job were finished, I might have thought twice about seeking reelection to this job. But we now have an economy that for the first time—well, let's put it this way, in the first half of 1980 gross national product was down a minus 3.7 percent.

The first half of '84 it's up 8.5 percent. Productivity in the first half of 1980 was down a minus 2 percent. Today it is up a plus 4 percent. Personal earnings after taxes per capita have gone up almost $3,000 in these four years. In 1980 or 1979 the person with a fixed income of $8,000 was $500 above the poverty line, and this maybe explains why there are the numbers still in poverty. By 1980 that same person was $500 below the poverty line.

We have restored much of our economy with regard to a business investment. It is higher than it has been since 1949. So there seems to be no shortage of investment capital. We have, as I said, cut the taxes, but we have reduced inflation and for two years now it has stayed down there, not a double digit but in the range of 4 or below.

We believe that we had also promised that we would make our country more secure. yes, we have an increase in the defense budget. But back then we had planes that couldn't fly for lack of spare parts or pilots. We had navy vessels that couldn't leave harbor, because of lack of crew or again, lack of spare parts. Today we're well on our way to a 600-ship navy. We have 543 at present. We have—our military, the morale is high, I think the people should understand that two-thirds of the defense budget pays for pay and salary—or pay and pension. And then you add to that food and wardrobe and all the other things and you only have a small portion going for weapons. But I am determined that if ever our men are called on they should have the best that we can provide in the manner of tools and weapons. There has been reference to expensive spare parts, hammers costing $500. Well, we are the ones who found those.

I think we've given the American people back their spirit. I think there is an optimisim in the land and a patriotism and I think that we're in a position once again to heed the words of Thomas Paine who said: "We have it in our power to begin the world over again."

MODERATOR: *Thank you Mr. Reagan. Mr. Mondale, the closing words are now yours.*

MONDALE: *I want to thank the League of Women Voters and the city of Louisville for hosting this evening's debate. I want to thank President Reagan for agreeing to debate. He didn't have to and he did, and we all appreciate it.*

The President's favorite question is, "Are you better off?" Well, if you're wealthy, you're better off. If you're middle income, you're about where you were, and if you're of modest income, you're worse off. That's what the economists tell us. But is that really the question that should be asked. Isn't the real question, "Will we be better off? Will our children be better off? Are we building the future that this nation needs?"

I believe that if we ask those questions that bear on our future—not just congratulate ourselves but challenge us to solve those problems—you'll see that we need new leadership.

Are we better off with this arms race? Will we be better off if we start this star wars escalation into the heavens? Are we better off when we de-empha-

size our values in human rights? Are we better off when we load our children with this fantastic debt? Would father and mothers feel proud of themselves if they loaded their children with debts like this nation is now, over a trillion dollars, on the shoulders of our children? Can we be—say, really say, that we will be better off when we pull away from sort of that basic American instinct of decency and fairness?

I would rather lose a campaign about decency than win a campaign about self-interest. I don't think this nation is composed of people who care only for themselves. And when we sought to assault Social Security and Medicare, as the record shows we did, I think that was mean spirited. When we terminated 400,000 desperate, hopeless, defenseless Americans who were on disability, confused and unable to defend themselves, and just laid them out on the streets as we did for four years, I don't think that's what America is all about. America is a fair society, and it is not right that Vice President Bush pays less in taxes than the janitor who helps him. I believe there's fundamental fairness crying out that needs to be achieved in our tax system.

I believe that we will be better off if we protect this environment. And contrary to what the president says I think their record on the environment is inexcusable and often shameful. These laws are not being enforced, have not been enforced and the public health and the air and the water are paying the price. that's not fair for our future.

I think our future requires the president lead us in an all-out search to advance our education, our learning and our science and training, because this world is more complex and we're being pressed harder all the time.

I believe in opening doors. We won the Olympics in part because we've had civil rights laws and the laws that prohibit discrimination against women. I have been for those efforts all my life. The president's record is quite different.

The question is our future. President Kennedy once said in response to similar arguments, we are great but we can be greater. We can be better if we face our future, rejoice in our strengths, face our problems and by solving them build a better society for our children.

Thank you.

MODERATOR: *Thank you Mr. Mondale, and thank you Mr. President, and our thanks to our panel members as well. And so we bring to a close this first of the League of Women Voters presidential debates of 1984. You two can go at each other again in the final League debate on October 21 in Kansas City, Missouri, and this Thursday night, October 11, at 9 P.M. Eastern daylight time, Vice President Bush will debate Congresswoman Geraldine Ferraro in Philadelphia. And I hope that you will all watch once again, no matter what the format, these debates are very important. We all have an extremely vital decision to make. Once more gentlemen, our thanks, once to you our thanks, and now this is Barbara Walters wishing you a good evening.*

League of Women Voters President Dorothy S. Ridings confers with moderator Sander Vanocur of ABC News minutes before the League-sponsored vice presidential debate on October 11, 1984 (LEAGUE OF WOMEN VOTERS EDUCATION FUND)

Transcript of Philadelphia Debate Between Bush and Ferraro, October 11, 1984

DOROTHY S. RIDINGS: *Good evening from the Civic Center in Philadelphia, Pennsylvania. I'm Dorothy Ridings, president of the League of Women Voters, the sponsor of tonight's vice-presidential debate between Republican George Bush and Democrat Geraldine Ferraro.*

Our panelists for tonight's debate are John Mashek, national correspondent for U.S. News & World Report; *Jack White, correspondent for* Time *magazine; Norma Quarles, correspondent for NBC News; and Robert Boyd, Washington bureau chief for Knight-Ridder Newspapers.*

Sander Vanocur, senior political correspondent for ABC News, is our moderator tonight. Sandy.

MODERATOR: *Thank you, Dorothy. A few words about the order of our format tonight. The order of questioning was determined by a toss of the coin. Congresswoman Ferraro won the toss. She elected to speak last. Therefore Vice-President Bush will get the first question.*

The debate will be built upon a series of questions from the four reporters on the panel. A reporter will ask a candidate a question, a followup question and then the same to the other candidate, then each candidate will get to rebut the other.

The debate will be divided into two parts. There'll be a section, the first one, on domestic affairs; the second on foreign affairs.

275

Now the manner of address was decided by the candidates. Therefore it will be Vice-President Bush, Congresswoman Ferraro.
And we begin our questioning with Mr. Mashek.

President-Vice President Relationship

Q: *John Adams, our nation's first president, once said: "Today I am nothing. Tomorrow I may be everything." With that in mind, I'd like to ask the following question: Vice President Bush, four years ago, you ran against Mr. Reagan for the Republican nomination. You disagreed with him on such issues as the Equal Rights Amendment, abortion, and you even labeled his economic policies as voodoo. Now you apparently agree with him on every issue. If you should be called upon to assume the presidency, would you follow Mr. Reagan's policies down the line or would you revert to some of your own ideas.*

BUSH: *Well, I don't think there's a great difference, Mr. Mashek, between my ideas and President Reagan's.*

One of the reasons I think we're an effective team is that I believe firmly in his leadership. He's really turned this country around. We agree on the economic program.

When we came into office, why, inflation was 21, 12½ percent interest rates wiping out every single American were 21½ percent if you can believe it. Productivity was down. Savings was down. There was despair. In fact, the leadership of the country told the people that there was a malaise out there.

And this president turned it around and I've been with him every step of the way. And of course I would continue those kinds of programs because it's brought America back. America's better off. People are going back to work. And why Mr. Mondale can't understand that there's a new enthusiasm in this country, that America is back, there's new strong leadership, I don't know.

He has one answer to the problem. Raise everybody's taxes. He looked right into that lens and he said out there in San Francisco, he said, "I'm gonna raise your taxes." Well he's had a lot of experience in that and he's sure gonna go ahead and do it. But I remember a statement of Lyndon Johnson's when he was looking around, why his party people weren't supporting him, and he said, "Hey, they painted their tails white and they ran with the antelopes." There's a lot of Democratic white tails running with the antelopes. Not one single Democrat has introduced the Mondale tax bill into the Congress.

Of course I support the president's economic program and I support him in everything else.

And I'm not sure, because of my concept of the vice presidency, that if I didn't, I'd go doing what Mr. Mondale has done with Jimmy Carter; jump away from him. I couldn't do that to Ronald Reagan, now, next year or any other time. I have too much trust in him. I have too much friendship for him. And I'd feel very uncomfortable doing that.

Q: *Well some Republicans have criticized Mr. Mondale for now claiming he disagreed privately with Jimmy Carter's decision to impose the grain embargo. Have you ever disagreed with any decision of the Reagan administration and its inner circles? And in following that up, where in your judgment does loyalty end and principle begin?*

BUSH: *I owe my president my judgment and then I owe him loyalty. You can't have the president of the United States out there looking over his shoulder wondering whether his vice president is going to be supporting him.*

Mrs. Ferraro has quite a few differences with Vice-President Mondale and I understood it when she changed her position on tuition tax credits. They're different on busing; she voted to extend the grain embargo; he now says that he was against it. If they win—and I hope they don't—but if they win, she'll have to accommodate some views. But she'll give him the same kind of loyalty that I'm giving President Reagan. One, we're not far apart on anything. Two, I can walk into that Oval Office anytime and give him my judgment and he might agree or he might not. But he also knows I won't be talking about it to the press or I won't be knifing in the back by leaking to make me look good and complicate the problems of the president of the United States.

Q: *Congresswoman Ferraro, your opponent has served in the House Of Representatives, he's been ambassador to the United Nations, ambassador to China, director of the Central Intelligence Agency and now he's been vice president for four years. How does your three terms in the House of Representatives stack up against experience like that?*

FERRARO: *Well, let me first say that I wasn't born at the age of forty-three when I entered Congress. I did have a life before that as well. I was a prosecutor for almost five years in the district attorney's office in Queens County and I was a teacher. There's not only what is on your paper résumé that makes you qualified to run for or to hold office. It's how you approach problems and what your values are. I think if one is taking a look at my career they'll see that I level with the people; that I approach problems analytically; that I am able to assess the various facts with reference to a problem, and I can make the hard decisions.*

I'm intrigued when I hear Vice-President Bush talk about his support of the president's economic program and how everything is just going so beautifully. I, too, recall when Vice President Bush was running in the primary against President Reagan and he called the program voodoo eco-

nomics, and it was and it is. We are facing absolutely massive deficits; this administration has chosen to ignore it; the president has failed to put forth a plan to deal with those deficits and if everything believes that everything is coming up roses, perhaps the vice-president should join me as I travel around the country and speak to people.

People in Johnstown, Pennsylvania, are not terribly thrilled with what's happening in the economy because they're standing in the light of a closed plant because they've lost their jobs. the people in Youngstown, Ohio, have stores that are boarded up because the economy is not doing well. It's not only the old industries that are failing, it's also the new ones. In San Jose, California, they're complaining because they can't export their high-tech qualities—goods—to Japan and other countries. The people in the Northwest—in the state of Washington and Oregon—are complaining about what's happening to the timber industry and to the agriculture industry. So, so things are not as great as the administration is wanting us to believe in their television commercials. My feeling, quite frankly, is that I have enough experience to see the problems, address them and make the tough decisions and level with people with reference to those problems.

Q: Despite the historic aspects of your candidacy, how do you account for the fact that a majority of women—at least according to the polls—favor the Reagan-Bush ticket over the Mondale-Ferraro ticket?

FERRARO: I don't. Let me say that I'm not a believer in polls and let me say further that what we are talking about are problems that are facing the entire nation. They're not just problems facing women. The issues in this campaign are the war-peace issues; the problems of deficits; the problems of trade deficits. We are now facing a $120 billion trade deficit in this country. We're facing problems of the environment. I think what we're going to be doing over the next several weeks—and I'm absolutely delighted that the League is sponsoring these debates and that we are, we are able to now speak to the American public and address the issues in a way such as this. I think you're going to see a change in those polls.

MODERATOR: Vice President Bush, you have one minute to rebuttal.

BUSH: Well, I was glad to get that vote of confidence from Mrs. Ferraro in my economic judgment. So let me make a statement on the economy.

The other day she was in a plant and she said to the workers, Why are you all voting for, why are so many of you voting for the Reagan-Bush ticket? And there was a long, deathly silence and she said come on, we delivered. That's the problem. And I'm not blaming her except for the liberal voting record in the House. They delivered. They delivered 21½ percent interest rates. They delivered what they called malaise. They delivered interest rates that were right off the charts. They delivered take-home pay, checks that were shrinking, and we've delivered optimism. People are going back to work; 6 million of them. And 300,000 jobs a month being

*created. That's why there was that deathly silence out there in that plant.
They delivered the wrong thing. Ronald Reagan is delivering leadership.*
MODERATOR: *Congresswoman Ferraro, one-minute rebuttal.*
FERRARO: *I, I think what I'm going to have to do is I'm going to start
correcting the vice-president's statistics. There are 6 million more people
who have jobs and that's supposed to happen in a growing economy. In fact
in the prior administration, with all their problems, they created 10 million
jobs. The housing interest rates during this administration, for housing for
middle-class Americans, was 14.5 percent. Under the prior administration,
with all their problems, the average rate was 10.6 percent. If you take a look
at the number of people living in poverty as a result of this administration, 6
million people, 500,000 people knocked off disability rolls. You know, it's,
you can walk around saying things are great and that's what we're going to
be hearing, we've been hearing that on those commercials for the past
couple of months. I expect they expect the American people to believe that.
I'll become a one-woman truth squad and we'll start tonight.*
MODERATOR: *Mr. White.*

Civil Rights, Education, and Poverty

Q: *Congresswoman Ferraro, I would like to ask you about civil rights. You
have in the past been a supporter of tuition tax credits for private parochial
schools. And also of a constitutional amendment to ban busing. Both these
measures are opposed not only by your running mate but by just about
every educational and civil rights organization in the country. Now that
you're Mr. Mondale's running mate have you changed your position on
either of those?*
FERRARO: *With reference to the busing vote that I cast in 1979, both Fritz
Mondale and I agree on the same goal and that is nondiscrimination. I just
don't agree on the same direction he does on how to achieve it. But I don't
find any problem with that. I think that's been something that's been handled by the courts, and not being handled by Congress and will not be
handled by the White House. But we both support nondiscrimination in
housing and integration of neighborhoods. The goals we both set forth.*

*With reference to tuition tax credits, I have represented a district in
Queens which is 70 percent Catholic. I represented my district. Let me say
as well that I have also been a great supporter of public school education
and that is something that Fritz and I feel very, very strongly about for the
future of this country. And this administration over the past several years
has gutted the educational programs available to our young people.*

*It has attempted to knock out Pell Grants, which are monies to young
individuals who are poor and who cannot afford to go to college. It has*

reduced by 25 percent the amount of monies going into college education and by a third those going into secondary and primary schools. But Fritz Mondale and I feel very strongly that if you educate your children that that's an effort and the way that you build up and make a stronger America.

With reference to civil rights I think you've got to go beyond that and if you take a look, also, at my record in the Congress and Fritz Mondale's record, both in the Senate and as vice president, we both have extremely strong civil rights records. This administration does not. It has come in in the Bob Jones on the side of segregated academies. It came in in the Grove City case on the side of discrimination against women, the handicapped, and the elderly. As a matter of fact, in the Congress we just passed over-whelmingly the Civil Rights Bill of 1984 and this administration, the Repub-lican-controlled Senate, just killed it in the last week or two in Congress. So there is a real difference between how the Mondale-Ferraro administration will address the problems of civil rights and the failure of this administration specifically in that particular area.

Q: In the area of affirmative action, what steps do you think government can take to increase the representation of minorities and women in the work force, and in colleges and universities, and specifically, would you support the use of quotas to achieve those goals?

FERRARO: I do not support the use of quotas. Both Mr. Mondale and I feel very strongly about affirmative action to correct inequities, and we believe that steps should be taken both through government—for instance, the Small Business Administration. We have supported set-asides for minority and women's businesses. That's a positive thing.

We don't feel that you're in any way hurting anybody else by reaching out with affirmative action to help those who've been disenfranchised. On the contrary, if you have a growing economy, if you create the jobs, if you allow for small business the opportunity with lower interest rates to reach out and grow, there will be more than enough space for everybody. And affirmative action is a very positive way to deal with the problems of discrimination.

Q: Vice-President Bush, many critics of your administration say that it is the most hostile to minorities in recent memory. Have you inadvertently perhaps encouraged that view by supporting tuition tax credits, the antibus-ing amendment, and siding with Bob Jones University in a case before the Supreme Court, your original opposition to the Voting Rights Act extension and so forth?

BUSH: No, Mr. White, I think our record on civil rights is a good record. You mentioned the Voting Rights extension; it was extended for the longest period of time by President Reagan. But we have some problems in attracting the black vote, and I think our record deserves better. We have done more for black colleges than any previous administration.

We favor enterprise zones to give—and it's been blocked by Tip O'Neill and that House of Representatives, those liberals in that House blocked a new idea to bring jobs into the black communities across the country. And because it's not an old handout, special federal spending program, it's blocked there—a good idea. And I'd like to see that tried.

We've brought more civil rights cases in the Justice Department than the previous administration by far. We believe in trying something new to help these black teenage kids; the minimum wage differential that says, "Look," to an employer, "hire these guys. And, yes, they're willing to work for slightly less than the minimum wage. Give 'em a training job in a private sector." We threw out that old CETA that didn't train people for jobs that existed, simply rammed them onto the government payroll, and we put in a thing called the Job Training Partnership Act. Wonderful, new legislation that's helping blacks more and more.

We think of civil rights as something like crime in your neighborhoods. And, for example, when crime figures are going in the right direction that's good, that's a civil right. Similarly, we think of it in terms of quality of life, and that means interest rates.

You know, it's funny, Mr. Mondale talks about real interest rates. The real interest rate is what you pay when you go down and try to buy a TV set or buy a car, or do whatever it is. The interest rates when we left office were 21½ percent. Inflation! Is it a civil right to have the going right off the chart so you're busting every American family, those who can afford it the less?

No, we've got a good record. We've got it on civil rights legislation, minority set-asides, more help for black colleges, and we've got it in terms of an economy that's offering people opportunity and hope instead of despair.

Q: *Along those lines, sir, many recent studies have indicated that the poor and minorities have not really shared in the new prosperity generated by the current economic recovery. Was it right for your administration to pursue policies, economic policies, that required those at the bottom of the economic ladder to wait for prosperity to trickle down from people who are much better off than they?*

BUSH: *Mr. White, it's not trickling down. And I'm not suggesting there's no poverty, but I am suggesting the way to work out of poverty is through real opportunity. And in the meantime, the needy are getting more help. Human resource spending is way, way up. Aid for Dependent Children spending is up. Immunization programs are up. Almost every place you can point, contrary to Mr. Mondale's—I gotta be careful—but contrary of how he goes around just saying everything bad. If somebody sees a silver lining, he finds a big black cloud out there. Whine on harvest moon! I mean, there's a lot going on, a lotta opportunity.*

MODERATOR: *Congresswoman Ferraro, your rebuttal.*

FERRARO: *The vice-president indicates that the President signed the Voting Rights Act. That was after he was—he did not support it while it was in the Congress, in the Senate, it was passed despite his opposition, and he did sign it because he was required to do so. In the civil rights cases that he mentioned, the great number of cases that they have enforced, the reason they enforced them because under the law they're required to do that. And I'm delighted that the administration is following the law.*

With reference . . .

MODERATOR: *Excuse me—this will be out of my time, not yours—knowing and cherishing the people of this city and knowing their restraint and diffidence about emotion especially of athletic contexts of which this is not one, I beseech you, try to hold your applause please. I'm sorry.*

FERRARO: *I just have to correct in my thirty seconds that are left the comment that the vice-president made with reference specifically to a program like AFDC. If you take AFDC, if you take food stamps, if you take—oh, go down the line on poor people's programs, those are the programs that suffered considerably under this administration's first budget cuts and those are the ones that in the second part of their part of their term, we were able to restore some of those terribly, terribly unfair cuts to the poor people of this country.*

MODERATOR: *Vice-President Bush.*

BUSH: *Well, maybe we have a factual—maybe we can ask the experts to go to the books. They'll do it anyway. Spending for food stamps is way, way up under the Reagan administration. AFDC is up under the Reagan administration, and I am not going to be found wrong on that. I am sure of my facts, and we are trying to help and I think we're doing a reasonable job. But we are not going to rest until every single American that wants a job and until this prosperity and this recovery that's benefiting many Americans, benefits all Americans.*

Religion and Politics

MODERATOR: *Miss Quarles*

Q: *Vice-President Bush, one of the most emotional issues in this campaign has been the separation of church and state. What are your views on the separation of church and state specifically with regard to abortion, and do you believe it was right for the archbishop of Philadelphia to have a letter read in 305 churches urging Catholics to fight abortion with their votes?*

BUSH: *I do believe in pluralism. I do believe in separation of church and state. I don't consider abortion a religious issue. I consider it a moral issue. I believe the archbishop has every right to do everything he wants in that direction, just as I never faulted Jesse Jackson from taking his message to the black pulpits all across this country, just as I never objected when the nuclear arms, the nuclear freeze or the antinuclear people—many of those movements were led by priests. Suddenly, because a Catholic bishop or an evangelist feels strongly on a political issue, people are saying it's merging of church and state.*

We favor—and I speak confidently for the president—we favor separation of church and state. We favor pluralism. Now somebody says you ought to restore prayer in schools. You don't think it's right to prohibit a kid from praying in schools. For years kids were allowed to pray in schools. We don't think that's a merger of church and state to have nonmandatory, voluntary, nongovernment-ordered prayer. And yet some are accusing us of injecting religion into politics. I have no problem with what the archbishop does, and I have no problem with what the evangelists on the right do and I have no problem what the priests on the left do.

And it didn't bother me when during the Vietnam War much of the opposition to the government—Democrat and Republican governments—was led by priests, encouraging people to break the law and the adage of the—you know—the civil disobedience thing.

So our position, separation of church and state, pluralism, so no little kid with a minority religion of some sort is going to feel offended or feel left out or feel uncomfortable. But, yes, prayer in school on a voluntary basis worked for many, many years until the Supreme Court ruled differently. And I'm glad we got this question because I think there's been too much said about religion and politics. We don't believe in denominationally moving in. It wasn't our tide that raised the question about our president whether he was a good Christian or not and so I, so that's our position—separation of church and state, pluralism, respect for all.

Q: *Vice-President Bush, four years ago you would have allowed federal financing of abortions in cases of rape and incest as well as when the mother's life was threatened. Does your position now agree with that of president Reagan who in Sunday's debate came very close to saying that abortion is murder?*

BUSH: *You know, there has been—I have to make a confession—an evolution in my position. there's been 15 million abortions since 1973, and I don't take that lightly. There's been a million and a half this year. The president and I do favor a human rights amendment. I favor one that would have an exception for incest and rape, and he doesn't, but we both—only for the life of the mother. And I agree with him on that. So, yes, my position's evolved, but I'd like to see the American who faced with 15 million abortions isn't rethinking his or her position and I'll just stand with the answer. I support the president's position—and comfortably—from a moral standpoint.*

Q: *So you belive it's akin to murder?*

BUSH: *No, I support the president's position.*

Q: *Fine. Congresswoman Ferraro, what are your views on the separation of church and state with regard to abortions, and do you believe it was right for the archbishop of Philadelphia to have those letters read in the pulpits and urged the voters to fight abortion with their vote?*

FERRARO: *Let me say first of all I believe very, very sincerely in the separation of church and state. I'm taking it from the historical viewpoint, if you go back to the 1600s when people came here, the reason they came to this country was to escape religious persecution, and that's the same reason why people are coming here today in the 1940s to escape Nazism, now in the 1980s and 1984 when they can get out of the country to escape communism so they can come here and practice their religion.*

Our country is founded on the principle that our government should be neutral as far as religion is concerned. Now what's happened over the past several years, and quite frankly I'm not going to let you lay on me the intrusion of state politics into religion or religion into politics by my comments with reference to the president's policies, because it started in 1980 when this administration was running for office and the Reverend Jerry Falwell became very, very involved in the campaign.

What has happened over the past four years has been I think a real fudging of that line with the separation of church and state. The actions of the archbishops let me say to you I feel that they have not only a right but a responsibility to speak up, and even though I've been the person that they're speaking up about, I feel they do have the responsibility to do so, and I have no problem with it, no more than I did a priest who marched at the time of Vietnam and no more than I did at the time when Martin Luther King marched at the time of the civil rights marches. I have absolutely no problem with them speaking up, I think they have an obligation as well as a right.

But what I do have a problem with is when the president of the United States gets up in Dallas and addresses a group of individuals and said to them that anybody who doesn't support his constitutional amendment for prayer in the schools is intolerant of religion.

Now there are numerous groups who don't support that prayer in the school, numerous religious groups. Are they intolerant of religion? Is that what the president is saying?

I also object, when I am told, that the Reverend Falwell has been told that he would pick two of our Supreme Court justices. That's going a little bit far. In that instance, let me say to you it is more than a fudging at the line, it is a total intrusion, and I think that it's in violation of our Constitution.

Q: *Congresswoman Ferraro, as a devout Catholic, does it trouble you that so many of the leaders of your church disagree with you, and do you think that you're being treated unfairly in any way by the Catholic church?*

FERRARO: *Let me tell you that I did not come to my position on abortion very lightly. I am a devout Catholic. When I was running for Congress in 1978 I sat and met with a person I felt very close to, a monsignor currently a bishop. I spoke to him about my personal feelings that I would never have an abortion, but I was not quite sure if I were ever to become pregnant as a result of a rape if I would be that self-righteous. I then spoke to him; he said, Gerry, that's not good enough. There you can't support that position. I said O.K. That's my religious view; I will accept the teaching of the church, but I cannot impose my religious views on someone else.*

I truly take an oath as a public official to represent all the people in my district, not only the Catholics. If there comes a time where I cannot practice my religion and do my job properly, I will resign my job.

MODERATOR: *Vice-President Bush, your rebuttal.*

BUSH: *Well I respect that statement, I really and truly do. We have a difference on a moral question here on abortion. I notice that Mr. Mondale keeps talking in the debate and now it's come here about Mr. Falwell. And I don't know where this canard could have come from about Mr. Falwell picking the Supreme Court justices. Ronald Reagan has made one superb, outstanding, the only one he's made, appointment to the Supreme Court, and that was Sandra Day O'Connor, and Mr. Falwell opposed her nomination. We still have respect for him, but he opposed it, and so I hope this lays to rest this slander against the president. We want justices who will interpret the Constitution, not legislate it.*

MODERATOR: *Congresswoman Ferraro, your rebuttal?*

FERRARO: *Yes, I still find it very difficult to believe because in the platform which this Republican party passed in Dallas—one of the things they did was they said that this position on abortion would be a litmus test, not only for Supreme Court justices but for other federal justices. That, again, seems to me a blurring of the line of the separation between church and state.*

MODERATOR: *The next questioning from Mr. Boyd.*

Candidate Financial Issues

Q: *Like many Americans, each of you has recently had an unhappy experience with the Internal Revenue Service. I'm going to prolong your ordeal. Congresswoman Ferraro, you disagree with the rule that says that a candidate must report the income or assets of his or her spouse if you get any benefit from them. Your husband's tax return showed that you did benefit because he paid the mortgage and the property taxes on your home. Now the ethics committee is examining this question, but it won't report its findings until after the election. Would you be willing to ask that committee, which is controlled by Democrats, to hurry up its work and report before the election.*

FERRARO: *Let me say to you that I already did that. I wanted them to move ahead. If you recall, I spent about an hour and 45 minutes speaking to 200 reporters on August 21, which is the day after I was required to file my financial statement, and I sat for as long as they had questions on the issue, and I believe that they were satisfied. I filed more information than any other candidate for a national office in the history of this country.*

Not only did I agree to file my tax returns, after a little bit of prodding my husband also agreed to file his with the—not only the ethics committee but the FEC. But the action that you're speaking about with the ethics committee was started by a right-wing legal organization—foundation—knowing that I would have to—that there would be an automatic inquiry. We have filed the necessary papers, I have asked them to move along. Unfortunately, the House, I believe, went out of session today, so I don't know if they will move. But quite frankly, I would like that to be taken care of anyway, because I just want it cleared up.

Q: *Since that famous August 21 press conference on your family finances, you filed a new report with the ethics committee, and this showed that your previous reports were full of mistakes and omissions. For example, you failed to report about twelve trips that were paid for by special interest groups. In at least eighteen cases your holdings were misstated. Do you think it showed good leadership or attention to duty to blame all this on sloppy work by your accountant?*

FERRARO: *Well, what it showed was that—and it was truly that I hired an accountant who had been with our family for well over forty years. He was filling out those ethics forms. I did not spend the time with him—I just gave him my tax information and he did it. I have to tell you what we have done since I have hired a marvelous accountant. I've spent a lot of money having him go through all those ethics forms and he will be doing my taxes over the next eight years while we're in the White House so that the American public can be sure it's all been taken care of.*

Q: *Vice-President Bush, last year you paid less than 13 percent of your income in federal taxes. According to the IRS, someone in your bracket normally pays about 28 percent of his income. Now what you did was perfectly legal, but do you think it was fair, and is there something wrong with our tax laws that allows such large deductions for wealthy taxpayers?*

BUSH: *What that figure—and I kind of like the way Mrs. Ferraro and Mr. Zaccaro reported—because they reported federal taxes, state and local taxes—gives people a clearer picture. That year I happened to pay a lot of state and local taxes, which as you know are deducted from the other, and so I looked it up the other day, and we had paid—I think it's 42 percent—of our gross income in taxes. Now Mr. Mondale the other night took what*

I—I'll be honest—I think it was a cheap shot—at me, and we did a little looking around to see about his. We can't find his 1981 tax return—it may have been released.

Maybe my opponent knows whether Mr. Mondale released it. But we did find estimates that his income for those three years is a million, four hundred thousand dollars, and I think he paid about the same percentage as I did in total taxes. He also made a reference that troubled me very much. Mr. Boyd. He started talking about my chauffeur, and you know, I'm driven to work by the Secret Service—so is Mrs. Ferraro—so is Mr. Mondale — they protected his life for four years and now they've done a beautiful job for Barbara and mine. They saved the life of the president of the United States. I think that was a cheap shot—telling the American people to try to divide class—rich and poor.

But the big question isn't whether Mrs. Ferraro is doing well. I think they're doing pretty well, and I know Barbara and I are doing well. And it's darn sure that Mr. Mondale is doing well, with a million four in income, but the question really is—after we get through this disclosure—is the tax cut fair? Are people getting a fair break, and the answer is the rich are paying 6 percent more on taxes and the poor are getting a better break. Those lower- and middle-income people that have borne the burden for a long time. So yes, I favor disclosure. I've always disclosed. This year I had my taxes and everything I own in a blind trust—so blind—blinder than the president's, so I didn't even sign my tax return. But there seemed to be an interest in it so we went to the government ethics committee—they agreed to change the trust. The trust has been revealed, and I was sure glad to see that I had paid 42 percent of my gross income in taxes.

Q: Mr. Vice-President, how can you claim that your home is in Maine for tax purposes and at the same time claim that your home is in Texas for voting purposes? Are you really a Texan or a New Englander?

BUSH: I'm really a Texan. But I got one house. And under the law, every taxpayer is allowed, when he sells a house, and buys another house, to get the rollover. Eveybody, if it turns out, and I may hire, I notice she said she has a new good accountant. I'd like to get his name and phone number because I think I've paid too much in the way of taxes. And residence, Mr. Boyd, legal residence, for voting, is very different. And the domicile, they call that, very different, than the house. That they say you're living in the vice-president's house. Therefore you don't get what every—I've got problems—what every other taxpayer gets. I got problems with the IRS, but so do a lot of people out there. I think I've paid too much. Nothing ethical. I'd like to get some money back.

MODERATOR: Congresswoman Ferraro, your rebuttal please.

FERRARO: Let me just say that I'd be happy to give the vice-president the name of my accountant, but I warn you, he's expensive.

I think the question is whether or not the tax cuts and the tax system that's currently in our government, that our government uses, is fair. I think the tax system is unfair. But it's not something that we can address in the short term. The tax cuts that Vice-President Bush and I got last, three years ago, that this president gave out, no, that's not fair. If you earn $200,000 a year, you got a $25,000 tax cut. If you earned between $20,000 and $40,000, you may have gotten about $1,000 between ten and twenty, close to a hundred dollars and if you made less than $10,000 with all the budget cuts that came down the line, you suffered a loss of $400. That's not fair. That's basically unfair and not only is it unfair, but economically it has darn near destroyed this country. There's a $750 billion tax cut over a five-year period of time. That's one of the reasons we're facing these enormous deficits that we have today.

MODERATOR: *Mr. Vice-President.*

BUSH: *No, I think I've said all I want to say. I do, I didn't fully address myself to Mr. Boyd's question no disclosure, I led the fight, I think, in 1968, in the House—I was in the House of Representatives for a couple of terms—and I led the fight for disclosure. I believe in it. Before I went into this job, I disclosed everything we had. We didn't have any private corporations, but I disclosed absolutely everything. Arthur Anderson made out a assets and liabilities statement that I believe went further than any other one. And then, to protect the public interest, we went into this blind trust. I believe in the blind trust because I believe a public official in this kind of job ought not to know whether he's gonna benefit, directly or indirectly, by some holding he might have or something of that nature. And, no, I support full disclosure.*

MODERATOR: *Thank you. That ends the part of this debate devoted to domestic affairs. We will now turn to foreign affairs and will begin the questioning with Mr. Mashek.*

Policy on Terrorism

Q: *Vice-President Bush, since your administration came to power the President has threatened a stern response against terrorism, yet murderous attacks have continued in Lebanon and the Middle East. Who's to blame, and you've been director of the Central Intelligence Agency. What can be done to stop it?*

BUSH: *Terrorism is very, very difficult to stop. And I think everybody knows that. We had ambassadors killed in Sudan and the Lebanon some time ago, a long time ago. When you see the Israeli building in Lebanon after the death of our marines you see that, hit by terrorism, the Israelis,*

*with all their experience fighting terrorism, you know it's difficult. When
you see Khomeini with his radical Islam resorting to government-sponsored
terrorism, it's very difficult. The intelligence business can do a good job,
and I'm always one that defends the Central Intelligence Agency. I believe
we ought to strengthen it and I believe we still have the best foreign intelligence business in the world. But it is very difficult to get the source information that you need to go after something as shadowy as international terror.*

*There was a difference between Iran and what happened in Lebanon. In
Iran you had a government holding a U.S. embassy; the government sanc-
tioning the takeover of that embassy by those students; the government
negotiating with the United States government for their release. In Lebanon,
in the terror that happened at the embassy, you have the government there,
Mr. Gemayel, that wants to help fight against terrorism. But because of the
melee in the Middle East, it's there today and has been there yesterday and
the day before, and everyone that's had experience in that area knows, it is a
very different thing. So what we've got to do is use absolutely the best
security possible. I don't think you can go assigning blame. The president,
of course, is the best I've ever seen at accepting that. He's been wonderful
about it in absolutely everything that happens. But I think fair-minded
people that really understand international terror know that it's very hard to
guard against. And the answer then really lies in the Middle East and
terrorism happening all over the world, is a solution to the Palestine question, the followon to Camp David under the umbrella of the Reagan September of 1982 initiative. That will reduce terror, it won't eliminate it.*

Q: *You mention Khomeini. Some Republicans charge the previous administration with being almost helpless against Khomeini and Libya's Quad-
dafi. Why hasn't your administration done something to take action against
Arab states that foment this kind of terrorism?*

BUSH: *What we've done is to support Arab states that want to stand up
against international terror, quite different. We believe in supporting, without jeopardizing the security of Israel in any way, because they are our one
strategic ally in the area, they are the one democracy in the area and our
relations with them has never been better. But we do believe in reaching out
to the, what they call the GCC, those Gulf Cooperative Council states, those
moderate Arab states in that world, and helping them with defensive weapons to guard against international terror or radical Islam perpetuated by
Khomeini. And because we've done that and because the Saudis chopped
down a couple of those intruding airplanes a while back, I think we have
helped keep the peace in the Persian Gulf.*

Q: *Congresswoman Ferraro, you and former Vice President Mondale have
criticized the president over the bombings in Lebanon, but what would you
do to prevent such attacks?*

FERRARO: *Let me first say that terrorism is a global problem, and let me say secondly that the—Mr. Bush has referred to the embassy that was held in Iran. Well, I was at the White House in January, I guess it was, in '81, when those hostages, all fifty two of them, came home alive. It was at that time that President Reagan gave a speech welcoming them home—as America did, we were so excited to see them back. But what he said was: The United States has been embarrassed for the last time. We're going to stand tall and if this ever happens again, there's going to be swift and immediate steps taken to address the wrong that our country has founded—has suffered.*

In April of 1983 I was in Beirut and visited the ambassador at the embassy. Two weeks later, that embassy was bombed. At that time—take a look at the crazy activities of terrorists, you can't blame that on anybody. They're going to do crazy things and you just don't know what's going to happen. The following October, there was another bombing and that bombing took place at the marine barracks, where there were 242 young men who were killed.

Right after that bombing occurred, there was a commission set up called the Long Commission. That commission did a study of the security arrangements around where the marines were sleeping and found that there was negligence, that they did not have proper gates up, proper precautions to stop those trucks from coming in. And so the Long Commission issued a report, and President Reagan got up and he said: I'm commander in chief. I take responsibility.

And we all waited for something to be done when he took responsibility. Well, last month we had our third bombing. The first time, the first embassy, there was no gate up. The second time, with our Marines, the gate was open. The third time, the gate was there but it had not been installed. And what was the president's reaction? Well, the security arrangements were not in, our people were placed in that embassy in an unsecured time, and the marines who were guarding it were left to go away and there were other people guarding the embassy.

Again the president said: I assume responsibility. I'd like to know what that means. Are we going to take proper precautions before we put Americans in situations where they're in danger, or are we just going to walk away, throwing our arms up in the air now—quite a reversal from the first time, from the first time when he said he was going to do something? Or is this President going to take some action?

Q: Some Democrats cringe at the words spying and covert activity. Do you believe both of them have a legitimate role in countering terrorist activity around the world.

Ferraro: I think they have a legitimate role in gathering information. And what had happened was the CIA, in the last bombing, had given information to our administration with reference to the actual threats that that embassy was going to be bombed. So it wasn't the CIA that was at fault.

There's legitimate reason for the CIA to be in existence, and that's to gather intelligence information for our security. But when I see the CIA doing things like they're doing down in Central America—supporting a covert war—no, I don't support that kind of activity. The CIA is there, it's meant to protect our government; not there to subvert other governments.

MODERATOR: *Vice-President Bush.*

BUSH: *Well, I'm surprised. I think I just heard Mrs. Ferraro say that she would do away with all covert actions, and if so, that has very serious ramifications, as the intelligence community knows. This is serious business. And sometimes it's quiet support for a friend, and so I'll leave that one there.*

But let me help you with the difference, Mrs. Ferraro, between Iran and the embassy in Lebanon. Iran—we were held by a foreign government. In Lebanon you had a wanton, terrorist action where the government opposed it. We went to Lebanon to give peace a chance, to stop the bombing of civilians in Beirut, to remove 13,000 terrorists from Lebanon—and we did.

We saw the formation of a government of reconciliation and for somebody to suggest, as our two opponents have, that these men died in shame—they better not tell the parents of those young marines. They gave peace a chance. And our allies were with us—the British, the French, and the Italians.

MODERATOR: *Congresswoman Ferraro.*

FERRARO: *Let me just say, first of all, that I almost resent, Vice President Bush, your patronizing attitude that you have to teach me about foreign policy. I've been a member of Congress for six years; I was there when the embassy was held hostage in Iran, and I have been there and I've seen what has happened in the past several months; seventeen months of your administration.*

Secondly, please don't categorize my answers, either. Leave the interpretation of my answers to the American people who are watching this debate. And let me say further that no one has ever said that those young men who were killed through the negligence of this administration and others ever died in shame. No one who has a child who is nineteen or twenty years old, a son, would ever say that at the loss of anybody else's child.

Central America

MODERATOR: *Mr. White.*

Q: *Congresswoman Ferraro, you've repeatedly said that you would not want your son to die in an undeclared war for an uncertain cause. But recently your running mate, Mr. Mondale, has suggested that it may become necessary to erect a military quarantine or blockade of Nicaragua. Under what circumstances would you advocate the use of military force, American combat forces, in Central America?*

FERRARO: *I would advocate the use of force when it was necessary to protect the security of our country, protect our security interest or protect our people or protect the interests of our friends and neighbors. When president—I'm jumping the gun a bit, aren't I?—when Mr. Mondale, Mr. Mondale referred to the quarantine of Central America, a country in Central America, what he is referring to is a last resort after all other means of attempting to settle the situation down in that region of the world had been exhausted.*

Quite frankly now what is being done by this administration is an Americanizing of a regional conflict. They're moving in militarily instead of promoting the Contadora process, which, as you know, is the process that is in place with the support of Mexico and Colombia and Panama and Venezuela.

Instead of supporting the process, our administration has in Nicaragua been supporting covert activities to keep that revolution going in order to overthrow the Sandinista government; in El Salvador was not pushing the head of the government to move toward correction of the civil rights, human rights problems that existed there, and now this administration seems almost befuddled by the fact that Nicaragua is moving to participate in the Contadora process, and El Salvador is, through its President Duarte, is reaching out to the guerrillas in order to negotiate a peace.

What Fritz Mondale and I feel about the situation down there is that what you do is you deal first through negotiation. That force is not a first resort but certainly a last resort in any instance.

MODERATOR: *A followup, please.*

Q: *Many times in its history the United States has gone to war in order to defend freedom in other lands. Does your answer mean that you would be willing to forgo the use of military force even if it meant the establishment of a Soviet-backed dictatorship so close to our own borders?*

FERRARO: *No, I think what you have to do is work with the government —I assume you're speaking about the government of Nicaragua—work with that government to achieve a pluralistic society. I mean they do have elections that are coming up on Nov. 4. I think we have to work with them to achieve a peaceful solution to bring about a pluralistic country.*

No, I'm not willing to live with a force that could be a danger to our country. Certainly, I would see that our country would be there putting all kinds of pressure on the neighboring countries of Honduras, of Costa Rica, of El Salvador, to promote the kind of society that we can all live with and security in this country.

Q: *Vice-President Bush, both Cuba and Nicaragua are reported to be making extensive preparations to defend themselves against an American invasion, which they claim could come this fall. And even some of your Democratic opponents in Congress have suggested that the administration may be planning a December surprise invasion. Can you tell us under what circumstances a reelected Reagan administration would consider the use of force in Central American or the Caribbean?*

BUSH: *We don't think we're to be required to use force. Let me point out that there are 2,000 Cuban military and 7,500 so-called Cuban advisers in Nicaragua. There are 55 American military in El Salvador.*

I went down, on the instructions of the president, to speak to the commandants in El Salvador and told them that they had to move with Mr. Magana, then the president of El Salvador, to respect human rights. They have done that. They're moving well. I'm not saying it's perfect, but the difference between El Salvador and Nicaragua is like the difference between night and day.

El Salvador went to the polls, Mr. Duarte was elected by 70 percent of the people in 70 percent voting in a certifiably free election. In Nicaragua, you have something very different. You have a Marxist-Leninist group, the Sandinistas, that came into power talking democracy. They have aborted their democracy. They have humiliated the Holy Father. They have cracked down on the only press organ there, La Prensa, censoring the press something that should concern every American.

They have not had any human rights at all. They will not permit free elections. Mr. Cruz, who was to be the only viable challenger to Nicaragua, the Sandinistas, to the junta, to Mr. Ortega, went down there and found that the ground rules were so unfair that he couldn't even wage a campaign. One country is devoid of human rights. The other is struggling to perfect their democracy.

We don't like it, frankly, when Nicaragua exports its revolution or serves as a conduit for supplies coming in from such "democracies" as North Korea, Bulgaria, the Soviet Union and Cuba, to tries to destabilize El Salvador.

Yes, we're concerned about that. Because we want to see this trend toward democracy continue. There have been something like thirteen countries since we've come in move toward the democratic route, and let me say that Grenada is not unrelated. And I have a big difference with Mrs. Ferraro on that one. We gave those four tiny Caribbean countries a chance. We saved the lives, and most of those thousand students said that they were in jeopardy. Grenada was a proud moment because we did stand up for democracy.

But in terms of threat of these countries, nuclear, I mean, weapons, no. There's not that kind of a threat. It's Mr. Mondale that proposed the quarantine, not Ronald Reagan.

Q: *Considering this country's long respect for the rule of international law, was it right for the United States to be involved in mining the harbors of Nicaragua, a country we're not at war with, and to subsequently refuse to allow the World Court to adjudicate that dispute and the complaint from Nicaragua?*

BUSH: *I support what we're doing. It was supported to the Congress and under the law. I support it. My only regret is that the aid for the contras, those people that are fighting, we call them freedom fighters. They want to see the democracy perfected in Nicaragua. Am I to understand from this assault on covert action that nowhere in the world would we do something that was considered just off base when Mrs. Ferraro said she's never support it? Would she never support it if the violation of human rights was so great and quiet support was necessary for freedom fighters?*

Yes, we're for the contras. *And let me tell you another fact about the* contras. *Everyone that's not for this, everyone who wants to let that Sandinista government prevail, just like that Castro did, all of that, the* contras *are not Somozistas. Less than 5 percent of the* contras *supported Somoza. These were people that wanted a revolution. These people that felt the revolution was betrayed. These are people that support human rights. Yes, we should support them.*

MODERATOR: *Congresswoman Ferraro.*

FERRARO: *I spent time in Central America in January and had an opportunity to speak to the* contras *after the incident in Nicaragua and in El Salvador. Let me just say that the situation as it exists now, because of this administration's policies, are not getting better. We're not moving toward a more secure area of the world. As a matter of fact the number of troops that the Sandinistas have accumulated since the administration started its covert activities has risen from 12,000 to 50,000, and of course the number of Soviet and Cuban advisors has also increased. I did not support the mining of the harbors in Nicaragua; it is a violation of international law. Congress did not support it and as a matter of fact, just this week, the Congress voted to cut off covert aid to Nicaragua unless and until a request is made and there is evidence of need for it, and the Congress approves it again in March. So if Congress doesn't get laid on, the covert activities which I opposed in Nicaragua, those CIA covert activities in that specific country, are not supported by the Congress. And believe it or not, not supported by the majority of people throughout the country.*

MODERATOR: *Vice-President Bush.*

BUSH: *Well, I would simply like to make the distinction again between those countries that are searching for democracy and the handful of countries that have totally violated human rights and are going the Marxist route. Ortega, the commandante who is head of the Nicaraguan Sandinistas, is an avowed Marxist. They don't believe in the church. They don't believe in free elec-*

tions. They don't believe in all of the values that we believe in. So it is our policy to support the democracy there, and when you have freedom fighters that want to protect that revolution, and go the democractic route, we believe in giving them support. We are for democracy in the hemisphere. We are for negotiations. $3 out of every $4 that we sent down there has been for economic aid to support the people's chance to eat and live and be happy and enjoy life. And one-fourth only was military. You wouldn't get that from listening to Mr. Mondale.

Arms Control Policy

MODERATOR: *Miss Quarles.*

Q: *Vice President Bush, the last three Republican administrations, Eisenhower, Nixon, and Ford, none of them soft on communism, met with the Soviets and got agreements on arms control. The Soviets haven't changed that much. Can you tell us why President Reagan has not met with the Soviet ministers at all and only met with Prime Minister Gromyko less than a month ago?*

BUSH: *Yes, I can. The, you mentioned the Gromyko meeting, those were broken off under the Carter-Mondale days. There had been three separate Soviet leaders. Mr. Brezhnev, Mr. Andropov, and now Chernenko. During their, that, in three and a half years, three separate leaders. The Soviets have not been willing to talk. We are the ones that went to the table in INF. We had a good proposal, a moral proposal. Ban an entire generation of intermediate nuclear force weapons and if you won't do that, don't leave your allies in Europe in a monopoly position. The Soviets with 1,200 of these things, and the alliance with none. We didn't think that's the way you deter aggression and keep the peace. The president went, the first thing he did when he came into office was make a proposal on the most destabilizing weapons of all, Start.*

And when the the strategic weapon and when the Soviets said, well, we don't like that proposal, we said all right, we'll be more flexible. I at the urging of the president went to Geneva and laid on the table a treaty to ban all chemical weapons. We don't want them to have a monopoly. We said look, let's come together. You come over here and see what we're doing; we'll go over there and see what you're doing. But let's save the kids of this world from chemical weapons. A brilliant proposal to get rid of all of them. And the Soviets nyet, nyet nyet. In the mutual balance force reduction to reduce conventional forces, they're not even willing to tell us the base. Mrs. Ferraro knows that, and how many troops they have. There's four sessions. We have had an agreement with them on the hot line. But Carter-Mondale made an agreement, the Salt II agreement, but the Democratic Senate, they were a Democratic administration, the Democratic Senate wouldn't even ratify that agreement. It was flawed, it was unverifiable and it was not good. Our president wants to reduce, not just to stop, he wants to reduce dramatically nuclear weapons. And when the Soviets know they're going to have this strong president to deal with, and when this new administration, Mr. Chernenko, given more than a few months in office can solidify its position, then they'll talk. But if they think the opposition, before they sit down, are going to give up the MX, give up the B-1, go for a freeze that locks in inferiority in Europe, all of these things, unilaterally, before they're willing to talk, they may just sweat it out for four more weeks. Who knows.

Q: You were once quoted as saying that a nuclear war is winnable. Is that still your belief, and if not, under what circumstances would you use nuclear weapons if you were president?

BUSH: No, I don't think it's winnable. I was quoted wrong, obviously, 'cause I never thought that. The Soviet planning, I did learn that when I was director of Central Intelligence, and I don't think there'd be any disagreement, is based on that ugly concept. But I agree with the president: It should never be fought.

Nuclear weapons should never be fought with, and that's our approach. So, therefore, let's encourage the Soviets to come to the table as we did at the Gromyko meeting. I wish everybody could have seen that one—the President, giving the facts to Gromyko in all of these nuclear meetings—excellent, right on top of that subject matter. And I'll bet you that Gromyko went back to the Soviet Union saying, "Hey, listen, this president is calling the shots; we'd better move."

But do you know why I think we'll get an agreement? Because I think it is in the interest of the Soviet Union to make it, just as it is in the United States. They're not deterred by rhetoric. I listened to the rhetoric for two years at the United Nations. I've lived in a Communist country. It's not rhetoric that decides agreements, it's self-interest of those countries.

Q: Congresswoman Ferraro, you and Mr. Mondale are for a verifiable nuclear freeze. Some Democrats have said that verification may not be possible. How would you verify such an agreement and make sure that the Soviets are not cheating?

FERRARO: Let me say first of all that I don't think there is any issue that is more important in this campaign, in this election, than the issue of war and peace. And since today is Eleanor Roosevelt's 100th birthday, let me quote her. She said, "It is not enough to want peace, you must believe in it. And it is not enough to believe in it, you must work for it." This administration's policies have indicated quite the opposite.

The last time I heard Vice-President Bush blame the fact that they didn't meet with the Soviet leader, and this is the first president in forty years not to meet with a Soviet counterpart. He said the reason was because there are three Soviet leaders in the past three and a half years. I went and got a computer printout. It's five pages of the leaders, world leaders, that the Soviet leaders have met with, and they're not little people. They're people like Mitterrand of France and Krohl of Germany and President Kiprianou of Cyprus—you go down the line, five pages of people that the Soviet leaders have managed to meet with and somehow they couldn't meet with the president of the United States.

In addition to not meeting with his Soviet counterpart, this is the first president—and you're right—since the start of negotiating arms control agreements who have not negotiated an arms control agreement. But not only has he not negotiated one, he's been opposed to every single one that every other president has negotiated, including Eisenhower, including Ford, and including Nixon.

Now, let me just say that with reference to the vice-president's comments about the intent and the desire of the United States and this administration, the Soviet Union did walk out of the talks. I agree. But it seems to me that 1982, when the administration presented its Start proposal, that it wasn't a realistic proposal. And that is the comment that was made by Secretary Haig after he left office, because what it dealt with was that it dealt just with land-based nuclear missiles, which is where the Soviets had the bulk of their missiles.

But that aside, in 1982, I believe it was, their own negotiator, Nitze, came out with a proposal called the "walk-in-the-woods proposal" which would have limited the number of nuclear arms in Europe. That proposal was turned down by the administration—a proposal presented by its own administrator.

Now I'm delighted that they met with Mr. Gromyko, but they could have had that opportunity to meet with him in 1981 when he came to the UN, which he had done with every other president before, and in 1982 as well. I guess my—

MODERATOR: *Congresswoman, I'm sorry. Speaking of limits, I have to impose a limit on you. Vice President Bush?*

BUSH: *Well, I think there's quite a difference between Mr. Kyprianou in Cyprus and the leader of the free world, Ronald Reagan, in terms of meeting. And the Soviet Union—the Soviet Union, the Soviet Union will meet with a lot of different people. We've been in very close touch with Mr. Mitterrand, Mr. Kohl, and others that have met with the leaders of the Soviet Union. But that's quite different than meeting with the president of the United States. The Soviets say we'll have a meeting when we think there can be progress and yet they left those talks.*

I'd like to correct my opponent on the walk in the woods. It was the Soviet Union that was unwilling to discuss the walk in the woods. They were the ones that gunned it down first and the record is very, very clear on that.

Miss Ferraro mentioned the inflexibility of our position on strategic arms. Yes, we offered first to get rid of all those—we tried to reduce the SS-18's and those weapons. But then we said if that's not good enough, there is flexibility, let's talk about the bombers and planes. So that's a very important point in terms of negotiation.

MODERATOR: *Congresswoman, he that taketh away has to give back. I robbed you of your rebuttal. Therefore, you will have two minutes to rebut. Forgive me.*

FERRARO: *I—You robbed me of my followup, that's what you robbed me, so why don't I let her give me the follow-up.*

MODERATOR: *All right, and then give your rebuttal.*

Q: *Congresswoman Ferraro, most polls show that the American— Americans feel that the Republicans, more than the Democrats are better able to keep the United States out of war. We've had four years of relative peace under President Reagan. How can you convince the American public that the world would be a safer place under Carter-Mondale? [sic]*

FERRARO: *I think first of all, you have to take a look at the current situation. We now have 50,000 nuclear warheads; we are building at the rate of five or six a day between us and we have been doing that since this administration came into office. I think what you can do is look at what they've done and recognize that they're not going to do very much in the future. And so, since they've done nothing, do we continue to build because an arms race doesn't lead to anything, it leads to another arms race and that's that.*

Vice-President Mondale has indicated that what he would do, first of all, as soon as he gets into office, is contact his Soviet counterpart and set up an annual summit meeting. That's Number one. I don't think you can start negotiating until you start talking. Secondly, he would issue a challenge, and the challenge would be in the nature of temporary, mutual, verifiable, moratoria to halt testing in the air, in the atmosphere, that would respond with a challenge from the Soviet Union, we hope, to sit down and negotiate a treaty. That was done in 1960.

I don't know what your lights are doing, Sander.

MODERATOR: *You have another minute.*

FERRARO: *O.K. I'm watching them blinking. So I have another minute. What that would do is it would give us the opportunity to sit down and negotiate a treaty. That was done in 1960 by President Kennedy—in 1963. What he did was he issued a challenge to the Soviet Union. He said we will not test in space—in the atmosphere, if you will not. They did not. In two months they sat down and they negotiated a treaty. We do not now have to worry about that type of testing. It can be done; it will be done, if only you have the will to do it. Again, remember it is mutual; it is verifiable and it is a challenge that once that challenge is not met, if testing were to resume, then we would continue testing as well.*

MODERATOR: *Our last series of questions on foreign affairs from Mr. Boyd.*

Q: *Congresswoman Ferraro, you have had little or no experience in military matters and yet you might someday find yourself commander-in-chief of the armed forces. How can you convince the American people and the potential enemy that you would know what to do to protect this nation's security, and do you think in any way that the Soviets might be tempted to try to take advantage of you simply because you are a woman.*

FERRARO: *Are you saying that I would have to have fought in the war in order to love peace?*

Q: *I'm not saying that, I'm asking you—you know what I asked.*

FERRARO: *All right. I think what happens is when you try to equate whether or not I have had military experience, that's the natural conclusion. It's about as valid as saying that you would have to be black in order to despise racism, that you'd have to be female in order to be terribly offended by sexism. And that's just not so.*

I think if you take a look at where I've been, both in the Congress and where I intend to go, the type of person I am—I think that the people of this country can rely upon the fact that I will be a leader. I don't think the Soviet Union for one minute can sit down and make determination on what I will do if I'm ever in a position to have to do something with reference to the Soviet Union. Quite frankly I'm prepared to do whatever is necessary in order to secure this country and make sure that security is maintained.

Secondly, if the Soviet Union were to ever believe that they could challenge the United States with any sort of nuclear forces or otherwise, if I were in a position of leadership in this country, they would be assured that they would be met with swift, concise and certain retaliation.

Let me just say one other thing now. The most important thing, though I think as a leader that what one has to do is get to the point where you're not put into that position. And the way you get to that position of moving away from having to make a decision—armed force or anything else—is by moving toward arms control. And that's not what's been done over the past four years. I think that if you were to take a look at the failures of this administration that would have to be number one. I will not put myself in that position as a leader in this country. I will move immediately toward arms control negotiations.

Question for the Other Candidate

Q: *For my follow, I'm going to borrow a leaf from the Sunday night debate between your principals and ask you what is the single question you would most like to ask your opponent here on foreign policy?*

FERRARO: *Oh, I don't have a single-most question. I guess the concern that I have is a concern not only as a vice-presidential candidate but as a citizen in this country. My concern is that we are not doing anything to stop the arms race, and it seems to me that if we keep talking about military inferiority—which we do not have, we are at a comparable level with the Soviet Union; our Joint Chiefs of Staff have said they'd never exchange our military power for theirs. I guess the thing that I'd want is a commitment that pretty soon they're going to do something about making this a safer world for all of us.*

Q: *Vice-President Bush, four years ago President Reagan insisted that a military buildup would bring the Soviets to negotiate seriously. Since then, we have spent almost a trillion dollars on defense but the Soviets are still building their military forces as rapidly as we are, and there are no negotiations. Was the president's original premise, his whole strategy, wrong?*

BUSH: *No, I think his strategy not only was correct but is correct. You've got to go back where we were. Clearly, when we came into office, the American people recognized that we had slipped into positions of inferiority on various things. Some of our planes, as the president points out, were older than the pilots; ships that couldn't go out to sea. And you had a major problem with the military. Actually, the morale wasn't very good either.*

So we have had to strengthen the military and we're well on the way to getting that job done. America is back in terms of military strength, in terms of our ability to deter aggression and keep the peace. At the same time, however, we have made proposals and proposals and proposals—sound proposals—on reducing nuclear weapons.

The Strategic Arms Reducation Talks were good proposals, and it's the Soviets who left the table. The Intermediate Nuclear Force Talks were sound talks, and I wish the Soviet Union had continued them. The chemical weapon treaty to ban all chemical weapons, it was our initiative, not the Soviets. And we wish they would think anew and move forward to verification so everybody would know whether the other side was keeping its word. But, much more important, you'd reduce the level of terror.

Similarly, we're reducing—trying to talk to them, and are talking to them, in Vienna, about conventional force reduction. We've talked to them about human rights. I've met with Mr. Andropov and Mr. Chernenko, and we mention and we try to do something about the human rights question. The suppression of Soviet Jews is absolutely intolerable and so we have to keep pushing forward on the moral grounds as well as on the arms reduction ground.

But it is my view that because this president has been strong, and because we've redressed, the imbalances—and I think we're very close to getting that job done—the Soviets are more likely to make a deal. The Soviets made an ABM treaty when they felt we were going to deploy an ABM system. So I am optimistic for the future, once they realize that they will have this strong, principled president to negotiate with, strong leadership, and yet with demonstrable flexibility on arms control.

MODERATOR: *And now, I'll give you a chance, Mr. Vice-President, to ask the question you'd most like to ask your opponent.*

BUSH: *I have none I'd like to ask of her, but I'd sure like to use the time, to talk about the World Series or something of that nature. Let me put it this way—I don't have any questions, but we are so different from—the Reagan-Bush administration is so different from the Carter-Mondale [sic] adminis-tration that the American people are going to have the clearest choice.*

It's a question of going back to the failed ideas of the past, where we came in—21½ percent on those interest rates, inflation, despair, malaise, no leadership, blaming the American people for failed leadership. Or another option—keep this recovery going until it benefits absolutely everybody. Peace at home—peace abroad—prosperity—opportunity. I'd like to hear her talk on those things, but I think the yellow light is flashing and so we'll leave it there.

MODERATOR: *Nothing on the World Series? Congresswoman Ferraro?*

FERRARO: *I think the vice-president's comment about the Carter-Mondale administration really typifies this administration. It's an administration that looks backwards, not forwards and into the future. I must say that I'm also tickled by their comments on human rights. The Soviet Union in 1979 allowed 51,000 people to emigrate, because, in large measure, this adminis-tration's policies over the past four years, 1,313 people got out of the Soviet Union in 1983 and 1984.*

That's not a great record on human rights and certainly not a record on human rights achievements. This administration spent a trillion dollars on defense, but it hasn't gotten a trillion dollars on national security.

MODERATOR: *Vice-President Bush, your rebuttal?*

BUSH: *No rebuttal.*

MODERATOR: *Well, we then can go to the closing statements. Each statement will be four minutes in length and we'll begin with the vice-president.*

Concluding Statements

BUSH: *Well, in a couple of weeks, you, the American people, will be faced, three weeks, with a choice. It's the clearest choice in some fifty years. And the choice is, do we move forward with strength and with prosperity or do we go back to weakness, despair, disrespect.*

Ronald Reagan and I have put our trust in the American people. We've moved some of the power away from Washington, D.C., and put it back with the people. We're pulling together. The neighborhoods are safer 'cause crime is going down. Your sons and daughters are doing better in school. Test scores are going up. There's a new opportunity lying out there in the future. Science, technology and space offering opportunity that, to everybody, all the young ones coming up. And abroad there's new leadership and respect. And Ronald Reagan is clearly the strong leader of the free world. And I'll be honest with you. It's a joy to serve with a president who does not apologize for the United States of America.

Mr. Mondale, on the other hand, has one idea. Go out and tax the American people. And then he wants to repeal indexing, to wipe out the one protection that those at the lowest end of the economic scale have protecting them against being rammed into higher and higher tax brackets. We just owe our country too much to go back to that kind of an approach.

I'd like to say something to the young people. I started a business. I know what it is to have a dream and have a job and work hard to employ others and really to participate in the American dream. Some of you out there are finishing high school or college and some of you are starting out in the working place. And we want for you America's greatest gift. And that is opportunity.

And then, peace. Yes, I did serve in combat. I was shot down when I was a young kid, scared to death. And all that did, saw friends die, but that heightened my convictions about peace. It is absolutely essential that we guarantee the young people that they will not know the agony of war. America's gift, opportunity and peace.

Now we do have some unfinished business. We must continue to go ahead. The world is too complex to go back to vacillation and weakness. We've too much going on to go back to the failed policies of the past. The future is too bright not to give it our best shot. Together we can go forward and lift America up to meet her greatest dreams. Thank you very much.

MODERATOR: *Thank you very much. I must say now in matters of equity you will be allowed applause at the end of your closing statement, so if you begin now, please.*

FERRARO: *I hope somebody wants to applaud. Being the candidate for vice-president of my party is the greatest honor I have ever had. But it's not only a personal achievement for Geraldine Ferraro—and certainly not only the bond that I feel as I go across this country with women throughout the country. I wouldn't be standing here if Fritz Mondale didn't have the courage and my party didn't stand for the values that it does—the values of fairness and equal opportunity. Those values make our country strong and the future of this country and how strong it will be is what this election is all about.*

Over the last two months I've been traveling all over the country talking to the people about the future. I was in Kentucky and I spoke to the

Dyhouse family. He works for a car dealer and he's worried about the deficits and how high interest rates are going to affect his job. Every place I go I see young parents with their children and they say to me what are we going to do to stop this nuclear arms race. I was in Dayton, Ohio, a week and a half ago and I sat with the Allen family who live next door to a toxic dump and they're very, very concerned about the fact that those toxics are seeping into the water that they and their neighbors drink. Now those people love this country and they're patriotic. But it's not the patriotism that you're seeing in the commercials as you watch television these days. Their patriotism is not only a pride in the country as it is, but a pride in this country that is strong enough to meet the challenges of the future.

Do you know when we find jobs for the eight and a half million people who are unemployed in this country, you know we'll make our economy stronger and that will be a patriotic act. When we reduce the deficits and we cut interest rates, and I know the president doesn't believe that, but it's so—we cut those interest rates young people can buy houses, that's pro-family and that will be a patriotic act. When we educate our children—good Lord, they're going to be able to compete in a world economy and that makes us stronger and that's a patriotic act. When we stop the arms race, we make this a safer, saner world, and that's a patriotic act, and when we keep the peace young men don't die, and that's a patriotic act.

Those are the keys to the future and who can be the leader for the future? When Walter Mondale was attorney general of Minnesota, he led the fight for a man who could not afford to get justice because he couldn't afford a lawyer; when he was in the Senate he fought for child nutrition programs, he wrote the Fair Housing Act, he even investigated the concerns and the abuses of migrant workers. And why did he do that? Those weren't popular causes. You know, no one had ever heard of Clarence Gideon, the man without a lawyer. Children don't vote and migrant workers aren't exactly a powerful lobby in this country, but he did it because it was right. Fritz Mondale has said that he would rather lose a battle for decency than win one over self-interest. Now I agree with him.

This campaign is not over. For our country, for our future, for the principles we believe in Walter Mondale and I have just begun to fight.
MODERATOR: *Thank you very much. I'd like to thank Vice-President Bush, Congresswoman Ferraro, the members of our panel for joining us in this League of Women Voters debate. I'd like to join you in thanking them, the city of Philadelphia and the League of Women Voters. The League of Women Voters' next debate, the presidential debate, will take place in Kansas City on October 21. The subject will be foreign affairs and it will begin at 8 P.M., Eastern time. Again our thanks. We hope you'll join us on the Twenty-first.*

Transcript of the Reagan-Mondale Debate on Foreign Policy, October 21, 1984

DOROTHY S. RIDINGS: *Good evening from the Municipal Auditorium in Kansas City. I am Dorothy Ridings, the president of the League of Women Voters, the sponsor of this final presidential debate of the 1984 campaign between Republican Ronald Reagan and Democrat Walter Mondale.*

Our panelists for tonight's debate on defense and foreign policy issues are Georgie Anne Geyer, syndicated columnist for Universal Press Syndicate; Marvin Kalb, chief diplomatic correspondent for NBC News; Morton Kondracke, executive editor of the New Republic *magazine; and Henry Trewhitt, diplomatic correspondent for the* Baltimore Sun.

Edwin Newman, formerly of NBC News and now a syndicated columnist for King Features, is our moderator. Ed.

EDWIN NEWMAN: *Dorothy Ridings, thank you. A brief word about our procedure tonight. The first question will go to Mr. Mondale. He'll have two and a half minutes to reply. Then the panel member who put the question will ask the followup. The answer to that will be limited to one minute. After that, the same question will be put to President Reagan. Again, there will be a followup and then each man will have one minute for rebuttal.*

The second question will go to President Reagan first. After, the alternating will continue. At the end there will be four-minute summations with President Reagan going last.

We have asked the questioners to be brief.

Let's begin. Miss Geyer, your question to Mr. Mondale.

Central America and the CIA

Q: *Mr. Mondale, two related questions on the crucial issue of Central America. You and the Democratic party have said that the only policy toward the horrendous civil wars in Central America should be on the economic developments and negotiations with, perhaps, a quarantine of Marxist Nicaragua. Do you believe that these answers would in any way solve the bitter conflicts there? Do you really believe that there is no need to resort to force at all? Are not these solutions to Central America's gnawing problems simply again too weak and too late?*

MONDALE: *I believe that the question oversimplifies the difficulties of what we must do in Central America. Our objectives ought to be to strengthen the democracy, to stop Communist and other extremist influences and stabilize the community in that area.*

To do that, we need a three-pronged attack. One is military assistance to our friends who are being pressured. Secondly, a strong and sophisticated economic aid program and human rights program that offers a better life and a sharper alternative to the alternative offered by the totalitarians who oppose us. And finally, a strong diplomatic effort that pursues the possibilities of peace in the area.

That's one of the big disagreements that we have with the President, that they have not pursued the diplomatic opportunities either within El Salvador or as between the country and have lost time during which we might have been able to achieve peace.

This brings up the whole question of what presidential leadership is all about. I think the lesson in Central America, this recent embarrassment in Nicaragua where we are giving instructions for hired assassins, hiring criminals and the rest—all of this has strengthened our opponent.

A president must not only assure that we're tough. But we must also be wise and smart in the exercise of that power. We saw the same thing in Lebanon, where we spent a good deal of America's assets but because the leadership of this government did not pursue wise policies, we have been humiliated and our opponents are stronger.

The bottom line of national strength is that the president must be command. He must lead. And when a president doesn't know that submarine missiles are recallable, says that 70 percent of our strategic forces are conventional, discovers three years into his administration that our arms control efforts have failed because he didn't know that most Soviet missiles were on land—these are things a president must know to command. A president is called the commander-in-chief. And he's called that because he's supposed to be in charge of facts and run our government and strengthen our nation.

Q: *Mr. Mondale, if I could broaden the question just a little bit. Since*

World War II, every conflict that we as Americans have been involved with has been in nonconventional or irregular terms and yet we keep fighting in conventional or traditional military terms. The Central American wars are very much in the same pattern as China, as Lebanon, as Iran, as Cuba in the early days. Do you see any possibility that we are going to realize the change in warfare in our time or react to it in those terms?

MONDALE: *We absolutely must, which is why I responded to your first question the way I did. It's much more complex. You must understand the region, you must understand the politics in the area, you must provide a strong alternative, and you must show strength—and all at the same time. That's why I object to the covert action in Nicaragua. That's a classic example of a strategy that's embarrassed us, strengthened our opposition and undermined the moral authority of our people and our country in the region.*

Strength requires knowledge, command. We've seen in the Nicaraguan example a policy that has actually hurt us, strengthened our opposition and undermined the moral authority of our country in that region.

Q: *Mr. President, in the last few months it has seemed more and more that your policies in Central America were beginning to work. Yet just at this moment we are confronted with the extraordinary story of the C.I.A. guerrilla manual for the anti-Sandinista* contras, *whom we are backing, which advocates not only assassinations of Sandinistas but the hiring of criminals to assassinate the guerrillas we are supporting in order to create martyrs. Is this not in effect our own state-supported terrorism?*

REAGAN: *No, but I'm glad you asked that question because I know it's on many people's minds. I have ordered an investigation; I know that that CIA is already going forward with one. We have a gentleman down in Nicaragua who is on contract to the CIA, advising supposedly on military tactics, the* contras. *And he drew up this manual. It was turned over to the agency head of the CIA in Nicaragua to be printed, and a number of pages were excised by that agency head there, the man in charge, and he sent it on up here to CIA where more pages were excised before it was printed. But some way or other, there were twelve of the original copies that got out down there and were not submitted for this printing process by the CIA. Now those are the details as we have them, and as soon as we have an investigation and find out where any blame lies for the few that did not get excised or changed, we certainly are going to do something about that. We'll take the proper action at the proper time.*

I was very interested to hear about Central America and our process down there, and I thought for a moment that instead of a debate I was going to find Mr. Mondale in complete agreement with what we're doing because the plan that he has outlined is the one we've been following for quite some time, including diplomatic processes throughout Central America and working closely with the Contadora group. So I can only tell you, about the manual, that we're not in the habit of assigning guilt before there has been proper evidence produced in proof of that guilt; but if guilt is established, whoever is guilty, we will treat with that situation then and they will be removed.

Q: *Well, Mr. President, you are implying then that the CIA in Nicaragua is directing the* contras *there. I'd also like to ask whether having the CIA investigate its own manual in such a sensitive area is not sort of like sending the fox into the chicken coop a second time.*

REAGAN: *I'm afraid I misspoke when I said a CIA head in Nicaragua. There's not someone there directing all of this activity. There are, as you know, CIA men stationed in other countries in the world, and certainly in Central America, and so it was a man down there in that area that this was delivered to. And he recognized that what was in that manual was a direct contravention of my own executive order in December of 1981, that we would have nothing to do with regard to political assassinations.*

MODERATOR: *Mr. Mondale, your rebuttal?*

MONDALE: *What is a president charged with doing when he takes his oath of office? He raises his right hand and takes an oath of, oath of office to take care, to faithfully execute the laws of the land. Presidents can't know everything but a president has to know those things that are essential to his leadership and the enforcement of our laws.*

This manual, several thousands of which were produced, was distributed ordering political assassination, hiring of criminals, and other forms of terrorism. Some of it was excised, but the part dealing with political terrorism was continued.

How can this happen? How can something this serious occur in an administration and have a president of the United States in a situation like this say he didn't know. A president must know these things.

I don't know which is worse—not knowing or knowing and not stopping it.

And what about the mining of the harbors in Nicaragua, which violated international law? This has hurt this country and a president's supposed to command.

Defense Policy and Arms Control

MODERATOR: *Mr. President, your rebuttal.*

REAGAN: *Yes. I have so many things there to respond to I'm going to pick out something you said earlier.*

You've been all over the country repeating something that I will admit the press has also been repeating—that I believe that nuclear missiles could be

*fired and then called back. I never conceived of such a thing. I never said
any such thing.*

*In a discussion of our strategic arms negotiations, I said that submarines
carrying missiles and airplanes carrying missiles were more conventional-
type weapons, not as destabilizing as the land-based missiles and that they
were also weapons that, or carriers, that, if they were sent out and there was
a change, you could call them back before they had launched their missiles.
But I hope that from here on, you will not longer be saying that particular
thing, which is absolutely false. How anyone could think that any sane
person would believe you could call back a nuclear missile I think is as
ridiculous as the, as the whole concept has been.*

*So thank you for giving me a chance to straighten the record. I'm sure
that you appreciate that.*

MODERATOR: *Mr. Kalb, your question to President Reagan.*

Q: *Mr. President, you have often described the Soviet Union as a powerful
evil empire intent on world domination. But this year, you have said, and I
quote, "If they want to keep their Mickey Mouse system, that's O.K. with
me." Which is it, Mr. President: Do you want to contain them within their
present borders and perhaps try to reestablish détente or what goes for
détente, or do you really want to roll back their empire?*

REAGAN: *I have said, on a number of occasions, exactly what I believe
about the Soviet Union. I retract nothing that I have said. I believe that
many of the things they have done are evil in any concept of morality that
we have. But I also recognize that as the two great superpowers in the
world, we have to live with each other. And I told Mr. Gromyko we don't
like their system. They don't like ours. And we're not gonna change their
system and they sure better not try to change ours. But, between us, we can
either destroy the world or we can save it. And I suggested that certainly it
was to their common interest, along with ours, to avoid a conflict and to
attempt to save the world and remove the nuclear weapons. And I think that
perhaps we established a little better understanding.*

*I think that in dealing with the Soviet Union, one has to be realistic. I
know that Mr. Mondale, in the past, has made statements as if they were
just people like ourselves and if we were kind and good and did something
nice, they would respond accordingly. And the result was unilateral disarmament. We canceled the B-1 under the previous administration. What
did we get for it? Nothing.*

*The Soviet Union has been engaged in the biggest military buildup in the
history of man at the same time that we tried the policy of unilateral
disarmament, of weakness, if you will. And now, we are putting up a
defense of our own. And I've made it very plain to them. We seek no
superiority. We simply are going to provide a deterrent so that it will be too
costly for them if they are nursing any ideas of aggression against us.*

Now they claim they're not. And I made it plain to them that we're not. But, this, there's been no change in my attitude at all. I just thought when I came into office it was time that there was some realistic talk to and about the Soviet Union. And we did get their attention.

Q: *Mr. President, on perhaps the other side of the coin, a related question, sir. Since World War II, the vital interests of the United States have always been defined by treaty commitments and by presidential proclamations. Aside from what is obvious, such as NATO, for example, which countries, which regions in the world do you regard as vital national interests of this country, meaning that you would send American troops to fight there if they were in danger?*

REAGAN: *Ah, well now you've added a hypothetical there at the end, Mr. Kalb, about that where we would send troops in to fight. I am not going to make the decision as to what the tactics could be, but obviously there are a number of areas in the world that are of importance to us.*

One of the Middle East. And that is of interest to the whole Western world and the industrialized nations, because of the great supply of energy upon which so many depend there.

The—our neighbors here in America are vital to us. We're working right now in trying to be of help in southern Africa with regard to the independence of Namibia and the removal of the Cuban surrogates, the thousands of them, from Angola.

So, I can say there are a great many interests. I believe that we have a great interest in the Pacific basin. That is where I think the future of the world lies.

But I am not going to pick out one and in advance and hypothetically say, oh, yes, we would send troops there. I don't—

MODERATOR: *Sorry, Mr. President. Sorry, your time was up.*

Q: *Mr. Mondale, you have described the Soviet leaders as, and I'm quoting, cynical, ruthless, and dangerous, suggesting an almost total lack of trust in them. In that case, what makes you think that the annual summit meetings with them that you've proposed will result in agreements that would satisfy the interests of this country?*

MONDALE: *Because the only type of agreements to reach with the Soviet Union are the types that are specifically defined, so we know exactly what they must do, subject to full verification. Which means we know every day whether they're living up to it, and follow-ups wherever we find suggestions that they're violating it, and the strongest possible terms.*

I have no illusions about the Soviet Union leadership or the nature of that state. They are a tough and a ruthless adversary, and we must be prepared to meet that challenge. And I would.

Where I part with the president is that despite all of those differences, we must, as past Presidents before this one have done, meet on the common ground of survival.

And that's where the president has opposed practically every arms control agreement, by every president of both political parties, since the bomb went off.

And he now completes this term with no progress toward arms control at all, but with a very dangerous arms race under way instead.

There are now over 2,000 more warheads pointed at us today than there were when he was sworn in, and that does not strengthen us.

We must be very, very realistic in the nature of that leadership, but we must grind away and talk to find ways to reducing these differences, particularly where arms races are concerned and other dangerous exercises of Soviet power.

There will be no unilateral disarmament under my administration. I will keep this nation strong. I understand exactly what the Soviets are up to. But that, too, is a part of national strength.

To do that, a president must know what is essential to command and to leadership and to strength. And that's where the president's failure to master, in my opinion, the essential elements of arms control has cost us dearly.

These four years—three years into this administration he said he just discovered that most Soviet missiles are on land and that's why his proposal didn't work.

I invite the American people tomorrow, because I will issue the statement quoting President Reagan. He said exactly what I said he said. He said that these missiles were less dangerous than ballistic missiles because you could fire them and you could recall them if you decided there'd been a miscalculation. A president must know those things.

MODERATOR: *I'm sorry.*

Q: *A related question, Mr. Mondale, on Eastern Europe: Do you accept the conventional diplomatic wisdom that Eastern Europe is a Soviet sphere of influence, and if you do, what could a Mondale administration realistically do to help the people of Eastern Europe achieve the human rights that were guaranteed to them as a result of the Helsinki accords.*

MONDALE: *I think the essential stretegy of the United States ought not accept any Soviet control over Eastern Europe. We ought to deal with each of these countries separately, we ought to pursue strategies with each of them—economic and the rest—that help them pull away from their dependence upon the Soviet Union.*

Where the Soviet Union has acted irresponsibly, as they have in many of those countries—especially recently in Poland—I believe we ought to insist that Western credits extended to the Soviet Union bear the market rate, make the Soviets pay for their irresponsibility. That is a very important objective to make certain that we continue to look forward to progress toward greater independence by these nations and work with each of them separately.

MODERATOR: *Mr. President, your rebuttal.*

REAGAN: *Yes, I'm not going to continue trying to respond to these repetitions of the falsehoods that have already been stated here, but with regard to whether Mr. Mondale would be strong, as he said he would be, I know that he has a commercial out where he is appearing on the deck of the* Nimitz *and watching the F-14's take off, and that's an image of strength—except that if he had had his way when the* Nimitz *was being planned he would have been deep in the water out there because there wouldn't have been any* Nimitz *to stand on. He was against it.*

He was against the F-14 fighter, he was against the M-1 tank, he was against the B-1 bomber, he wanted to cut the salary of all of the military, he wanted to bring home half of the American forces in Europe, and he has a record of weakness with regard to our national defense that is second to none. Indeed, he was on that side virtually throughout all his years in the Senate and he opposed even President Carter when toward the end of his term President Carter wanted to increase the defense budget.

MODERATOR: *Mr. Mondale, your rebuttal.*

MONDALE: *Mr. President, I accept your commitment to peace, but I want you to accept my commitment to a strong national defense. I propose a budget, I have proposed a budget, which would increase our nations's strength by, in real terms, by double that of the Soviet Union. I tell you where we disagree. It is true, over ten years ago I voted to delay production of the F-14 and I'll tell you why. The plane wasn't flying the way it was supposed to be, it was a waste of money.*

Your definition of national strength is to throw money at the Defense Department. My definition of national strength is to make certain that a dollar spent buys us a dollar's worth of defense. There's a big difference between the two of us. A president must manage that budget. I will keep us strong, but you'll not do that unless you command that budget and make certain we get the strength that we need. When you pay $500 for a $5 hammer, you're not buying strength.

MODERATOR: *I would ask the audience not to applaud. All it does is take up time that we would like to devote to the debate. Mr. Kondracke, your question to Mr. Mondale.*

Using Military Force

Q: *Mr. Mondale, in an address earlier this year you said that before this country resorts to military force, and I'm quoting, American interests should be sharply defined, publicly supported, congressionally sanctioned, militarily feasible, internationally defensible, open to independent scrutiny, and alert to regional history. Now aren't you setting up such a gauntlet of tests here that adversaries could easily suspect that as president you would never use force to protect American interests?*

MONDALE: *No; as a matter of fact, I believe every one of those standards is essential to the exercise of power by this country. And we can see that in both Lebanon and in Central America. In Lebanon this president exercised American power all right, but the management of it was such that our marines were killed, we had to leave in humiliation, the Soviet Union became stronger, terrorists became emboldened, and it was because they did not think through how power should be exercised, did not have the American public with them on a plan that worked, that we ended up the way we did.*

Similarly, in Central America, what we're doing in Nicaragua with this covert war which the Congress, including many Republicans, have tried to stop is finally end up with the public definition of American power that hurts us, where we get associated with political assassins and the rest. We have to decline for the first time in modern history jurisdiction of the World Court because they'll find us guilty of illegal actions, and our enemies are strengthened from all of this.

We need to be strong. We need to be prepared to use that strength, but we must understand that we are a democracy; we are a government by the people, and when we move, it should be for very severe and extreme reasons that serve our national interest and end up with a stronger country behind us. It is only in that way that we can persevere.

Q: *You've been quoted as saying that you might quarantine Nicaragua. I'd like to know what that means. Would you stop Soviet ships as President Kennedy did in 1962 and wouldn't that be more dangerous than President Reagan's covert war?*

MONDALE: *What I'm referring to there is the mutual self-defense provisions that exist in the inter-American treaty, the so-called Rio Pact, that permits the nations, our friends in that region, to combine to take steps, diplomatic and otherwise, to prevent Nicaragua when she acts irresponsibly in asserting power in other parts outside of her border, to take those steps, whatever they might be, to stop it.*

The Nicaraguans must know that it is the policy of our government that those people, that that leadership must stay behind the boundaries of their nation, not interfere in other nations. And by working with all of the nations in the region, unlike the policies of this administration and unlike the president said they have not supported negotiations in that region, we will be much stronger because we'll have the moral authority that goes with those efforts.

Q: *President Reagan, you introduced U.S. forces into Lebanon as neutral peace keepers, but then you made them combatants on the side of the Lebanese government. Eventually you were forced to withdraw them under fire and now Syria, a Soviet ally, is dominant in the country. Doesn't Lebanon represent a major failure on the part of your administration and raise serious questions about your capacity as a foreign policy strategist and as commander-in-chief?*

REAGAN: *No, Morton, I don't agree to all of those things. First of all, when we and our allies, the Italians, the French, and the United Kingdom, went into Lebanon, we went in there at the request of what was left of the Lebanese government, to be a stabilizing force while they tried to establish a government. But first, pardon me, the first time we went in, we went in at their request because the war was going on right in Beirut between Israel and the PLO terrorists. Israel could not be blamed for that. Those terrorists had been violating their northern border consistently and Israel chased them all the way to there.*

Then, we went in, with the multinational force, to help remove and did remove more than 13,000 of those terrorists from Lebanon. We departed and then the government of Lebanon asked us back in as a stabilizing force while they established a government and sought to get the foreign forces all the way out of Lebanon and that they could then take care of their own borders. And we were succeeding. We were there for the better part of a year. Our position happened to be at the airport or there were occasional snipings and sometimes some artillery fire, but we did not engage in conflict that was out of line with our mission.

I will never send troops anywhere on a mission of that kind without telling them that if somebody shoots at them they can darn well shoot back. And this is what we did. We never initiated any kind of action, we defended ourselves there. But, we were succeeding to the point that the Lebanese government had been organized, if you will remember there were the meetings in Geneva in which they began to meet with the hostile factional forces and try to put together some kind of a peace plan. We were succeeding and that was why the terrorist acts began. There are forces there—and that includes Syria, in my mind—who don't want us to succeed, who don't want that kind of a peace with a dominant Lebanon, dominant over its own territory. And so the terrorist acts began and led to the one great tragedy when they were killed in that suicide bombing of the building. Then the multilateral force withdrew for only one reason. We withdrew because we were no longer able to carry out the mission for which we had been sent in. But we went in in the interest of peace and to keep Israel and Syria from getting into the sixth war between them. And I have no apologies for our going on a peace mission.

Policy on Terrorism

Q: *Mr. President, four years ago you criticized President Carter for ignoring ample warning that our diplomats in Iran might be taken hostage. Haven't you done exactly the same thing in Lebanon, not once, but three times, with 300 Americans, not hostages, but dead? And you vowed swift retaliation against terrorists, but doesn't our lack of response suggest that you're just bluffing?*

REAGAN: *Morton, no. I think there's a great difference between the government of Iran threatening our diplomatic personnel and there is a government that you can see and can put your hand on. In the terrorist situation there are terrorist factions all over—in a recent thirty-day period thirty-seven terrorist actions in twenty countries have been committed. The most recent has been the one in Brighton. In dealing with terrorists, yes, we want to retaliate, but only if we can put our finger on the people responsible and not endanger the lives of innocent civilians there in the various communities and in the city of Beirut where these terrorists are operating. I have just signed legislation to add to our ability to deal, along with our allies, with this terrorist problem, and it's going to take all the nations together, just as when we banded together we pretty much resolved the problem of skyjackings some time ago. Well, the red light went on—I could have gone on forever.*

MODERATOR: *Mr. Mondale, your rebuttal?*

MONDALE: *Groucho Marx said, Who do you believe, me or your own eyes? And what we have in Lebanon is something that the American people have seen. The Joint Chiefs urged the president not to put our troops in that barracks because they were undefensible. They urged—they went to five days before they were killed and said please take them out of there. The secretary of state admitted that this morning. He did not do so. The report following the explosion in the barracks disclosed that we had not taken any of the steps that we should have taken. That was the second time. Then the embassy was blown up a few weeks ago and once again none of the steps that should have been taken were taken and we were warned five days before that explosives were on their way and they weren't taken. The terrorists have won each time. The president told the terrorists he was going to retaliate. He didn't. They called their bluff. And the bottom line is the United States left in humiliation and our enemies are stronger.*

MODERATOR: *Mr. President, your rebuttal?*

REAGAN: *Yes, first of all, Mr. Mondale should know that the president of the United States did not order the marines into that barracks. That was a command decision made by the commanders on the spot and based with what they thought was best for the men there. That is one. On the other things that you've just said about the terrorists—I'm tempted to ask you what you would do. These are unidentified people, and after the bomb goes off they're blown to bits because they are suicidal individuals who think that they're going to go to paradise if they perpetrate such an act and lose their life in doing it. We are going to, as I say—we are busy trying to find the centers where these operations stem from and retaliation will be taken, but we are not going to simply kill some people to say, oh look, we got even. We want to know when we retaliate that we're retaliating with those who are responsible for the terrorist acts. And terrorist acts are such that our own United States Capitol in Washington has been bombed twice.*

MODERATOR: *Mr. Trewhitt, your question to President Reagan?*

Age and Leadership

Q: *President, I want to raise an issue that I think has been lurking out there for two or three weeks, and cast it specifically in national security terms. You already are the oldest president in history, and some of your staff say you were tired after your most recent encounter with Mr. Mondale. I recall, yes, that President Kennedy, who had to go for days on end with very little sleep during the Cuba missile crisis. Is there any doubt in your mind that you would be able to function in such circumstances?*

REAGAN: *Not at all, Mr. Trewhitt and I want you to know that also I will not make age an issue of this campaign. I am not going to exploit for political purposes my opponent's youth and inexperience.*

If I still have time, I might add, Mr. Trewhitt, I might add that it was Seneca or it was Cicero, I don't know which, that said if it was not for the elders correcting the mistakes of the young, there would be no state.

Q: *Mr. President, I'd like to head for the fence and try to catch that one before it goes over but—without going to another question. The—you and Mr. Mondale have already disagreed about what you had to say about recalling submarine-launched missiles. There's another similar issue out there that relates to your—you said at least that you were unaware that the Soviet retaliatory power was based on land-based missiles. First, is that correct? Secondly, if it is correct, have you informed yourself in the meantime and, third, is it even necessary for the president to be so intimately involved in strategic details?*

REAGAN: *Yes. This had to do with our disarmament talks and the whole controversy about land missiles came up because we thought that the strategic nuclear weapons—the most destabilizing are the land-based. You put your thumb on a button and somebody blows up twenty minutes later.*

So we thought that it would be simpler to negotiate first with those, and then we made it plain, a second phase, take up the submarine-launched—the airborne missiles. The Soviet Union, to our surprise and not just mine—made it plain when we brought this up that they placed, they thought, a greater reliance on the land-based missiles and therefore they wanted to take up all three and we agreed. We said all right, if that's what you want to do.

But, it was a surprise to us because they outnumbered us sixty-four to thirty-six in submarines and 20 percent more bombers capable of carrying nuclear missiles than we had. So, why should we believe that they had placed that much more reliance on land-based? But even after we gave in and said all right, let's discuss it all, they walked away from the table. We didn't.

Q: *Mr. Mondale, I'm going to hang in there. Should the president's age and stamina be an issue in the political campaign?*

MONDALE: *No. And I have not made it an issue nor should it be. What's at issue here is the president's application of his authority to understand what a president must know to lead this nation, secure our defense, and make the decisions and judgments that are necessary.*

A minute ago, the president quoted Cicero, I believe. I want to quote somebody a little closer home, Harry Truman. He said the buck stops here. We just heard the president's answer for the problems at the barracks in Lebanon where 241 marines were killed. What happened?

First, the Joint Chiefs of Staff, with the president, said don't put those troops there. They did it. And then five days before the troops were killed, they went back to the president, through the secretary of defense, and said please, Mr. President, take those troops out of there because we can't defend them. They didn't do it. And we know what's—what happened.

After that, once again our embassy was exploded. This is the fourth time this has happened—an identical attack in the same region, despite warnings even public warnings from the terrorists. Who's in charge? Who's handling this matter. That's my main point.

Now on arms control—we're completing four years—this is the first administration since the bomb went off that made no progress. We have an arms race under way instead. A president has to lead his government or it won't be done. Different people with different views fight with each. For three and a half years, this administration avoided arms control, resisted tabling arms control proposals that had any hope of agreeing, rebuked their negotiator in 1981 when he came close to an agreement, at least in principle, on medium-range weapons and we have this arms race under way. And a recent book that just came out by, perhaps, the nation's most respected author in this field, Strobe Talbott, called Deadly Gambit, *concludes that this president has failed to master the essential details needed to command and lead us both in terms of security and terms of arms control. That's why they call the president the commander-in-chief. Good intentions, I grant, but it takes more than that. He must be tough and smart.*

Q: *This question of leadership keeps arising in different forms in this discussion already. And the president, Mr. Mondale, has called you whining and vacillating, among the more charitable phrases—weak, I believe. It is a question of leadership. And he has made the point that you have not repudiated some of the semidiplomatic activity of the Reverend Jackson, particularly in Central America. Do you, did you approve of his diplomatic activity? And are you prepared to repudiate him now?*

MONDALE: *I, I read his statement the other day. I don't admire Fidel Castro at all. And I have said that. Ché Guevara was a contemptible figure in civilization's history. I know the Cuban state as a police state. And all my life, I've worked in a way that demonstrates that.*

But Jesse Jackson is an independent person. I don't control him. And, let's talk about people we do control. In the last debate, the vice-president of the United States said that I said the marines had died shamefully and died in shame in Lebanon. I demanded an apology from Vice-President Bush because I had instead honored these young men, grieved for their families, and think they were wonderful Americans that honored us all. What does the president have to say about taking responsibility for a vice-president who won't apologize for something like that?

MODERATOR: *Mr. President, your rebuttal.*

REAGAN: *Yes, I know it'll come as a surprise to Mr. Mondale, but I am in charge. And as a matter of fact we haven't avoided arms control talks with the Soviet Union. Very early in my administration, I proposed—and I think something that had never been proposed by any previous administration—I proposed a total elimination of intermediate-range missiles where the Soviets had better than a, and still have better than a, ten-to-one advantage over the allies in Europe. When they protested that and suggested a smaller number, perhaps, I went along with that. The so-called negotiation that you said I walked out on was the so-called "walk in the woods" between one of our representatives and one of the Soviet Union and it wasn't me that turned it down. The Soviet Union disavowed it.*

MODERATOR: *Mr. Mondale, your rebuttal.*

MONDALE: *There are two distinguished authors of arms control in this country. There are many others, but two that I want to cite tonight. One is Strobe Talbott in his classic book* Deadly Gambit. *The other is John Newhouse, who's one of the most distinguished arms control specialists in our country. Both said that this administration turned down the "walk in the woods" agreement first and that would have been a perfect agreement from the standpoint of the United States and Europe and our security. When Mr. Nitze, a good negotiator, returned, he was rebuked and his boss was fired. This is the kind of leadership that we've had in this administration in the most deadly issue of our time. Now we have a runaway arms race. All they've got to show for four years in U.S.-Soviet relations is one*

meeting in the last weeks of an administration and nothing before. They're tough negotiators, but all previous presidents have made progress. This one has not.
MODERATOR: *Miss Geyer, your question to Mr. Mondale.*

Immigration Policy

Q: *Mr. Mondale, many analysts are now saying that actually our number one foreign policy problem today is one that remains almost totally unrecognized. Massive illegal immigration from economically collapsing countries. They are saying that it is the only real territorial threat to the American nation-state. You yourself said in the 1970s that we had a "hemorrhage on our borders" yet today you have backed off any immigration reform such as the balanced and highly crafted Simpson-Mazzoli bill. Why? What would you do instead today if anything?*
MONDALE: *Ah, this is a very serious problem in our country and it has to be dealt with. I object to that part of the Simpson-Mazzoli bill which I think is very unfair and would prove to be so. That is the part that requires employers to determine the citizenship of an employee before they're hired. I am convinced that the result of this would be that people who are Hispanic, people who have different languages or speak with an accent, would find it difficult to be employed.*

I think that's wrong. We've never had citizenship tests in our country before. And I don't think we should have a citizenship card today. That is counterproductive. I do support the other aspects of the Simpson-Mazzoli bill that strengthen enforcement at the border, strengthen other ways of dealing with undocumented workers in this difficult area and dealing with the problem of settling people who have lived here for many many years and do not have an established status. I further strongly recommend that this administration do something it has not done. And that is to strengthen enforcement at the border, strengthen the officials in this government that deal with undocumented workers and to do so in a way that's responsible and within the Constitution of the United States.

We need an answer to this problem. But it must be an American answer that is consistent with justice and due process. Everyone in this room, practically, here tonight, is an immigrant. We came here loving this nation, serving it and it has served all of our most bountiful dreams. And one of those dreams is justice. And we need a measure, and I will support a measure that brings about those objectives, but avoids that one aspect that I think is very serious.

The second part is to maintain and improve relations with our friends to the south. We cannot solve this problem all on our own. And that's why the failure of this administration to deal in an effective and good-faith way with Mexico, with Costa Rica, with the other nations in trying to find a peaceful settlement to the dispute in Central America has undermined our capacity to effectively to deal diplomatic in this, diplomatically in this area as well.

Q: *Sir, people as well-balanced and just as Father Theodore Hesburgh at Notre Dame, who headed the Select Commission on Immigration, have pointed out repeatedly that there will be no immigration reform without employer sanctions because it would be an unbalanced bill and there would be simply no way to enforce it. However, putting that aside for the moment, your critics have also said repeatedly that you have not gone along with the bill, or with any immigration reform, because of the Hispanic groups—or Hispanic leadership groups, who actually do not represent what the Hispanic Americans want because polls show that they overwhelmingly want some kind of immigration reform. Can you say, or how can you justify your position on this, and how do you respond to the criticism that this is another, or that this is an example of your flip-flopping and giving in to special interest groups at the expense of the American nation?*

MONDALE: *I think you're right that the polls show that the majority of Hispanics want that bill, so I'm not doing it for political reasons. I'm doing it because all my life I've fought for a system of justice in this country, a system in which every American has a chance to achieve the fullness of life without discrimination. This bill imposes upon employers the responsibility of determining whether somebody who applies for a job is an American or not, and just inevitably they're going to be reluctant to hire Hispanics or people with a different accent.*

If I were dealing with politics here, the polls show the American people want this. I am for reform in this area, for tough enforcement at the border, and for many other aspects of the Simpson-Mazzoli bill, but all my life I've fought for a fair nation and, despite the politics of it, I stand where I stand, and I think I'm right. And before this fight is over, we're going to come up with a better bill, a more effective bill, that does not undermine the liberties of our people.

Q: *Mr. President, you too have said that our borders are out of control. Yet this fall, you allowed the Simpson-Mazzoli bill, which would at least have minimally protected our borders and the rights of citizenship because of a relatively unimportant issue of reimbursement to the states for legalized aliens. Given that, may I ask what priority can we expect you to give this forgotten national security element; how sincere are you in your efforts to control, in effect, the nation's states, that is, the United States.*

REAGAN: *Georgie, and we, believe me, supported the Simpson-Mazzoli bill strongly, and the bill that came out of the Senate. However, there were things added in in the House side that we felt made it less of a good bill; as a matter of fact, made it a bad bill. And in conference, we stayed with them in conference all the way to where even Senator Simpson did not want the bill in the manner in which it would come out of the conference committee. There were a number of things in there that weakened that bill—I can't go into detail about them here. But it is true our borders are out of control, it is also true that this has been a situation on our borders back through a number of administrations.*

And I supported this bill, I believe in the idea of amnesty for those who have put down roots and who have lived here, even though some time back they may have entered illegally. With regard to the employer sanctions, we must have that—not only to ensure that we can identify the illegal aliens but also, while some keep protesting about what it would do to employers, there is another employer that we shouldn't be so concerned about, and these are employers down through the years who have encouraged the illegal entry into this country because they then hire these individuals and hire them at starvation wages and with none of the benefits that we think are normal and natural for workers in our country. And the individuals can't complain because of their illegal status. We don't think that those people should be allowed to continue operating free, and this was why the provisions that we had in with regard to sanctions and so forth.

And I'm going to do everything I can, and all of us in the administration are, to join in again when Congress is back at it to get an immigration bill that will give us once again control of our borders. And with regard to friendship below the border with the countries down there, yes, no administration that I know has established the relationship that we have with our Latin friends. But as long as they have an economy that leaves so many people in dire poverty and unemployment, they are going to seek that employment across our borders. And we work with those other countries.

Q: Mr. President, the experts also say that the situation today is terribly different—quantitatively, qualitatively different—from what it has been in the past because of the gigantic population growth. For instance, Mexico's population will go from about 60 million today to 120 million at the turn of the century. Many of these people will be coming into the United States not as citizens but as illegal workers. You have repeatedly said recently that you believe that Armageddon, the destruction of the world, may be imminent in our times. Do you ever feel that we are in for an Armageddon or a situation, a time of anarchy, regarding the population explosion in the world?

REAGAN: *No, as a matter of fact the population explosion, if you look at the actual figures, has been vastly exaggerated—overexaggerated. As a matter of fact, there are some pretty scientific and solid figures about how much space there still is in the world and how many more people can have.*

It's almost like going back to the Malthusian theory, when even then they were saying that everyone would starve with the limited population they had then.

But the problem of population growth is one here with regard to our immigration. And we have been the safety valve, whether we wanted to or not, with the illegal entry here; in Mexico, where their population is increasing and they don't have an economy that can absorb them and provide the jobs. And this is what we're trying to work out, not only to protect our own borders but to have some kind of fairness and recognition of that problem.

MODERATOR: *Mr. Mondale, your rebuttal.*

MONDALE: *One of the biggest problems today is that the countries to our south are so desperately poor that these people who will almost lose their lives if they don't come north, come north despite all the risks. And if we're going to find a permanent, fundamental answer to this, it goes to American economic and trade policies that permit these nations to have a chance to get on their own two feet and to get prosperity so that they can have jobs for themselves and their people.*

And that's why this enormous national debt, engineered by this administration, is harming these countries and fueling this immigration.

These high interest rates, real rates, that have doubled under this administration, have had the same effect on Mexico and so on, and the cost of repaying those debts is so enormous that it results in massive unemployment, hardship, and heartache. And that drives our friends to the north—to the south—up into our region, and we need to end those deficits as well.

MODERATOR: *Mr. President, your rebuttal.*

REAGAN: *Well, my rebuttal is I've heard the national debt blamed for a lot of things, but not for illegal immigration across our border, and it has nothing to do with it.*

But with regard to these high interest rates, too, at least give us the recognition of the fact that when you left office, Mr. Mondale, they were 22½, the prime rate; it's now 12¼, and I predict it'll be coming down a little more shortly. So we're trying to undo some of the things that your administration did.

MODERATOR: *Mr. Kalb. No applause, please. Mr. Kalb, your question to President Reagan.*

Armageddon and Nuclear War

Q: *Mr. President, I'd like to pick up this Armageddon theme. You've been quoted as saying that you do believe deep down that we are heading for some kind of biblical Armageddon. Your Pentagon and your secretary of defense have plans for the United States to fight and prevail in a nuclear war. Do you feel that we are now heading, perhaps, for some kind of nuclear Armageddon? And do you feel that this country and the world could survive that kind of calamity?*

REAGAN: *Mr. Kalb, I think what has been hailed as something I'm supposedly, as president, discussing as principle is the result of just some philosophical discussions with people who are interested in the same things. And that is the prophecies down through the years, the biblical prophecies of what would portend the coming of Armageddon and so forth. And the fact that a number of theologians for the last decade or more have believed that this was true, that the prophecies are coming together that portend that.*

But no one knows whether Armageddon—those prophecies—mean that Armageddon is a thousand years away or day after tomorrow. So I have never seriously warned and said we must plan according to Armageddon.

Now, with regard to having to say whether we would try to survive in the event of a nuclear war—of course we would. But let me also point out that to several parliaments around the world, in Europe and in Asia, I have made a statement to each one of them, and I'll repeat it here: A nuclear war cannot be won and must never be fought.

And that is why we are maintaining a deterrent and trying to achieve a deterrent capacity to where no one would believe that they could start such a war and escape with limited damage. But the deterrent—and that's what it is for—is also what led me to propose what is now being called the "Star Wars" concept, but propose that we research to see if there isn't a defensive weapon that could defend against incoming missiles. And if such a defense could be found, wouldn't it be far more humanitarian to say that now we can defend against a nuclear war by destroying missiles instead of slaughtering millions of people?

Q: *Mr. President, when you made that proposal, the so-called "Star Wars" proposal, you said, if I'm not mistaken, that you would share this very supersophisticated technology with the Soviet Union. After all of the distrust over the years, sir, that you have expressed toward the Soviet Union, do you really expect anyone to take seriously that offer—that you would share the best of America's technology in this weapons area with our principal adversary?*

REAGAN: *Why not? What if we did and I hope we can, we're still researching. What if we come up with a weapon that renders those missiles obsolete? There has never been a weapon invented in the history of man that has not led to a defensive, a counterweapon, but suppose we came up with that. Now, some people have said, ah, that would make a war imminent because they would think that we could launch a first strike because we could defend against the enemy. But why not do what I have offered to do and asked the Soviet Union to do? Say look, here's what we can do, we'll even give it to you, now will you sit down with us and once and for all get rid—all of us—of these nuclear weapons and free mankind from that threat. I think that would be the greatest use of a defensive weapon.*

Q: *Mr. Mondale you've been very sharply critical of the president's strategic defense initiative and yet what is wrong with a major effort by this country to try to use its best technology to knock out as many incoming nuclear warheads as possible?*

MONDALE: *First of all, let me sharply disagree with the president on sharing the most advanced, the most dangerous, the most important technology in America with the Soviet Union. We have had, for many years, understandably, a system of restraints on high technology because the Soviets are behind us and any research or development along the "Star Wars" schemes would inevitably involve our most advanced computers, the most advanced engineering and the thought that we would share this with the Soviet Union is, in my opinion, a total nonstarter. I would not let the Soviet Union get their hands on it at all.*

Now, what's wrong with "Star Wars"? There's nothing wrong with the theory of it. If we could develop a principle that would say both sides could fire all their missiles and no one would get hurt, I suppose it's a good idea. But the fact of it is, we're so far away from research that even comes close to that that the director of engineering research in the Defense Department said to get there we would have to solve eight problems, each of which are more difficult than the atomic bomb and the Manhattan Project. It would cost something like a trillion dollars to test and deploy weapons. The second thing is this all assumes that the Soviets wouldn't respond in kind, and they always do. We don't get behind, they won't get behind and that's been the tragic story of the arms race. We have more at stake in space satellites than they do. If we could stop right now the testing and the deployment of these space weapons and the president's proposals go clear beyond research. If it was just research, we wouldn't have any argument, because maybe some day somebody will think of something. But to commit this nation to a buildup of antisatellite and space weapons at this time in their crude state would bring about an arms race that's very dangerous indeed.

One final point: The most dangerous aspect of this proposal is for the first time we would delegate to computers the decision as to whether to start a war. That's dead wrong. There wouldn't be time for a president to decide. It would be decided by these remote computers. It might be an oil fire, it might be a jet exhaust, the computer might decide it's a missile and off we go. Why don't we stop this madness now and draw a line and keep the heavens free from war?

The Nuclear Freeze

Q: *Mr. Mondale, in this general area, sir, of arms control, President Carter's national security adviser, Zbigniew Brzezinski, said, "A nuclear freeze is a hoax," yet the basis of your arms proposals as I understand them is a mutual and verifiable freeze on existing weapons systems. In your view, which specific weapons systems could be subject to a mutual and verifiable freeze and which could not?*

MONDALE: *Every system that is verifiable should be placed on the table for negotiations for an agreement. I would not agree to any negotiations or any agreement that involved conduct on the part of the Soviet Union that we couldn't verify every day. I would not agree to any agreement in which the United States' security interest was not fully recognized and supported. That's why we say mutual and verifiable freezes.*

Now, why do I support the freeze? Because this ever-rising arms race madness makes both nations less secure, it's more difficult to defend this nation it is putting a hair trigger on nuclear war. This administration, by going into the "Star Wars" system, is going to add a dangerous new escalation. We have to be tough on the Soviet Union, but I think the American people and the people of the Soviet Union want it to stop.

MODERATOR: *Time is up, Mr. Mondale. President Reagan your rebuttal.*

REAGAN: *Yes, my rebuttal once again is that this invention that has just been created here of how I would go about rolling over to the Soviet Union. No, Mr. Mondale, my idea would be with that defensive weapon, that we would sit down with them and then say, now, are you willing to join us? Here's what we can—give them a demonstration, and then say, here's what we can do. Now, if you're willing to join us in getting rid of all the nuclear weapons in the world, then, we'll give you this one so that we would both know that no one can cheat—that we've both got something that if anyone tries to cheat—but when you keep star-warring it—I never suggested where the weapons should be or what kind. I'm not a scientist. I said, and the Joint Chiefs of Staff agreed with me, that it was time for us to turn our research ability to seeing if we could not find this kind of a defensive weapon. And suddenly somebody says, oh, it's got to be up there—"Star Wars"—and so forth. I don't know what it would be, but if we can come up with one, I think the world will be better off.*

MODERATOR: *Mr. Mondale, your rebuttal?*

MONDALE: *Well, that's what a president's supposed to know—where those weapons are going to be. If they're space weapons, I assume they'll be in space. If they're antisatellite weapons, I assume they're going to be armed against any satellite. Now, this is the most dangerous technology that we possess. The Soviets try to spy on us—steal this stuff—and to give them technology of this kind, I disagree with. You haven't just accepted research,*

Mr. President, you've set up a strategic defense initiative and agency. You're beginning to test. You're talking about deploying. You're asking for a budget of some $30 billion for this purpose. This is an arms escalation, and we will be better off—far better off—if we stop right now, because we have more to lose in space than they do. If someday somebody comes along with an answer, that's something else, but that there would be an answer in our lifetime is unimaginable. Why do we start things that we know the Soviets will match and make us all less secure? That's what a president is for.

MODERATOR: *Mr. Kondracke, your question to Mr. Mondale?*

Q: *Mr. Mondale, you say that with respect to the Soviet Union, you want to negotiate a mutual nuclear freeze. Yet you would unilaterally give up the MX missile and the B-1 bomber before the talks have ever begun, and you have announced in advance that reaching an agreement with the Soviets is the most important thing in the world to you. Now aren't you giving away half the store before you even sit down to talk?*

MONDALE: *As a matter of fact we have a vast range of technology and weaponry right now that provides all the bargaining chips that we need, and I support the air-launch cruise missile, ground-launch cruise missile, Pershing missile, the Trident submarine, the D-5 submarine, the Stealth technology, the Midgetman—we have a whole range of technology. Why I disagree with the MX is that it's a sitting duck. It'll draw an attack. It puts a hair trigger, and it is a dangerous, destabilizing weapon. And the B-1 is similarly to be opposed because for fifteen years the Soviet Union has been preparing to meet the B-1, the secretary of defense himself said it would a suicide mission, if it were built. Instead, I want to build the Midgetman which is mobile and thus less vulnerable, contributing to stability, and a weapon that will give us security and contribute to an incentive for arms control. That's why I'm for Stealth technology to build the Stealth bomber, which I supported for years, that can penetrate the Soviet air defense system without any hope that they can perceive where it is because their radar system is frustrated. In other words, a president has to make choices. This makes us stronger.*

The final point is that we can use this money that we save on these weapons to spend on things that we really need. Our conventional strength in Europe is understrength. We need to strengthen that in order to assure our Western allies of our presence there, a strong defense, but also to diminish and reduce the likelihood of a commencement of a war and the use of nuclear weapons. It's by this way by making wise choices that we're stronger, we enhance the chances of arms control. Every president until this one has been able to do it, and this nation, the world is more dangerous as a result.

Q: *I want to follow up on Mr. Kalb's question. It seems to me that on the question of verifiability that you do have some problems with the extent of the freeze. It seems to me, for example, that testing would be very difficult to verify because the Soviets encode their telemetry. Research would be impossible to verify, numbers of warheads would be impossible to verify by satellite except with on-site inspection, and production of any weapon would be impossible to verify. Now in view of that, what is going to be frozen?*

MONDALE: *I will not agree to any arms control agreement, including a freeze, that's not verifiable. Let's take your warhead principle. The warhead principle, they've been counting rules for years. Whenever a weapon is tested, we counted the number of warheads on it, and whenever that warhead is used we count that number of warheads, whether they have that number or less on it or not. These are standard rules. I will not agree to any production restrictions or agreement unless we have the ability to verify those agreements. I don't trust the Russians. I believe that every agreement we reach must be verifiable, and I will not agree to anything that we cannot tell every day. In other words, we've got to be tough, but in order to stop this arms madness we've got to push ahead with tough negotiations that are verifiable so that we know the Soviets are agreeing and living up to their agreements.*

Human Rights

Q: *Mr. President, I want to ask you about negotiating with friends. You severely criticized President Carter for helping to undermine two friendly dictators who got into trouble with their own people, the shah of Iran and President Somoza of Nicaragua. Now there are other such leaders heading for trouble, including President Pinochet of Chile and President Marcos of the Philippines. What should you do and what can you do to prevent the Philippines from becoming another Nicaragua?*

REAGAN: *Morton, I did criticize the President because of our undercutting of what was a stalwart ally, the shah of Iran. And I am not at all convinced that he was that far out of line with his people or that they wanted that to happen.*

The shah had done our bidding and carried our load in the Middle East for quite some time and I did think that it was a blot on our record that we let him down. Had things gotten better, the shah, whatever he might have done, was building low-cost housing, had taken land away from the mullahs and was distributing it to the peasants so they could be landowners, things of that kind. But we turned it over to a maniacal fanatic who has slaughtered thousands and thousands of people calling it executions.

The matter of Somoza, no, I never defended Somoza. And as a matter of fact, the previous administration stood by and so did I—not that I could have done anything in my position at that time. But for this revolution to take place and the promise of the revolution was democracy, human rights, free labor unions, free press. And then just as Castro had done in Cuba, the Sandinistas ousted the other parties to the revolution. Many of them are now the contras. *They exiled some, they jailed some, they murdered some. And they installed a Marxist-Leninist totalitarian government.*

And what I have to say about this is, many times—and this has to do with the Philippines also—I know there are things there in the Philippines that do not look good to us from the standpoint right now of democratic rights. But what is the alternative? It is a large Communist movement to take over the Philippines.

They have been our friend for—since their inception as a nation. And I think that we've had enough of a record of letting, under the guise of revolution, someone that we thought was a little more right than we would be, letting that person go and then winding up with totalitarianism pure and simple as the alternative and I think that we're better off, for example, with the Philippines of trying to retain our friendship and help them right the wrongs we see rather than throwing them to the wolves and then facing a Communist power in the Pacific.

Q: *Mr. President, since the United States has two strategic bases in the Philippines, would the overthrow of President Marcos constitute a threat to vital American interests, and, if so, what would you do about it?*

REAGAN: *Well, as I say we have to look at what an overthrow there would mean and what the government would be that would follow. And there is every evidence, every indication that that government would be hostile to the United States and that would be a severe blow to the—to our abilities there in the Pacific.*

Q: *And what would you do about it?*

MODERATOR: *Sorry, sorry, you've asked the followup question. Mr. Mondale, your rebuttal.*

MONDALE: *Perhaps in no area do we disagree more than this administration's policies on human rights. I went to the Philippines as vice-president, pressed for human rights, called for the release of Aquino, and made progress that had been stalled on both the Subic and the Clark airfield bases.*

What explains this administration cozying up to the Argentine dictators after they took over? Fortunately a democracy took over, but this nation was embarrassed by this current administration's adoption of their policies. What happens in South Africa, where, for example, the Nobel Prize winner two days ago said this administration is seen as working with the oppressive government of that region, of South Africa.

That hurts this nation. We need to stand for human rights. We need to make it clear we're for human liberty. National security and human rights must go together, but this administration time and time again has lost its way in this field.

MODERATOR: *President Reagan, your rebuttal.*

REAGAN: *Well, the invasion of Afghanistan didn't take place on our watch. I have described what has happened in Iran and we weren't here then either. I don't think that our record of human rights can be assailed. I think that we have observed ourselves and have done our best to see that human rights are extended throughout the world.*

Mr. Mondale has recently announced a plan of his to get the democracies together and to work with the whole world to turn to democracy. And I was glad to hear him say that because that's what we've been doing ever since I announced to the British Parliament that I thought we should do this.

And human rights are not advanced when at the same time you then stand back and say, "Whoops, we didn't know the gun was loaded," and you have another totalitarian power on your hands.

"Star Wars" and Deterrence

MODERATOR: *In this, in this segment, because of the pressure of time, there will be no rebuttals and there will be no followup questions. Mr. Trewhitt, your question to President Reagan.*

Q: *One question to each candidate?*

MODERATOR: *One question to each candidate.*

Q: *Mr. President, could I take you back to something you said earlier? And if I'm misquoting you please correct me. But I understood you to say that if the development of space military technology was successful, you might give the Soviets a demonstration and say, "Here it is," which sounds to me as if you might be trying to gain the sort of advantage that would enable you to dictate terms, and which I would then suggest to you might mean scrapping a generation of nuclear strategy called mutual deterrence, in which we in effect hold each other hostage. Is that your intention?*

REAGAN: *Well, I can't say that I have round-tabled that and sat down with the Chiefs of Staff, but I have said that it seems to me that this could be a logical step in what is my ultimate goal, my ultimate dream. And that the elimination of nuclear weapons in the world. And it seems to me that this could be an adjunct, or certainly a great assisting agent, in getting that done. I am not going to roll over, as Mr. Mondale suggests, and give them something that could turn around and be used against us. But I think it's a very interesting proposal to see if we can find first of all something that renders those weapons obsolete, incapable of their mission.*

But Mr. Mondale seems to approve MAD—MAD is Mutual Assured Destruction, meaning if you use nuclear weapons on us, the only thing we have to keep you from doing it is that we'll kill as many people of yours as you will kill of ours. I think that to do everything we can to find, as I say, something that would destroy weapons and not humans is a great step forward in human rights.

Q: *Mr. Mondale, could I ask you to address the question of nuclear strategy. Formal doctrine is very arcane, but I'm going to ask you to deal with it anyway. Do you believe in MAD, Mutual Assured Destruction, mutual deterrence, as it has been practiced for the last generation?*

MONDALE: *I believe in a sensible arms control approach that brings down these weapons to manageable levels. I would like to see their elimination. And in the meantime, we have to be strong enough to make certain that the Soviet Union never attempts this.*

Now here we have to decide between generalized objectives and reality. The president says he wants to eliminate or reduce the number of nuclear weapons, but in fact these last four years have seen more weapons built, a wider and more vigorous arms race than in human history. He says he wants a system that will make nuclear arms wars safe, so nobody's going to get hurt. Well, maybe someday somebody can dream of that. But why start an arms race now? Why destabilize our relationship? Why threaten our space satellites, upon which we depend? Why pursue a strategy that would delegate to computers the question of starting a war.

A president, to defend this country and to get arms control, must master what's going on. I accept his objective and his dreams, we all do. But the hard reality is that we must know what we're doing and pursue those objectives that are possible in our time. He's opposed every effort of every president to do so; in the four years of his administration he's failed to do so. And if you want a tough president who uses that strength to get arms control, and draws the line in the heavens, vote for Watler Mondale.

Concluding Statements

MODERATOR: *Please, I must again ask the audience not to applaud, not to cheer, not demonstrate its feelings in any way. We've arrived at the point in the debate now where we call for closing statements. You have the full four minutes, each of you, Mr. Mondale, will you go first.*

MONDALE: *I want to thank the League of Women Voters, the good citizens of Kansas City, and President Reagan for agreeing to debate this evening.*

This evening we talked about national strength. I believe we need to be strong, and I will keep us strong. But I think strength must also require wisdom and smarts in its exercise—that's key to the strength of our nation.

A president must know the essential facts, essential to command. But a president must also have a vision of where this nation should go.

Tonight, as Americans you have a choice. And you're entitled to know where we would take this country if you decide to elect us.

As president, I would press for long-term vigorous economic growth. That's why I want to get these debts down and these interest rates down, restore America's exports, help rural America which is suffering so much, and bring the jobs back here for our children.

I want this next generation to be the best educated in American history; to invest in the human mind and science again, so we're out front.

I want this nation to protect its air, its water, its land and its public health. America is not temporary. We're forever. And as Americans, our generation should protect this wonderful land for our children.

I want a nation of fairness, where no one is denied the fullness of life or discriminated against, and we deal compassionately with those in our midst who are in trouble.

And above all, I want a nation that's strong. Since we debated two weeks ago, the United States and the Soviet Union have built 100 more warheads, enough to kill millions of Americans and millions of Soviet citizens.

This doesn't strengthen us, this weakens the chances of civilization to survive.

I remember the night before I became vice-president. I was given the briefing and told that any time, night or day, I might be called upon to make the most fateful decision on earth—whether to fire these atomic weapons that could destroy the human species.

That lesson tells us two things. One, pick a president that you know will know, if that tragic moment ever comes, what he must know. Because there'll be no time for staffing committees or advisers; a president must know right then.

But above all, pick a president who will fight to avoid the day when that God-awful decision ever needs to be made. And that's why this election is so terribly important.

America and Americans decide not just what's happening in this country; we are the strongest and most powerful free society on earth. When you make that judgment, you are deciding not only the future of our nation; in a very profound respect, you're providing the future—deciding the future of the world.

We need to move on. It's time for America to find new leadership. Please join me in this cause to move confidently and with a sense of assurance and command to build the blessed future of our nation.

MODERATOR: *President Reagan, your summation, please.*

REAGAN: *Yes, my thanks to the League of Women Voters, to the panelists, to the moderator, and to the people of Kansas City for their warm hospitality and greeting.*

I think the American people tonight have much to be grateful for: an economic recovery that has become expansion, freedom, and most of all, we are at peace. I am grateful for the chance to reaffirm my commitment to reduce nuclear weapons and one day to eliminate them entirely.

The question before us comes down to this: do you want to see America return to the policies of weakness of the last four years, or do we want to go forward marching together as a nation of strength and that's going to continue to be strong?

We shouldn't be dwelling on the past or even the present. The meaning of this election is the future, and whether we're going to grow and provide the jobs and the opportunities for all Americans and that they need. Several years ago I was given an assignment to write a letter. I was to go into a time capsule and would be read in 100 years when that time capsule was opened. I remember driving down the California coast one day. My mind was full of what I was going to put in that letter about the problems and the issues that confront us in our time and what we did about them, but I couldn't completely neglect the beauty around me—the Pacific out there on one side of the highway shining in the sunlight, the mountains of the coast range rising on the other side, and I found myself wondering what it would be like for someone, wondering if someone 100 years from now would be driving down that highway and if they would see the same thing.

And with that thought I realized what a job I had with that letter. I would writing a letter to people who know everything there is to know about us. We know nothing about them. They would know all about our problems. They would know how we solved them and whether our solution was beneficial to them down through the years or whether it hurt them. They would also know that we lived in a world with terrible weapons, nuclear weapons of terrible destructive power aimed at each other, capable of crossing the ocean in a matter of minutes and destroying civilization as we know it.

And then I thought to myself: what are they going to say about us? What are those people 100 years from now going to think? They will know whether we used those weapons or not. Well, what they will say about us 100 years from now depends on how we keep our rendezvous with destiny. Will we do the things that we know must be done and know that one day down in history 100 years, or perhaps before, someone will say, Thank God for those people back in the 1980s, for preserving our freedom, for saving for us this blessed planet called earth with all its grandeur and its beauty.

You know, I am grateful for all of you for giving the opportunity to serve you for these four years and I seek reelection because I want more than anything else to try to complete the new beginning that we charted four years ago.

George Bush, who I think is one of the finest vice-presidents this country has ever had, George Bush and I have crisscrossed the country and we've had in these last few months a wonderful experience. We have met young America. We have met your sons and daughters.

MODERATOR: *Mr. President, I'm obliged to cut you off there under the rules of the debate. I'm sorry.*

REAGAN: *All right, I was just going to—*

MODERATOR: *Perhaps I should point out that the rules under which I did that were agreed upon by the two campaigns.*

REAGAN: *I know, yes.*

MODERATOR: *Thank you, Mr. President. Thank you, Mr. Mondale. Our thanks also to the panel, finally to our audience. We thank you, and the League of Women Voters asks me to say to you, Don't forget to vote on November 6.*

Selected Bibliography

Bates, Stephen and Edwin Diamond. *The Spot: The Rise of Political Advertising on Television*. Cambridge, MA: MIT Press, 1984.

Bagdikian, Ben. *The Media Monopoly*. Boston: Beacon Press, 1983.

Boller, Paul F. Jr., *Presidential Campaigns*. New York: Oxford University Press, 1984.

Brew, Douglas and George Church. "Fast and Loose with Facts." *Time*, 5 November 1984.

Broder, David. "When Ideology Faded in 1984," *Washington Post*, National Weekly Edition, 26 November 1984.

Cannon, Lou. "Phantom of the White House." *Washington Post*, National Weekly Edition, 24 December 1984.

Clancey, Maura and Michael Robinson. "General Election Coverage: Part One." *Public Opinion*, December/January 1985.

Clymer, Adam. "30 - Second Politics." *New York Times Book Review*, 21 October 1984.

Cobb, Edwin L., *No Ceasefires: The War On Poverty In Roanoke Valley*. Cabin John, MD: Seven Locks Press, 1985.

Collier, Peter and David Horowitz. "Confessions of Two New-Left Radicals: Why We Voted for Reagan." *Washington Post*, National Weekly Edition, 8 April 1985.

Collins, Tom. "The Reagan Team Hit a New Low." *Newsday* reprint, *Seattle Times*, 9 January 1985.

———. "The Us-Them Gulf is Widened." *Newsday* reprint, *Seattle Times*, 19 November 1984.

Cowden, Dick. "Enterprise Zones deserve a real chance." *Letters to the Editor*, *Wall Street Journal*, 10 April 1985.

Cronkite, Walter. "Dialogues on America's Future Series." *Congressional Clearinghouse on the Future*, 15 March 1985.

Cross, Donna Woolfolk. *Media-Speak*. New York: Coward-McCann, 1983.

Dickenson, James. "A Bare-Knuckle Conservative Brawler." *Washington Post*, National Weekly Edition, 18 February 1985.

Epstein, Jack and James Evans. "A Hero to Many South Americans." *Seattle Times*, 21 November 1984.

Garment, Suzanne. "Seeking the Needle of Bias in TV News Haystack." (Capital Chronicle), *Wall Street Journal*, 28 September 1984.

Goodman, Ellen. "No Public Anger Over Hungry Kids." *Boston Globe* reprint, *Seattle Times*, 16 April 1985.

Greenberger, Robert and Clifford Krauss. "Despite Fears of U.S., Soviet Aid to Nicaragua Appears to be Limited." (Latin Focus), *Wall Street Journal*, 3 April 1985.

Greenfield, Meg. "The 'Mondale' Issue," (interview with Walter Mondale). *Washington Post*, National Weekly Edition, 8 October 1984.

Griffith, Thomas. "Proving Lincoln was Right." (Newswatch), *Time*, 22 October 1984.

———. "From Monitor to Public Echo." (Newswatch), *Time*, 12 November 1984.

———. "Television News Without Blinkers." (Newswatch), *Time*, 29 April 1985.

Harrington, Michael. *The Other America*. New York: Macmillan, 1961, Revised edition, Pelican, 1971-1981.

Holmgren, Rod and William Norton. *The Mass Media Book*. Englewood Cliffs: Prentice Hall, 1972.

Hunt, Al. "Campaign Notes," (Politics '84). *Wall Street Journal*, 2 November 1984.

Jamieson, Kathleen Hall. *Packaging the Presidency: A History and Criticism of Presidential Campaign Advertising*. New York: Oxford University Press, 1984.

Kerner, Otto, Chairman. *Report of the Presidential Commission on Civil Disorders*. U.S. Government, 1968.

Kuttner, Robert. *The Economic Illusion: False Choices Between Prosperity and Social Justice*. Boston: Houghton Mifflin, 1984.

———. "A Flawed Case for Scrapping What's Left of the Great Society." *Washington Post*, National Weekly Edition, 17 December 1984.

Linowitz, Sol, Chair. *Report of the Presidential Commission on World Hunger*. U.S. Government, 1980.

Luttwak, Edward. *The Pentagon and the Art of War: The Question of Military Reform*. New York: Simon & Schuster, 1985.

Manchester, William. *American Caesar*. Boston: Little, Brown, 1978.

Matusow, Barbara. *The Evening Stars*. Boston: Houghton Mifflin, 1983.

Mayer, Jane. "How TV Viewed the Candidates" (Politics '84). *Wall Street Journal*, 24 September 1984.

Morrow, Lance. "Poof!" The Phenomenon of Public Vanishing." *Time*, 13 May 1985.

Murray, Charles. *Losing Ground: American Social Policy. 1950-1980*. New York: Basic Books, 1984.

Powell, Jody. "A Little Advice for the Winners." *Los Angeles Times* Syndicate, *Seattle Times*, 21 November 1984.

Raines, Howell. "Reagan Appears to Succeed by Avoiding Specific Issues." *New York Times*, 23 September 1984.

———. "As Campaign Ends, Parties Prepare for a New Political Era." *New York Times*, 4 November 1984.

Reeves, Richard. "America's Choice: What It Means." *New York Times* Magazine, 4 November 1984.

———. "Democrats Still Haven't Learned." *Universal Press* Syndicate, *Seattle Times*, 25 February 1985.

Reston, James. "We'll Sing A Different Tune Next Week." *New York Times*, 20 January 1985.

Rosenbaum, David. "Moynihan Reassessing Problems of Families." *New York Times*, 7 April 1985.

Schram, Martin. "Carter Commission Renews the War Against Hunger." *Washington Post*, 3 June 1979.

———. "Meet Mondale's Message Man." *Washington Post*, National Weekly Edition, 17 September 1984.

Sheperd, Jack. "When Foreign Aid Fails." *Atlantic Monthly*, April 1985.

Sidey, Hugh. "When the Elite Loses Touch." (The Presidency). *Time*, November 1984.

Sloan, John. "Enterprise Zones May Not Be the Bargain That's Advertised." *Wall Street Journal*, 26 March 1985.

Smith, Hedrick. "The Politics Of Blame." *New York Times Magazine*, 7 October 1984.

Sussman, Barry. "What Americans Think." *Washington Post*, National Weekly Edition, 12 November 1984.

———. "What Americans Think." *Washington Post*, National Weekly Edition, 7 January 1985.

Talbott, Strobe. *Deadly Gambits: The Reagan Administration and the Stalemate in Nuclear Arms Control*. New York: Alfred A. Knopf, 1984.

———. "A Partisan Gloss on the Globe." *Time*, 29 October 1984.

Tarolsovsky, Rich and David Shribman. "Mondale Campaign May Just Benefit From Newest Issue: Alleged Dirty Tricks." *Wall Street Journal*, 24 September 1984.

Traub, James. "That (Too Long?) One-Hour News Show." *Columbia Journalism Review*, January/February 1985.

Unger, Arthur. "Public TV is Feeling Heat From Reagan." *Christian Science Monitor* reprint, *Seattle Times*, 20 November 1984.

Weaver, David and Cleve Wilhoit. *The American Journalist*. Bloomington: Indiana University Press, 1985.

Weisman, Stephen. "The President and the Press: The Art of Controlled Access." *New York Times*, 14 October 1984.

White, Theodore. *America in Search of Itself: The Making of the President 1956-1980*. New York: Harper & Row, 1982.

———. "The Shaping of the Presidency 1984." *Time*, 19 November 1984.

Will, George. "The Great 49-State Non-Mandate." *Newsweek*, 19 November 1984.

About the Author

Keith Blume is the founder and executive director of Planet Earth Foundation, a non-profit organization concerned with public education through media on U.S. policy choices related primarily to global issues. He has written and produced documentaries broadcast on commercial and public television addressing the issues of world hunger and the nuclear arms race. In 1977 his production The Hungry Planet *led to the initiation by President Carter of the White House Hunger Working Group. In 1983 he hosted the program* Round Table: The Nuclear Arms Race *on PBS affiliate WNVC in the Washington, D.C. area. He has interviewed on camera presidential candidates Gerald Ford, Walter Mondale, Hubert Humphrey, Robert Dole and John Glenn, as well as other national and international public figures. His work has included research and film production in India, Thailand, Indonesia, Ethiopia, Kenya, Egypt, Israel, Cyprus and Greece. His home is in Seattle.*

Index

Aaron, David (former National Security staff member), 92–95
Abortion, 18, 51, 59–60, 78–80, 190, 258–61; Catholics for a Free Choice, 59
Accuracy in Media, 225
Age and leadership, 101, 122, 130, 131, 132, 162, 197, 315–18
Aid to Families with Dependent Children, 105, 106
America in Search of Itself, 184
American Catholic bishops, 50, 59–60
American Enterprise Institute, 189–92
American Legion Convention, 33, 40, 48, 57
Arledge, Roone, 27
Arms control. *See* Nuclear arms control

Bagdikian, Ben, 238
Bates, Stephen, 9
Bay of Pigs, 65
Big Brother watching TV, 239
Black Caucus, 53
Blackout on blacks, 57, 104–14
Blackwell, Morton (former White House aide), 79
Bluestone, Barry (Social Welfare Institute), 31–32
Boller, Paul F., 11
Bombing of U.S. embassy in Beirut, 76, 90, 190, 200
Brackett, Elizabeth (PBS), 141–43
Brinkley, David (ABC), 97
Brokaw, Tom (NBC), 33, 35, 96, 167–68, 229–30, 241; debate, 167–68; dirty tricks, 77–78; nuclear arms control, 96, 229–30
Bruno, Hal (ABC), 13, 14
Buchanan, John (former congressman from Alabama): Moral Christian Report Cards, 52–55
Buchanan, Patrick (Reagan's director of communications), 59, 222
Budget, the, 244–47
Bureau of Labor Statistics, 112
Burford, Anne (former director of the Environmental Protection Agency), 19
Bush campaign, 27
Bush-Ferraro debate, 14, 136, 137, 140–46; nuclear arms race, 137, 138. *See* Appendix for complete transcripts of the debates
Bush, Vice President George, 23, 30, 139, 140–46

Cannon, Lou *(Washington Post),* 81, 82
Carlough, Edward (Sheet Metal Workers Union), 31
Carter, Hodding (former State Department spokesman), 223–24, 226
Carter, President Jimmy, 22, 32, 54, 56, 90, 201
Center on Budget and Policy Priorities Report, 109

Central America, 19, 148–58, 160
Central America and the CIA, 291–95
Chancellor, John (NBC), 127, 141
Chase, Rebecca (ABC), 100
Chernenko, Konstantin, Soviet Premier, 83
Christian community, 59
Christian fundamentalists, 34, 52–56
Christian Minister Letter, 48–49, 56
Civil rights, 19, 86
Clancey. *See* Robinson and Clancey report
Clymer, Adam *(New York Times),* 11
Cobb, Edwin L., 106
Collins, Tom *(Newsday),* 188, 193, 194
Commerce, Department of, 31
Commercials, campaign: *The Spot: The Rise of Political Advertising on TV* (by E. Diamond and S. Bates), 9
Congressional Budget Office report, 111
Constitution, 45, 46, 56, 59
Constitutional amendment to balance the budget, 71
Contadora negotiating process, 137, 149, 150, 154
Controversy, media search for, 28
Crime, environmental causes of, 109
Criswell, Rev. W. A. (First Baptist Church, Dallas), 56
Critique of TV news, 182, 193, 197, 201–3, 234–35
Cronkite, Walter, 227; criticism of presidential campaigns, 202–03
Cross, Donna Woolfolk, 238, 239
Cuba: anti-Castro violence, 65; naturalization ceremony, 64
Cuomo, Governor Mario, 22; Supreme Court, 97, 98

Dean, Robert (State Department), 92–95
Deaver, Mike (White House aide), 83, 193, 219
Debates. *See* Appendix for complete transcripts of the debates
Defense, 40–42, 44
Deficit, the, 17, 22, 43, 44, 61, 69–72, 158, 218; debate, 124, 125, 244–47; State of the Union address, 232
Democratic convention, 20
Democratic primaries, 20
Diamond, Edward, 9, 135
Dirty tricks, Republican, 68, 77–79, 180
Distortions in reporting, 40, 192; Iranian hostage crisis, 184
Dole, Senator Robert, 8, 117
Donahue, Phil, 241
Donaldson, Sam (ABC), 30, 33, 34, 47, 127; age issue, 169–70; Grand Ole Opry, 60–61; nuclear

arms control, 169–70; Reagan campaign, 80–82; Reagan on the economy, 60–61
Donovan, Raymond (Secretary of Labor), 97
Dowe, David (CBS), 65
Dugger, Ronnie (CNN), 119–20

East, Senator John, 50–51
Economy, the, 16, 43, 71, 96, 158, 196, 232; State of the Union address, 233. *See* Appendix for complete transcripts of the debates
Eisenhower, President Dwight, 13, 16, 17
El Salvador, 150–51, 156, 157, 158, 212; Duarte meeting guerrillas, 148, 155–56
Environment, the, 19, 37, 86, 199
Equal Rights Amendment, 54, 55
Evening Stars, The, 234

Fairness issue, 28, 128, 139
Fairness in Media (Senator Jesse Helms), 225
Falwell, Jerry, 45, 50, 55, 86, 99; Moral Majority Report, 54; "Presidential Biblical Scorecard," 49
Farmer subsidy, 81
Farrakhan, Louis, 21
Federal Trade Commission, 239
Ferraro, Geraldine, 22–23, 28, 102, 137–39; Republican dirty tricks, 68, 77–79, 186. *See* Appendix for complete transcripts of the debates
Fineman, Howard *(Newsweek),* 69
Fire Unleashed, The, 236
First Amendment, 50–51, 55; and the press, 226–29
Ford, President Gerald, 8, 13, 16, 44, 90, 117, 134, 159
Foreign aid, 205, 206, 207, 212, 213–14
Fox, Anne (Massachusetts chairperson of Citizens for Life), 79
Freedom of Information Act, 227
Friendly dictators, 152, 153, 166, 171, 201, 208–9
Friendly, Fred, 228–29, 234
Fundamentalist christians. *See* Christian fundamentalists

Garment, Suzanne *(Wall Street Journal),* 189, 192–93
Gault, Charlayne Hunter (PBS), 158
Glenn, Senator John, 8, 20
Goldberg, Bernard (CBS), 240; impact of television on election, 87
Goldwater, Senator Barry, 17, 131, 151
Goodman, Ellen *(Boston Globe),* 105, 106
Graham, Fred (CBS), 97–99
Greenberger, Robert *(Wall Street Journal),* 150–151
Greenfield, Jeff (ABC), 140
Greenstein, Robert (former head of food stamps program), 110–14
Grenada, 19, 34, 101, 226, 228–29
Griffith, Thomas *(Time),* 181–82
Gromyko, Andrei (Foreign Minister USSR), 69, 76, 80, 83, 90, 91

Harrington, Michael, 105, 107
Hart, Senator Gary, 8, 18, 21; primary campaign, 188–89
Helms, Senator Jesse, 105, 189, 222

Human rights issue, 155, 201, 326–28
Hume, Britt (ABC), 36, 64, 66, 76, 87, 89, 122; foreign policy, 170–71
Humphrey, Vice President Hubert, 8, 16, 29, 86
Hunger. *See* World hunger
Hunger Project (Werner Erhard), 215
Hungry Planet, The, 206

Image making, 127, 131
Image over substance, 178, 180, 184, 193, 194, 234, 240
Immigration policy, 166, 318–21
Impact of TV news, 2, 4, 7, 9–12, 179, 181, 182, 204; Kennedy-Nixon debates, 8
Inflation, 70, 85, 111, 112
Iranian hostage crisis, 2
Isaacs, Maxine (Mondale campaign staff), 39, 64
Israel, 46, 63, 200
Issues, lack of coverage, 34, 36, 40, 42, 44, 80, 102, 133

Jackson, Reverend Jesse, 20, 21, 22, 104
Jamieson, Kathleen Hall, 9
Jennings, Peter (ABC), 26; Mondale campaign, 114–17
Jewish organizations, 34, 45–48; B'nai Brith, 39, 46–52
Johnson, Jim, 37–38
Johnson, President Lyndon, 13, 16, 58, 105, 107, 112; Tonkin Gulf speech, 229
Journalism, television, 12, 14, 57–58, 62, 109, 114; abortion issue, 60, 190; control of outcome, 39; image selling, 8, 10, 73, 185, 223; labeling, 25, 68, 100, 123, 178, 183; "one-liners" on candidates, 33, 36, 39, 40, 96, 161; religion issue, 28; replay, 133–34; selling news, 69

Kalb, Marvin, 156–57, 164–65
Kaufman, Henry (Wall Street analyst), 85
Kennedy-Nixon television debates, 8
Kennedy, President John F., 13, 16, 41, 56, 59, 84, 105, 107
Kennedy, Senator Robert, 7, 107, 108, 109; and civil rights, 108
Kerner Commission on Civil Disorders, 109
King, Reverend Martin Luther, Jr., 107, 108
Kissinger, Henry, 83, 84, 149
Koppel, Ted (ABC, "Nightline"), 26, 33, 235; inaccurate scoop retracted, 39; South Africa program, 185
Kraft, Gerald, 46
Krauss, Clifford *(Wall Street Journal),* 150–52
Krushchev, Nikita, Soviet Premier, 41

Lahaye, Reverend Tim, 52–55; liberal secular humanists, 54
Lake, James (Reagan campaign spokesman), 82
Lance, Bert (former Carter aide), 21–22
Land reform, 209–12
"Latenight America", 235
Laxalt, Senator Paul: *Dear Christian Minister* letter, 48, 49, 56
League of Women Voters. *See* Appendix for complete transcript of the debates

Leahy, Senator Patrick: moral McCarthyism, 50–52

Lebanon, 19, 90, 101, 166, 200

Lehrer, Jim (PBS), 31, 47–52

Leone, Richard (Mondale adviser), 24

Leubsdorf, Carl (CNN), 179

Linowitz, Sol, 6, 7, 208

Locigno, Paul (Teamsters Union), 31

Losing Ground: American Social Policy, 1950–1980, 106

Luttwak, Edward, 198

MacNeil-Lehrer NewsHour (PBS), 30, 32, 201; blacks and poverty, 110-14; Central America, 149, 154, 155, 156–57; impact of debates, 134–35, 141–145; Mondale campaign style, 67–69; nuclear arms control, 92–95; religion and politics, 47–55; unemployment, 31

Malle, Louis, 210–11

Mannatt, Charles (national Democratic party chairman), 21

Marrow, Lance *(Time),* 2

Mass Media Book, The, 228–29

Matusow, Barbara, 234

Mayer, Jane *(Wall Street Journal),* 12

Mayne, William *(Foreign Affairs Quarterly),* 83

Media Monopoly, The, 238

Media Speak, 238–39

Medicare, 60, 63, 105, 124, 198

Middle East policy, 63, 90, 199, 200

Military power, use of, 166; war in Nicaragua, 19

Minnow, Newton (CBS Board of Directors), 88

Minorities, 124

Mondale campaigning: American Legion, Salt Lake City, 40–41; B'nai B'rith, Washington, D.C., 45, 47–52; Davenport, Iowa, 68; Long Beach, Calif., 35, 36–37; Minneapolis, Minn., 49; New York Labor Day Parade, 28, 68

Mondale-Ferraro campaign, 12, 13, 16–25, 27, 69, 196; after first debate, 126, 127

Mondale, Vice Pres. Walter: defamed, 17, 35, 164, 170, 172; need for debates, 36–37; voter reaction to policies, 119, 196

"Moral Christian Report Cards", 52–53

"Moral McCarthyism," 49, 50, 53–54

Morton, Bruce (CBS): nuclear arms control, 160–61

Moyers, Bill (CBS): party of religion, 58–59

Moynihan, Senator Daniel Patrick, 106

Mudd, Roger (NBC), 117

Murray, Charles, 106

Murrow, Edward R., 88, 230–31, 234

Mutual Assured Destruction (MAD): scrapped by Reagan, 172, 175

Myers, Lisa (NBC), 29, 38, 87; religion and politics, 45–46

NATO deployment of Pershing missiles, 90–91

Nelson, Jack *(Los Angeles Times),* 123

Neoconservatives, 18

New Deal, 17, 18

Newscasts: reinforcing negative image of candidates, 37–38, 66–68, 87, 185, 197; reinforcing positive image of candidates, 82, 185, 197

Nicaragua, 19, 81, 150, 163–64, 212; CIA manual for assassination, 163, 171; CIA mining of ports, 151, 152; Cuban and Soviet influence, 149, 150, 151, 152; quarantine, 160

Nixon President Richard, 13, 16, 78, 83, 84

No Ceasefires: The War on Poverty in Roanoke Valley, 106

Nofziger, Lyn (Reagan-Bush campaign consultant), 77–78, 98, 186–87

Nuclear arms control, 22, 30, 42, 64, 76, 86, 96, 236, 295–99; Bush on, 137; in debate, 159–60, Mondale on, 91, 171–173; Reagan on, 92–95, 165, 169–70, 174–76, 198, 217; treaties, 92–95

Nuclear freeze, 37, 41, 160, 164, 324–26

Oliphant, Tom *(Boston Globe),* 67, 68

Oliver, Don (NBC), 37

Ortner, Robert (Commerce Department), 31–32

O'Neill, Representative Thomas "Tip", 39–40

Orwell, George: prophecy of, 75

Other America, The, 105

Packaging the presidency, 9, 10

Participatory democracy, 14, 216; decreasing voter turnout, 11, 12

Peace and Freedom Party, 7

Penner, Ralph (Congressional Budget Office chief), 85

Pentagon and the Art of War, The, 198

Peterson, Barry, 29

"Phantom India," 210–11

Physicians Task Force on Hunger, 105, 106

Plante, Bill (CBS), 27, 33, 35, 76

Platform, Democratic, 17

Platform, Republican, 17, 23–24

Political parties and the electorate. *See* Appendix for complete transcripts of the debates

"Politics of Blame, The," 40

Polls, 37, 116, 134, 182, 183, 194; debates, 169; Gallup, 41; Harris, 99, 119, 130; *New York Times,* 132; *Newsweek,* 122; *Washington Post,* 115

Poverty, 104–14, 124, 265–68

Powell, Jody (Carter press secretary), 6, 194, 197

Pravda, 226

"Presidential Biblical Scorecard," 49

Presidential Campaigns, 11

Presidential Commission on World Hunger, 5, 6, 205–09, 214, 215

Presidential debates: Carter and Ford, 134. *See* Appendix for the complete transcripts of the 1985 presidential debates

Presidential press conferences: Carter, 7; Reagan, 38

Primaries, Democratic, 19, 20

Public broadcasting appropriation veto, 223

Qualities required of presidents, 14, 16, 17, 18, 24, 75

Raines, Howell *(New York Times),* 13–14, 67, 123, 129, 167

Rather, Dan (CBS), 33, 159; impact of the first debate, 128; Reagan campaign, 101–02; Reagan on the press, 73–75

Ratings control news reporting, 27, 229, 233, 239–40

Reagan-Bush campaign, 16–25; strategy, 12, 13, 24, 27, 132

Reagan campaigning: American Legion, Salt Lake City, 33–35; B'nai B'rith, Washington, D.C., 46, 47–52; prayer meeting, Dallas, 54, 55; Grand Ole Opry, 61; Miami, 64–65; Orange County Calif, 29–30

Reagan-Mondale debates, 115, 118, 119, 12?, 167, 168, 169; domestic issues, 25, 125; ne... mentary, 134–35; nuclear arms con... See Appendix for complete transcri... bates

Reagan, President Ronald: budget... appearances, 61, 64, 88, 101; evading ... 49, 69, 71, 81, 101, 102; German military ce... etery controversy, 224; Great Communicator, 18, 68, 119; policies turnabout, 86; sequestered from press, 29, 37, 73, 80, 81, 188, 219–20; State of the Union address, 232

Recession, 70

Regan, Secretary of Treasury Donald, 35

Reich, Ambassador Otto (State Department co-ordinator for Latin America), 154

Reporters, role of, 158, 179–83, 184, 185, 186, 187, 225; educating public, 234–35

Reporting, quality of, 87, 181, 192

Reporting in depth, 185, 236–37, 241–42

Republican Convention, 27

Reynolds, Dean (ABC): dirty tricks, 79

Robinson and Clancey report, 189–93

Rohatyn, Felix (financial expert), 85

Rollins, Ed (Reagan adviser), 77–78

Roosevelt, President Franklin, 16, 86

Rose, Charlie (CBS), 221

Safire, William (New York Times), 80

Saperstein, Rabbi David, 57

Schieffer, Bob (CBS): Mondale campaign, 132–33; religion and politics, 56–57

Schneider, William (American Enterprise Institute), 57

Schoenbrun, David, 234, 237–38

School prayer amendment, 48, 51–52

Schram, Martin (Washington Post), 24, 179

Sheperd, Jack (Atlantic Monthly), 213

Secular humanism, 53–55

Sensationalism in reporting, 26, 62; Robert Kennedy primary, 7, 8

Sidey, Hugh (Time), 179–81

Sloan, John (president of National Federation of Independent Business), 106, 107

Smith, Hedrick (New York Times), 40

Social policy, 18, 104, 124, 195, 197–98, 218, 219

Social Security issue, 60, 63, 105, 113, 124, 198, 218

Social Welfare Research Institute, 31

South Africa, 185, 201

Sovie...

S...

Tax issue, ...
dale's plan, 70–7...,

Terrorism, 288–91

Third World, 6; aid to, 205–7, 20...

Thomas, Helen (UPI), 221

Threlkeld, Richard (ABC, "Issues 84"): deficit, 69–72, 115

Toote, Dr. Gloria: follows Reagan idiom, 111–14

Trewhitt, Henry (Baltimore Sun), 172, 173

UNESCO, U.S. withdrawal from, 226–27

Urban Institute study, 111–12

USSR. See Soviet Union

Vance, Cyrus (former Secretary of State), 84

Vietnam, 6, 17, 51

Wallace, Chris (NBC), 33–34, 46, 61; B'nai B'rith speeches, 46; constitutional amendment for balanced budget, 43–44

War, nuclear, 321–23

War on Poverty: Kennedy and Johnson, 105

Watergate, 17, 78

Watt, James (former Secretary of Interior), 19

Wertheimer, Linda (National Public Radio), 68

When Foreign Aid Fails, 213

White House Hunger Working Group, 206–08

White Revolution, Iran, 208

White, Theodore, 184

Will, George (ABC), 118, 123, 176, 183, 194

Wolkee, Dr. John (president National Right to Life Committee), 80

Women's rights, 19, 99

Woodruff, Judy (PBS), 37, 63; Reagan's economic policy, 85; Mondale on campaign style, 67–69; Reagan campaign, 80–83

World Court and international law, 153

World hunger, 6, 205–16, 236

World War II, 65

Yuppies, 18

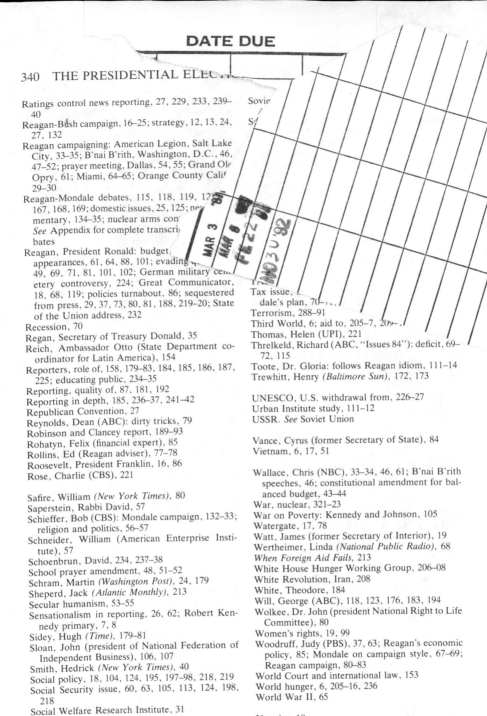